a new introduction to GEOGRAPHY

for OCR GCSE Specification A

FOUNDATION EDITION

Edited by:
Keith Flinders

Written by:
John Belfield, Keith Flinders and Emma Gobourn

Hodder Murray
A MEMBER OF THE HODDER HEADLINE GROUP

Acknowledgements

The Publishers would like to thank the following for permission to reproduce copyright material:

Fig 1.11 (top) George Hall/Corbis; Fig 1.11 (btm) Roger Ressmeyer/Corbis; Fig 1.22 Gary Rosenquist/USGS; Figs 1.23, 1.24, 1.25 Lyn Topinka/USGS; Fig 1.27 USGC; Fig 1.30 Thomas Raupach/Still Pictures; Fig 1.31 Associated Press AP; Figs 1.36, 1.37, 1.38 Nic Howes; Fig 1.43 Skyscan Photolibrary/William Cross; Fig 1.46 Popperfoto; 1.48 Reuters Jasper Juinen/Reuter; Figs 1.52, 1.53 Associated Press AP; Fig 1.54 Jim Holmes/Panos Pictures; Figs 1.57, 1.59, 1.67 Skyscan Photolibrary; Fig 1.69 Trackair Aerial Surveys; Figs 1.71, 1.72 Ross-Parry Picture Agency; Fig 1.78 Hull Daily Mail Publications Ltd; Figs 1.79, 1.81, 1.84, 1.89, 1.91, 1.92, 1.93, 1.95 John Pallister; 1.96 S.J. Sibley; Fig 2.29 Annie Griffiths Belt/CORBIS; Fig 2.30 Robert Harding; Fig 2.37 Caroline Penn/CORBIS; Figs 2.40, 2.41, 2.42, 2.43 Keith Flinders; Fig 2.44 Courtesy of the City and County of Swansea; Figs 2.45, 2.46, 2.48, 2.49, 2.50 Keith Flinders; Fig 2.52 Val Flinders; Figs 2.54, 2.56, 2.57, 2.58, 2.59 Keith Flinders; Figs 2.61, 2.65, 2.66, 2.68, 2.71 John Pallister; Fig 2.69 and pp126-127 Keith Flinders; Fig 3.11 Still Pictures Jorgen Schytte/Still Pictures; Figs 3.25, 3.27 David Gardner; Fig 3.29 Joerg Boethling/Still Pictures; Fig 3.30 Emma Lee/Life File; Figs 3.35, 3.37 Sealand Aerial Photography; Fig 3.39 Keith Flinders; Fig 3.40 A.J. Williamson; Fig 3.41 Keith Flinders; Fig 3.44 Stephen Hardy; Fig 3.45 Judith Capton; Figs 3.51, 3.52, 3.57 Keith Flinders; Fig 3.61 Richard Bird Photography; Figs 3.62, 3.63 Keith Flinders; Figs 3.65, 3.66, 3.67 John Pallister; pp178-179 Keith Flinders; Figs 4.11, 4.13, 4.14, Sue Cunningham/SCP; Fig 4.12 Andrew Ward/Life File; Fig 4.17 Mark Edwards/Still Pictures; Fig 4.18 Nigel Dickinson/Still Pictures; Figs 4.20, 4.22, 4.23 Keith Flinders; Figs 4.25, 4.26 Associated Press EFE; Fig 4.27 Associated Press AP; Figs 4.28, 4.29 ©2000 German Aerospace Center (DLR); Fig 4.31 Chinch Gryniewicz Ecoscene/CORBIS; Fig 4.32 University of Dundee; Fig 4.33 Bryan Pickering, Eye Ubiquitous/CORBIS; Fig 4.35 Ecoscene/Leeney; Fig 4.37 Ecoscene/Schaffer; Fig 4.42 Associated Press/Greenpeace via PA; Fig 4.44 Andrew Testa/The Observer; Fig 4.48 John Pallister; 4.52a Greenpeace/Morgan; pp220 Brian Smith; pp224-225, Keith Flinders; p226 Emma Gobourn, p229 S.J. Sibley.

The authors and publisher are also grateful to the following for permission to reproduce their copyright materials either in their original form or in a form adapted for the purposes of this book:

Fig 1.11 (home page) Mount St. Helens Tours Inc; Fig 1.11 based on a graphic © Times Newspapers Limited, 19th October 1989; Fig 1.12 San Francisco Chronicle; Fig 1.13 Los Angeles Times Syndicate; Fig 1.14 San Francisco Chronicle; Fig 1.17 Los Angeles Times Syndicate; Fig 1.19 USGS; Fig 1.26 Haraldur Sigurdsson; Fig 1.29 © Times Newspapers Limited, 8th December 1998; Fig 1.77 based on a graphic © Telegraph Group Ltd; Fig 2.31 © Based on Bartholomew Digital Database. Reproduced by permission of HarperCollins Publishers; Fig 2.32 Longman Geography for GCSE, p120, Longman; Fig 3.9 Hamish McRae/The Independent Syndication; Fig 3.17 © Times Newspapers Limited, 25th October 1998; p147 FAO (Food and Agriculture Organization of the United Nations); p150 BBC Online News; Fig 3.32 © Times Newspapers Limited, 13th November 1994; Fig 3.33 cartoon by Austin, eds. J. Porritt, and R. Maynard, *Earth Mirth*, 1986, Friends of the Earth; Fig 3.59 Sheffield Telegraph; p187 BBC Online News; Fig 4.19 Lagamar Expeditions; p191 BBC Online News; Fig 4.38 © Telegraph Group Ltd, 2000; Fig 4.38 (inset) Climatic Research Unit, University of East Anglia; Fig 4.41 US Department of Commerce: National Oceanic and Atmospheric Administration/The Telegraph Group Limited/Richard Burgess; Fig 1 p212, Oliver & Boyd, GCSE Copymasters, Addison Wesley Longman Ltd; Fig 2 p213 Greenpeace UK; Fig 7 p237 *Energy Resources for a Changing World*, JE Allan, 1992, Cambridge University Press.

Maps reproduced from Ordnance Survey mapping with permission of the Controller of Her Majesty's Stationery Office © Crown copyright Licence Number 399450: OS Landranger 1:50 000 series: Fig 1.63, Fig 2.55, p121, Fig 3.64; OS Explorer 1:25 000 series: Fig 1.43; OS Outdoor Leisure 1:25 000 series: p230.

Ordnance Survey Key
A key to the OS Landranger maps can be found on page 123

Every effort has been made to trace all copyright holders, but if any have been inadvertently overlooked the Publishers will be pleased to make the necessary arrangements at the first opportunity.

All internal artwork by Peters and Zabransky
Cartography by Jillian Luff, MAPgrafix
Although every effort has been made to ensure that website addresses are correct at time of going to press, Hodder Murray cannot be held responsible for the content of any website mentioned in this book. It is sometimes possible to find a relocated web page by typing in the address of the home page for a website in the URL window of your browser.

Orders: please contact Bookpoint Ltd, 130 Milton Park, Abingdon, Oxon OX14 4SB. Telephone: (44) 01235 827720. Fax: (44) 01235 400454. Lines are open from 9.00–6.00, Monday to Saturday, with a 24-hour message answering service. Visit our website at www.hoddereducation.co.uk.

© Keith Flinders, John Belfield and Emma Gobourn 2005
First published in 2005 by
Hodder Murray, a member of the Hodder Headline Group
338 Euston Road
London NW1 3BH

Impression number   10 9 8 7 6 5 4 3 2 1
Year   2010 2009 2008 2007 2006 2005

All rights reserved. Apart from any use permitted under UK copyright law, no part of this publication may be reproduced or transmitted in any form or by any means, electronic or mechanical, including photocopy, recording, or any information storage and retrieval system, without permission in writing from the publisher or under licence from the Copyright Licensing Agency Limited. Further details of such licences (for reprographic reproduction) may be obtained from the Copyright Licensing Agency Limited, of 90 Tottenham Court Road, London W1T 4LP.

Cover photo by Steve Rawlings of Debut Art www.debutart.com
Typeset in 12 Garamond by Pantek Arts Ltd, Maidstone, Kent
Printed in Italy

A catalogue record for this title is available from the British Library

ISBN-10: 0 340 88674 9
ISBN-13: 9 780340 886748

Words in bold
Words that appear in bold are key syllabus words that are either explained in the text, or in the glossary on page 239.

Contents

UNIT 1   PEOPLE AND THE PHYSICAL WORLD

Plate Tectonics   6
   What causes volcanoes and earthquakes?   6
   Plate boundaries   8
   What is an earthquake?   10
   Why do many people continue to live at risk from earthquakes?   12
   Volcanoes   16
   Mount St Helens   16
   Volcanoes and satellite imagery   20
   Why do people live near volcanoes?   22

Rivers   24
   The hydrological cycle   24
   River processes   26
   Transport processes   26
   River deposition   27
   River landscape features   28
   Upper course features   28
   Lower course features   30
   Why rivers flood   32
   Flooding in the Netherlands, 1995   32
   Flooding in Bangladesh, July–September, 1998   36

Coasts   40
   Wave power   40
   Wearing the coast away   42
   Features produced by erosion   44
   Moving and depositing material   46
   Erosion of the Holderness Coast   48

Advice   52
   Coursework for Rivers   52
   Coursework for Coasts   60
   Examination technique – Unit 1   62
   The Entry Level Certificate   66

UNIT 2   PEOPLE AND PLACES TO LIVE

Population   68
   Where do people live?   68
   Population distribution in the UK   70
   Changing populations   72
   Population issues   74
   Family planning in China   77
   Migration   78
   Mexicans to the USA   80

Settlement — 82

- What is urbanisation? — 82
- Megacities — 83
- Rural to urban migration in LEDCs — 84
- Problems of cities in LEDCs — 85
- Squatter settlements — 88
- The Central Business District — 90
- The inner zone — 92
- Suburbs — 94
- Traffic in an urban area — 96
- The provision of services — 100
- Rural services fight back — 101
- North Worcestershire, a case study — 102
- Urban to rural migration — 105

Advice — 108

- Coursework for Settlement — 108
- Examination technique – Unit 2 — 116
- The Entry Level Certificate — 126

UNIT 3   PEOPLE AND THEIR NEEDS

The Quality of Life — 128

- What is quality of life? — 128
- Comparing the UK with Burkina Faso — 132
- Economic indicators of development — 134
- Industrialisation and economic growth — 136
- South Korea — 138

Economic Activities — 140

- Farming systems — 140
- A commercial farm in an MEDC — 141
- Subsistence rice farming in India, an LEDC — 144
- The Green Revolution — 145
- Changes in farming in an MEDC — 148
- The environmental impact of farming — 150
- The location of industry — 152
- Argos Distribution warehouse, Stafford — 153
- Alcan smelter, Lynemouth — 154
- The effects of tourism – Menorca — 156
- The effects of tourism – Kenya — 158

Energy — 160

- Changing energy use in the UK — 160
- Meeting future energy demands — 162
- Holmewood — 164
- Consett after coal and steel — 166

Advice — 168

- Coursework for Economic Activities — 168
- Examination technique – Unit 3 — 170
- The Entry Level Certificate — 178

UNIT 4 PEOPLE AND THE ENVIRONMENT

Local Environments — 180
  Limestone — 180
  Tropical rainforests — 182
  Development projects in the Amazon — 184
  Environmental consequences — 186
  Stewardship and sustainable development — 188
  Land use conflicts in national parks — 192
  Dartmoor — 194
  Water pollution — 196
  Spanish sludge spill, April 1998 — 197
  Pembrokeshire coast oil spill, Wales — 200

The Global Environment — 202
  The causes of acid rain — 202
  The effects of acid rain — 203
  Tackling acid rain — 204
  Global warming — 206
  The potential consequences of global warming — 208
  How to deal with the effects of global warming — 209

Advice — 210
  Coursework for the environmental effects of people — 210
  Examination technique – Unit 4 — 212
  The Entry Level Certificate — 218

GUIDANCE — 222
  Coursework ideas — 222
  The coursework process — 223
  Using ICT in coursework — 224
  Coursework assessment — 226
  How to be successful in the examinations — 228
  The examination questions — 232
  Using question resources — 236
  Using case studies — 238
  Common examination errors — 238

GLOSSARY — 239
PLACE INDEX — 240

one
People and the Physical World
Plate tectonics

WHAT CAUSES VOLCANOES AND EARTHQUAKES?

SUMMARY We live on the outside layer of the earth. This is called the crust. The crust is broken into sections which are called plates. These plates move very slowly. Where plates meet they move in different directions. This causes volcanoes and earthquakes to happen.

To understand why volcanoes and earthquakes happen, we need to understand what is happening beneath the earth's surface.

We don't know much about the inside of the earth. We cannot get very far down into the earth. We do know that the earth is made up of layers of different rocks. It is more than 6 000 km from the surface of the earth to its centre. Figure 1.1 is a slice (or cross-section) through the earth. There are three main parts. They are the core, mantle and the crust. Each of these layers is different.

The **core** is in the centre. Here it is very hot. Some of the core is solid rock and the rest is rock which is partly melted.

The **mantle** is the middle layer between the core and the crust. It is the thickest layer. It is made mainly of solid rocks, but the part nearest the crust is not solid. This outside part is a layer of molten rock, which means it is partly melted. It is called magma. The magma moves slowly underneath the crust.

The **crust** is the outside. It is a very thin layer of solid rock. The crust is not one piece of rock. It is

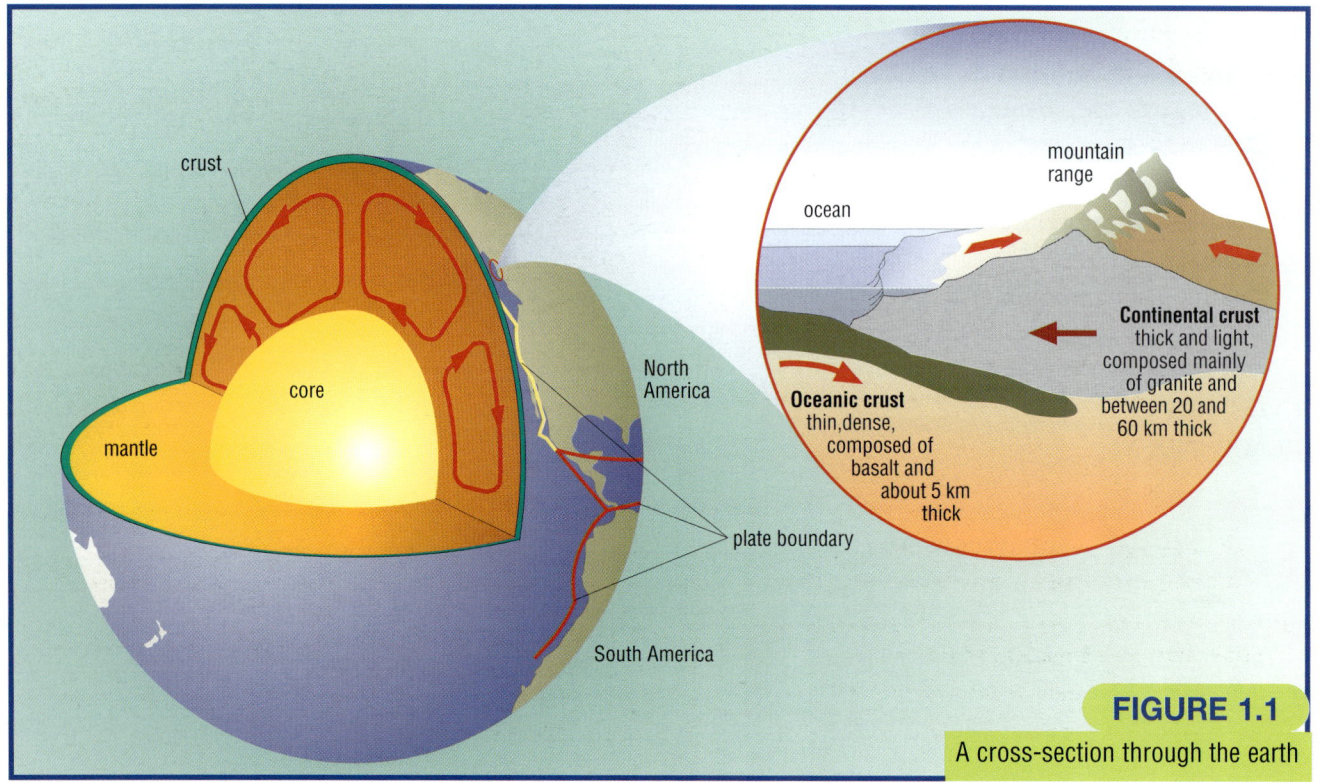

FIGURE 1.1
A cross-section through the earth

What causes volcanoes and earthquakes? 7

broken into several large pieces. These pieces of crust are called **plates**. The plates fit together like pieces of a jigsaw puzzle. They float on the molten rock of the mantle. They move very slowly, maybe a few centimetres every year. As the plates move they may move apart, move closer together, or slide past each other. The plates meet at a plate boundary. Most earthquakes occur and volcanoes erupt at plate boundaries which form long, narrow belts around the world.

Plates are made of two types of crust: continental crust and oceanic crust. Continental crust is lighter than oceanic crust. Where the two types of plate meet, the heavier oceanic crust sinks into the mantle.

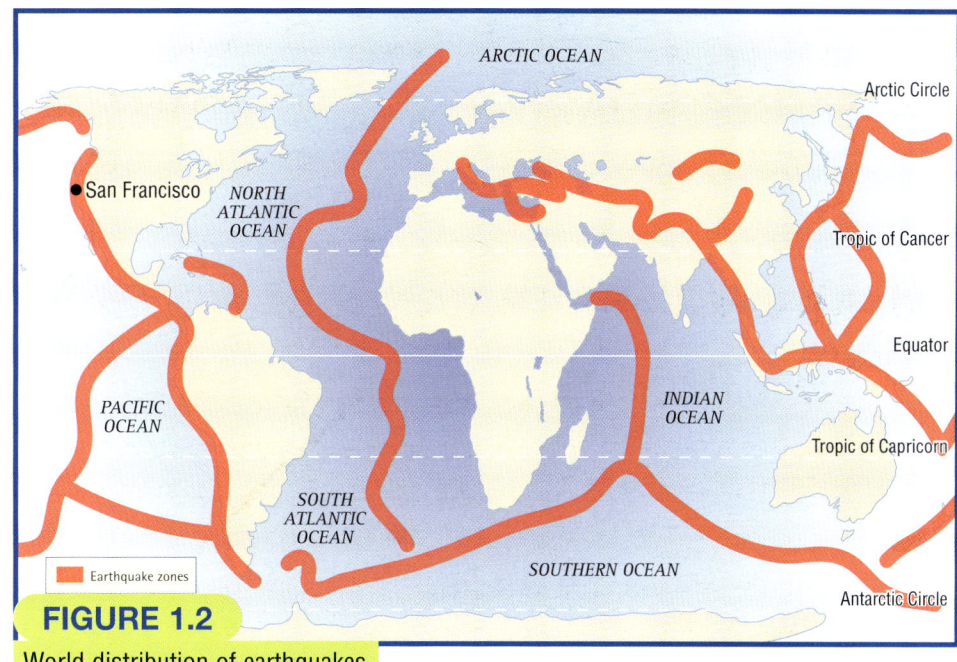

FIGURE 1.2
World distribution of earthquakes

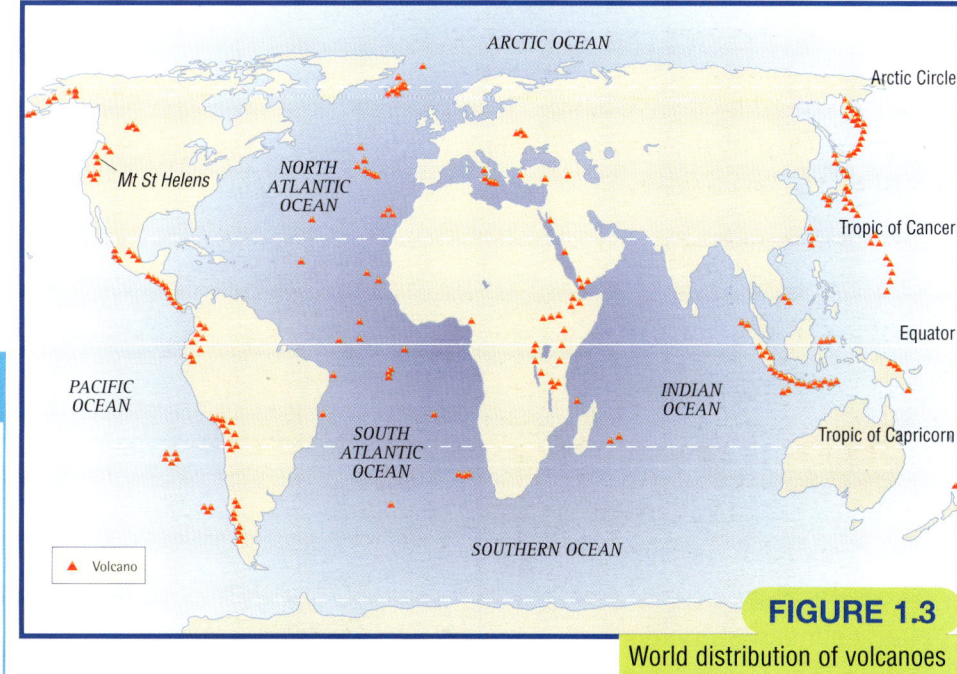

FIGURE 1.3
World distribution of volcanoes

TASKS

1. Match the following 'heads and tails':

The crust	is the hottest part of the earth.
The mantle	is the thin outside layer of the earth.
The core	is molten where it is nearest to the crust.

2. Look at Figures 1.2 and 1.3. What do you notice about where earthquakes happen and volcanoes erupt?

3. Complete the following sentence which describes the distribution of earthquakes and volcanoes.

   'Both earthquakes and volcanoes occur in l_____, n_____ belts around the world.'

4. Use an atlas to describe accurately areas where both volcanoes and earthquakes happen. One area is given below as an example. You should describe two more.
   'Volcanoes and earthquakes both happen down the western side of North America.'

5. Name one area of the world where volcanoes erupt but there are no earthquakes.

one
People and the Physical World
Plate tectonics

PLATE BOUNDARIES

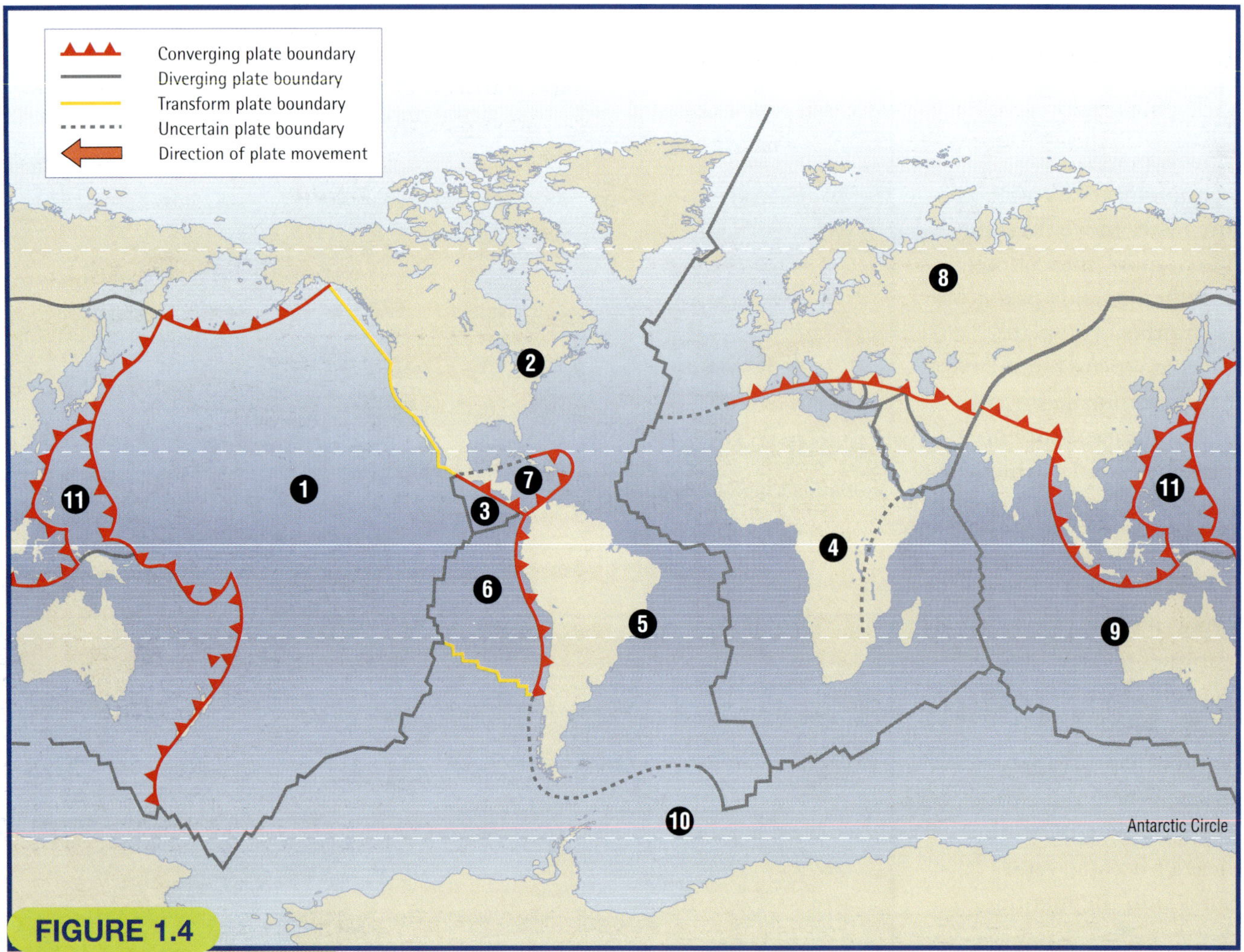

Legend:
- ▲▲▲ Converging plate boundary
- ── Diverging plate boundary
- ── Transform plate boundary
- ┄┄ Uncertain plate boundary
- ⬅ Direction of plate movement

FIGURE 1.4
Major plates of the earth's crust

SUMMARY

Earthquakes and volcanoes often happen in the same places. These are usually near plate boundaries. There are three types of plate boundary. At a convergent boundary the plates move towards each other. At a divergent boundary the plates move away from each other. At a transform boundary the plates move past each other.

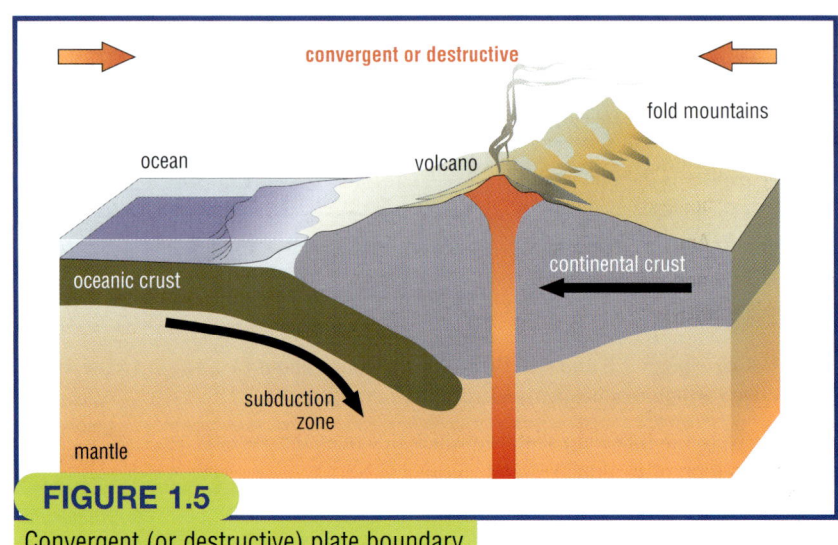

FIGURE 1.5
Convergent (or destructive) plate boundary

Plate boundaries

Earthquakes and volcanoes often occur in the same places around the world. These are usually near plate boundaries or the edges of plates. Figure 1.4 shows the main plates of the earth's crust. The key to the map shows that there are three types of plate boundary: convergent, divergent and transform.

At a **convergent** boundary one plate collides with another. Figure 1.5 shows heavier oceanic crust colliding with continental crust. The oceanic crust sinks underneath the lighter continental crust. The oceanic crust is forced downwards into the mantle and melts. This is called a subduction zone.

At a **divergent** plate boundary the two plates move away from each other. Figure 1.6 shows new magma creating new crust.

At a **transform** plate boundary the two plates move sideways past each other. Figure 1.7 shows this happening, but here the Pacific plate is 'overtaking' the North American plate.

FIGURE 1.6 Divergent (or constructive) plate boundary

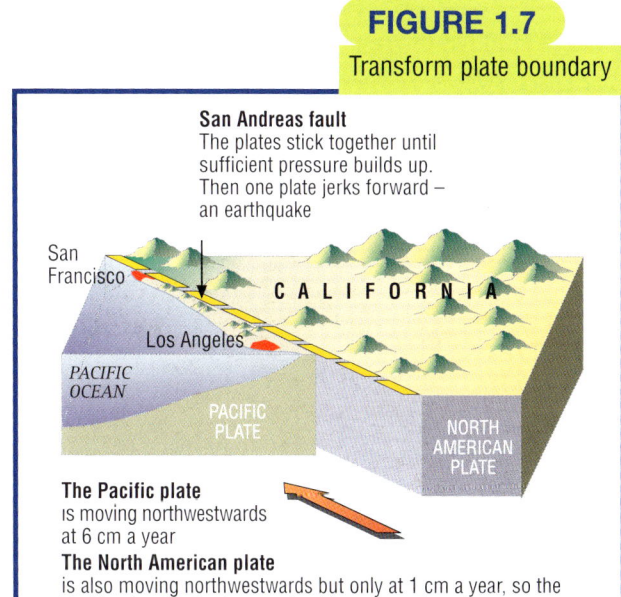

FIGURE 1.7 Transform plate boundary

TASKS

1. On a blank outline map of the world draw in the plate boundaries shown in Figure 1.4.
2. On Figure 1.4, the names of the plates have been labelled 1–11. Using an atlas and the list of names given below, label the names of the plates on your map.

   Eurasian, North American, South American, African, Pacific, Indo-Australian, Nazca, Cocos, Antarctic, Philippine, Caribbean

3. Use Figure 1.4 to copy and complete the following table. The first one has been done for you.

Plate boundary	Type of plate boundary	Direction of plate movement
North American and Eurasian	Diverging	← →
Nazca and _____		→ ←
Indo-Australian and Eurasian		
African and South American		
North American and _____		← ←

one

People and the Physical World

Plate tectonics

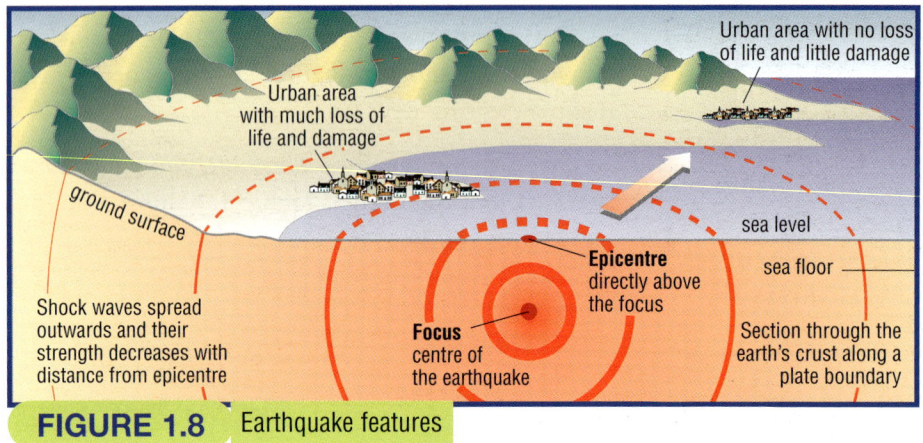

FIGURE 1.8 Earthquake features

WHAT IS AN EARTHQUAKE?

SUMMARY An earthquake is a giant vibration. It is caused when the plates of the earth's crust move. Pressure between the plates builds up until suddenly they move with a jerk. A seismograph measures the strength of an earthquake. It is recorded on the Richter scale.

An earthquake is a sudden movement in the earth's crust. This movement causes shock waves. The centre of the earthquake, where the shock waves come from, is called the **focus**. The point on the earth's surface straight above the focus is the **epicentre**. The shock waves are strongest here. As shock waves spread out from the centre they become weaker and cause less damage.

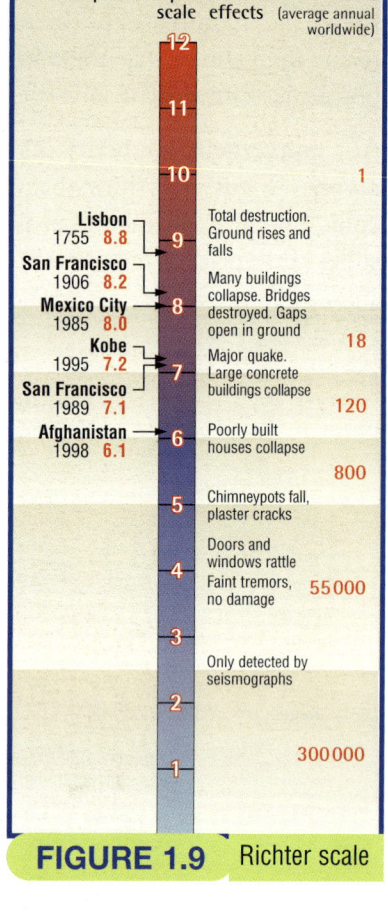

FIGURE 1.9 Richter scale

How are earthquakes measured?

A **seismograph** is an instrument which measures how strong an earthquake is. The strength of the earthquake is identified using the **Richter** scale. An earthquake which measures 7 on the scale is ten times stronger than an earthquake which measures 6.

Year	Place	No. of deaths	Richter scale
1964	Alaska, USA	131	8.3
1970	Peru	66 000	7.8
1985	Mexico City	9 500	8.1
1988	Armenia	25 000	6.9
1989	San Francisco, USA	67	7.1
1990	Iran	50 000	7.3
1993	Latur, India	10 000	6.5
1995	Kobe, Japan	5 477	7.2
1998	Afghanistan	4 000	6.1

Figure 1.10

TASKS

1 Use Figure 1.8 to match the following 'heads and tails':

The focus	get weaker as they spread out.
Most damage	is on the crust above the centre of the earthquake.
The epicentre	is where the shock waves come from.
Shock waves	happens in places near the centre of the earthquake.

2 Use the information in Figure 1.10 to plot a scattergraph. Copy the axes below.

Number of deaths

Strength measured on Richter scale

Use your completed graph to answer the following questions.

3 What is the link between the strength of the earthquake and the number of deaths?

What is an earthquake? 11

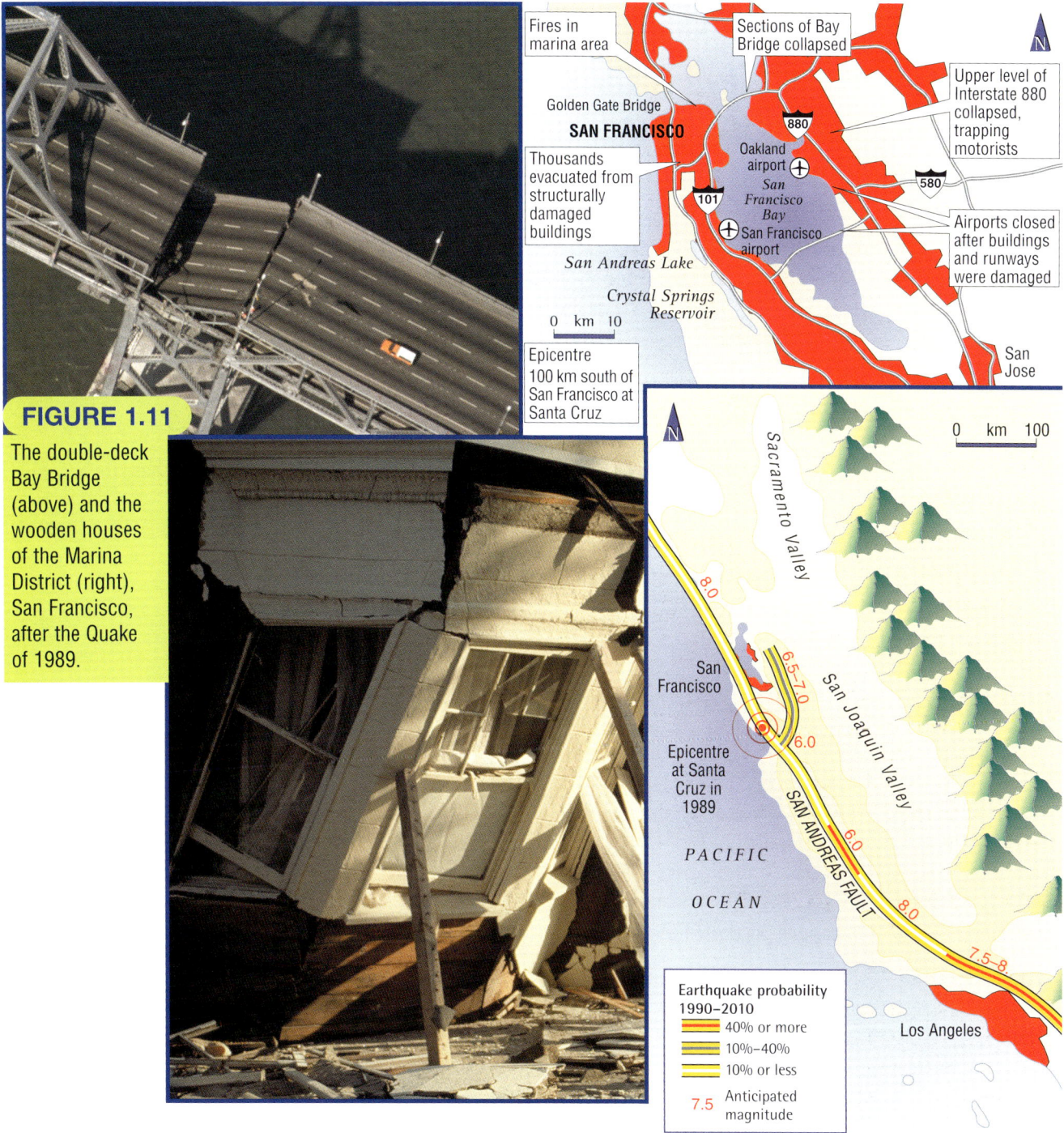

FIGURE 1.11
The double-deck Bay Bridge (above) and the wooden houses of the Marina District (right), San Francisco, after the Quake of 1989.

TASKS

4 Why is there this link between the strength of the earthquake and the number of deaths?

5 Suggest two reasons why some powerful earthquakes cause fewer deaths.

6 Look at the resources in Figure 1.11. They are all about an earthquake which struck San Francisco in 1989. The earthquake measured 7.1 on the Richter scale. What caused the earthquake? (Look back at Figure 1.7 for more information.)

7 Describe the damage done by the San Francisco earthquake.

You might want to record your investigation in the form of a newspaper report. To find out more about this earthquake, type 'San Francisco earthquake 1989' into a search engine.

one People and the Physical World
Plate tectonics

WHY DO MANY PEOPLE CONTINUE TO LIVE AT RISK FROM EARTHQUAKES?

> **SUMMARY** Many people still live in areas where earthquakes happen. They live with the risk because they think that the advantages are greater than the dangers. Earthquakes cannot be prevented but people can prepare for them.

There are many big cities in earthquake zones, but millions of people still live in them. San Francisco in California was almost completely destroyed by an earthquake in 1906. The city was rebuilt on the same land, even though people knew that further earthquakes were likely to happen there.

In Turkey, many people have left the countryside and moved to Istanbul. Now more than 10 million people live in the city. A disastrous earthquake hit Istanbul in 1999, but 15 years earlier a warning had been given of a future earthquake. Despite the warning, poor-quality homes were built in the city for people moving there. This increased the risk of more people dying and being injured during the earthquake.

People are prepared to live with the risk. They think that getting better jobs and a higher standard of living are worth the risk. After all, the earthquake might not happen in their lifetime.

It is not possible to stop earthquakes happening. They usually happen without any warning. All people can do is:

- prepare for them and make sure that the emergency services are ready
- try to predict where and when an earthquake will happen.

Prediction is very difficult, so preparation is best.

Earthquake proof buildings

In big cities in MEDCs (see page 130) new buildings are designed to survive earthquakes. When the earthquake struck San Francisco in 1989 (see page 11) skyscraper buildings in the city centre shook but did not collapse. People in these buildings were frightened but not killed or injured. This is because the skyscrapers were designed to cope with the shock waves. Engineers can now design and build stronger buildings.

San Francisco Chronicle (adapted)   **Thursday October 17 1996**

Few ready for the next big one, poll finds

Charles Petit

If the 1989 earthquake was a wake-up call to Northern California, most people seem to have gone back to sleep. Even the government is cutting funds for earthquake studies.

   A poll being released today by the American Red Cross and Pacific Gas and Electric Co. shows that 82% of Northern and Central California residents say that they are 'not very well prepared' for the next big disaster, and only 25% believe a major disaster is likely in the next 10 years. In fact, some scientists have estimated the risk of an earthquake in the immediate San Francisco Bay area as high as 90% during the next 30 years.

   The Red Cross survey found a variety of reasons why people are not ready for a big quake. They include a feeling that it's not worth their time (19%); don't know what to do (17%); laziness (11%); no time to do it (11%); no money to do it (10%); belief no disaster will happen (6%), and others (26%).

   Those under the age of 35, who presumably have experienced fewer disasters, are the least prepared, with 95% saying they have done little or nothing to get ready.

Figure 1.12

Why do many people continue to live at risk from earthquakes?

L.A. Subject to Same Jolt but is Better Built

Thursday, August 19, 1999 — *Los Angeles Times* (adapted)

By ROBERT LEE HOTZ, *Times* Science Writer

On any day in Los Angeles, there are half a dozen faults capable of creating an earthquake like the explosive strength 7.4 tremor that struck Turkey before dawn on Tuesday, killing thousands. But a similar earthquake here would have far less disastrous results, said earthquake experts.

The reason is because of better building. When it comes to earthquake engineering, California has perhaps the world's strictest building codes, which have been updated regularly over the years. More importantly, those codes have been more strictly enforced, several experts said.

In Southern California, more people also live in flexible, wood-frame homes, not the concrete high-rise apartments common in cities in Turkey.

The poor quality of housing construction may have been the key factor in the high number of deaths during the recent earthquake disaster in the cities in Turkey. 'We are better prepared because we are better off economically and have more funds to put into each building,' said UCLA geophysicist David Jackson.

Figure 1.13

READY OR NOT

Rick DelVecchio, *San Francisco Chronicle* Sunday, January 10, 1999 (adapted)

Bay Area earthquake researchers are racing against the clock, gathering information they hope will cut down the damage and suffering when a big one rips the East Bay's Hayward Fault

To many people, earthquakes don't seem real. It's difficult to grasp how serious they are, and the big ones are so infrequent that most people don't remember them.

Recent earthquakes in the San Francisco Bay Area, have, for most people, been like rolling on a water bed. But a truly major earthquake will be a different experience. Thousands of people, if not millions, will feel as if they have been seized by the collar and tossed into the air. A half-minute of shaking will cause death, injury and widespread economic loss, but its effects won't be spread out evenly across the region.

Both close to the epicentre and far from it, some spots will be hit far worse than others, and scientists are in a hurry to try to work out the likely patterns.

Within a year, the U.S. Geological Survey hopes to publish new detailed seismic geology maps. Their maps will also show new data on the risk of earthquake-related landslides in the East Bay hills.

Such maps would help in designing and upgrading buildings to withstand different levels of damage. A city with many thousands of buildings built or strengthened according to these principles would be able to recover more quickly from disaster.

Figure 1.14

One of the best ways to reduce the effect of an earthquake is not to build in high-risk areas. During an earthquake the shock waves cause water under the ground to rise to the surface. If this happens where the surface rock is clay, the water turns the clay into mud. Any buildings built on clay will sink into the mud and collapse. This happened in the Marina District in San Francisco (see Figure 1.11). These were the only buildings which collapsed during the 1989 earthquake.

Improved preparation

In many places where earthquakes might happen, people try to prepare themselves. In Japan, 1 September is Disaster Day. The day is a public holiday, when Japanese people practise earthquake drill. They practise what they would do if an earthquake happened. This includes how to put out fires and give first aid. In the USA there is a website that has information about what to do before, during and after an earthquake. The website address is http://quake.usgs.gov/

People and the Physical World
Plate tectonics

FIGURE 1.15 Earthquake survival kit

Shelf-life
- 3 months
- 6 months
- 1 year

Top
- Batteries, with tester
- Flashlight
- Portable radio
- First aid kit

Middle
- Food and water for pets, manual can opener, dry food (pasta, rice)
- Instant food, water, purification tablets
- Canned food

Bottom
- Blanket
- Tarpaulin
- Extra clothing, shoes
- Premoistened towelettes
- Items for personal hygiene: toilet tissue and heavy-duty plastic bags for disposal

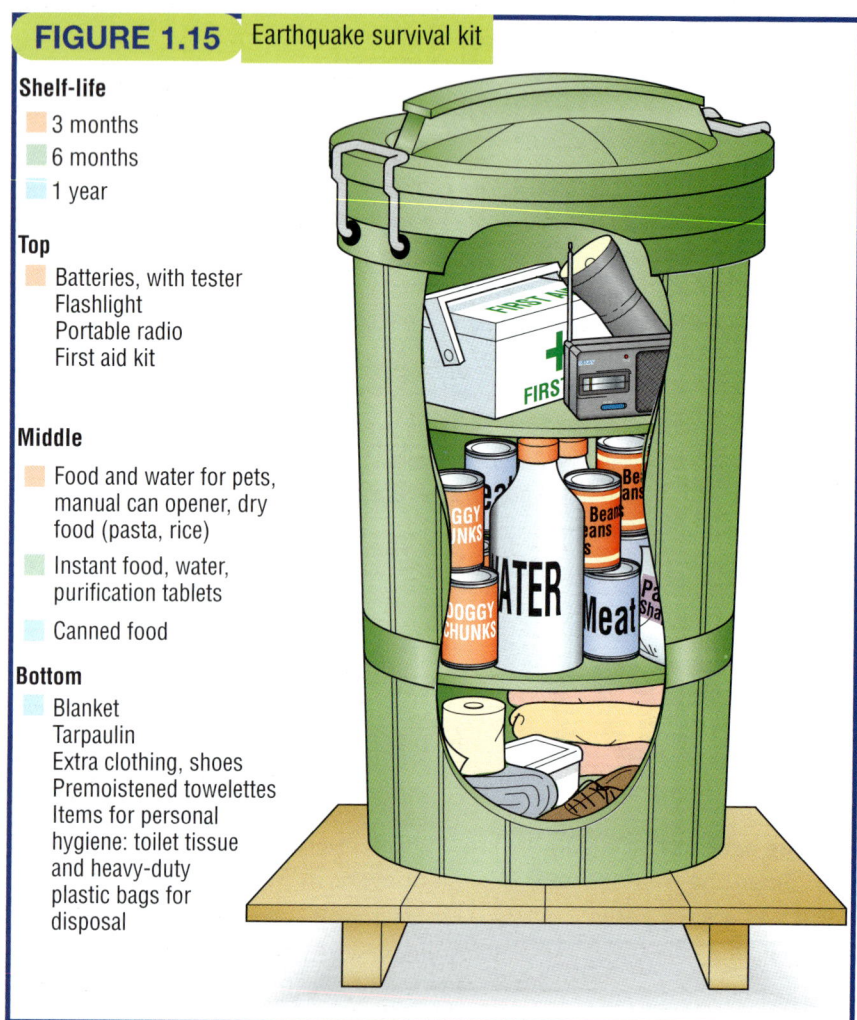

EARTHQUAKE KIT

A Guide to Updating Emergency Supplies
Los Angeles Times Earthquake Safety Guide *(adapted)*

Preparing for an earthquake consists of a series of precautions in the form of survival kits. They can usually be started or replenished with supplies already on the shelf. Encourage the next-door neighbours to update their emergency supplies too.

Recommendations vary as to the appropriate amount of emergency food and water to store. Many experts advise one gallon of water per person per day for three to seven days. Also store enough food for the same period of time.

Use a large container such as a cupboard or dustbin. Label each food and water item with the date of purchase or the last date it should be used. Place the container in a cool, dark place, such as a garage, on something to raise it off the ground.

MARK HAFER / *Los Angeles Times*

Figure 1.16

Los Angeles Times Earthquake Safety Guide

What to do during an earthquake

1 If you are INDOORS – STAY THERE! (Get under a desk or table and hang on to it, or move into a hallway or get against an inside wall. STAY CLEAR of windows, fireplaces, and heavy furniture or appliances. GET OUT of the kitchen, which is a dangerous place (things can fall on you). DON'T run downstairs or rush outside while the building is shaking or while there is danger of falling and hurting yourself or being hit by falling glass or debris.

2 If you are OUTSIDE – get into the OPEN, away from buildings, power lines, chimneys, and anything else that might fall on you.

3 If you are DRIVING – stop, but carefully. Move your car as far out of traffic as possible. DO NOT stop on or under a bridge or overpass or under trees, light posts, power lines, or signs. STAY INSIDE your car until the shaking stops. When you RESUME driving watch for breaks in the pavement, fallen rocks, and bumps in the road at bridge approaches.

4 If you are in a MOUNTAINOUS AREA – watch out for falling rock, landslides, trees, and other debris that could be loosened by quakes.

Figure 1.17

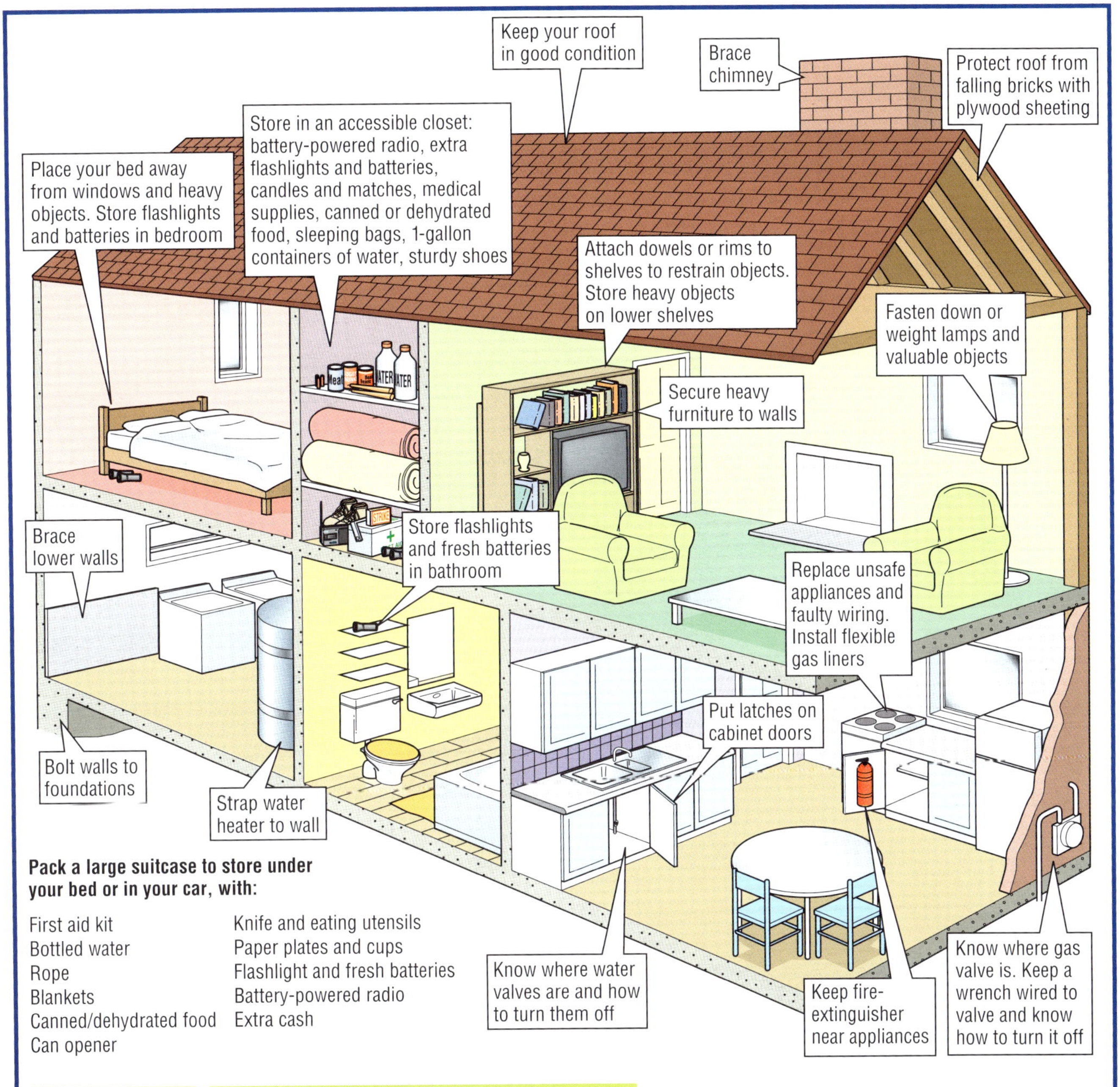

● Why do many people continue to live at risk from earthquakes? 15

FIGURE 1.18 Preparing your house to survive an earthquake

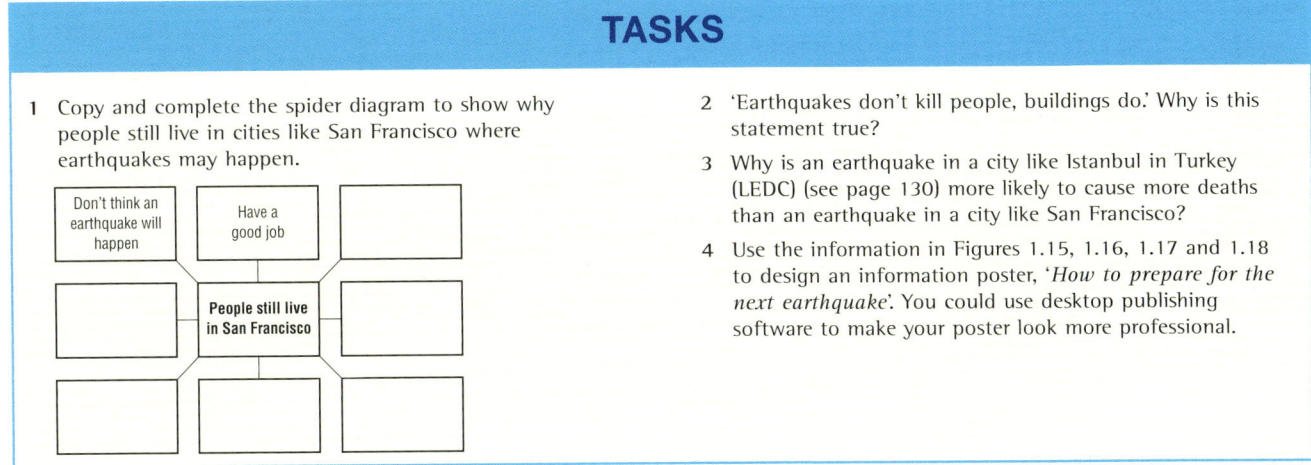

TASKS

1. Copy and complete the spider diagram to show why people still live in cities like San Francisco where earthquakes may happen.

   - Don't think an earthquake will happen
   - Have a good job
   - People still live in San Francisco

2. 'Earthquakes don't kill people, buildings do.' Why is this statement true?

3. Why is an earthquake in a city like Istanbul in Turkey (LEDC) (see page 130) more likely to cause more deaths than an earthquake in a city like San Francisco?

4. Use the information in Figures 1.15, 1.16, 1.17 and 1.18 to design an information poster, 'How to prepare for the next earthquake'. You could use desktop publishing software to make your poster look more professional.

one
People and the Physical World
Plate tectonics

VOLCANOES

SUMMARY Volcanoes are mountains. When a volcano erupts it throws out lava, ash and dust. These build up to form a volcanic cone. There are different types of volcanic eruption. Mount St Helens is a volcano in the Rocky Mountains in North America. When it erupted in 1980 it affected a large area.

Each time a volcano erupts, lava, volcanic bombs, ash, dust and gases are thrown out of the **vent**. The vent is the pipe which links the top of the mountain to the reservoir of molten (or melted) rock underneath the surface of the earth.

Some volcanic eruptions are explosive but others are not. The force of an eruption depends on how sticky the **magma** (or molten rock) is. If magma is thin and runny it flows out of the volcano. If magma is thick and sticky, gases cannot easily escape from it, so pressure builds up under the earth's surface until the gases escape violently and explode.

TASK

1 Use the information above to complete the following statements.
   - A volcano is ...
   - When a volcano erupts the following are thrown out: ...
   - The _____ links the top of the mountain to the reservoir of _____
   - The force of an eruption depends on how _____ the magma is.
   - Magma flows out of a volcano if it is _____ and _____
   - If the magma is _____ and _____ pressure builds up and it erupts _____

MOUNT ST HELENS

Cause of the eruption

Mount St Helens is in the Rocky Mountains in North America. The area is on a convergent plate boundary where two plates are moving towards each other. (Look at Figure 1.5 on page 8 to remind yourself about this type of plate boundary.) A small plate called the Juan de Fuca Plate is moving towards the North American Plate. These plates are colliding and the heavier oceanic crust (Juan de Fuca) is forced downwards into the mantle. It is very hot in the mantle and this crust is melted and turned into magma. The magma is pushed up the vent and causes the volcanic eruption. Each time the volcano erupts another layer of lava, ash or dust covers the earth's surface.

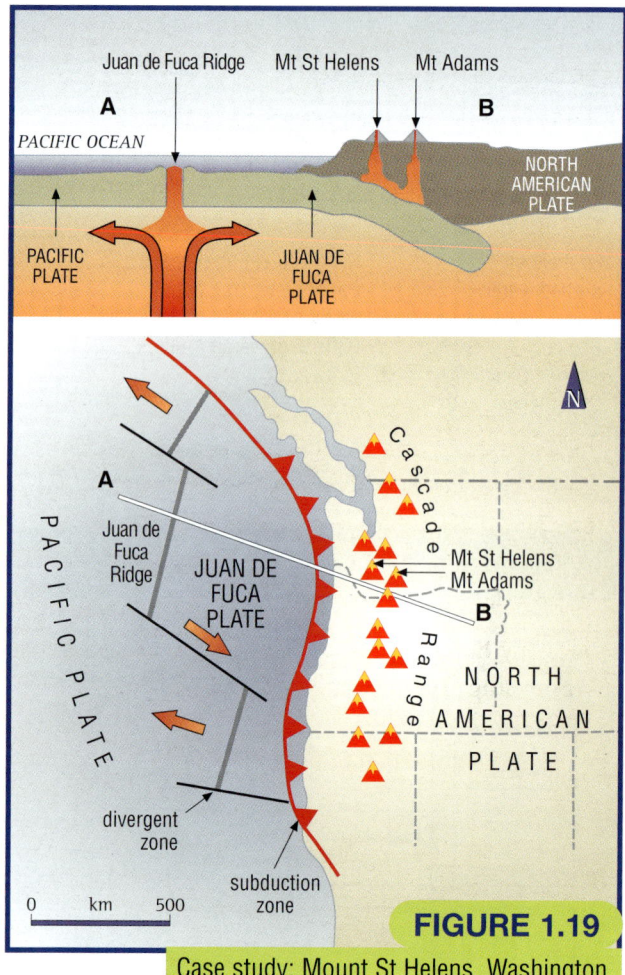

FIGURE 1.19

Case study: Mount St Helens, Washington

Mount St Helens

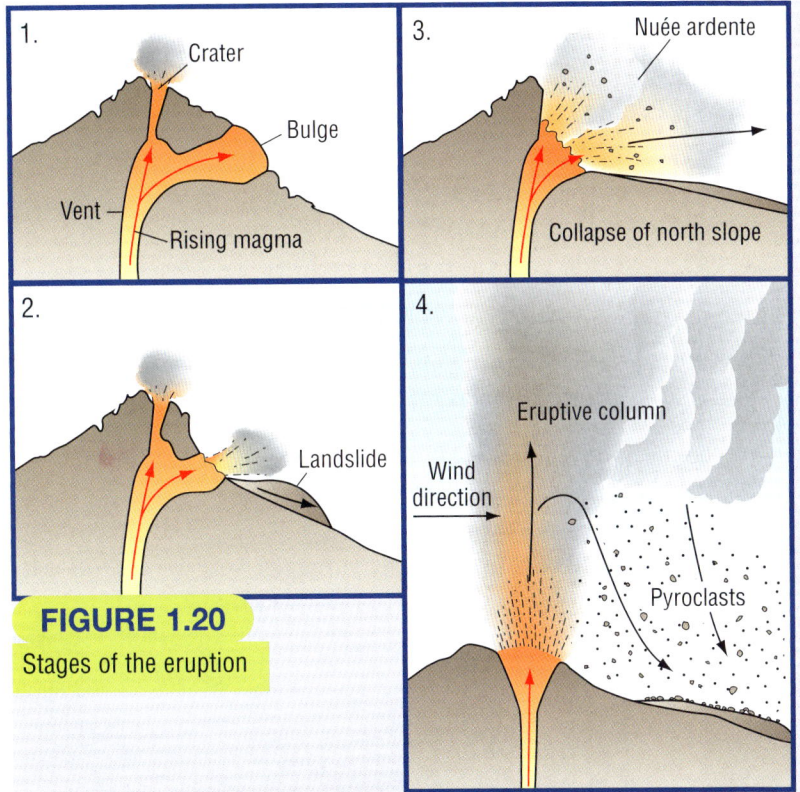

FIGURE 1.20 Stages of the eruption

The eruption

20 March, 1980. At 3:47 pm Pacific Standard Time, a powerful 4.2 earthquake (Richter scale) was the first signal of the reawakening of the volcano. A number of smaller earthquakes followed over the next few days.

1. 27 March. Mount St Helens began to throw out ash and steam, marking the first significant eruption.

Early May. The northern side of Mount St Helens began to bulge by 1.5 m a day. Public authorities closed the area surrounding the mountain after being told by geologists of the volcano's past violent behaviour. This proved unpopular with some local people.

18 May 8.30 am. Small ash and steam eruptions were rising from the crater of the volcano.

2. 18 May 8.32 am. An earthquake (measured at 5 on the Richter scale) caused the bulging northern slope to move forwards and downwards. This became a great landslide of soil, glacier ice, snow and rock, which raced down the mountainside to fill in Spirit Lake. This material, together with the water flung out of the lake by the landslide, then moved down the Toutle valley as a mudflow. This eventually blocked the channel on the Columbia River 60 km away.

3. 18 May 8.33 am. The landslide exposed magma in the volcano's vent. It exploded sideways, sending out a gigantic blast of hot volcanic gases, steam, dust and rock fragments, moving at speeds of over 100 kph. It flattened trees up to 24 km away. Every form of life – plant and animal – within this range was destroyed.

4. Rest of the morning. A vertical eruption rose to a height of more than 20 km, depositing ash over a wide area. In the town of Yakima, 120 km away, the ash deposits were 1 cm thick, and the inhabitants could only go out if they wore face masks. Volcanic debris, formed from the solidifying magma, fell from the eruption, onto the remains of the northern slope of the mountain. These deposits are known as volcanic bombs or pyroclasts. Near the volcano, the swirling ash particles in the atmosphere caused lightning, which in turn started many forest fires.

Early on 19 May the eruption had stopped. By that time, the ash cloud had spread to the central United States. Two days later, fine ash was detected in several cities of the north-eastern United States. Some of the ash drifted around the globe within about 2 weeks.

one
People and the Physical World
Plate tectonics

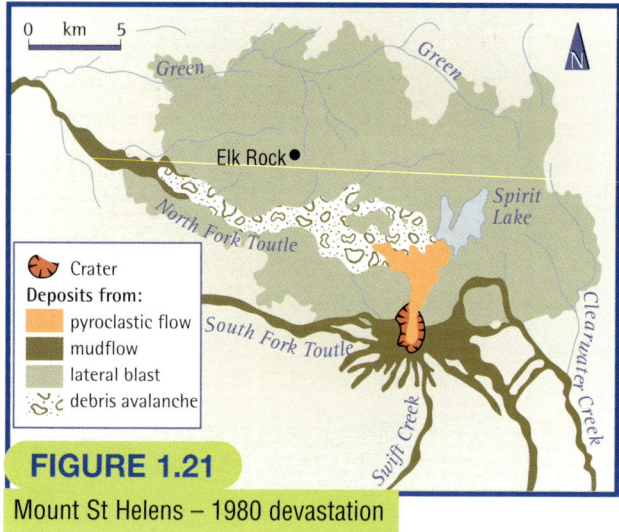

FIGURE 1.21
Mount St Helens – 1980 devastation

- more than 200 houses and cabins
- over 185 miles of roads
- 15 miles of railways
- 27 bridges over the rivers
- a large area of forest
- crops of wheat, apples, potatoes and alfalfa.

The ash from the volcano reduced visibility which affected transport:

- many roads were closed because drivers could not see where they were going
- several airports in the area were closed for up to 2 weeks because the runways were covered in ash and visibility was too poor to fly.

FIGURE 1.23
Mount St Helens – blowdown

At first the eruption stopped tourism, an important industry in the area. However, as things got back to normal tourism increased because of the eruption. Many people wanted to see Mount St Helens for themselves and thousands of visitors came to the area. Tourism increased so much that in 1982 a large area around the volcano was made into a national park. Many walking trails, viewpoints, information stations, campgrounds, and picnic areas have been created.

FIGURE 1.22
Mount St Helens as seen from Johnston Ridge, 18 May

Effects of the eruption

Mount St Helens erupted on 18 May 1980. It was a powerful eruption and caused destruction over a wide area. The volcano erupted sideways not upwards. Many people were injured and 61 people died. Some died because they choked by breathing in hot volcanic ash, and others were burnt to death. 7 000 animals also died including deer, elk and bears. Damage to the local area included the destruction of:

FIGURE 1.24
Mount St Helens – volcanic ash

Mount St Helens

FIGURE 1.25
Mount St Helens – the morning after

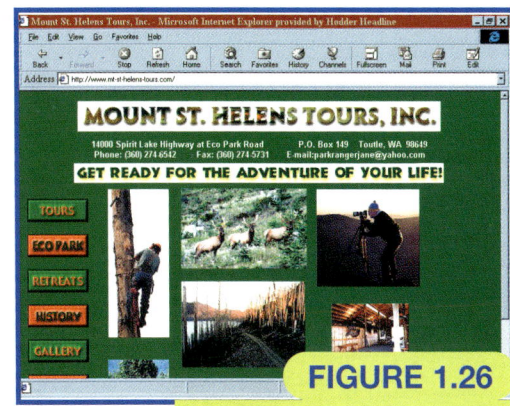

FIGURE 1.26
Mount St Helens Tours website

TASKS

1 Use Figure 1.20 to put the following events into a timeline. Copy the timeline below into your books. The first event has been added for you.

Timeline to show the eruption of Mount St Helens: 18 May 1980	
Early May	The northern side of the mountain bulged outwards.
18 May: 8.30 am	
18 May: 8.32 am	
18 May: 8.33 am	
Rest of morning	

Add these events to the timeline:

- The volcano exploded sideways.
- The north slope became a landslide of soil, ice, rock and snow.
- Ash erupted into the air and covered a wide area.
- Small ash and steam eruptions came out of the crater at the top of the mountain.
- Volcanic bombs fell onto what was left of the north slope of the mountain.
- The landslide mixed with water from Spirit Lake to make a mudflow.
- Hot gases, steam, dust and rock moved sideways at over 100 km per hour.
- Forest fires started near the volcano.
- All trees, plants and animals up to 24 km away from the volcano were killed.
- The mudflow blocked the Columbia River 60 km away.

2 A mind map is a good way to help develop your understanding. It allows you to write down what you know in any order. The topics help you to organise the details and make links.

Copy and complete the mind map below to describe the effects of the Mount St Helens eruption. Some ideas have been included to get you started. See how one idea leads to more detail.

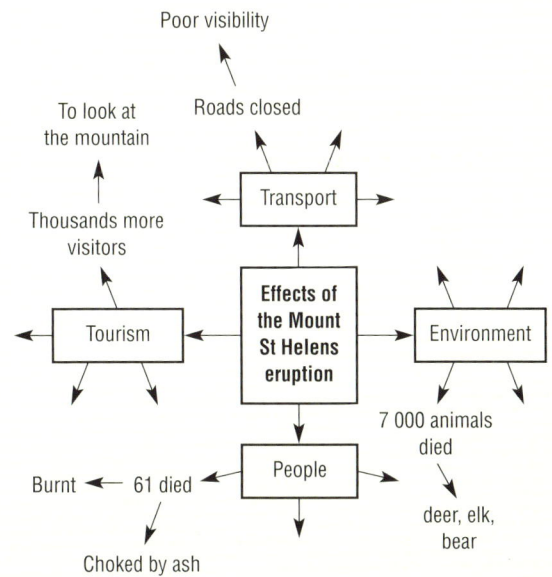

3 The following websites contain lots of information about the 1980 eruption at Mount St Helens:

Cascades Volcano Observatory –
http://vulcan.wr.usgs.gov/home.html

Volcano World– http://volcano.und.nodak.edu/
http://www.mountsthelens.com/

If you visit these websites you can find out much more about the eruption. Add these new ideas to your timeline and mind map.

one
People and the Physical World
Plate tectonics

VOLCANOES AND SATELLITE IMAGERY

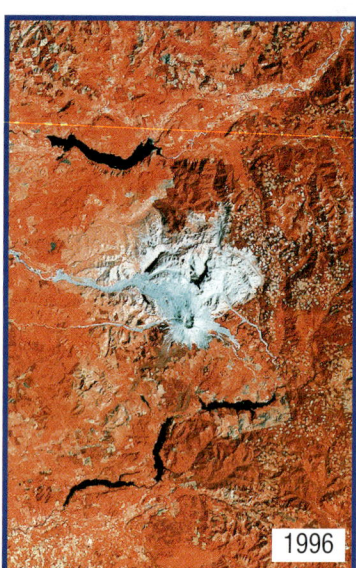

FIGURE 1.27 1973   1983   1996

Ash, mudslides, and mud-laden rivers show as greyish blue.
Water looks black.
Ice and snow are white.
Gradual vegetation regrowth show as light red and pink, in the devastated area.

SUMMARY Satellite images are pictures taken from outer space. They can be used to spot volcanoes which may be ready to erupt. Some people living in the area can be warned of a possible volcanic eruption.

The three satellite images of Mount St Helens in 1973, 1983 and 1996 were taken from an Internet site in the USA: USGS Earthshots Satellite Images of Environmental Change
http://edcwww.cr.usgs.gov/earthshots/slow/tableofcontentstext

These satellite images show the area around Mount St Helens before and after its eruption on 18 May 1980. The main colour on the three images is red, which shows vegetation. Look at the difference between the amount of red in 1973 and 1983, before and after the eruption.

TASKS

1. Look at the 1973 image. How can you spot Mount St Helens?
2. Look at the 1983 image. What has happened to the vegetation around the mountain?
3. How can you tell that Mount St Helens has erupted?
4. Look at the 1996 image. How can you tell that the vegetation is re-growing?

Volcanoes and satellite imagery 21

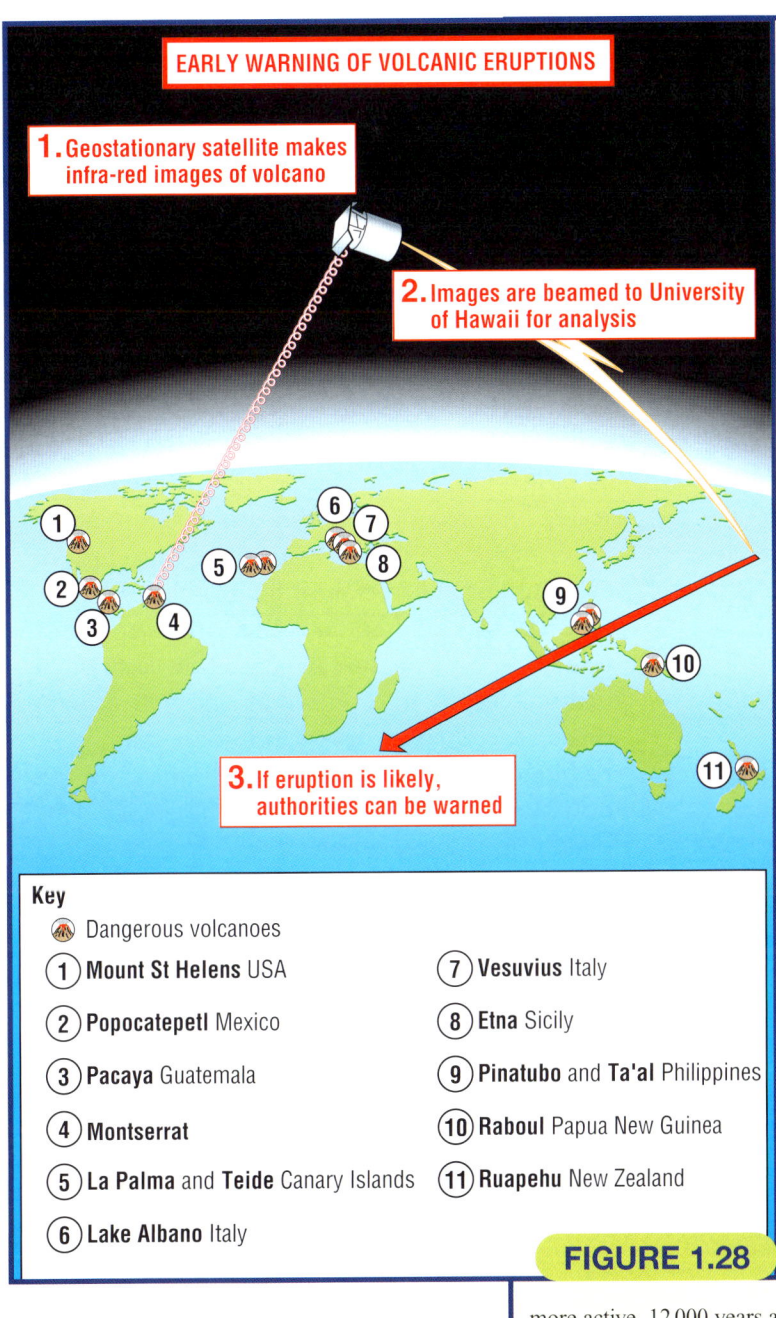

FIGURE 1.28

Satellites spot volcano ready to erupt (adapted)

A volcanic eruption has been successfully predicted with the use of satellites. Researchers said yesterday that they had detected the eruption of Pacaya, in Guatemala, a week before it began.

The team, using satellites with infra-red detectors, picked up a heat signal on May 13. This showed that hot magma was bubbling towards the surface. The volcano erupted on May 20, sending an ash cloud over Guatemala City and the airport 13 miles away.

The breakthrough, by British and American scientists, may lead to the establishment of a worldwide automatic forecasting system for the 600 active volcanoes and many others considered to be potentially active.

The team also spotted the eruption of Popocatepetl, near Mexico City, from space. The satellites detected a moderate eruption on the morning of November 24 this year. Local ground-based teams recorded the same event and sounded the alarm one minute earlier. But many parts of the world where volcanoes could burst into life are too dangerous to have trained staff in place.

The satellite system, even if it spots an eruption only as it occurs, may give emergency services vital hours or days to get people cleared from a likely lava flow.

A scientist said that about seven satellites would be needed to create a global volcano early-warning system. 'At the moment we are only really covering the Americas and the Caribbean.'

About 360 million people live on or near dangerous volcanoes, from Etna in Sicily to Mount St Helens in the USA. In recent years volcanoes have killed about 25 000 people.

Aircraft are also at risk. In 1982 a British Airways Boeing 747 nearly fell from the sky over Java after volcanic dust got into the jet engines.

The search for an early-warning system for volcanic eruptions is now more urgent after signs that rising sea levels because of global warming may make volcanoes more active. 12 000 years ago, when sea levels rose by 38 ft in two centuries, volcanic activity increased.

FIGURE 1.29

Nick Nuttall, *The Times*, 8 December 1998

TASK

With a partner, read through Figure 1.29. It is taken from a newspaper article about trying to predict when volcanoes will erupt. Use the framework below to pick out the main ideas from the article.

- Two dangerous volcanic eruptions have been correctly predicted by scientists. These eruptions were at the _____ and _____ volcanoes.

- The satellites can predict volcanic explosions by _____

- It is important to give people an early warning of a possible eruption so that _____

- Millions of people live near dangerous volcanoes, and recent eruptions have killed _____

- It is now more urgent to set up an early-warning system for volcanic eruptions because _____

People and the Physical World
Plate tectonics

WHY DO PEOPLE LIVE NEAR VOLCANOES?

SUMMARY Millions of people live near volcanoes. They think that they will be safe because they will be given warning of a future eruption. People live near to volcanoes for many reasons. They may be farmers using the fertile soil to grow crops. They may use the electricity and hot water created underground. They may work in mines. They may make a living from the expanding tourist industry.

About 500 million people now live in areas at risk from volcanic hazards. In the past 500 years, over 200 000 people have been killed by the effects of volcanic eruptions. An average of 845 people died each year between 1900 and 1986 from volcanic hazards. The number of deaths for these years is far greater than the number of deaths for previous centuries. Why? The reason for this increase is not due to an increase in volcanic eruptions. It is because more people now live on the sides of active volcanoes and in valleys near to volcanoes. There are advantages of living near volcanoes.

The plus side of volcanoes

Fertile soils

Over thousands of years, volcanic rocks have been weathered into very fertile soils. These soils attract many farmers. The soils on the slopes of Vesuvius in Southern Italy are used to grow crops of olives, fruit, vines and nuts. One in five people on the island of Sicily lives on the slopes of Mount Etna to farm on the fertile soils, even though the volcano erupts on average once every 10 years. Some of the best rice-growing regions of Indonesia are around **active** volcanoes (Figure 1.30).

Geothermal energy

Geothermal energy comes from heat underneath the earth's surface. This heat is usually created by active volcanoes. Water stored underground in permeable rocks is heated by magma to form steam. Boreholes are drilled into the permeable rocks to tap the steam. This steam can be used to drive turbines in power stations to produce electricity, or to provide hot water for radiators, heat for greenhouses and industrial uses, and hot or warm springs at tourist resort spas. This method of generating electricity is used successfully in countries like New Zealand and Iceland. Geothermal heat warms more than 70% of the homes in Iceland. The great advantages of this form of energy are that it is environmentally friendly and almost limitless.

FIGURE 1.30
A lush rice paddy in central Java, Indonesia. Sundoro volcano looms in the background. The most highly prized rice-growing areas have fertile soils formed from the breakdown of young volcanic deposits

Minerals

Lava in volcanoes can eventually turn into minerals, like gold, silver, diamonds, copper and zinc. Therefore, **dormant** or **extinct** volcanoes are excellent places for mining. This creates job opportunities, leading to the development of mining towns near volcanoes.

Tourism

People are fascinated by volcanoes, so many tourists visit areas where volcanoes are still erupting. This brings in a lot of money for the country. It is not only volcanoes which attract tourists. Hot springs and geysers also bring tourists to volcanic areas to visit health spas. Old Faithful, a geyser in Yellowstone National Park in the USA, which erupts at regular intervals, is a famous tourist attraction. Since the early 1980s, thousands of visitors have gone to the area surrounding Mount St Helens to see the effects of the eruption. More than 1.5 million visitors have gone to the Visitor Centre since it was opened in 1986.

Monitoring and predicting eruptions

The main reason why scientists study and monitor volcanoes is so that people living near active volcanoes will know about the hazards they produce. It is important that scientists tell local authorities and the general public about the dangers the volcanoes may bring. Each volcano has its own set of hazards. When scientists study volcanoes, they draw maps of deposits left by previous eruptions. They use satellites to look at ash clouds and gases coming out of the vent. They also study and monitor streams and lakes near the volcano for more clues about a possible eruption.

By studying volcanic deposits, scientists can produce hazard maps. These maps give some clues about the types of hazards that can be expected the next time a volcano erupts. By watching and measuring a volcano over a long time, we can learn how it is changing. These changes can help in predicting when an eruption may occur.

FIGURE 1.31

The eruption of Popocatepetl in Mexico in November 1998 was predicted from satellite evidence and warnings were issued

TASKS

1 Three different ways of describing a volcano are active, dormant and extinct. Use the Internet or other resources to find out what these words mean. Write out a definition of each word. Give an example of a volcano which matches each description.

2 WEARS is a good word to help you remember why people live near to volcanoes. It is an example of a mnemonic. Each letter stands for a reason. Copy and complete the table below to summarise why people live near volcanoes.

W	Warning	People believe they will be safe
E	Energy	
A	Attracts tourists	
R	Resources	
S	Soils	

one
Rivers
People and the Physical World

THE HYDROLOGICAL CYCLE

> **SUMMARY** A drainage basin is an area of land drained by a river and its tributaries. The drainage basin shows how the hydrological cycle works. Water flows in a cycle from the clouds to the sea and back to the clouds. In the drainage basin there is a balance between inputs and outputs. A hydrograph shows how the river discharge varies with the amount of rainfall.

The **drainage basin** is an area of land which collects rainwater and feeds it into a network of streams. The boundary of the basin is the **watershed**.

The water balance

The system in a drainage basin has:

- **inputs** – water entering the system, e.g. rainfall
- **flows** – water running through the system, e.g. overland flow, throughflow
- **stores** – water is held in the system, e.g. lake
- **outputs** – water leaving the system, e.g. river flowing to the sea, evaporation.

The storm hydrograph

A hydrograph shows how **discharge** changes over time. Discharge is the amount of water flowing down a river.

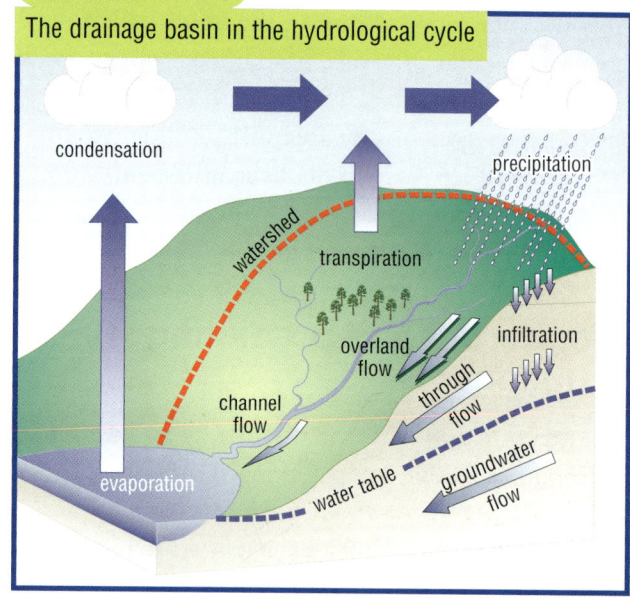

FIGURE 1.32 The drainage basin in the hydrological cycle

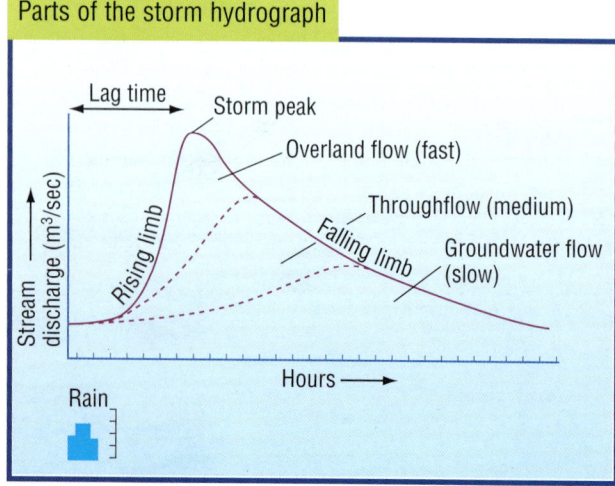

FIGURE 1.34 Parts of the storm hydrograph

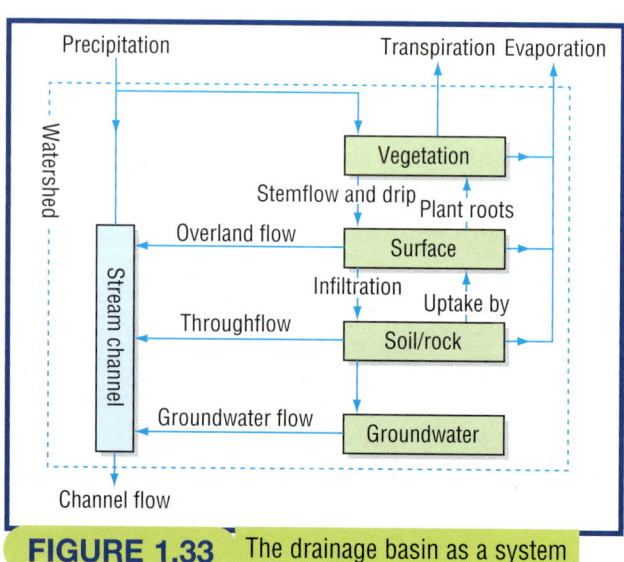

FIGURE 1.33 The drainage basin as a system

Analysing storm hydrographs

Hydrographs vary in the detail of their shapes. Figure 1.35 shows two hydrographs with several differences:

- A has a shorter lag time than B. The lag time is the period between rainfall and peak stream discharge.
- A is a flashy hydrograph whereas B is subdued.
- B's response to the rain lasts longer then A's.
- A has a higher peak discharge than B.
- A's rising and falling limbs are steeper than B's.

The shorter the time lag and the steeper the rising limb, the greater is the risk of flooding.

FIGURE 1.35
Two contrasting hydrographs

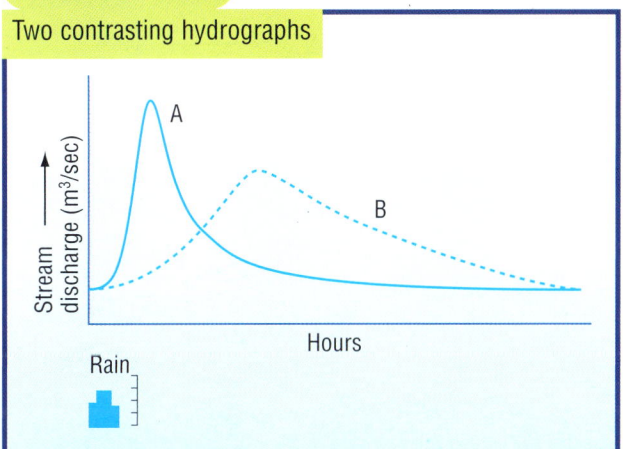

FIGURE 1.36
The old Wye Bridge, Hereford, at high flow

FIGURE 1.37
The Old Wye Bridge, Hereford, at low flow

Variations can be caused by:

- **Land use.** Vegetation intercepts rain so that less water arrives at the ground surface. This reduces overland flow (= a **subdued** hydrograph). The concrete and tarmac surfaces in urban areas do not allow water to soak in. This increases overland flow (= a **flashy** storm hydrograph).
- **Type of rain.** A heavy downpour means that some of the rain will not soak away, so overland flow increases (= a **flashy** storm hydrograph).
- **Soil moisture.** When soil is saturated, rain cannot infiltrate, so overland flow increases (= a **flashy** storm hydrograph).

TASKS

1. Make four headings:

   Inputs, Flows, Stores, Outputs

   Put as many as you can of the following words under the correct heading.

precipitation	vegetation	infiltration	tributary
groundwater flow	condensation	throughflow	lake
evaporation	drainage basin	water table	hydrological cycle
river	transpiration	watershed	channel flow

2. Which three words do not fit under any of the four headings?

3. Look at the two river hydrographs in Figure 1.35. Select the correct alternative from each of the statements in the table below.

Subdued storm hydrograph	Flashy storm hydrograph
longer / shorter lag time	longer / shorter lag time
lower / higher peak discharge	lower / higher peak discharge
Rainfall reaches river channel slowly / quickly	Rainfall reaches river channel slowly / quickly
low / high flood risk	low / high flood risk
gentle / steep rising and falling limbs	gentle / steep rising and falling limbs
Rainwater is taken away over a longer / shorter time	Rainwater is taken away over a longer / shorter time

one
People and the Physical World
Rivers

RIVER PROCESSES

SUMMARY A river gets its energy from flowing downhill. This energy helps it to erode the bed and banks of its channel. A river can also transport the material it has eroded. When a river loses energy it will deposit its load. A river erodes in four different ways. It also has four methods of transporting its load. When the river no longer has enough energy to transport its load it deposits the heavier stones first and lighter particles later.

From its **source** to its **mouth** a river channel is a system. Its energy comes from water flowing down towards sea level. A river's energy lets it change the land.

- **Erosion** happens when the running water wears away the river's bed and banks. **Vertical erosion** happens when the river cuts downwards into its bed. **Lateral erosion** happens when the river cuts sideways into its banks.
- **Transport** happens when the river carries material (**load**) that it has already eroded. The size and number of particles that can be carried depends on the speed of the river.
- **Deposition** happens when the river loses energy, stops eroding and puts down load it has been carrying.

Erosion processes

A river erodes in four ways:

- **Abrasion** is when pebbles are carried by the flow of the river. These are thrown and rolled against the bed and banks with sufficient force to wear them away.
- **Attrition** is the wearing down of pebbles which the river transports. As they hit the bed, banks or other pebbles, they gradually become rounder and smaller.
- **Solution** is a chemical process. The weak acids in the river water dissolve the minerals in the rock of the river's bed and banks. Some rocks – such as limestone – are easy to dissolve.
- **Hydraulic action** is the banging effect of rough water on the bed and banks. This hammering loosens particles that are eventually pulled out into the flow of water.

FIGURE 1.38
The Holford River in its middle course

TRANSPORT PROCESSES

A river transports material in four ways:

- **Dissolved load** is the material which cannot be seen but is dissolved in the river water.
- **Suspended load** is the material which is light enough to be carried by the river's current.
- **Bedload** is material which is too heavy to be carried by the river's current. Instead it rolls along the river bed.
- **Saltation load** is material which moves by bouncing along the river bed in short 'hops'.

The last three methods of transport depend on the speed of the river's flow. A small pebble may be lying still on the river bed. If the river's speed increases (as it will in a rising storm hydrograph), the pebble may start rolling (bedload) before bouncing (saltation load) and then finally being carried by the flow (suspended load).

RIVER DEPOSITION

If the river slows down it will lose energy. It will no longer be able to carry out so much erosion and transportation. As the river slows down larger stones, which are heavier, will be deposited first. There are two main reasons why a river slows down:

- The river's volume gets less
- There has been an increase in friction due to the river becoming shallower.

In both cases the river will start to deposit the material that it was carrying (load). This often happens on the inside of a bend (Figure 1.38).

In Figure 1.39 the river is doing two things:

- cutting down into its bed so it is always getting lower
- removing its own eroded material and the material which has been brought to it by erosion on the slopes beside it.

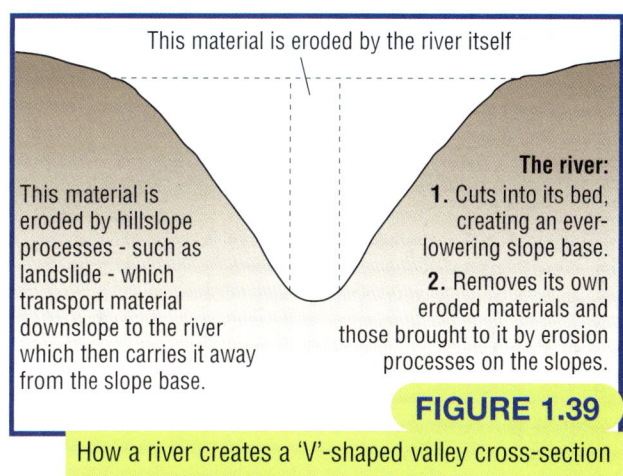

FIGURE 1.39
How a river creates a 'V'-shaped valley cross-section

TASKS

1. a Draw a simple sketch of a river bend.
   b Label the following on your sketch:
      - where the water is flowing fastest
      - a steep bank
      - a gently sloping bank
      - lateral erosion cutting under the bank
      - material deposited in slow-moving water.
2. Copy the table below and match the key words with their correct definitions.

Erosion processes	Definition
Abrasion	
Attrition	
Solution	
Hydraulic action	
Transport processes	**Definition**
Dissolved load	
Suspended load	
Bedload	
Saltation load	

Definitions:
- Water hammers the bed and banks and loosens small pebbles.
- Large stones are rolled along the river bed.
- Invisible load carried by the river.
- Pebbles carried by the river are thrown at the bed and banks.
- Minerals dissolved by weak acid in the water.
- Light particles carried along in the water.
- Lighter stones bounce along the river bed.
- Pebbles in the river are rounded off as they hit the bed and banks.

3. Give two reasons why a river deposits its load.
4. Put these materials in the correct order that they will be deposited by the river.

   pebble, grain of sand, particle of soil, large stone

Deposited first	
Deposited second	
Deposited third	
Deposited fourth	

one
People and the Physical World
Rivers

RIVER LANDSCAPE FEATURES

SUMMARY The land around a river changes as it flows from the hills through lowland plains and eventually to the sea. This is because the river processes change. Erosion is the most important process in the upper course. Erosion and deposition both happen in the lower course. Therefore different river features are formed in the upper and lower courses.

The river landscape changes as the water flows from its upper course, through its middle and lower courses and into the sea. Features of the landscape are:

- **Upper course**
  waterfalls, rapids, large bedload, bare rock bed, steep gradient, V-shaped valley, interlocking spurs.

- **Middle course**
  small meanders, narrow floodplain, moderate gradient.

- **Lower course**
  more winding meanders, wide floodplain, gentle gradient, levées, oxbow lakes.

UPPER COURSE FEATURES

The river's energy is used to cut down vertically into its bed. This means that the bed is often made of eroded bare rock.

The river flows in a fairly straight line in its upper course. It flows at the bottom of a **V-shaped valley** between **interlocking spurs**. Look at the area south of grid line 41 on Figure 1.42 (opposite) and find some upper course features.

Waterfalls are sometimes found in the upper course of a river. They are formed where the river crosses a hard layer of rock lying on top of softer rock. Figure 1.41 shows how the soft rock is worn away more than the hard rock. The hard rock eventually collapses because it is no longer supported underneath. The waterfall gradually moves back upstream from its original position, leaving behind a narrow, steep-sided gorge.

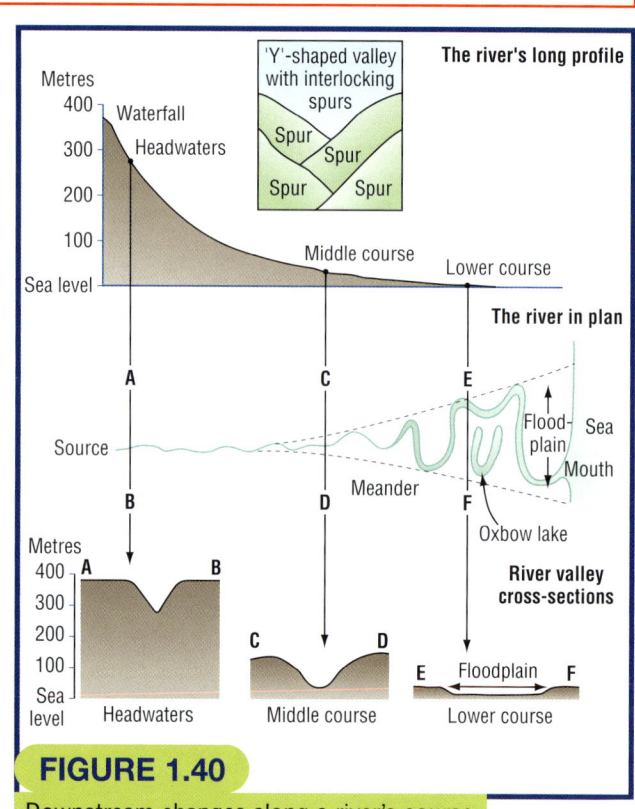

FIGURE 1.40
Downstream changes along a river's course

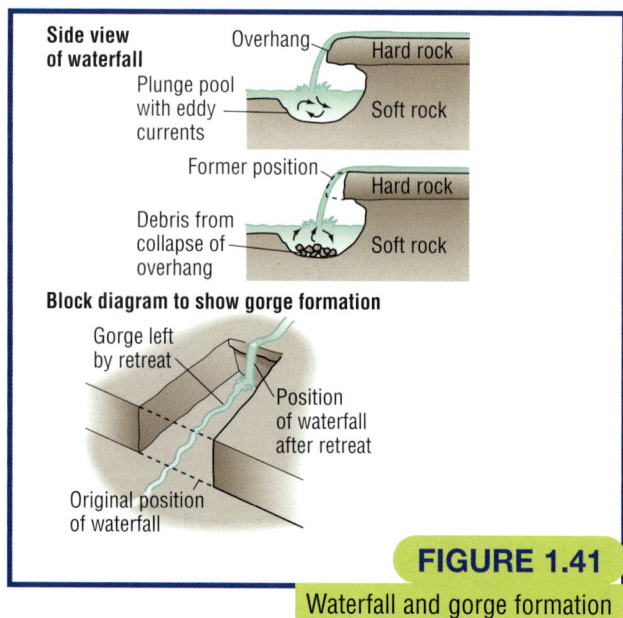

FIGURE 1.41
Waterfall and gorge formation

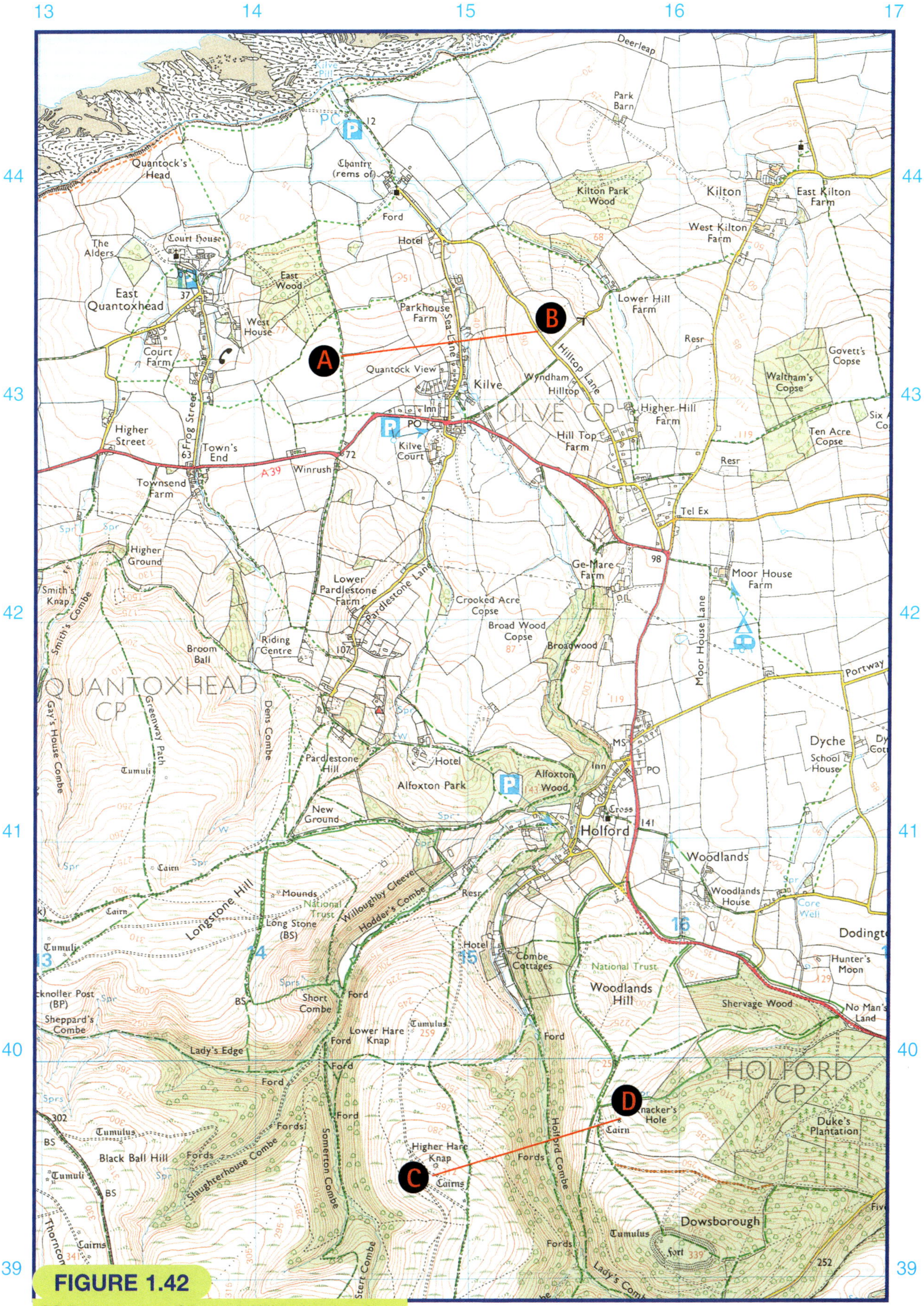

FIGURE 1.42

OS Explorer map, Quantock Hills, showing the catchment of the Holford River, Somerset

People and the Physical World
Rivers

LOWER COURSE FEATURES

In its lower course the river's energy is concentrated on cutting sideways into its banks. This means that it creates a flat **floodplain** across which the river winds in loops known as **meanders** (see Figure 1.43).

Running water flows fastest on the outside of a bend, as Figure 1.45 shows. The fast-flowing water on the outside of the bend causes erosion. The slower flow on the inside of the bend causes deposition.

Occasionally, a great flood may cut through the narrow neck of a meander. When the flood goes down, the river may follow a new route (see Figure 1.44). The old route of the river is left as a horseshoe-shaped pool known as an **oxbow lake**.

Every time the river floods over its banks the water velocity will slow down. This is because there is friction with the floodplain. Deposition happens on top of both river banks, forming low ridges known as **levées**.

The course taken by the fast-moving water through a series of meanders causes erosion on the outside banks and deposition on the inside banks. This causes the meanders to slowly widen the floodplain.

FIGURE 1.43
The River Swale in its lower course

Lower course features

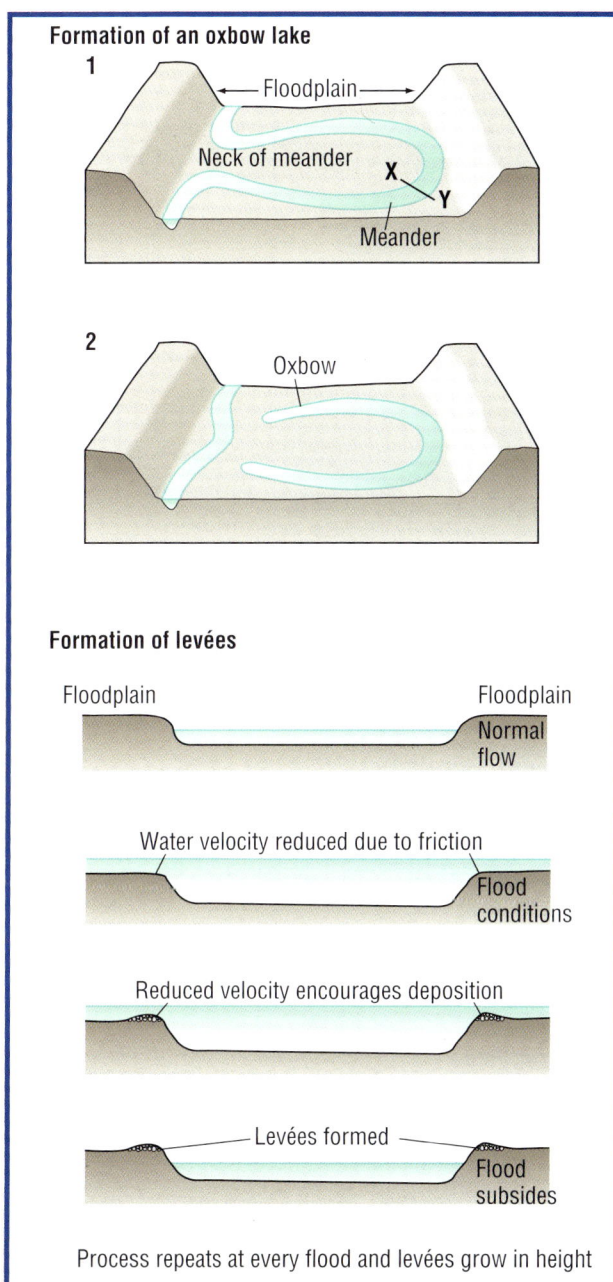

FIGURE 1.44 Floodplain features

TASKS

1. Make a large, simple sketch of the river in Figure 1.43. On your sketch, label the following:
   - a meander
   - the oxbow lake
   - where another oxbow lake may form
   - the floodplain.

   Why do you think the floodplain is given this name?

2. Look at the diagrams which show how an oxbow lake is formed in Figure 1.44.

   Sort out the following boxes into the correct order to show how an oxbow lake is formed.

   - The river erodes the narrow piece of land.
   - The meander is cut off.
   - An oxbow lake is formed.

   - As the river winds across the floodplain it begins to erode the outside bend.
   - The river begins to deposit material on the inside bend.

   - Erosion wears away the meander.
   - The outside bends move towards each other.

   - A narrow piece of land is left.
   - Erosion further wears away the meander neck.
   - Deposition occurs and begins to block off the meander.

3. Explain how these four features are formed: *waterfall, meander, levée, V-shaped valley*

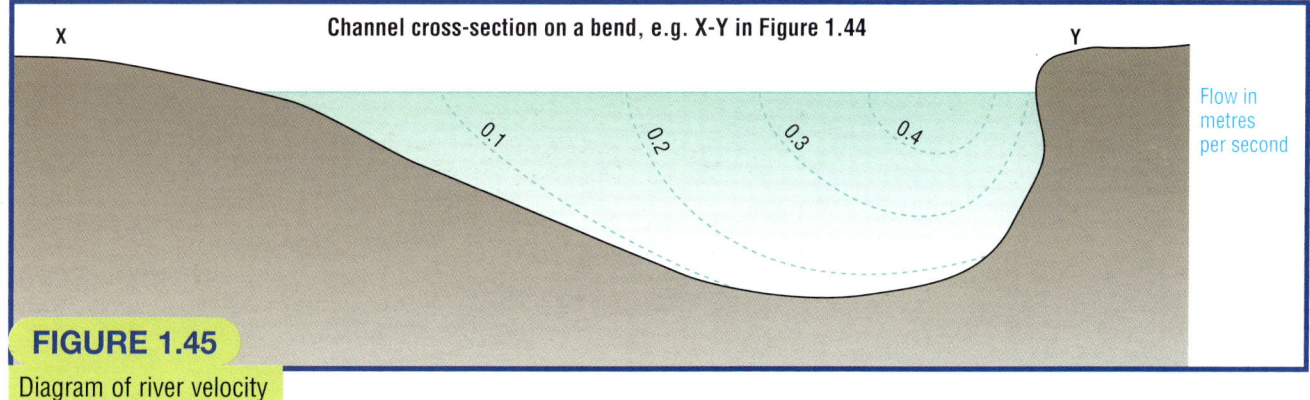

FIGURE 1.45 Diagram of river velocity

one People and the Physical World

Rivers

WHY RIVERS FLOOD

SUMMARY There are many causes of river flooding. Large-scale flooding is usually caused by a mixture of natural and human factors. Areas which are in danger of serious flooding need to have short-term and long-term protection plans in place. The Netherlands is one country which has suffered from large-scale flooding and has made plans for the future.

A river flood is when a river spills out over its banks and flows onto areas which are not usually covered by water. The main causes of river floods are:

- heavy rainfall
- rapidly melting snow
- soil saturation
- deforestation (removing trees)
- ploughing farmland
- a burst dam
- urbanisation (extending built-up areas).

FLOODING IN THE NETHERLANDS, 1995

Natural causes

In early 1995, there was heavy rain over much of Europe. In some parts, it was almost continuous from November 1994 to February 1995.

Switzerland received three times its January average. Snow melted early and quickly in the Alps. The ground was saturated because of the heavy rain. Therefore further rain was rapidly transferred to rivers as overland flow.

Some people feel that the floods are evidence of the effects of global warming. In the last 100 years:

- Average temperatures have risen by about 1°C in southern Germany.

- Winter precipitation (rain and snow) in the Rhine catchment area has increased by 40%.

FIGURE 1.46
Flooding in the Netherlands (note the protective dyke around the farmhouse)

Flooding in the Netherlands, 1995

Human causes

- Pressure to use the land as farmland or for building. This means that the Rhine has lost much of its riverside marsh and floodplain which used to hold back floodwater.
- Improved flood protection measures upstream, such as higher embankments. This means that floodwater moves downstream more quickly than it used to.
- Improved navigation for shipping. This has involved straightening the river so water moves downstream more quickly.
- Generating hydro-electric power. Ten power stations use a new channel parallel to the old river. This means that water goes downstream more quickly.
- Flood surges. The same volume of water is moving further in a shorter time. This causes a dramatic rise in the river's level.
- The change from pastoral (animals) to arable (crops) land use in rural areas. This has led to the removal of hedgerows and meadows. They have been replaced by ploughed fields with a reduced capacity for interception and infiltration. So a greater percentage of the rain falling on the Rhine catchment enters the river.
- Urbanisation. This has led to a dramatic increase in built-up areas. The concrete and tarmac send more water to the river than the fields which they replaced.

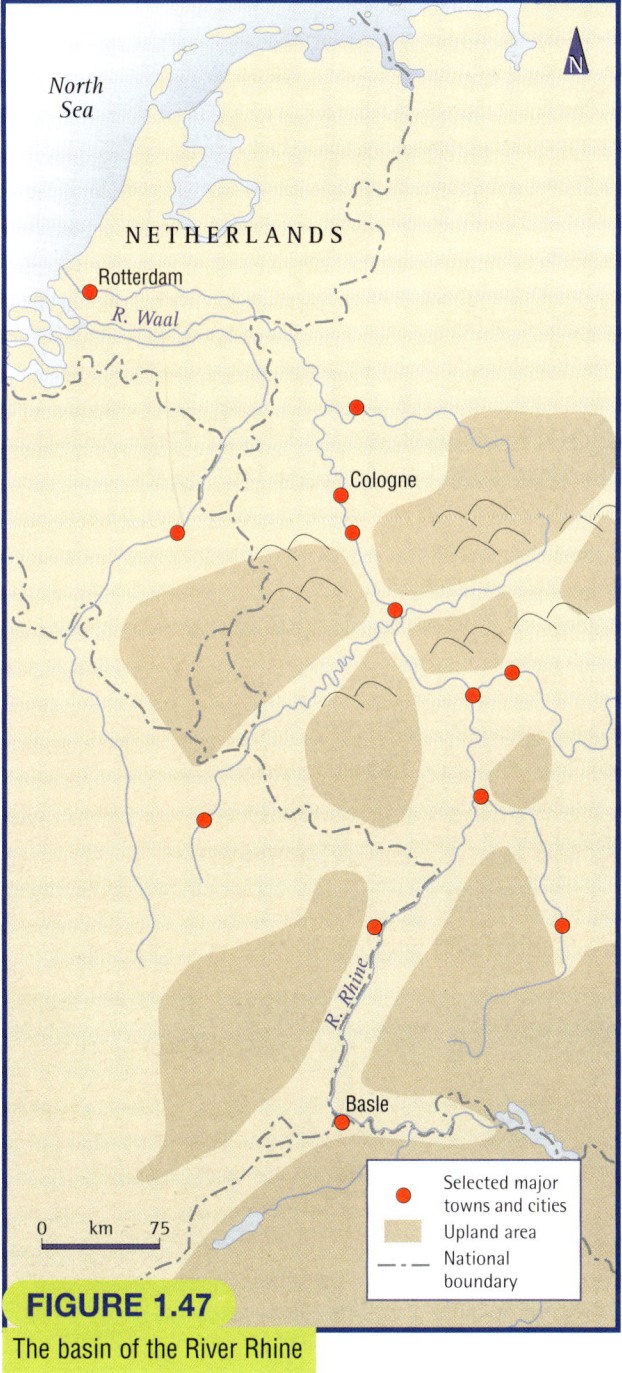

FIGURE 1.47
The basin of the River Rhine

TASKS

1 Below are four possible causes of flooding. Match the correct 'heads and tails' to explain what they mean.

Possible causes of flooding	Explanation
Soil saturation	The increase in impermeable concrete and tarmac sends more water into the river.
Deforestation	With less grassland for interception and less infiltration, more water is able to enter the river.
Ploughing	Trees intercept water in the drainage basin. When they are cut down more water goes into the river.
Urbanisation	Water cannot soak into the soil so it quickly runs across the surface and into the river.

2 Look at Figure 1.46. How has the flood risk been reduced?

3 Trace the map in Figure 1.47 and use an atlas to name and label:
- major towns and cities
- upland areas
- tributaries of the River Rhine
- the countries shown on the map.

People and the Physical World
Rivers

The Netherlands flood, 1995

On 31 January 1995, the Rhine burst its banks at the point where it enters the Netherlands. Much of the land around the river are **polders**. These are low-lying areas enclosed by embankments called **dykes**. The water table is kept below the surface of the polders by continuous pumping.

- Many of the polders were flooded.
- Four people were killed.
- Some roads became impassable.
- Many of the dykes are made of sand and clay. These became saturated because of high river levels for a long time. This made them more likely to collapse so that emergency reinforcement work had to be carried out.
- 250 000 people were evacuated. Police and soldiers guarded the empty houses against looters.
- Many homes were flooded.
- Greenhouses were flooded and stocks of flowers, fruit and vegetables were lost.
- One million cattle were evacuated. This led to some of them being infected with foot rot and reduced milk yields because of the disturbance.
- Waterways were closed to ships for two weeks. Many oil and dry bulk barges were stranded.
- Flood damage cost millions of pounds.
- A full-scale disaster was avoided because the authorities and emergency services were well-prepared.

FIGURE 1.49 Rainfall upstream at Cologne, Germany and discharge along the River Rhine from mid-January to mid-February, 1995

Date	Two-day total rainfall at Cologne (mm)	Discharge along the River Rhine (m^3/second)
15.1.95	0	2 200
17.1.95	0	3 500
19.1.95	5	2 500
21.1.95	0	2 200
23.1.95	18	3 000
25.1.95	19	3 000
27.1.95	22	6 800
29.1.95	16	6 500
31.1.95	0	9 500
2.2.95	0	11 500
4.2.95	3	11 000
6.2.95	1	8 000
8.2.95	9	6 000
10.2.95	7	4 200
12.2.95	0	4 000

Short-term flood relief measures in the Netherlands in 1995

- Sandbags and temporary barriers across doors and windows
- Evacuation of people and livestock
- Removing carpets and furniture to higher floors
- Constructing temporary dykes
- Clear underground car parks
- Clear subways and underpasses
- Close roads at risk of flooding
- Install portable pumps
- Seal door and window frames with putty or foam.

FIGURE 1.48 Temporary flood protection measures in use

TASK

Look at Figure 1.49.
- Between which dates did it rain most heavily?
- Between which dates was discharge highest?
- Describe the relationship between peak rainfall and peak discharge.
- Suggest why there is this relationship.
- How could this information be useful to governments in Germany and the Netherlands?

Flooding in the Netherlands, 1995

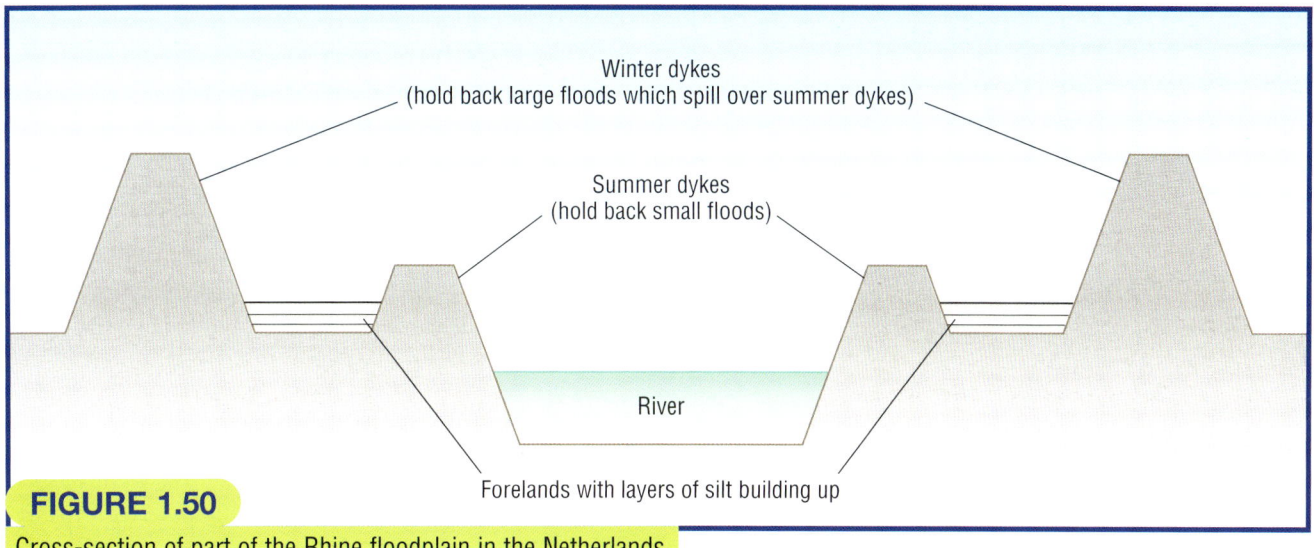

FIGURE 1.50
Cross-section of part of the Rhine floodplain in the Netherlands

Long-term flood relief plans in the Netherlands

- Recognise that countries need to work together in order to control flooding in the Rhine valley.
- Encourage **afforestation** (tree planting) in the Rhine drainage basin. This will increase the amount of rain which is intercepted.
- Encourage land uses in the Rhine basin which increase the amount of water that soaks into the ground, e.g. increase the area of parks and gardens in urban areas.
- Reinforce earth dykes with steel piling and stone blocks.
- Build flood retention basins. These are areas of riverside land which are enclosed with dykes. They have floodwater drained onto them. This will reduce the level of the river. When the flood level goes down, the water from the basin is slowly released into the channel.
- Allow the river to flow back through former marshland areas to absorb more floodwater and create an area for wildlife.
- Limit house building in areas which are likely to flood.
- Encourage individual households to reduce flood damage, e.g. tiled floors downstairs with removable items of furniture, and kitchen cupboards fixed to the wall, not resting on the floor.
- A further £1 billion worth of flood protection was planned after the 1995 floods.
- An early warning system should improve public confidence. But only if its predictions are accurate and the warnings are given to people.

TASK

A mind map is a good way to help develop your understanding. It allows you to write down what you know in any order. The topics help you to organise the details and make links.

Copy and complete the mind map below to describe the long-term flood protection measures in the Netherlands. Some ideas have been included to get you started. See how one idea leads to more detail.

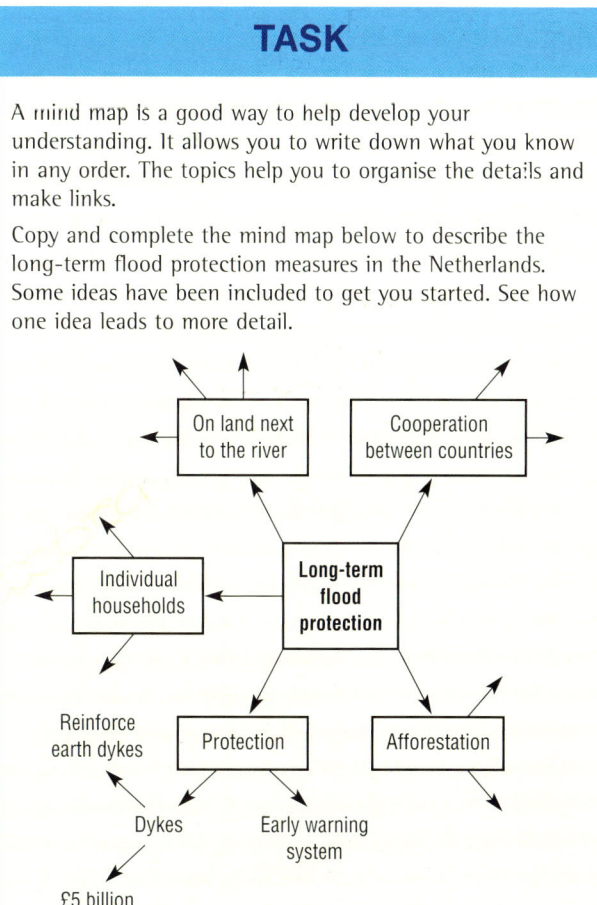

one
People and the Physical World
Rivers

FLOODING IN BANGLADESH, JULY–SEPTEMBER 1998

FIGURE 1.51
Bangladesh and the drainage basins of the Ganges and Brahmaputra

> **SUMMARY** Bangladesh is an LEDC and is one of the poorest countries in the world. It has suffered many disastrous floods. As in the Netherlands, flooding is due to a combination of natural and human causes. It also has long-term protection plans in place. Unfortunately, because Bangladesh is poor these plans cannot be carried out.

Natural causes

- Melting snow in the Himalayan mountains was adding water to the Ganges and Brahmaputra rivers which flow through Bangladesh.
- The monsoon (seasonal) rains in the region were very heavy from July onwards.
- More than half of Bangladesh is under 5 m above sea level.
- The country lies across a huge **river delta** (a low-lying flat area formed from sediment which has been deposited by a river as it enters the sea).
- Some flooding is normal. It helps the economy of the area by providing fresh nutrients in the deposited river silt and by increasing the soil depth.

Human causes

- Over 90% of the area of the drainage basins which feed water into Bangladesh is in other countries (see Figure 1.51).
- Deforestation in the Himalayan foothills means more rainwater enters the Ganges and Brahmaputra because there is less interception by tree leaves.
- Some experts believe that the scale and effect of deforestation has been exaggerated.
- The Ganges has been diverted for irrigation (bringing water to fields of crops), which has removed silt from the river's load and prevented the building up of the floodplain.
- 100 000 new wells have lowered the water table and caused the land to sink at 2.5 cm per year.
- Bangladesh is heavily in debt and there is no money available for flood protection measures.
- Bangladesh spends money on supporting exports rather than building and maintaining flood defences.
- Many of the existing flood defences do not work.
- Corruption is taking money away from flood protection schemes.

Flooding in Bangladesh, 1998

The effects of flooding in Bangladesh

FIGURE 1.52 Muslim women wade through floodwaters in Dhaka

The number of people who died was relatively low but the damage was devastating:

- 130 million cattle killed
- 1040 people dead in floods
- Two-thirds of the country flooded
- 23.5 million people homeless
- Worst floods this century
- More than 1000 schools damaged
- 2½ million farmers affected
- 6500 bridges damaged
- 11 000 km of roads damaged
- Some areas underwater now for two months

People and the Physical World
Rivers

FIGURE 1.53
Dhaka residents queueing for emergency meals

After the flood

Health

Water supplies were contaminated for a quarter of a million people. This was because of polluted wells, flooded sewers and floating bodies of people and cattle. Young children and the elderly were most at risk. A quarter of a million people were affected by diarrhoea. Health problems were made worse by thousands of people having to live in crowded flood shelters.

Relief

Relief efforts were difficult because of the damage to communication links. The main port of Chittagong was closed for weeks, and roads and railways were cut off.

Economy

Over 400 clothing factories closed. Shipping was impossible through Chittagong, the main port. Electricity supplies were also disrupted.

TASKS

1. Learning a case study means knowing some details. One way to remember lots of ideas is to summarise them by picking out the key words or phrases. Practise this skill using the information on page 36 which describes the causes of flooding in Bangladesh.

   A summary table which highlights the natural and human causes is started below. Draw your own table and complete it.

Natural causes	Human causes
Melting snow	Floodwater comes from other countries
Heavy monsoon rains	Deforestation in the Himalayas

2. List five pieces of evidence to show that the effects of flooding in Bangladesh in 1998 were much worse than in the Netherlands in 1995.

Floods in Bangladesh, 1998

Short-term flood-relief measures in Bangladesh in 1998

- 350 000 tonnes of cereal were bought by the Bangladesh Government to feed people.
- The UK Government gave £21 million.
- More than a million tonnes of international food aid was given.
- The World Health Organization appealed for £5.2 million to buy water purification tablets.
- The Bangladesh Government gave free seeds to farmers.
- Engineers and volunteers worked long hours to repair the flood damage.

Long-term flood protection measures in Bangladesh

- Plans to cope with future floods have been made to give warnings and organise rescue and relief services.
- After the 1998 floods, a 50 km embankment around the city of Dhaka was planned, but there was no money to build it.
- Shelters were constructed (see Figure 1.54).
- Dams and embankments were planned to hold back some of the flood water but the cost was too much and they were never built.

TASK

3. Work with a partner to draw up a list of reasons why flooding is likely to be a bigger problem in Bangladesh than in the Netherlands.

   Think about:
   - the physical geography of the two countries
   - the natural causes of the floods
   - how rich the two countries are
   - the long-term protection plans for the future.

FIGURE 1.54
A flood shelter

one
People and the Physical World
Coasts

WAVE POWER

SUMMARY Waves have a massive amount of energy to change the shape of the coastline. Waves start far out at sea but it is only when they break near the coastline that they use their energy. Like rivers, waves erode the land, move the sediment and deposit it elsewhere.

Coastal areas are always changing. The continuous impact of waves and daily tides erodes the coast. They move sediment and deposit it elsewhere. Sometimes these changes are hardly noticeable but stormy weather conditions can cause rapid changes to a coastline.

Waves

Waves are formed by wind blowing over the surface of the sea. This causes a drag or friction on the water, creating a swell in the water. The size and strength of the wave depends on three factors:

- The strength of the wind – the stronger the wind, the bigger the wave.
- How long the wind has been blowing. More energy is transferred to the wave over a longer time.
- How far the wave has travelled. This is called the **fetch**. The longer the fetch, the larger the wave is likely to be (Figure 1.55).

When the wave reaches shallow water, friction between the sea bed and the wave slows it down.

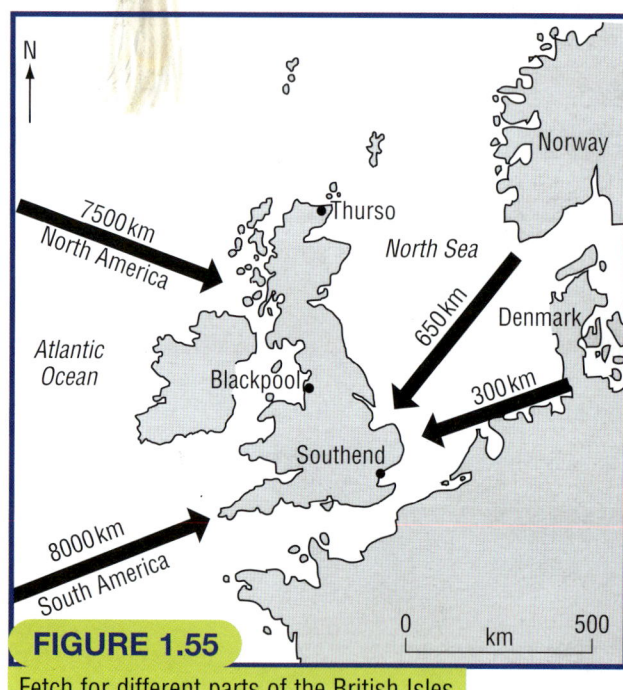

FIGURE 1.55
Fetch for different parts of the British Isles

The water begins to pile up and the tops of the waves begin to break as the wave becomes unstable and topples forward (Figure 1.56).

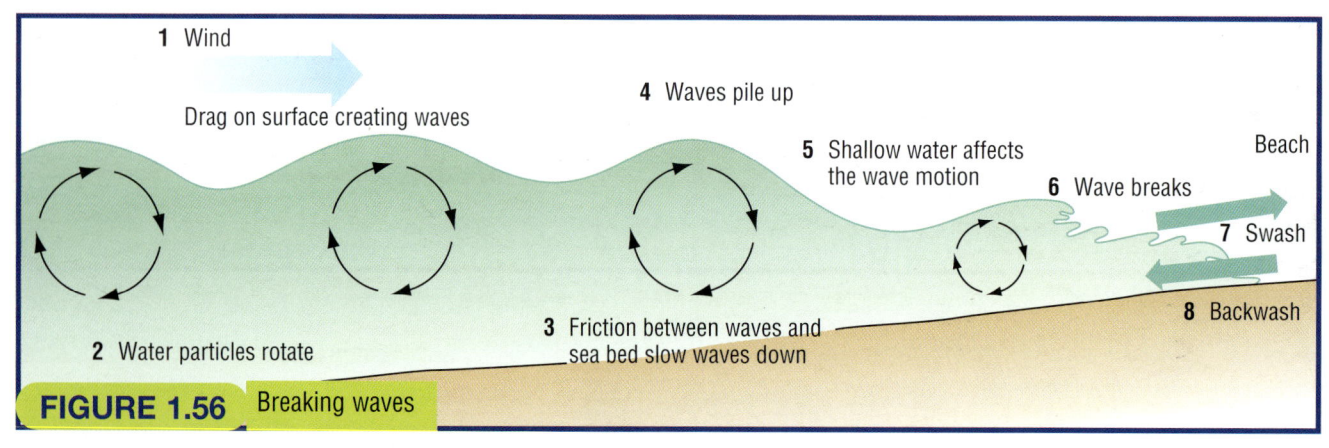

FIGURE 1.56 Breaking waves

1 Wind
Drag on surface creating waves
2 Water particles rotate
3 Friction between waves and sea bed slow waves down
4 Waves pile up
5 Shallow water affects the wave motion
6 Wave breaks
7 Swash
8 Backwash
Beach

Wave power 41

FIGURE 1.57
Wave refraction at St Ives, Cornwall

As the sea becomes shallower, the waves change direction to follow the shape of the coastline. This is called **wave refraction**. When a wave approaches a coastline, the headlands slow the wave. The wave, though, continues to roll at a faster rate in the bay. Wave refraction concentrates the wave energy on the headland (Figure 1.57).

As the wave reaches the coast, it breaks and the water runs up the beach. This is called the **swash**. The water drains back down into the sea. This is called the **backwash**. Waves which arrive at a rate of more than eight per minute are usually caused by strong winds over a long fetch. They will cause erosion. Waves arriving at a rate fewer than eight have less energy. They will deposit sediment and build up a coastline.

TASKS

1. Complete the sentences below to explain what decides the size and strength of waves.
   - The stronger the wind _____
   - Winds blowing over the waves for a long time _____
   - The further the wave has travelled _____

2. Match the following 'heads and tails'. They are definitions of four key words about waves.

Key word	Definition
Fetch	Waves change direction to follow the shape of the coast
Wave refraction	Water from the wave drains back down the beach
Swash	How far the wave has travelled
Backwash	Water runs up the beach as the wave breaks

3. Look at Figure 1.57. What is happening to the waves as they approach the coast?

People and the Physical World
Coasts

WEARING THE COAST AWAY

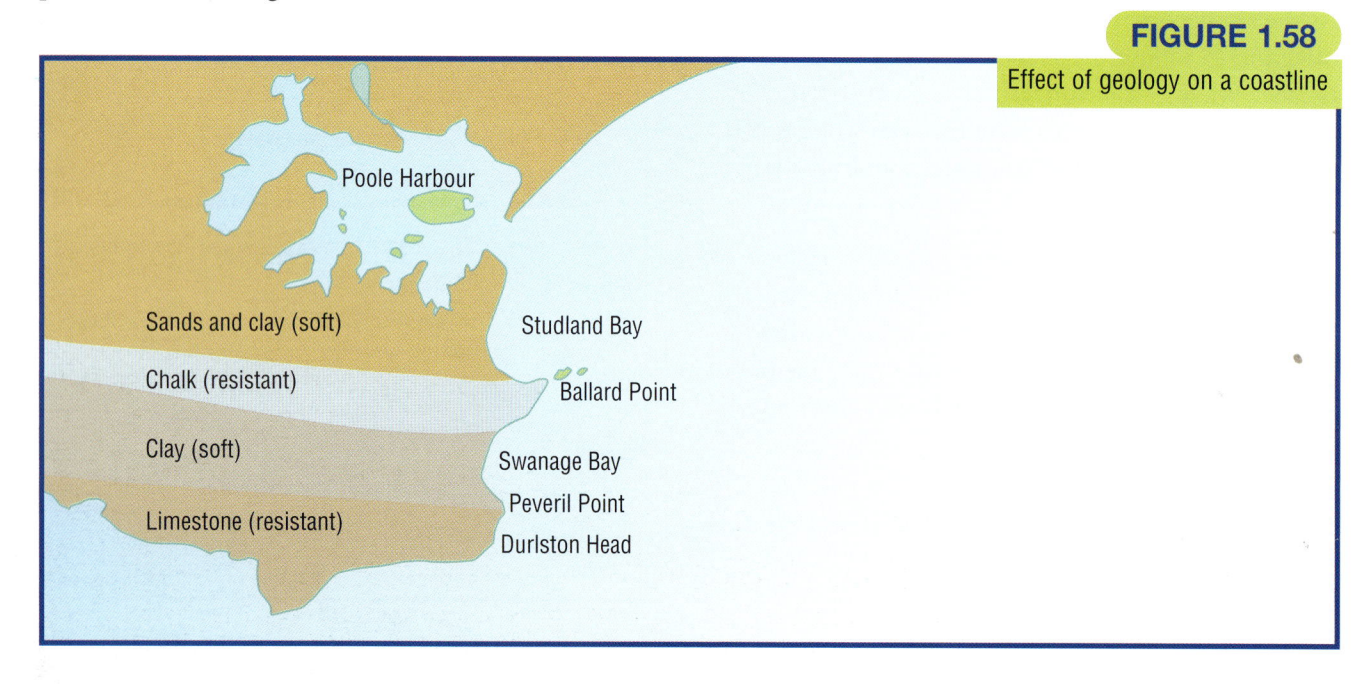

> **SUMMARY** The sea erodes some coastlines more easily than others. The type and structure of the rock, and the shape of the coastline affect how quickly erosion happens. Like a river, the waves erode in a few different ways.

What affects the rate of coastal erosion?

Some coastlines are eroded by the sea more easily than others. The rock type, the rock structure (geology) and the shape of the coastline are important factors in the rate of erosion.

Rocks such as limestone, chalk and granite are hard to erode. These rocks often form cliffs and headlands. Softer rocks, such as clay or shale, are more easily eroded by the sea. These often form wide beach areas and low cliffs.

The rock structure can help shape the coastline. Figure 1.58 shows part of Dorset known as the Isle of Purbeck. The rocks are in lines from west to east. The rocks erode at different rates. In the east, there are headlands of hard rock, like chalk, and bays of soft rock, like clay. A hard rock, limestone, produces cliffs along the south coast.

FIGURE 1.59 Cliffs in Pembrokeshire

FIGURE 1.58 Effect of geology on a coastline

- Poole Harbour
- Sands and clay (soft)
- Chalk (resistant)
- Studland Bay
- Ballard Point
- Clay (soft)
- Swanage Bay
- Peveril Point
- Limestone (resistant)
- Durlston Head

42

Wearing the coast away

How the sea erodes

The main cause of erosion is the impact of waves crashing on the rock:

- **Corrasion/abrasion**. Waves scoop up stones and rock fragments and hurl these at the cliffs. This chips away at the rock, eventually breaking pieces off.
- **Scouring**. Waves at the **base** of a cliff remove loose rock.
- **Hydraulic action**. Waves trap air in cracks. The pressure forces the cracks to open and weakens the rock.
- **Solution** Some rocks contain chemicals which salt water can dissolve. This weakens the rock. In chalk and limestone, the calcium carbonate is dissolved.
- **Attrition**. Rock fragments collide and wear down. Eventually the fragments are reduced to sand or silt. These fragments are sorted by the sea. The heaviest and largest material is left near the cliff. The finest material is deposited as sand off the coast (Figure 1.60).

As well as the sea at work, other weathering processes such as the wind, rain and frost also wear away the cliffs.

TASKS

1. Here is a mnemonic to help you to remember the five ways that the sea erodes the coast.

   Can Students Have Shorter Afternoons

   Are you able to think of a better one?

2. Copy and complete the spider diagram which describes the five erosion processes.

3. Look at Figure 1.60. Why does erosion happen at the base (bottom) of the cliff?
4. How are beach materials graded (sorted)?

FIGURE 1.60
Grading of beach material

Sand — Pebbles — Smaller stones — Large stones — Erosion at the base of the cliff

Large boulders from cliff collapse

Attrition reduces and rounds stones
Backwash carries the lighter material out to sea

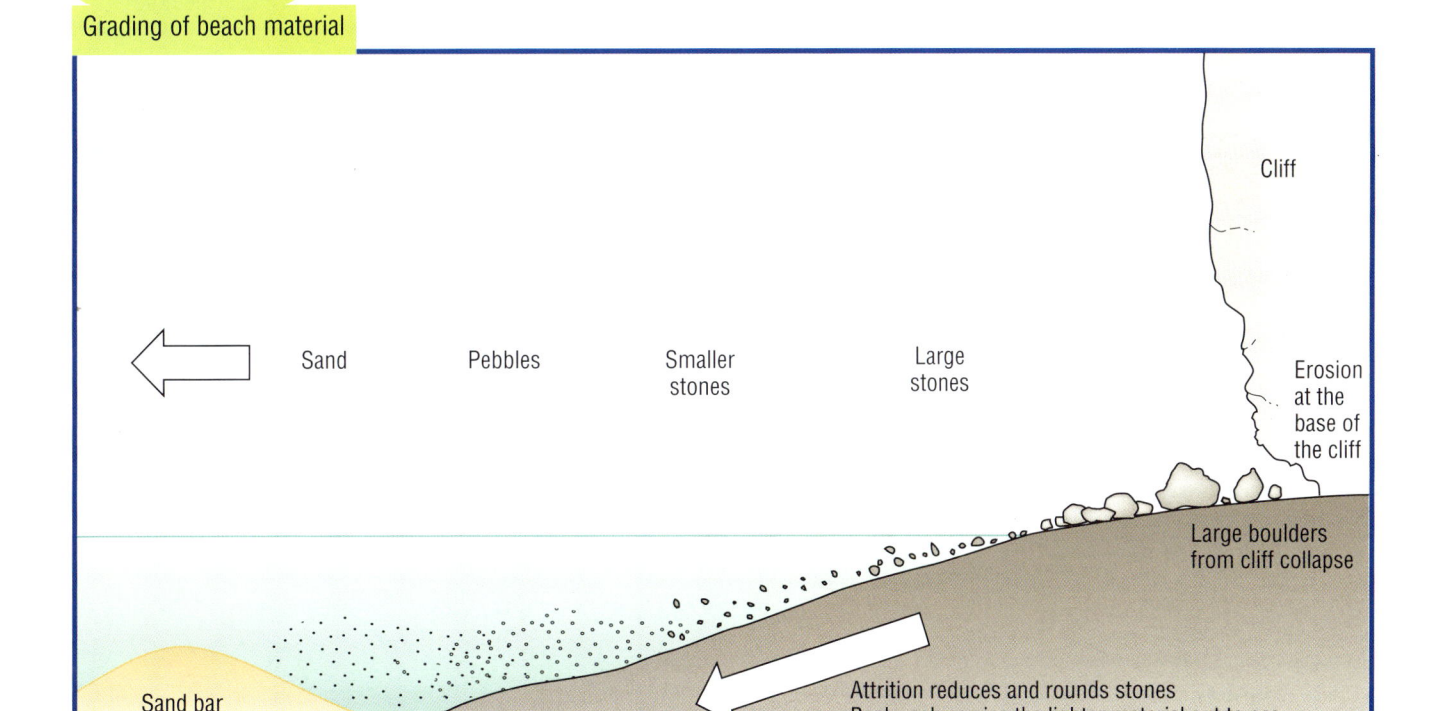

Sand bar

one
Coasts
People and the Physical World

FEATURES PRODUCED BY EROSION

> **SUMMARY** When waves erode the coast they attack both hard and soft cliffs. Caves, arches, stacks, stumps and wave-cut platforms are cut from the harder rock. Where cliffs are made of softer rock slumping happens. The cliffs collapse into the sea.

The erosion of the coast produces cliffs, headlands, caves, arches, stacks and wave-cut platforms. There is an order to their formation, shown in Figure 1.61.

FIGURE 1.61 Headland erosion

1. Waves crash on to the headland. Weak areas are opened to form a cave
2. The sea enlarges the cave to form an arch. New cave forming
3. The arch collapses. The seaward side left standing. This is a stack. New arch forming
4. Headland retreating. The stack is eroded down to form a stump. A shallow rock ledge develops to form a wave-cut platform

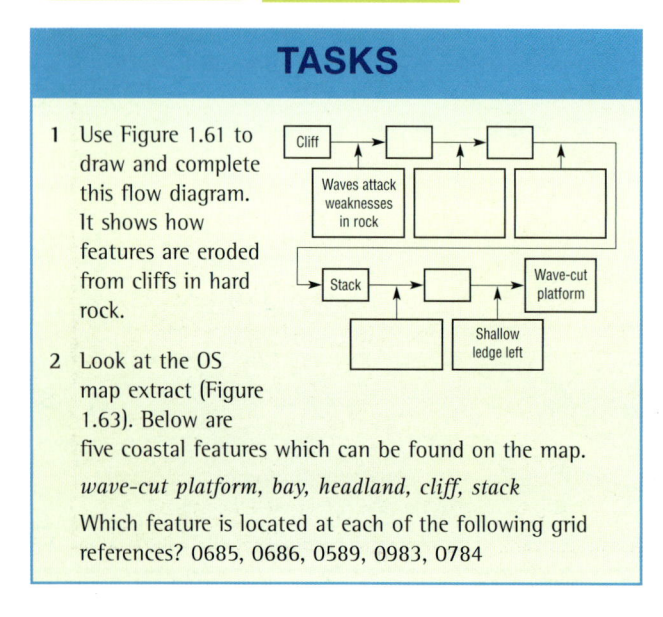

The OS map extract shows a coastal area south of Scarborough where the coastline is being eroded. This area has hard limestone rock and some thinner layers of softer clay. Along the coastline there are headlands, cliffs, bays and wave-cut platforms.

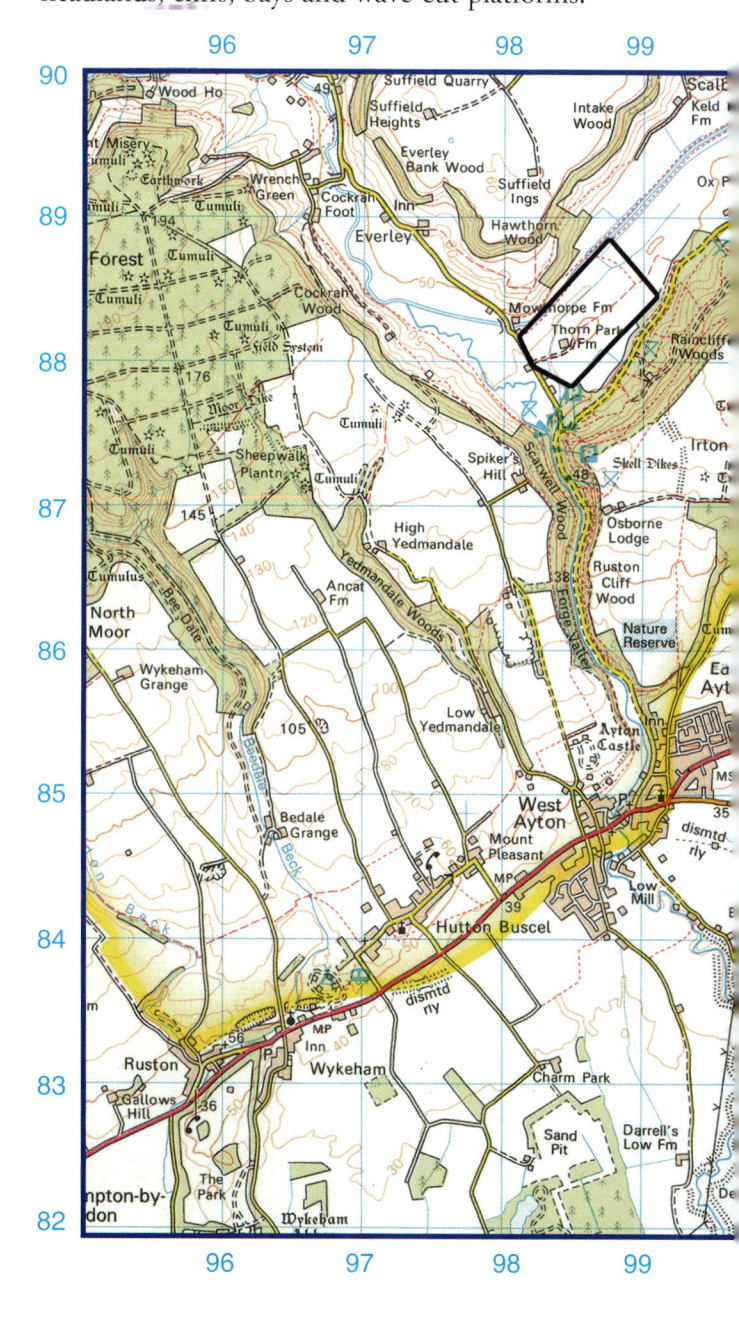

TASKS

1. Use Figure 1.61 to draw and complete this flow diagram. It shows how features are eroded from cliffs in hard rock.

   Cliff → Waves attack weaknesses in rock → ... → ...
   → Stack → ... → Wave-cut platform
   Shallow ledge left

2. Look at the OS map extract (Figure 1.63). Below are five coastal features which can be found on the map.
   wave-cut platform, bay, headland, cliff, stack
   Which feature is located at each of the following grid references? 0685, 0686, 0589, 0983, 0784

Features produced by erosion   45

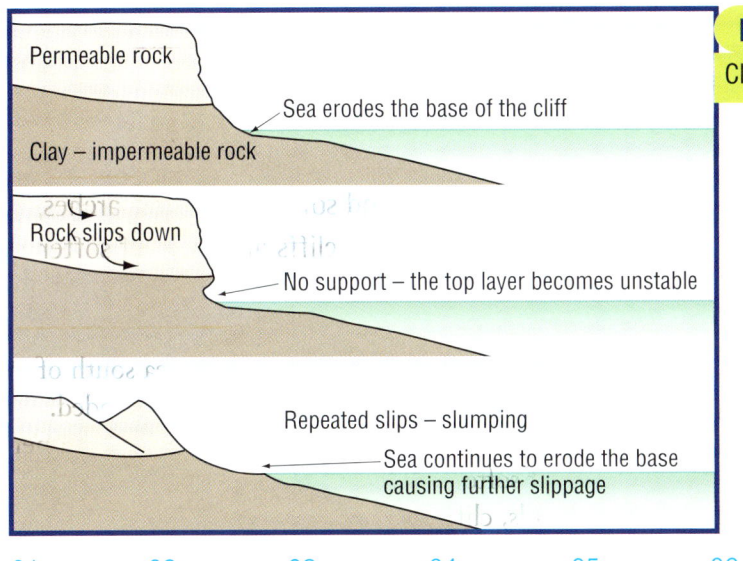

FIGURE 1.62
Cliff slumping

In the area around Scarborough there are several areas where the cliff has slipped, for example, Tenants' Cliff (0684) and at Holbeck Hall on the South Cliffs in 1993. This is called **slumping**. It happens when the sea erodes the base of the cliff. The rocks above become unstable. Limestone is a **permeable** rock (it allows water to soak through it). The water collects in the underneath layer of rock which is clay. Clay is **impermeable** (it does not let water soak through it). This provides a surface for the unstable rocks above to slip down (Figure 1.62).

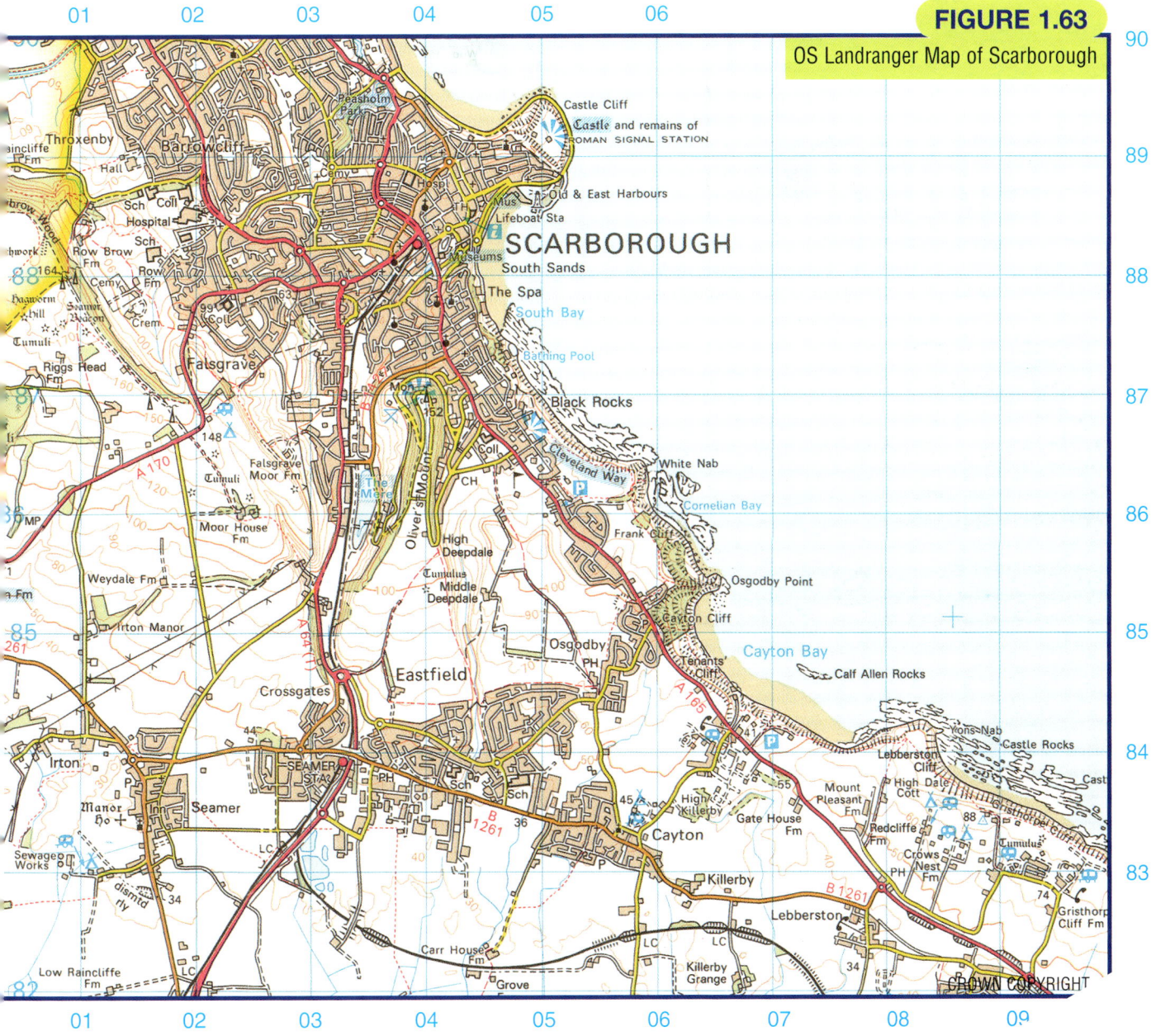

FIGURE 1.63
OS Landranger Map of Scarborough

People and the Physical World

Coasts

MOVING AND DEPOSITING MATERIAL

SUMMARY Waves move eroded material along the coast. This process is called longshore drift. Like a river, waves move material in different ways. When the waves cannot carry the eroded material any further it is deposited. These deposits produce some landscape features, like spits, beaches, bars and tombolos.

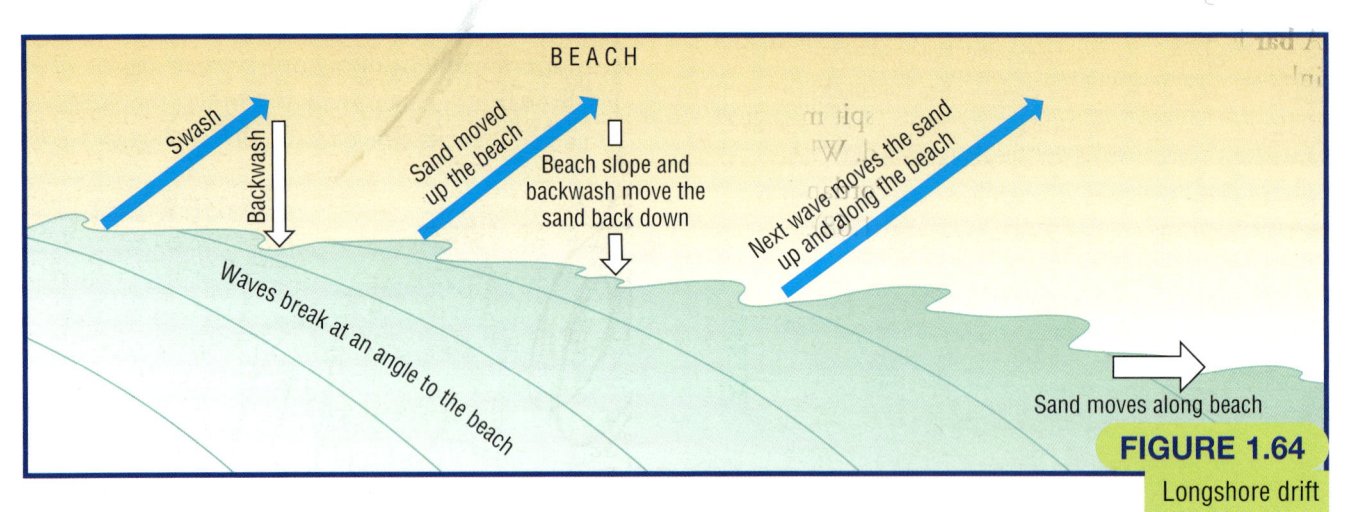

FIGURE 1.64 Longshore drift

Longshore drift

Longshore drift is at work when waves break at an angle to the beach. The **swash** runs up the beach at an angle. However, the **backwash** flows straight back due to the beach's slope. A pebble being moved along has a zig-zag path (Figure 1.64).

Moving material

Like rivers, waves move material in different ways. This depends on the size of the material and how much energy there is (Figure 1.65).

- **Solution**. Minerals which cannot be seen are dissolved in the water.
- **Suspension**. Light materials can be carried by waves.
- **Saltation**. Material which is just too heavy to be carried in suspension will be bounced along the sea bed.
- **Traction**. Heavier material is rolled along the sea bed by the strongest waves.

FIGURE 1.65 How sediment is moved by the sea

1 Fine sediment held in suspension

2 Saltation – pebbles, which are too heavy to be in suspension but too light to sink, are bounced along

3 Traction – heavy and large sediment rolled along the sea bed

Moving and depositing material

Features produced by deposition

Sand dunes form when winds blow sand from the beaches to the land behind. Here it piles up as dunes.

A **spit** may form when there is a gap in the coastline, for example where a river enters the sea (estuary). Longshore drift deposits material across the estuary faster than the river can remove it. Gradually a piece of land develops across the estuary. Plants begin to grow on this land (Figure 1.66).

A **bar** is where the spit has formed across a bay or inlet creating a lagoon (lake) and **salt marsh** behind it (Figure 1.68). Sometimes a spit may grow out from the land to connect an island. When Chesil Beach joined with the Isle of Portland, it formed a **tombolo** (Figures 1.67 and 1.68).

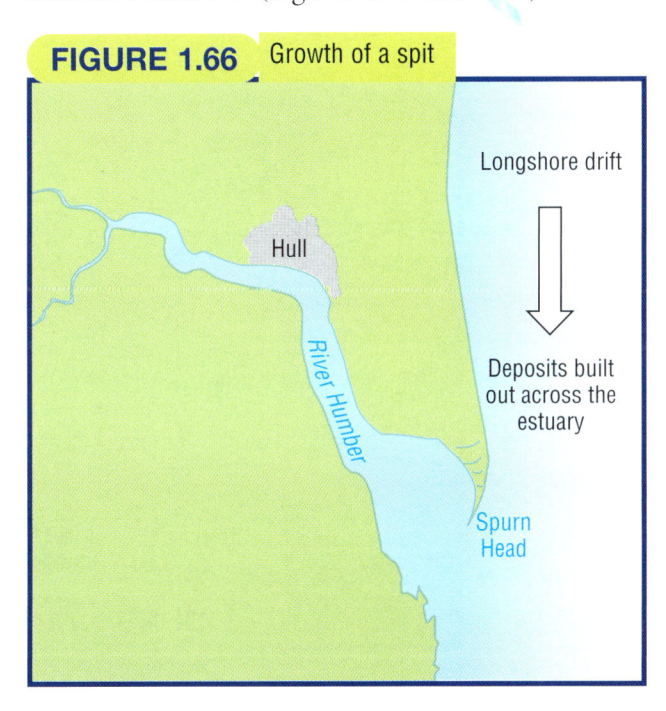

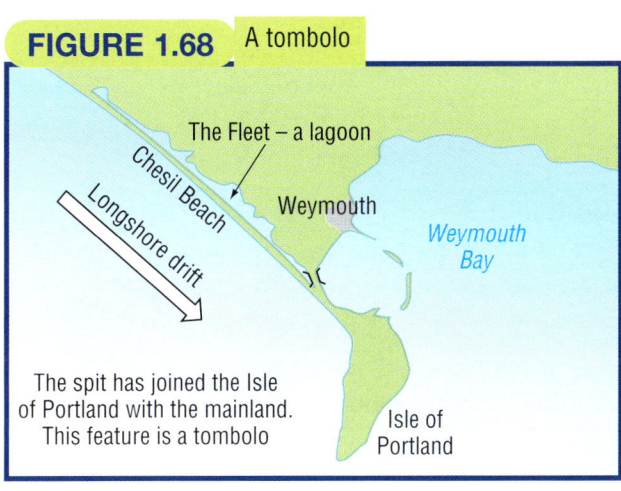

FIGURE 1.66 Growth of a spit

FIGURE 1.67 Chesil Beach

FIGURE 1.68 A tombolo

The spit has joined the Isle of Portland with the mainland. This feature is a tombolo.

TASKS

1 Describe the process of longshore drift. Include the words below.

   pebble, beach, straight back, waves, along, swash, angle, zig-zag, backwash, sand

2 Copy and complete the table below. It is a summary of features produced by wave deposition.

Feature	Example	Definition
Bar	Chesil Beach	
Spit		Deposits built across an estuary
Tombolo	Chesil Beach	
Lagoon		Part of the sea is cut off to form a lake

one
People and the Physical World
Coasts

EROSION OF THE HOLDERNESS COAST

The Holderness coast is on the eastern side of the UK. It is south of Scarborough and faces the North Sea (see Figure 1.70). Along most of the coast are cliffs which are between 20 m and 30 m high. At the estuary of the River Humber an impressive spit – called Spurn Head – has been formed (Figure 1.69).

The cliffs of the Holderness coast have been eroding at a rapid rate for thousands of years. They are being worn back by 1.2 m each year.

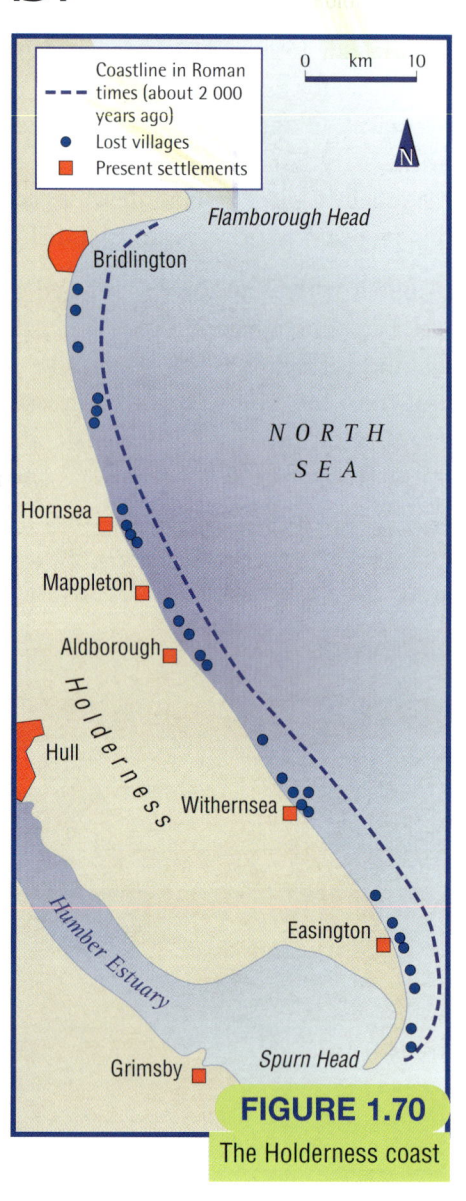

FIGURE 1.69 Spurn Head, a spit

FIGURE 1.70 The Holderness coast

Causes of rapid cliff erosion at Holderness

The area is made of soft material called boulder clay. The cliffs are easily undercut by wave action. They collapse in a series of slips and slumps. This is worse when the material is weakened by waterlogging after heavy rain (see Figure 1.71).

The coast is often attacked by powerful waves. These are driven by strong winds blowing across the North Sea. The destructive power of the waves may be increasing because of a slow rise in sea level. The waves erode the base of the cliffs by means of hydraulic action and abrasion (see page 43).

Much of the eroded material is fine clay which is carried out to sea. The rest of the eroded material is heavier sand which settles to form a thin beach. Longshore drift moves the sand south. This removal of sand means that wide beaches cannot form. So there is nothing to reduce wave energy by friction.

Erosion of the Holderness coast

FIGURE 1.71 Sue Earle's farm, on the Holderness coast

The effects of rapid cliff erosion at Holderness

A strip of land 4 km wide has been eroded since Roman times. Many villages and farms have disappeared under the sea (see Figure 1.70).

The North Sea gas terminal at Easington is where gas pipelines from North Sea drilling platforms come ashore. It is very important for supplying gas throughout the UK. However, it is threatened because of its location on the top of cliffs.

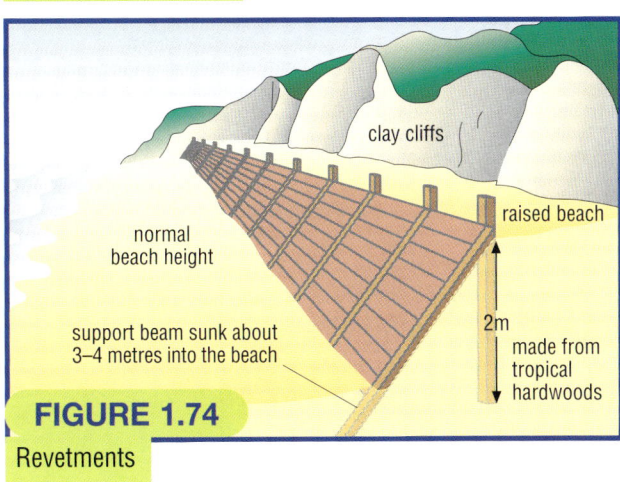

FIGURE 1.73 Sea wall and groynes

FIGURE 1.72 Rock barrier to protect caravan site

Coastal towns, including Withernsea and Hornsea, farms, roads and tourist facilities such as caravan sites are under threat from the advancing sea (see Figures 1.71 and 1.72).

Attempts to control coastal erosion at Holderness

Attempts have been made to reduce the force of waves hitting the cliff by:

- building **sea walls** (see left-hand side of Figure 1.73) and **revetments** (sloping wooden barriers, see Figure 1.74) along the bottom of the cliffs
- building barriers called **groynes** which will trap beach material moved by longshore drift (see right-hand side of Figure 1.73 and also Figure 1.76).

FIGURE 1.74 Revetments

(Diagram labels: clay cliffs; normal beach height; support beam sunk about 3–4 metres into the beach; raised beach; 2m; made from tropical hardwoods)

People and the Physical World
Coasts

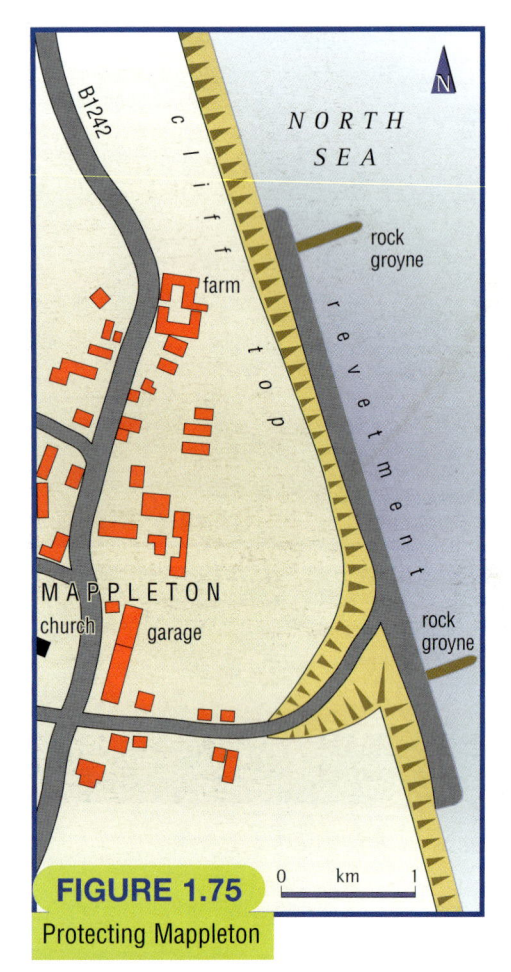

It is very expensive to protect the coast. There are arguments about who should pay. Should it be the local authorities or the government?

Only the most valuable sections of the coast where most people live are fully protected. Remote, unpopulated farmland may be left unprotected. Withernsea and Hornsea have expensive protection measures. It will cost £4.5 million to protect the Easington gas terminal by a 1 km sea wall. In some places, concrete blocks and rubble have been dumped in front of the cliff base to absorb wave energy (see Figure 1.72).

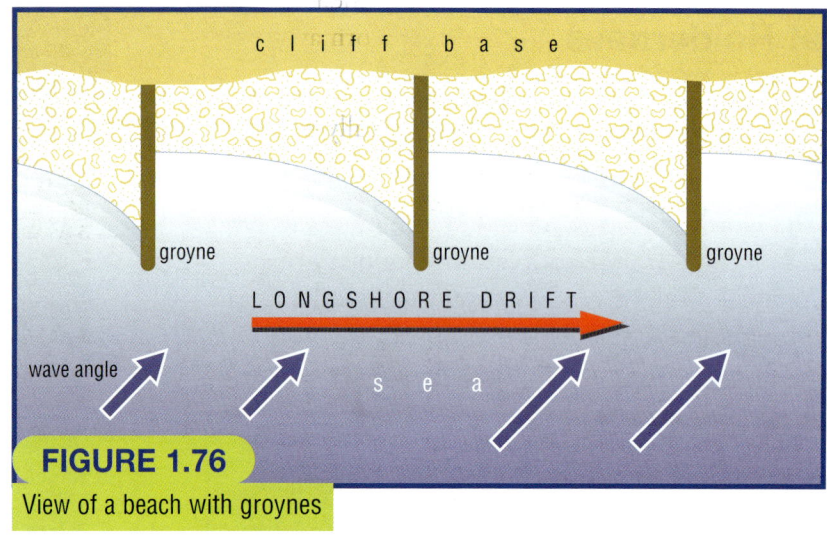

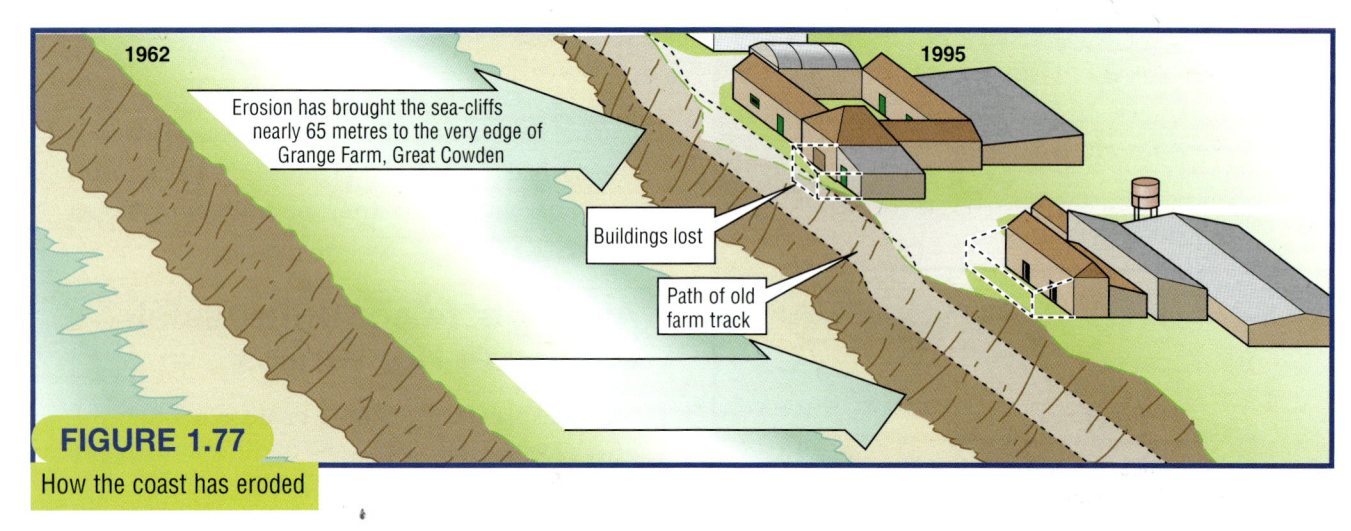

FIGURE 1.75 Protecting Mappleton

FIGURE 1.76 View of a beach with groynes

FIGURE 1.77 How the coast has eroded

Erosion has brought the sea-cliffs nearly 65 metres to the very edge of Grange Farm, Great Cowden

By 1988 the cliff top had been worn back to within 500 m of the main coast road (B1242) through the village of Mappleton. It was too expensive to move the road and build new houses for people, so a rock barrier was built in 1991 (see Figure 1.75).

Erosion of the Holderness coast

The possible 'knock-on' effects of coastal protection at Holderness

People who live along the coast south of Mappleton are worried. They think that the building of the rock groyne (see Figure 1.75) in 1991 has speeded up erosion of their cliffs to a rate of 10 m per year. It has stopped longshore drift moving sand along the coast. So the cliffs have lost the beach which protected them. Farmers Sue Earle and her uncle were forced to abandon fields, farm buildings and – eventually, in 1996 – their farmhouse as the cliffs were quickly worn away (see Figure 1.71).

It is important that people think carefully before trying to interfere with natural processes. Protecting the coastline in one place may increase erosion elsewhere.

FIGURE 1.78
Wave damage to the road along Spurn Head

TASKS

1. Fact or fiction? Holderness case study.

    Do this exercise with a partner. Both of you write 20 statements about Holderness on cards.

    - Some could be useful **facts**, e.g. the cliffs are easily worn away because they are made of boulder clay.
    - Others could be **opinions**, e.g. the money spent on protecting the coastline has been wasted.
    - Others could be **false**, e.g. Hornsea, Mappleton and Withernsea were villages which have collapsed into the sea.
    - Others could be **irrelevant**, e.g. global warming may cause a rise in sea level.

    When you have written your set of statements, you can swap the cards and decide which types of statement each one is. Agree with your partner which are important facts, then make a list of them to learn. It is also useful to remember some opinions, especially if they show different points of view.

2. A good way to learn a case study is to create a summary page in your book or file. Use the following outline (or template) to make your own summary. Some sections have examples to get you started.

Name of case study The Holderness coast	Location map
Key idea Coastal erosion and protection	
Key words Hydraulic action Sea walls	
Key questions Why is the Holderness coast being eroded so quickly? What can be done to protect the coastline?	
Causes Powerful waves from the North Sea	Effects Farms and villages fallen into the sea
Possible solutions Build new sea walls and revetments	Knock-on effects Other places may lose their beach

one
People and the Physical World
Advice

COURSEWORK FOR RIVERS

River- or stream-based coursework is very popular. Most people live fairly close to a suitable river. River-based coursework can focus on physical or human themes or both.

River studies are good for:

- collecting data in a group
- measuring and observing
- collecting lots of data for graphs and analysis.

Suggested titles

Coursework can be based on a general title such as:

- A study of stream A from X to Y
- A study of river B and its valley from source to mouth
- A study of flood prevention measures along river C.

A question can provide a good title for coursework:

- How and why does stream width vary with distance from the source?
- How and why does stream depth vary with distance from the source?
- How and why does stream velocity vary with distance from the source?
- How and why does the wetted perimeter (see page 54) change with distance from the source?
- How and why does bedload size vary with distance from the source?
- How and why does bedload shape vary with distance from the source?
- How is the river channel different above and below point D?

If a small stream is chosen (under 10 km long), sites can be selected from start to end. If a longer stream or river is chosen, a section can be selected for study.

FIGURE 1.79
Measuring channel width. This is probably the largest sized river in which it is safe to take measurements

The coursework process for a river study

There are six stages in the process.

1 Find a title
Think of a general title or question. You can change it slightly later if you need to.

> **Advice**
> The title must make your purpose clear.

2 Think about the practical issues
Choose a river of suitable size which is easy to get to.

> **Advice**
> Is it possible to collect enough data easily and safely there?

3 Plan the work
- Find the stream or river on an OS map.
- Select five or six sites to study.
- Write three or four aims to support your title.
- Decide what information you are going to collect.
- Design data recording sheets.
- Get the equipment you need.

> **Advice**
> Think about what you expect to find out. As you move downstream, the river may:
> - become deeper and wider and less steep
> - have increased velocity
> - have smaller boulders.

4 Collect the data
Be as careful and accurate as you can. Use the same methods at each site.

> **Advice**
> Never work alone. Take photographs or draw labelled field sketches.

5 Process and present the data
Calculations such as averages can be done. Tables, maps, sketches, labelled photographs and graphs can be produced.

> **Advice**
> Try to include at least four different types of data presentation.

6 Write up the work
You need at least four sections:

- Introduction
- Data Collection
- Analysis and Interpretation of the Results
- Conclusion.

People and the Physical World

Advice

Methods of measurement

Figure 1.80 shows examples of what can be measured at each site.

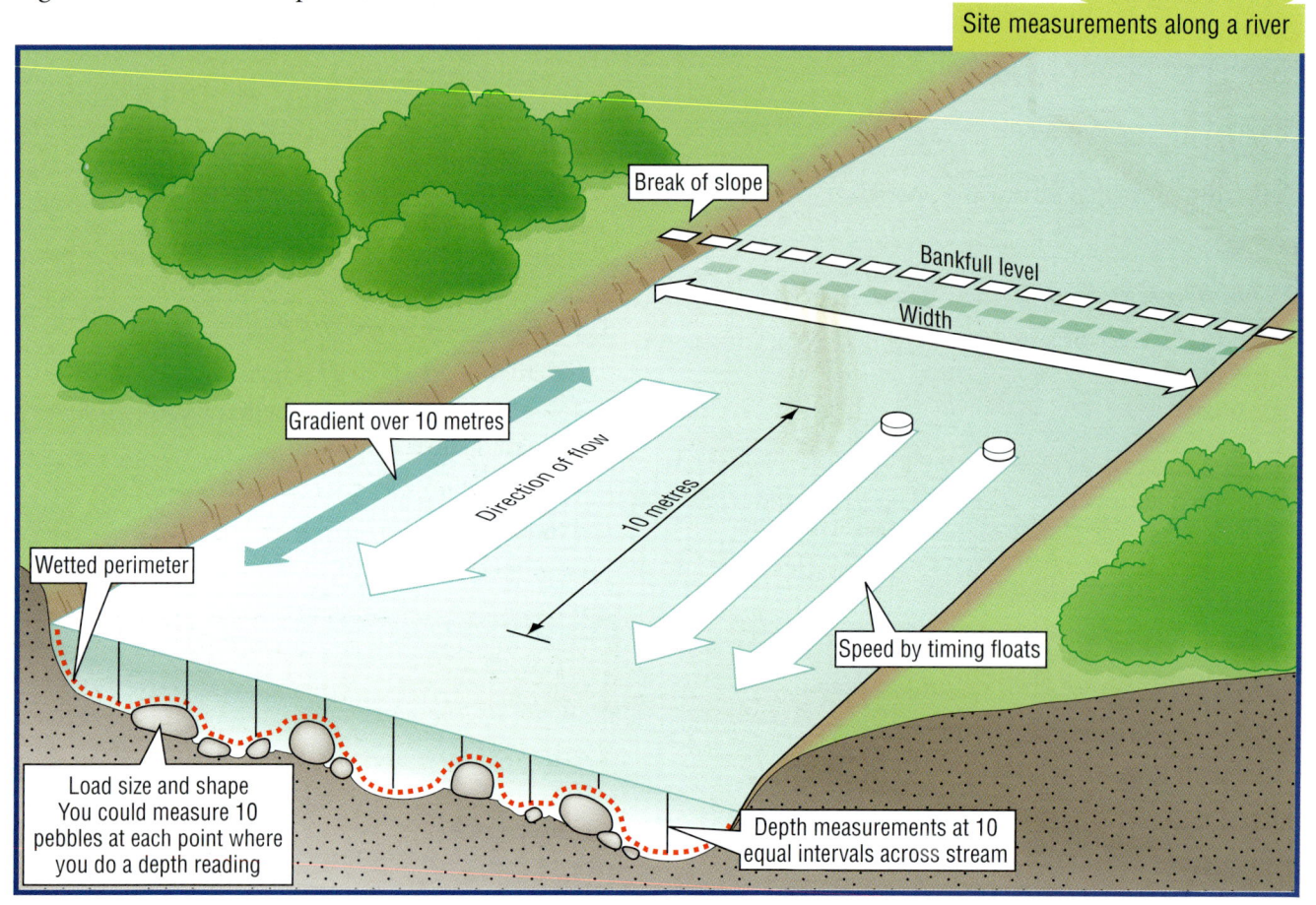

FIGURE 1.80
Site measurements along a river

Labels on figure: Break of slope; Bankfull level; Width; Gradient over 10 metres; Direction of flow; 10 metres; Speed by timing floats; Wetted perimeter; Load size and shape — You could measure 10 pebbles at each point where you do a depth reading; Depth measurements at 10 equal intervals across stream.

Measurement	Method
Width	Measure along the water surface from bank to bank with a tape or rope.
Depth	Measure the depth of water at regular intervals across the channel.
Wetted perimeter	Lay a rope or chain across the river bed then measure its length.
Velocity (speed of flow)	Time how long it takes for a float (e.g. an orange) to travel 10 m. You could do this several times and calculate the average. Overall velocity = $\frac{distance}{time} \times 0.85$
Gradient	Use a clinometer to measure the angle between two poles.
Load size	Collect random pebbles and measure the length or width and work out averages.

Coursework advice – Rivers

Collecting data

Advice
- Take safety seriously.
- Wear Wellington boots.
- Do not make channel measurements when the river is in flood.
- Always have someone there to help you with the measurements.
- Wear warm clothing.
- Pick the right time for doing the fieldwork.
- A fine day without too much wind makes measuring and recording easier.
- Try to do the fieldwork after rainfall when there is a sufficient flow of water.
- Do all the work in one or two days so that readings from different sites can be compared.
- Don't go near a stream with bankfull or flood conditions.

FIGURE 1.81 Measuring a stream's gradient

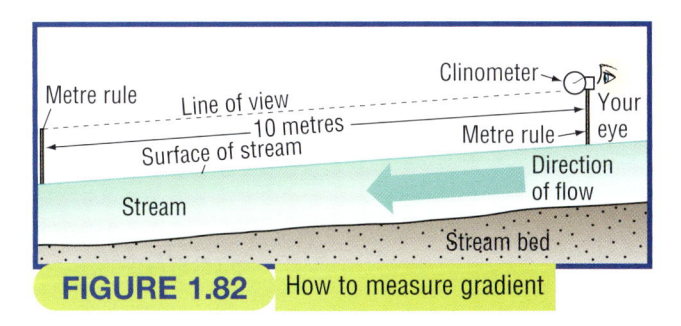

FIGURE 1.82 How to measure gradient

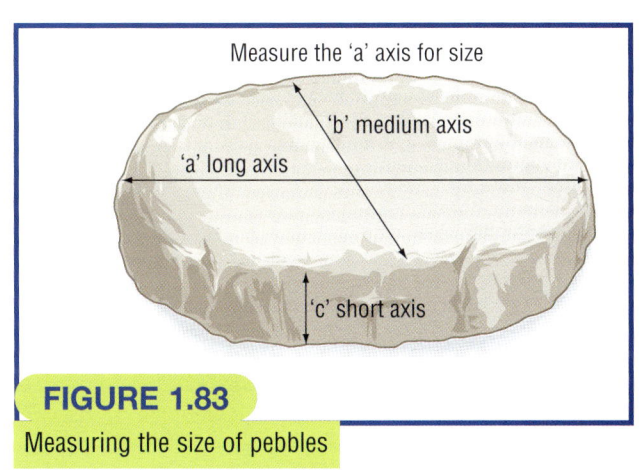

FIGURE 1.83 Measuring the size of pebbles

FIGURE 1.84 This is only a small stream, but high water levels make it too dangerous for taking measurements

Make an equipment checklist similar to the one below:

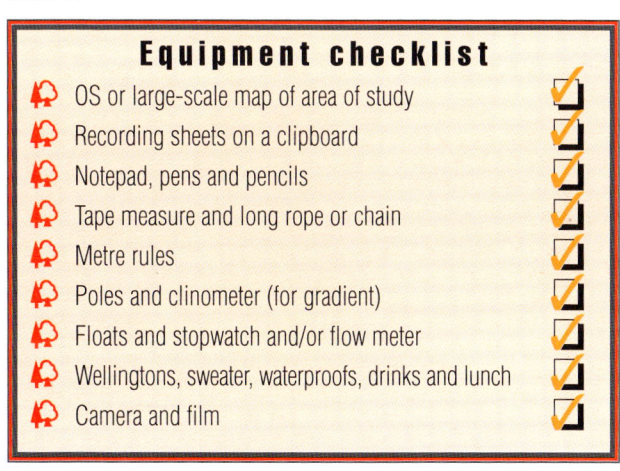

Equipment checklist
- OS or large-scale map of area of study
- Recording sheets on a clipboard
- Notepad, pens and pencils
- Tape measure and long rope or chain
- Metre rules
- Poles and clinometer (for gradient)
- Floats and stopwatch and/or flow meter
- Wellingtons, sweater, waterproofs, drinks and lunch
- Camera and film

People and the Physical World

Advice

Make a recording sheet for each site. Figure 1.85 is an example. You could include a sketch or photograph and observations. Use a notebook to describe each site before taking measurements.

Site number					Grid reference		
Date:					Weather:		
Notes about the site							
Width:					Gradient:		
Depth (cm) (m from bank)	0.5	1.0	1.5	2.0	2.5	3.0	3.5 4.0
Float times (seconds) (m from bank)		1.0		2.0		3.0	
Stone long axis (cm) Stones		1	2	3	4	5	
at 1.0m from bank							
at 2.0m from bank							
at 3.0m from bank							

FIGURE 1.85
Example of a recording sheet for rivers

Site	1	2	3	4	5	6	7	8
River width (m)	1.7	2.7	5.2	4.3	5.2	7.1	8.2	7.0
Depth (cm) at:								
0.5m	20	10	10	10	10	6	5	12
1m	25	15	10	10	12	7	6	10
1.5m	15	20	11	11	15	7	6	10
2m		10	12	12	17	8	5	10
2.5m		10	14	12	22	8	4	9
3m			15	10	27	8	4	10
3.5m			15	11	28	10	4	10
4m			13	10	25	15	7	11
4.5m			12		20	17	9	14
5m			10		7	20	12	16
5.5m						19	13	20
6m						19	16	23
6.5m						18	18	17
7m						14	20	0
7.5m							24	
8m							20	

FIGURE 1.86
River measurements at eight sites

Processing and presenting the data

Firstly, put all of your results into one table such as Figure 1.86. You could use a spreadsheet for this. This will make it easier to process your results and produce graphs. Figure 1.87 shows how cross-sections can be drawn using the data. It is important to keep the same scale at each site so they can be compared.

Draw at least three different types of graphs. For example:

- scattergraph of distance and width (or velocity or depth or average stone size)
- bar graph of average depth at each site
- cross-section for each site.

FIGURE 1.87
Channel cross-sections

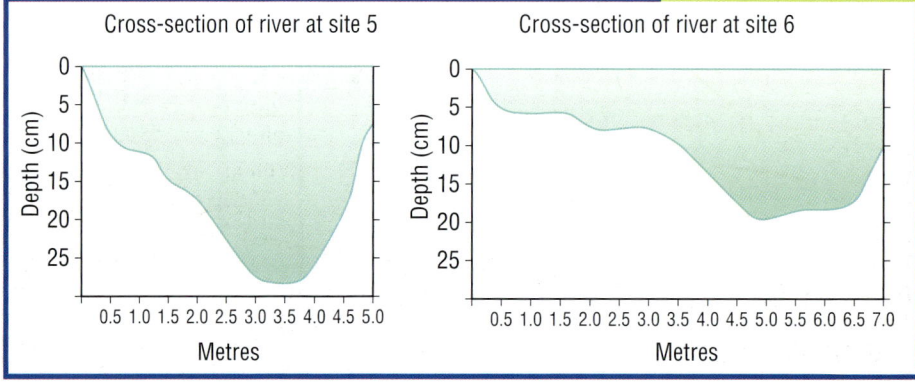

Cross-section of river at site 5

Cross-section of river at site 6

Coursework advice – Rivers

Choose photographs or sketches to label. Make sure you *use* them to gain marks by using geographical words as labels and explaining what you found at each site. Figure 1.89 shows an annotated photograph.

Advice
- Pick the best photographs – don't include too many.
- Place the photographs next to the information about each site. Don't put all of your photographs together at the back.
- Label each one to help meet your aims.

FIGURE 1.88
Drainage basin of the river used in the study

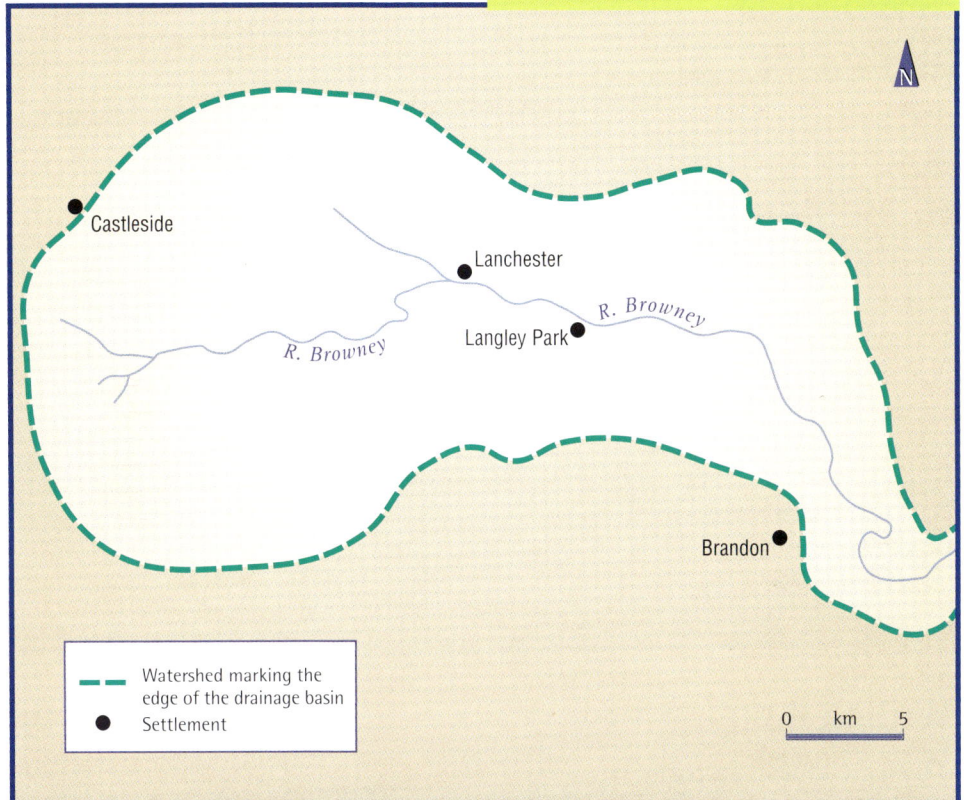

- Castleside
- Lanchester
- Langley Park
- Brandon
- R. Browney

--- Watershed marking the edge of the drainage basin
● Settlement

0 km 5

Labels on photograph:
- Small meander
- Bank eroded
- Steep bank
- Gentle valley sides
- Slip-off slope forming
- Deposition on the edge of the channel
- Riffles

FIGURE 1.89
A stream in its middle course

People and the Physical World

Advice

FIGURE 1.90
Locations of the study sites

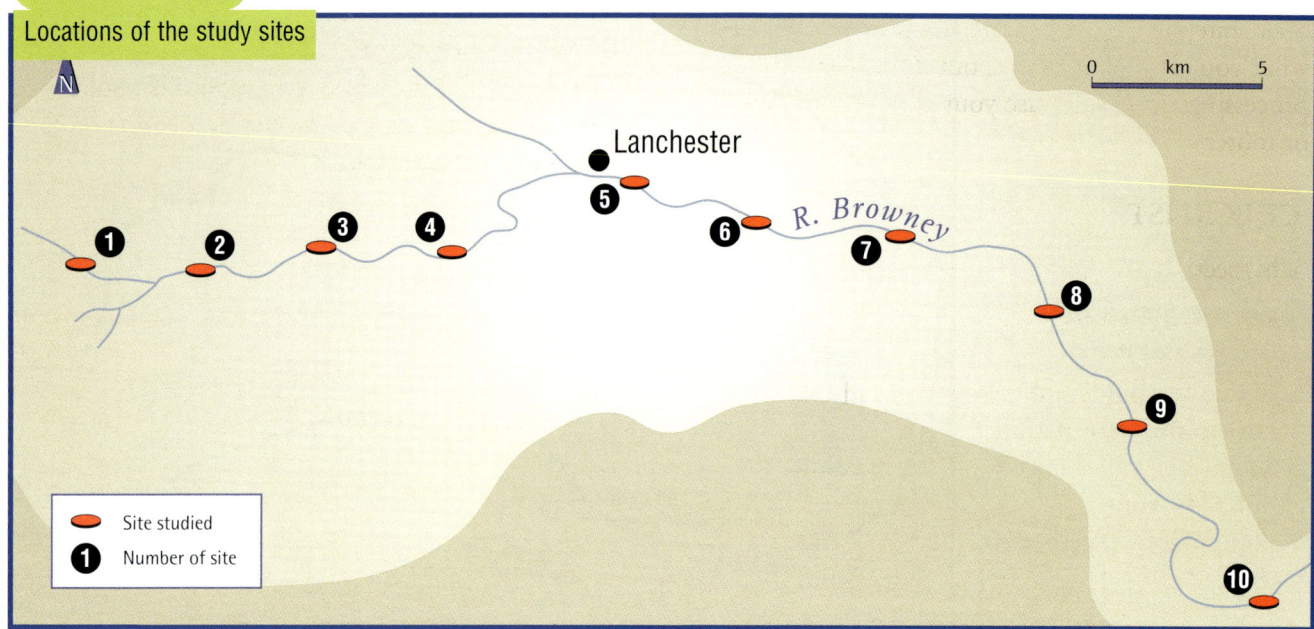

Writing it up

There are four main parts.

The Introduction and Data Collection sections are worth 40% of the marks.

1 Introduction

CHECKLIST

The Introduction should include:
- a title
- main aims
- information about the study area
- a map showing the location of the river and sites studied
- background theory.

Include a map showing the whole river basin (such as Figure 1.88) as well as a site map (such as Figure 1.90). Either add your own title and labels to a printed map or draw your own sketch map. Always include a title, key, scale and North arrow. Explain the geography theory about rivers including keywords. Make it clear what you expect to find as you move downstream.

2 Data Collection

This section may be longer than the Introduction.

It is really important to explain *why* each method was used or *why* a place was chosen.

CHECKLIST

In the Data Collection section, you should:
- describe and explain data collection methods
- say where and why the stream and sites were chosen
- include detail such as dates and times of data collection and why you chose these.

3 Analysis and Interpretation of the Results

This section includes maps, graphs, photographs and written analysis. Write your title and aims on a separate piece of paper and use it to remind you what you are trying to find out. If you are word processing, you could use your title as a header or footer.

CHECKLIST

This section should include:
- a description of what every map, photograph and graph shows
- an explanation of the patterns found
- a comparison of the sites.

Try to put each figure near to the writing which explains what it shows.

4 Conclusion

This section sums up what you have found out. You could use a labelled sketch or map for this. The Conclusion must be linked clearly to the title of your coursework. You should try to refer to theory and also explain any unexpected results. This section includes an evaluation of what worked well and what did not.

FIGURE 1.91
River in its upper course

Labels on figure:
- Not typical of an upper course: gentle slopes and flat land on valley floor
- Typical of an upper course: shallow water; boulders in the bed

one
People and the Physical World
Advice

COURSEWORK FOR COASTS

The scenery at the coast of the British Isles is attractive and varied. Some of the coast is protected. There are opportunities for physical and human coursework projects.

Suggested titles

A Physical
- What are the similarities and differences between two stretches of coastline?
- What are the features of the beach and cliffs along a stretch of coastline and how were they formed?

B Mainly human
- How and why has the coast been protected between X and Y?
- What problems are caused by people living along and visiting a stretch of coastline?

C Mixed physical and human
- What are the physical features of beach X and how do people use it?
- What evidence is there of coastal erosion and what has been done to manage it?

FIGURE 1.92
Off Flamborough Head. Which landforms can you recognise?

FIGURE 1.93
Coastal protection at Eastbourne

Advice

Don't try to predict the future or say how successful projects such as defences have been. It is difficult to measure their success.

Coursework advice – Coasts

Methods of data collection

Data can be collected using primary methods, such as taking measurements. Secondary data can help support your findings.

Primary data collection

- Measuring pebble sizes and shapes (see Figure 1.83)
- Observing features of coastal erosion and deposition
- Observing methods of coastal protection
- Carrying out a questionnaire survey of locals and visitors
- Taking photographs or drawing labelled sketches
- Measuring beach and cliff profiles.

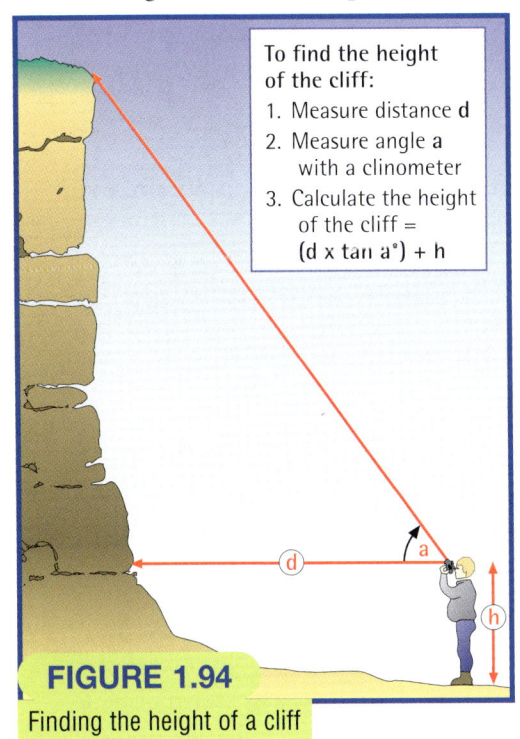

FIGURE 1.95
Shingle beach showing changes in slope downshore

To find the height of the cliff:
1. Measure distance d
2. Measure angle a with a clinometer
3. Calculate the height of the cliff = (d × tan a°) + h

FIGURE 1.94
Finding the height of a cliff

Secondary data collection

- OS and geology maps
- newspaper reports and visitor guides
- coastal defences information
- council visitor surveys.

Cliff profiles

1. Estimate the height of the cliff (Figure 1.94). Use an OS map to check it.
2. Sketch the cliff and label where the slope angle changes and features such as caves and joints.
3. Try to explain the cliff profile. Is there evidence of landslips?

Beach surveys

Take measurements in a line (transect) down the beach.

1. Use a clinometer to find the angle from the edge of the cliff to the low water mark.
2. Record the angle of slope each time the slope changes gradient (see Figure 1.95) and measure the distance between each point.
3. At regular intervals down the beach, randomly select five pebbles to measure the long axis and shape.
4. Carry out a questionnaire survey of beach users. You may want to design one survey for locals and one for visitors.

People and the Physical World

Advice

EXAMINATION TECHNIQUE – UNIT 1

Now that you have learned about 'People and the Physical World' it is time to see how you can use your knowledge and understanding to answer GCSE questions.

All GCSE questions use geographical resources. There is always at least one question which includes a photograph. There is only a small chance that you will have seen the photograph before. The questions begin with shorter sections to get you used to the photograph and question topic.

The following questions are based on a photograph.

> **1 (a)** Study Figure 1.96

Figure 1.96

The **question theme** is obviously rivers. On careful reading, the theme can be divided into two parts:
1 river features
2 river flooding.

> **(i)** What is the source of a river? [1]

The starter question tests your knowledge of **geographical words**. It is a good idea to make a **glossary** of geographical words which will include 'source'. There is only 1 mark allocated to this question so a definition or short description is needed.

> **(ii)** Describe three natural features of the river and its valley. [3]

You must study the photograph to answer this question. When you have identified three different features from the photograph you must describe them. Write in full sentences. Do not use one-word answers when you are asked to describe.

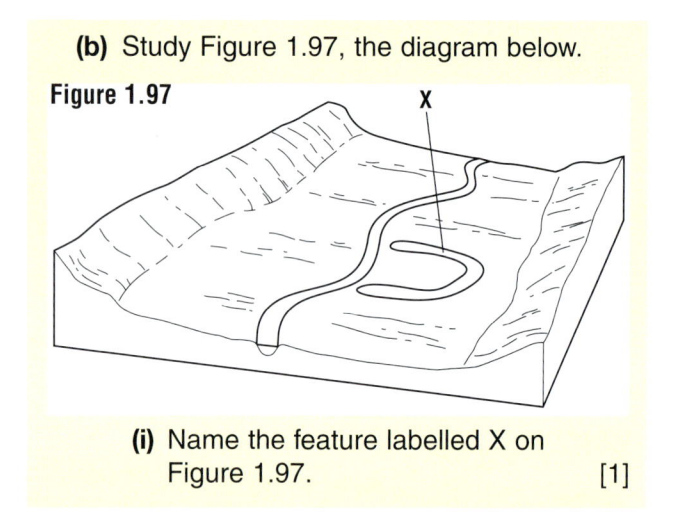

> **(b)** Study Figure 1.97, the diagram below.
>
> **Figure 1.97**
>
> **(i)** Name the feature labelled X on Figure 1.97. [1]

The **command word** 'name' instructs you to answer briefly.

> **(ii)** On Fig. 1.97 label the floodplain. [1]

Questions b(i) and b(ii) are testing what you know about river features.

> **(c)** Name a river which has flooded. Describe the effects of the flood on people who live near the river. [5]

The final question has the largest share of marks and tests your knowledge of a **case study**. You may choose any river which you have studied that has flooded. This might be a river in your local area or a major river of the world such as the Mississippi. Although there is no mark just for naming the river, the name will help to make your case study 'place specific'. This means it is about a particular river.

The case study will be marked in 'levels' which means you will get a better mark if you give more details. You will only score 1 or 2 marks for simple ideas. To score high marks you must include details about your chosen river.

Examination advice – Unit 1

The question tests what you know about how flooding affected people who live in the area around the river.

Look at the following question. See how the examiner is testing you in different ways.

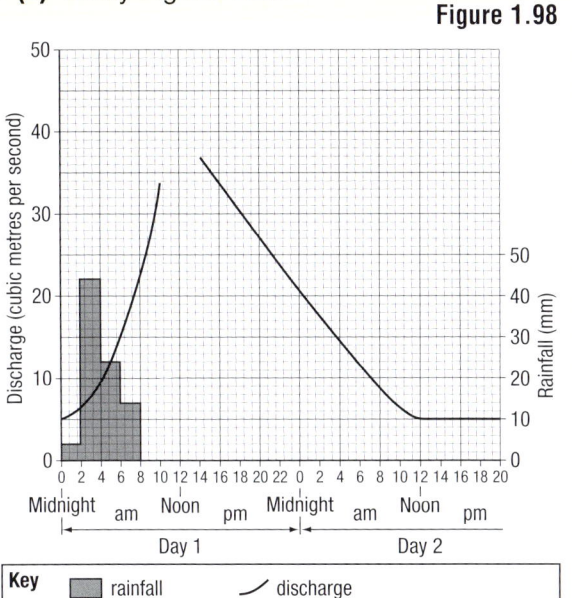

2 (a) Study Figure 1.98.

Figure 1.98

Key: rainfall ▬ discharge ╱

(i) What does 'discharge' mean? [1]

You need to **know** this key word. You cannot work it out from the graph. Write down what it means in your glossary.

(ii) Use the following information to complete Figure 1.98:

Time on Day 2	12 noon
Discharge (cumecs)	40

[1]

(iii) How much rain fell between 6 am and 8 am on Day 1?
_____ mm [1]

(iv) How long after peak rainfall does peak discharge occur? Put a circle around your answer.

9 hours   12 hours   15 hours [1]

These three questions all test your graph **skills**.

(v) The table below gives information about the area of the river basin. How does each characteristic explain the shape of the hydrograph?

1	The area is mostly covered by concrete and tarmac	so water cannot soak into the ground.
2	It has been raining for much of the week before	
3	There are many steep slopes in the area	

[2]

Your **understanding** is being tested. The first answer is completed to show you how to answer the question.

(b) (i) Give three reasons why rivers often flood. [3]

(ii) Suggest two ways to prevent rivers from flooding. [2]

The **focus** of the question has changed to flooding. You need to write a sentence for each answer, not just one or two words. For example:

'Melting snow means that a lot of extra water goes into the river', not just 'too much water'.

'Build a dam across the river to hold back the extra water and control the river' is a much better answer than 'make a dam'.

(c) For a named river in an MEDC describe the effects of flooding. [5]

This is obviously the **case study**. Be careful that you choose a river in an MEDC, not an LEDC.

(d) Why are the effects of river flooding usually greater in an LEDC than in an MEDC? [2]

People and the Physical World

Advice

The final part is testing whether you can **understand** how the level of development of a country can make the effects of flooding different.

The following question tests your knowledge of a **case study**.

> **3** Name an area which has been affected by erosion by the sea. Describe the effects of erosion on people in that area. [5]

Study the three answers below.

Answer from candidate 1

> **Name of area:** Mappleton in Yorkshire, the Holderness coast
> **Effects on people:**
> This coast is made of boulder clay, it has been eroding ever since Roman times. Many of the homes which gathered close to the cliff edge as it eroded were destroyed. People living in these homes were forced to move out. The erosion eroded away about ten homes and properties in a year, even the farmland collapsed into the sea causing the farmer to lose money. Now the erosion is getting even worse as it reaches the main road towards the village centre of Mappleton so traffic had to be diverted.

Examiner's comment

The candidate begins in the best way possible by naming the area which has been studied. The rest of the answer then refers to this chosen area. Effects on people are clearly described and the ideas are specific:

- Homes were destroyed **so** people had to move out.
- Farmland collapsed into the sea **so** farmers lost money.
- Main road into Mappleton was worn away **so** traffic had to be diverted.

This candidate scored the maximum 5 marks by naming an area and describing the effects in detail.

Answer from candidate 2

> **Name of area:** Bay Beach
> **Effects on people:**
> The houses fell down the cliffs. The road had to be shut off due to it being half broken down. Most people were scared due to their houses and farmland having to be abandoned. There would not be much beach left so not many people went there, the land has been getting smaller. People lost money because tourist shops went out of business. The people were forced to move somewhere else because no one knew when more collapse would happen.

Examiner's comment

Although the candidate includes some effects which are specific, the answer is restricted to Level 2 (3 or 4 marks) because no area is named. The ideas are general and do not describe any particular coastal area. Good ideas include:

- The road had to be abandoned because it was broken down.
- People were scared because they had to abandon their homes.
- People lost money because shops had to close.

Answer from candidate 3

> **Name of area:** Devon cliffs
> **Effects on people:**
> The land gets smaller and smaller each year and will affect people that live close by the cliffs.

Examiner's comment

This is a poor answer which does not score above Level 1 (1 or 2 marks). The named area is vague and the effects are described very simply:

- Land gets smaller ('land' is too general).
- This affects people that live close to the cliffs (how are they affected?).

Both these ideas could have been developed into a much better answer.

Examination advice – Unit 1

TASKS

The following examination questions are all linked to the theme of plate tectonics. Read all the questions but do not attempt to answer them.

a Define the term 'plate margin'. [1]

b Use the map (Figure 1.4 on page 8) to name two plates which are next to each other. Describe the movement along the plate margin where they meet. [1]

c Use the following information to plot on the graph (right) an earthquake which occurred in Mexico in 1985.

   Intensity measured on Richter scale   8.1
   Number of deaths   9500 [1]

d Identify the earthquake which measured the same power on the Richter scale as the one in Italy but caused fewer deaths. [1]

e Give two reasons why the number of deaths may vary between earthquakes of the same power. [2]

f Explain how volcanoes are formed at plate margins. [3]

g Why do many people live near active volcanoes? [4]

h Name a city which is at risk from earthquakes. Explain why people still live there. [5]

i Name an area which you have studied which has been affected by an earthquake. Describe the effects of the earthquake on the people who live there. [5]

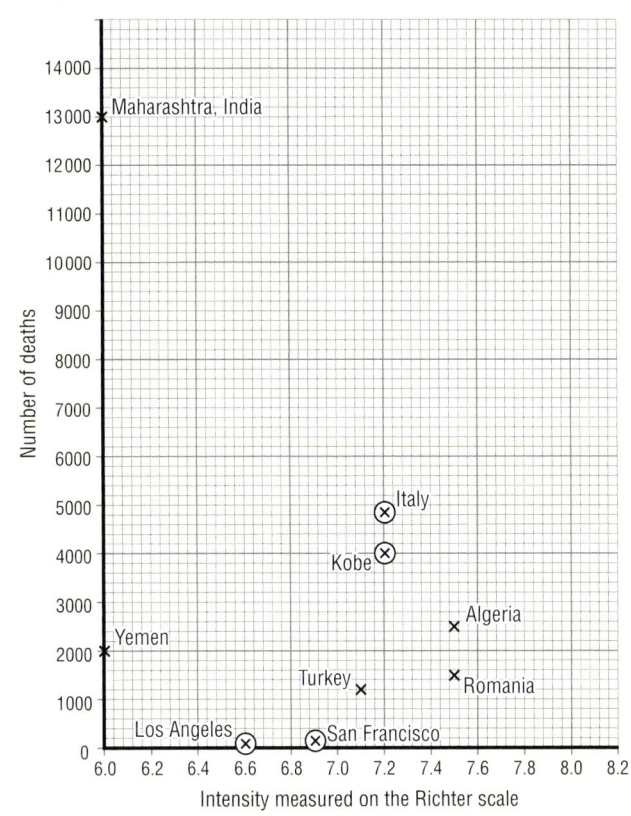

Now attempt the following tasks.

1 Make a list of the different **command** words (page 232 will help you to do this).
2 Make a list of the **geographical** words. Find the meanings of any words you do not know.
3 Look at the number of **marks** allocated to each question. What do you notice about how the marks vary? Why does this happen?
4 Two questions require you to use an example or **case study**. With your partner decide which examples you would use and discuss the main ideas you would include in your answer.

Key
× LEDCs
⊗ MEDCs

People and the Physical World

Advice

THE ENTRY LEVEL CERTIFICATE

If you choose to enter for the Entry Level Certificate, rather than GCSE, you will study the same Units, but not in the same depth. On this page, you can see the sort of activities for Entry Level.

People and the physical environment – rivers

Rivers flow from the mountains to the sea. As they do, they pass farms, factories and people living in towns and cities. A river changes the land and is used by people in different ways along its journey.

In the mountains when the river starts – at the **source** – it is fast and powerful. It wears away the land. This is called **erosion**. Over long periods of time, this makes channels or valleys through the land which help to move the water more easily. As the river gets nearer to the sea, these valleys become deeper and wider.

The rock that is worn away does not stay in one place. It is moved by the river. This is called **transportation**. Sometimes strong rivers move large rocks and boulders. Small rivers, which are less powerful, will only be able to move small particles of soil and mud. Over many years, much of this material – the **load** – is moved downstream.

As rivers get nearer the sea and lose some of their power, they cannot carry as much of the load as they used to. The heaviest rocks are put down first. This is called **deposition**.

The smaller particles of sand and mud will be deposited as the river gets near the end of its journey – the **mouth** or **estuary** – and finally flows into the sea.

Rivers are very important to people. We have used them for thousands of years to carry goods by boat. Many settlements are next to rivers so that people have a supply of water every day. Over many years, our use of water and of rivers has changed. Today, we use lots of water in factories and use rivers for enjoyment.

TASKS

4. Why were many settlements built near to rivers? Write down two reasons.
5. Draw a picture to show the ways that people use rivers. Write labels on your picture.

As rivers flow across lowlands, getting nearer to the sea, they lose a lot of their power. They develop large bends called **meanders**. These meanders move slowly down the valley and across it. This makes the valley a lot wider and flatter than before. This part of the river valley is called the **flood plain**.

The land is flat, so it is easy to build on, but, when the river level rises, this area is easily flooded. Homes, shops and factories would be under water. In some parts of the world, when a river floods it can kill thousands of people and cause millions of pounds' worth of damage.

TASKS

1. a Copy the map opposite.
   b In the correct places, write *source* and *mouth* on your map.
2. The work of a river is *eroding*, *transporting* and *depositing*. Write a sentence for each to explain what it means.
3. On your map, write *eroding*, *transporting* and *depositing* where the river is doing it.

TASKS

6. What problems can a river cause when it floods?
7. What can people do to stop a river from flooding?
8. Look at the information on pages 32–39 about the flooding in the Rhine valley or Bangladesh. Choose one of them. Do a newspaper front page about it. You could produce it on computer.

Certificate advice 67

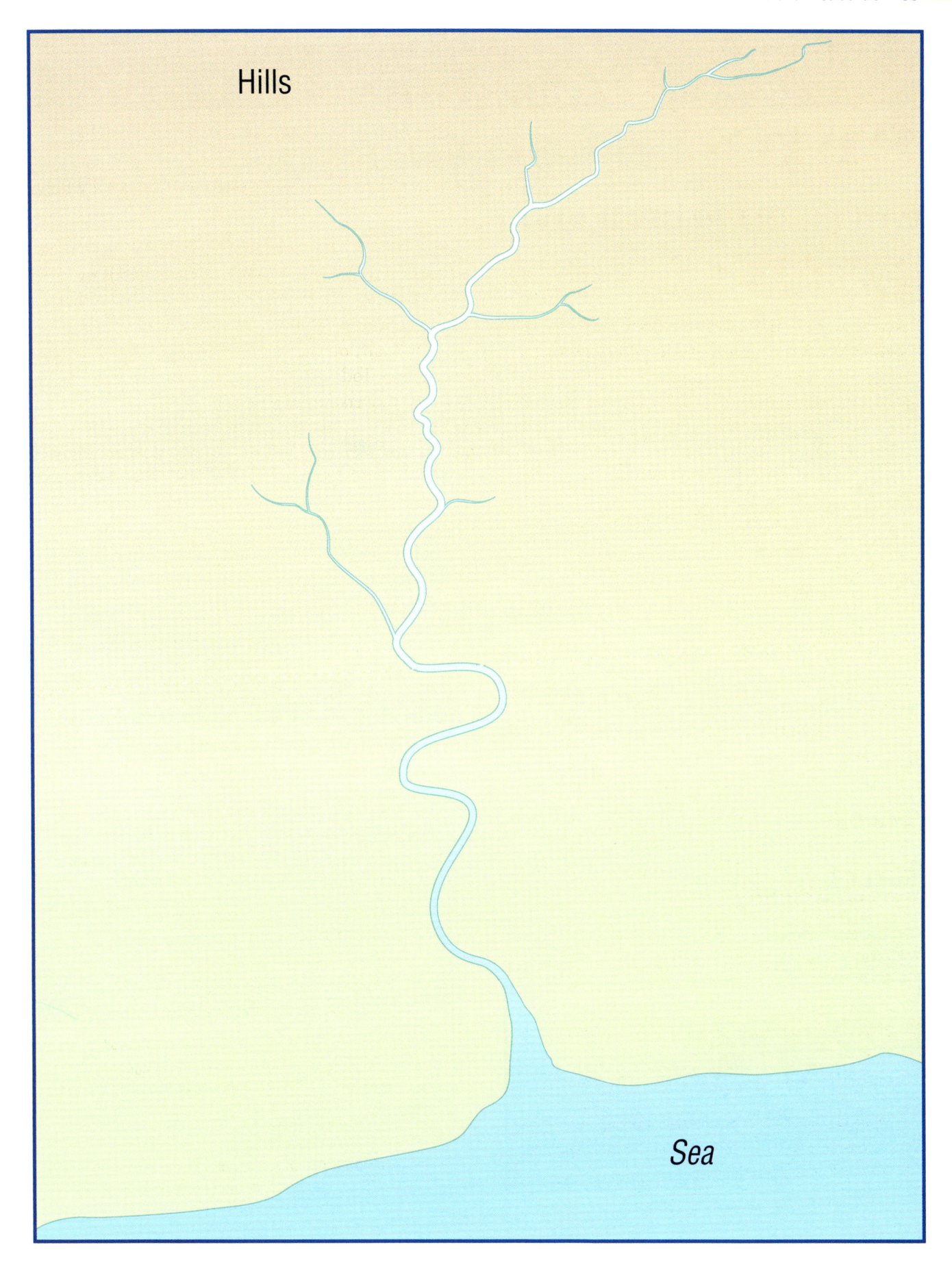

Hills

Sea

two
People and Places to Live
Population

WHERE DO PEOPLE LIVE?

> **SUMMARY** Some areas have many people. There may be resources for industries, so there are lots of jobs. The soil may be fertile and the climate may suit farming. Some areas have only a few people, such as deserts or mountain areas.

The world's population is now more than 6 billion. This population is not evenly spread. At present 50% of the population live on about 5% of the planet. Some areas have a **dense population**, a large population crowded into a small area, while other areas have a **sparse population**, an area with very few people living there. About 80% of the world's population live in LEDCs (Figure 2.1).

Region	Population density (per sq. km)	Percentage of the world's population
Africa	14	10
North America	11	6
South America	16	8
Asia	84	59
Europe/Russia	39	16
Oceania	3	1

Figure 2.1 Where are the people?

FIGURE 2.2 Population density

Population density by country
- Areas of dense population
- Areas of moderate population
- Areas of sparse population

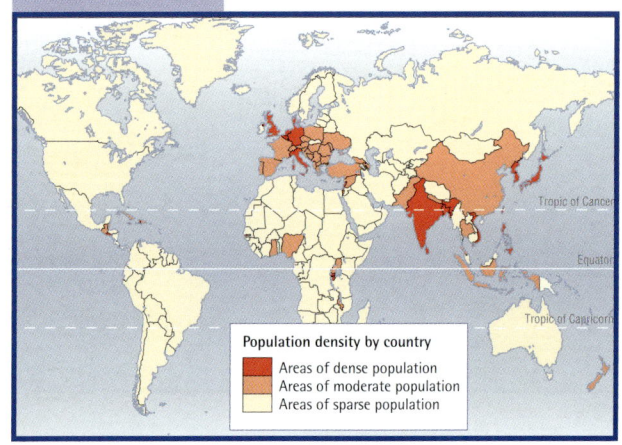

Figure 2.2 shows the countries where people are crowded together, and the countries where there is a lot of land but not many people. However, within each country, there are areas of dense population (the cities) and other areas of sparse population (the countryside). People live where they can make a living, such as where they can grow crops.

TASKS

1 Look at Figure 2.1.
   a Which region has 6% of the world's population?
   b Which region has the highest population density?
   c More than half of all the people in the world live in which region?

2 a Draw a grid of 20 squares (make the grid 5 cm by 4 cm) to represent the earth's land surface.
   b Draw a line down the middle so that there are ten squares each side of the line.
   c On one side of the line, put a dot in one of the squares.
   d On the other side of the line, put a dot in nine of the ten squares.
   e Label half of your diagram 'Dense population' and the other half 'Sparse population'.

3 a Identify where the USA is on Figure 2.2. Try to draw the shape of the USA onto a page of your notebook.
   b Now use an atlas to find where, in the USA, there are lots of cities. On the map you have drawn, colour these areas in red.
   c Find, from the atlas, the areas of the USA which are mountains. Colour these areas in yellow.
   d Colour the other parts of USA in orange.
   e Copy the key from Figure 2.2.
   f Decide the title for your map.

Where do people live?

70%	of the planet is ocean
30%	of the planet is land

29%	too dry
17%	too cold
11%	too mountainous
9%	poor soil

11%	is used to grow crops
23%	could be used to grow crops but isn't yet

Figure 2.3 Living on planet earth

The **environment** provides reasons why people choose to live in certain areas. Figure 2.4 shows why difficult areas, like hot deserts, are hard to farm and have a sparse population.

Social and **economic** factors can help to explain why urban areas attract large numbers of people. There are lots of jobs in manufacturing and service industries. For example, in the UK 98% of jobs are manufacturing or services.

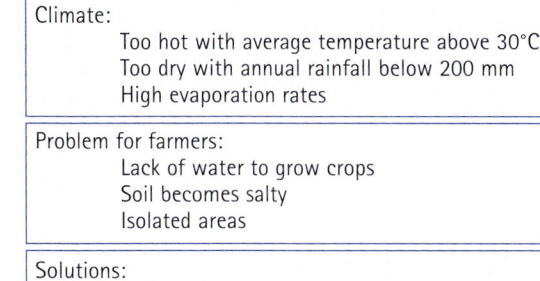

Climate:
- Too hot with average temperature above 30°C
- Too dry with annual rainfall below 200 mm
- High evaporation rates

Problem for farmers:
- Lack of water to grow crops
- Soil becomes salty
- Isolated areas

Solutions:
- Build wells and pump water for irrigation

Problem:
- Costly
- Low yields
- Little grass for grazing
- Food shortage

Population density:
- Few people are attracted to live in hot deserts
- Hot deserts can only support a low population density

Figure 2.4 Why hot deserts have a sparse population

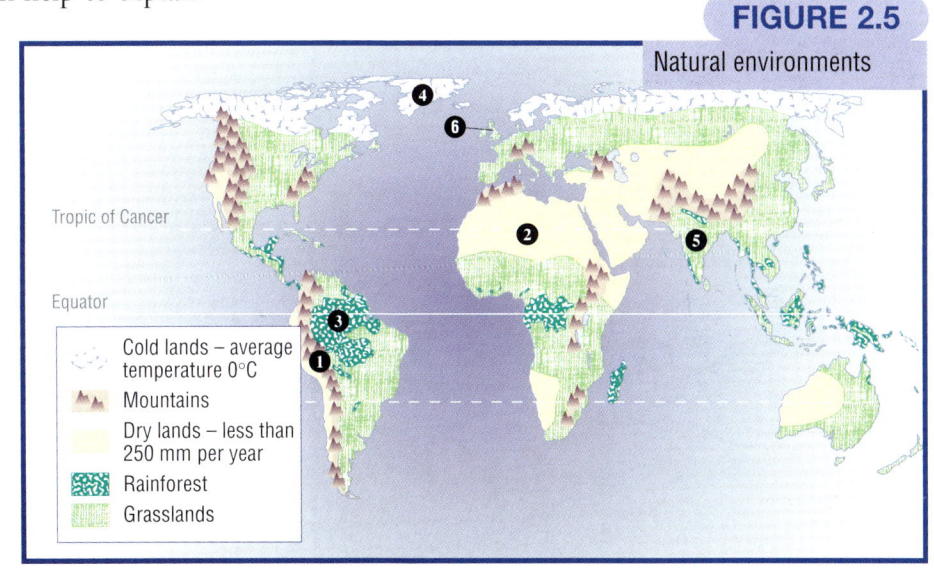

FIGURE 2.5 Natural environments

Legend:
- Cold lands – average temperature 0°C
- Mountains
- Dry lands – less than 250 mm per year
- Rainforest
- Grasslands

TASKS

4 a Write a sentence to show how the environment can affect the population density of an area.

   b Name an area where the population density is affected by social and economic factors (it could be where you live). Suggest reasons why the area has many, or few, jobs.

5 Look at Figure 2.3. Use an atlas to find areas of the USA where some of these phrases apply. On your map of the USA (task 3), use arrows to label three of these areas.

6 Using an atlas, locate Areas 2–6 shown on Figure 2.5. For each area, decide whether it would have a high population density (dense) or a low population density (sparse) and suggest why. Area 1 is done for you.

Location	Dense or sparse	Reason
Andes	Sparse	Mountainous. Too steep and cold for much farming.

two
■ People and Places to Live

Population

POPULATION DISTRIBUTION IN THE UK

SUMMARY Half of the people in England live in conurbations. Many conurbations were close to coal mines. The coal once provided the fuel for factories.

Some parts of the UK have few people. Some parts are crowded. On average, there are 243 people per square kilometre. In England, the **population density** is even higher. Here 89% live in urban areas. More than half of these people live in **conurbations**, where towns have grown until they join together. These are the large, red areas on Figure 2.7. They grew because there was coal for industries or ports for trade.

Country	Area (sq. km)	Population	Pop. density
England	130 423	47 million	376
Wales	20 766	2.8 million	141
Scotland	78 133	5 million	66
N. Ireland	14 160	1.5 million	117

Figure 2.8 Population data for the UK in 1991

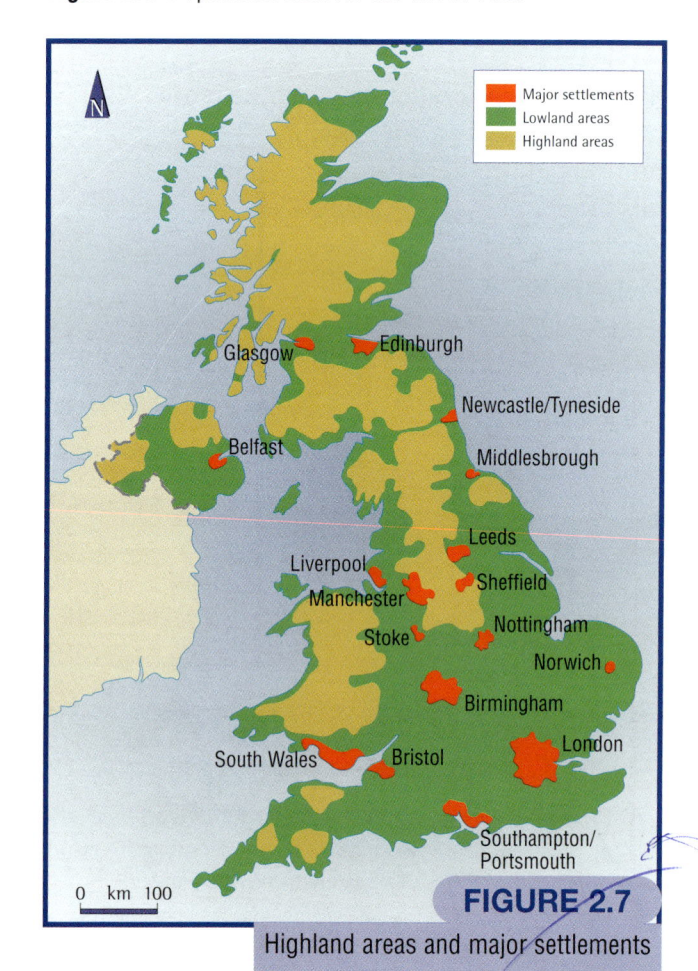

FIGURE 2.6 Population density

FIGURE 2.7 Highland areas and major settlements

TASKS

1. What is meant by a 'conurbation'?
2. Use an atlas to identify four of the conurbations shown on Figure 2.6. Write down their names (these may be the names of their largest cities).
3. Which of the countries of the UK has the most conurbations?
4. Look at Figure 2.8. Which part of the UK has the lowest population density?
5. Look at the large areas on Figure 2.6 which have less than 10 people per square kilometre. Now look at the same areas on Figure 2.7. What factors link these to each other?

Population distribution in the UK

Derbyshire's population pattern

In Derbyshire, few people live in the Peak District, a hilly area. The high land is cool and wet. Soil is thin and poor. To the south and east, farming is easier. More people live here. The densest population is in the east of Derbyshire, where coal used to be mined. This was used by industries in the towns which are now close to the M1 motorway.

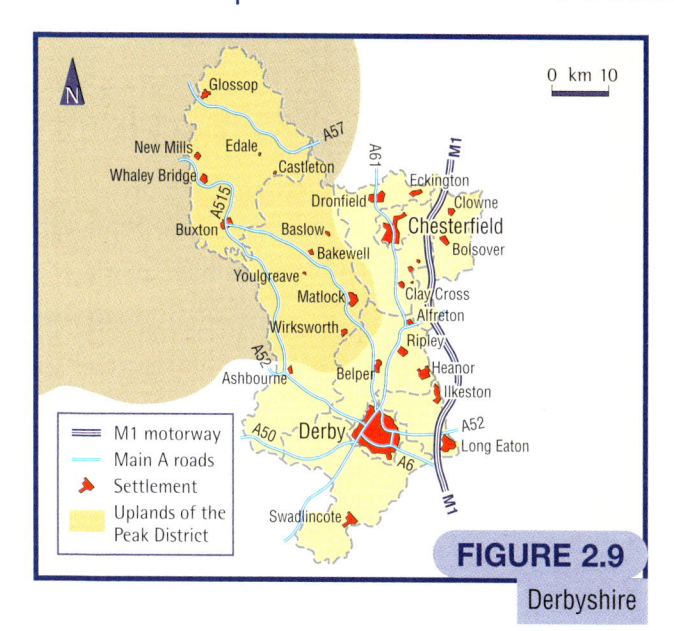

FIGURE 2.9 Derbyshire

TASKS

6 a Use Figure 2.9 to name the two largest places in Derbyshire.

 b Think about their location, then suggest why they grew large.

7 Make two copies of Figure 2.10. Choose colours or shading to show 'the higher, the darker'. Add a key to each map.

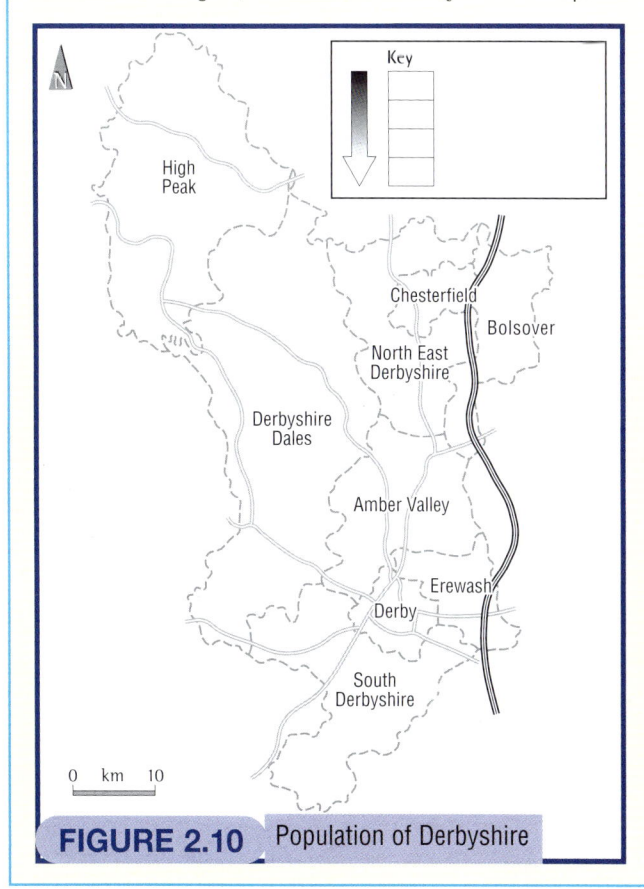

FIGURE 2.10 Population of Derbyshire

a Plot the actual population data using this scale:
- above 200 000
- 100 001 to 200 000
- 80 000 to 100 000
- less than 80 000.

b Plot the density of population data using this scale:
- above 10 per hectare
- 5.1 to 10 per hectare
- 3 to 5 per hectare
- below 3 per hectare.

c Describe and explain the pattern shown by each map.

District	Population 1991 (thousands)	Population density numbers per ha.
Amber Valley	111.9	4.1
Bolsover	70.4	4.3
Chesterfield	99.4	15.1
Derby	218.8	27.4
Derbyshire Dales	67.6	0.9
Erewash	106.1	9.5
High Peak	85.1	1.5
N E Derbyshire	97.5	3.5
S Derbyshire	71.8	2.1
County (average)	28.6	3.5

Figure 2.11 Population data for Derbyshire

8 For the area in which you live, write down reasons to explain its population density. Think about its location, how good the area is for farming and the things industries need.

two — People and Places to Live
Population

CHANGING POPULATIONS

> **SUMMARY** The population of the world is increasing. The countries which are growing fastest are LEDCs where families have many children and old people are living longer.

The population of the world increases by 78 million every year. More people are born than die. This is called **natural increase**. The population can also change because of migration.

Year	Population (billions)
AD 1	0.3
1000	0.4
1600	0.5
1700	0.7
1800	0.9
1900	1.7
1950	2.3
1960	3.0
1970	3.9
1987	5.0
1999	6.0
2010	8.0
2050	8.9

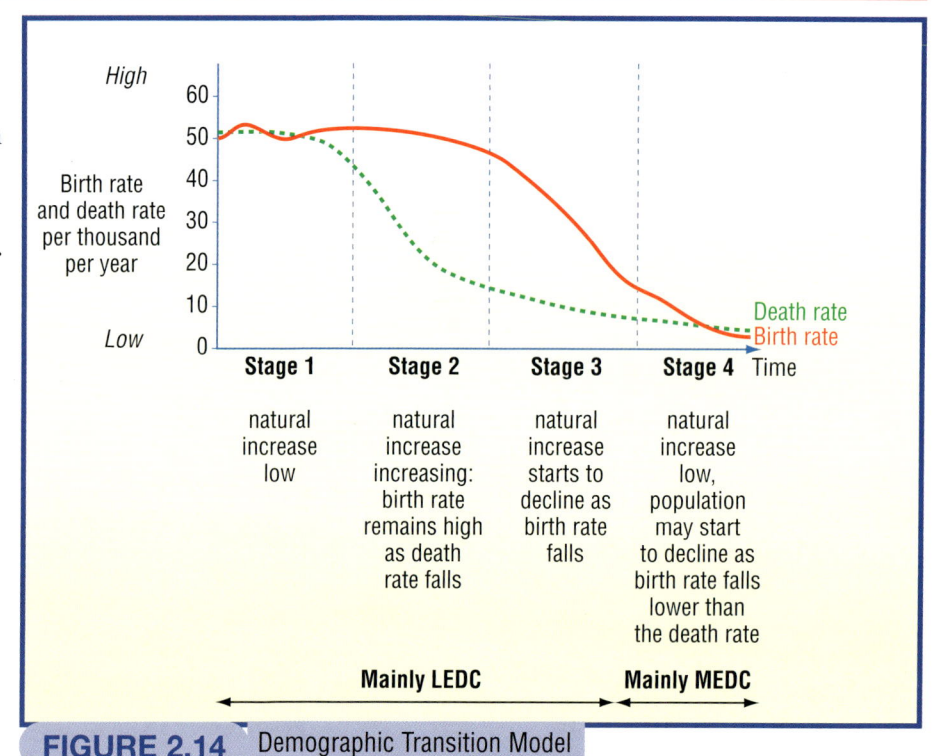

Figure 2.12 World population growth

FIGURE 2.14 Demographic Transition Model

Stage 1: natural increase low
Stage 2: natural increase increasing: birth rate remains high as death rate falls
Stage 3: natural increase starts to decline as birth rate falls
Stage 4: natural increase low, population may start to decline as birth rate falls lower than the death rate

Mainly LEDC ← Stages 2–3 → Mainly MEDC

Figure 2.14 shows how populations change. The death rate becomes lower when living conditions, food and medical care improve. The birth rate is lower where education (especially of girls) has improved and family planning is available. People are living longer as their quality of life improves.

Continent	Birth rate	Death rate	Natural increase	Life expectancy	Doubling time
Asia	24	8	1.6	65	44
Africa	40	14	2.6	53	26
North America	14	9	0.6	73	117
South America	25	7	1.8	69	38
Europe	10	12	-0.1	70	–
Oceania	19	8	1.1	74	63

Figure 2.13 Population growth rates

TASKS

1. Look at Figure 2.12. How many years did it take for the population of the world to double from 3 billion to 6 billion?

2. Use Figure 2.12 to draw a line graph to show world population growth. Annotate the finished graph to highlight:

   slow growth, rapid growth, long doubling time, short doubling time

3. Copy the information below and match up these words. One is done for you.

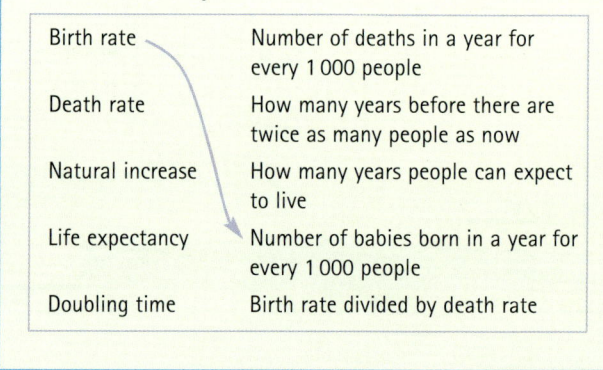

Birth rate	Number of deaths in a year for every 1 000 people
Death rate	How many years before there are twice as many people as now
Natural increase	How many years people can expect to live
Life expectancy	Number of babies born in a year for every 1 000 people
Doubling time	Birth rate divided by death rate

Changing populations

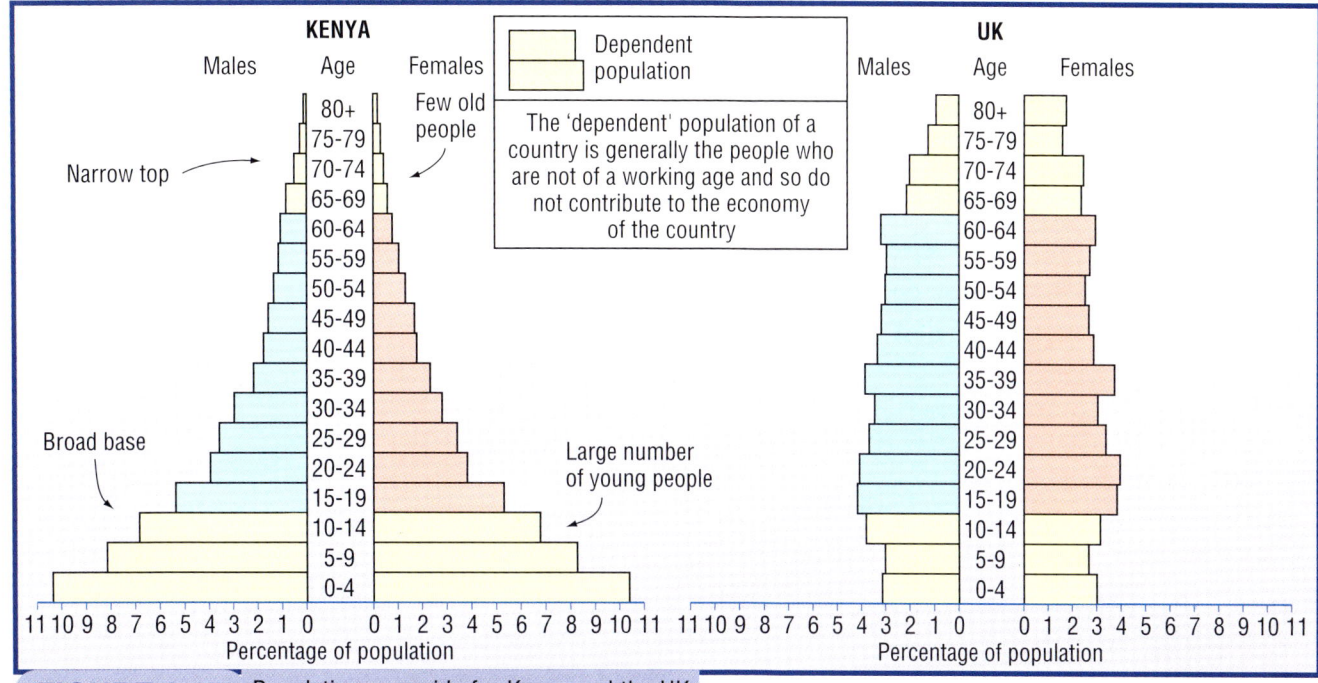

FIGURE 2.15 Population pyramids for Kenya and the UK

Kenya pyramid labels: Narrow top; Broad base; Few old people; Large number of young people.

Dependent population: The 'dependent' population of a country is generally the people who are not of a working age and so do not contribute to the economy of the country.

Kenya is an LEDC. Its **population pyramid** (Figure 2.15) shows that more than half of the population is under 16. The broad base of the pyramid means that the birth rate is high and there are large families. The narrow top to the pyramid shows that the death rate is high, with few people surviving to old age. Those too young or too old to work are called **dependent**.

In MEDCs, the number of births and deaths are about the same, so there is no natural increase. There is still a large dependent population but, unlike Kenya, it includes many old people.

TASKS

Country	Birth rate	Death rate	Natural increase
Nigeria	43	13	
Mali	50	20	
Germany	10	11	
Italy	9	9	

4 a Make a copy of the table above and work out the natural increase for each country.
  b Which of the countries are MEDCs and which are LEDCs?
5 Look at Figure 2.13.
  a Which continent has the fastest population growth?
  b How can you tell from Figure 2.13 that Europe's population is reducing?

two

■ People and Places to Live

Population

POPULATION ISSUES

SUMMARY Changes in population can present problems to MEDCs. Although the total population may not rise, there will be many more old people and not enough workers for all the jobs. In LEDCs, the population continues to grow as fewer people die young. Birth control and better education will reduce the size of families.

How many people could the world feed? When will there be too many people for the resources that can be provided? Will more people mean more polluting of the environment?

Every minute, 170 babies are born, but only 80 people die. The increase is mostly in LEDCs. Here, already one in five go hungry. As the population rises in LEDCs, their governments struggle to provide for many more old people.

In MEDCs, like the UK, families are having fewer children (Figure 2.16). To replace those who die, mothers need to have 2.4 children each on average. Family planning is freely available. Fewer women are now willing to give up, or take a break from, their careers to have large families. Many cannot afford to.

In 2008, there will be more pensioners living in the UK than children. There will also be 2 million fewer workers, so the government will get less tax to spend on looking after all the old people – the **greying population** (Figure 2.17).

FIGURE 2.17
The 'greying population'

FIGURE 2.16
Shrinking UK families

TASKS

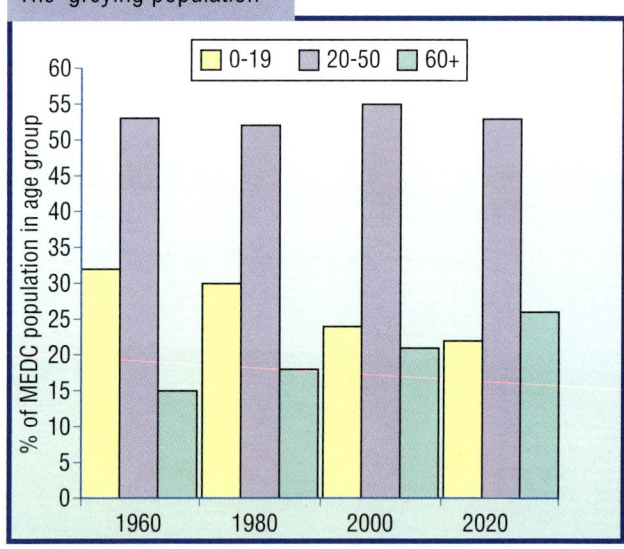

1 Look at how family size has changed in the UK (Figure 2.16).
   a How many children on average did a woman have in 1880?
   b Ask the people around you how many children their mothers have had. What number is the most common answer?
2 Look at Figure 2.17.
   a What two colours show the dependent population?
   b What percentage in 1960 were aged 60+?
   c What has happened to the 60+ population since then?
   d Between 2000 and 2020, what will happen to the number of people aged 20–50?
   e The shortage of workers will encourage migration from LEDCs. Why is this bad for LEDCs but good for MEDCs?

Population issues

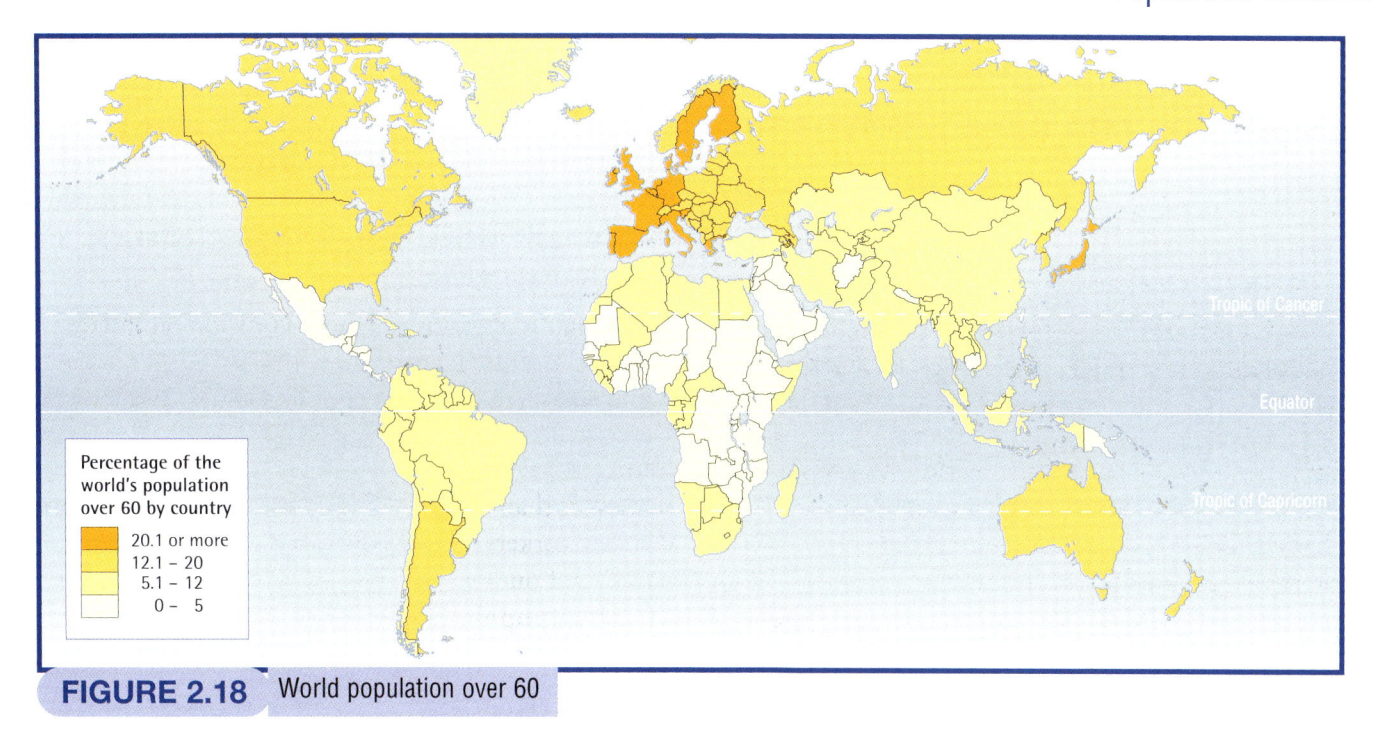

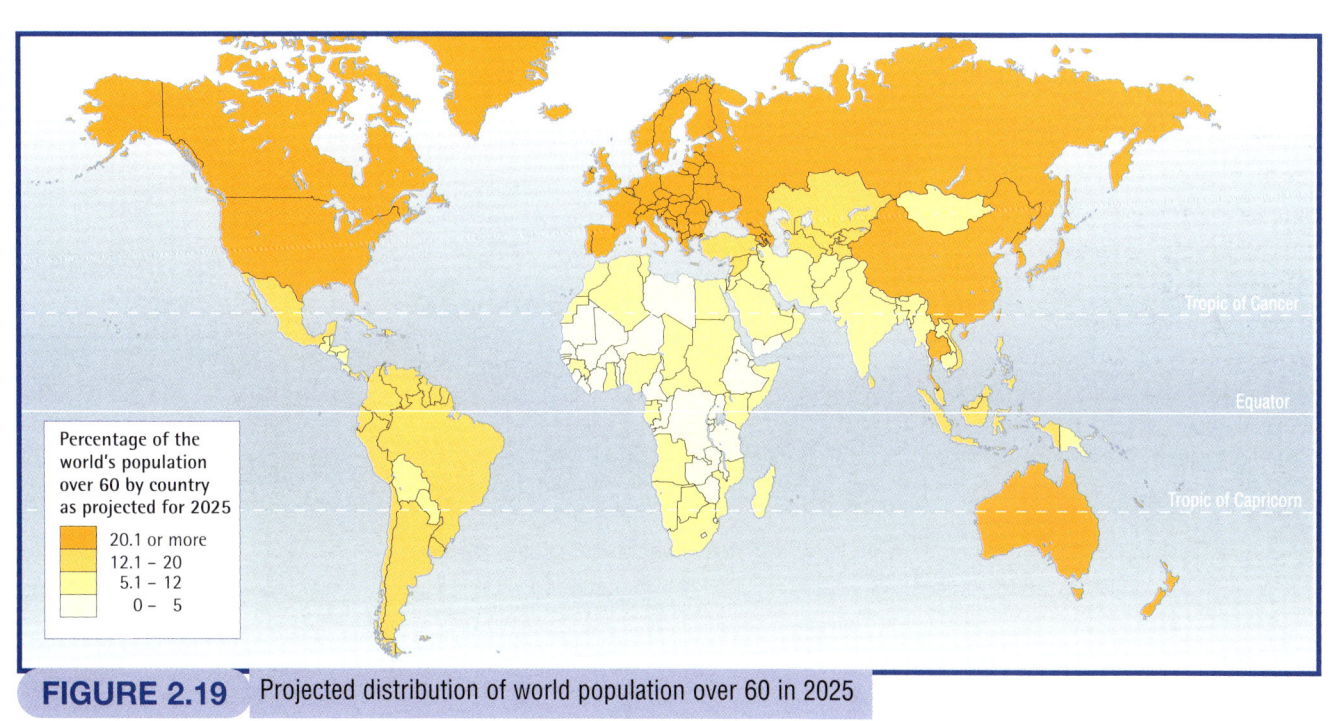

FIGURE 2.18 World population over 60

Percentage of the world's population over 60 by country
- 20.1 or more
- 12.1 – 20
- 5.1 – 12
- 0 – 5

FIGURE 2.19 Projected distribution of world population over 60 in 2025

Percentage of the world's population over 60 by country as projected for 2025
- 20.1 or more
- 12.1 – 20
- 5.1 – 12
- 0 – 5

Birth control

Many LEDCs are encouraging family planning. The governments of Mexico and Thailand are educating women so they know that the fewer children they have, the healthier the children will be. Sometimes the traditions of the country and the religion make it difficult for women to have fewer children. In some countries, the government has tried to force people to limit their families. Page 77 tells you about China.

two

People and Places to Live

Population

Population and the environment

Many areas are **overpopulated**. People struggle to make a living and the environment gets damaged. For example, the Sahel in Africa is turning into a desert. There are too many animals eating the grass down to its roots. The grass dies. Firewood is used for cooking. It is scarce. There are now few trees left. Droughts are more common now. Lack of water affects health and stops food crops growing.

Figure 2.20 shows what happens when the population grows too big for the amount of food available. The poorest people die from famine and diseases. Relief aid can increase the food supply for a short while only.

Although the graph suggests that food production can be increased, Africa now has 10% less food available than ten years ago. It also has countries at war, which makes things worse.

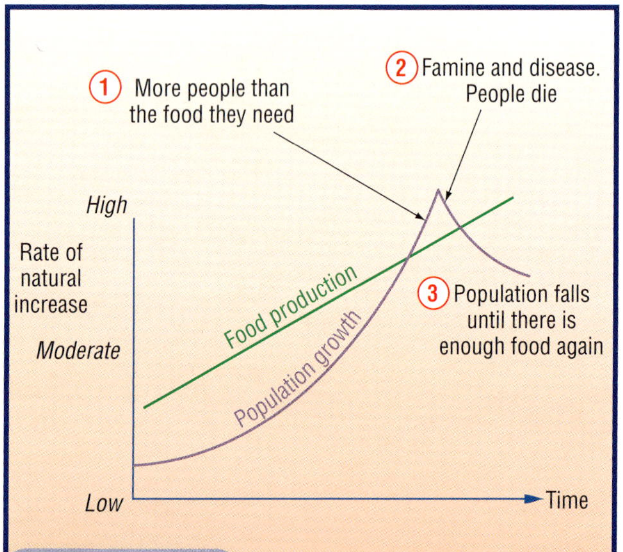

FIGURE 2.20
Population growth linked to food production

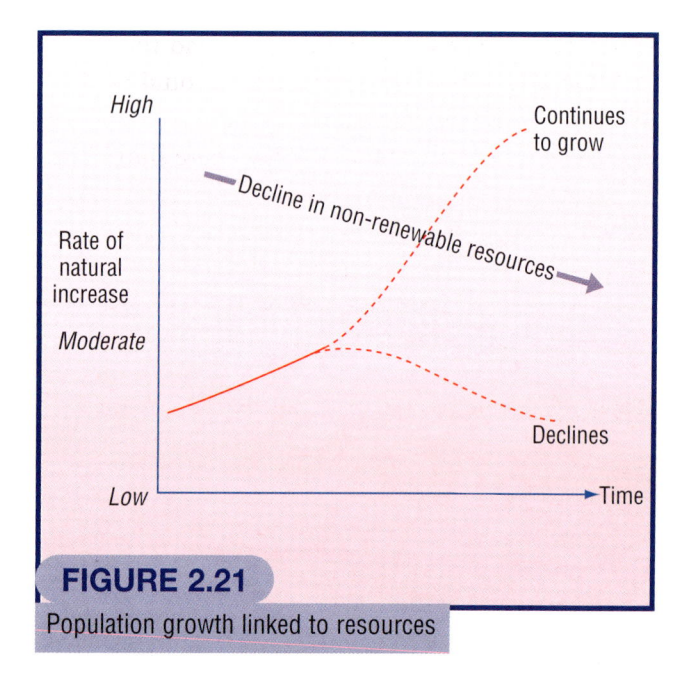

① More people than the food they need
② Famine and disease. People die
③ Population falls until there is enough food again

FIGURE 2.21
Population growth linked to resources

Decline in non-renewable resources
Continues to grow
Declines

TASKS

1. Use an atlas to identify two countries which now have more than 20% of their populations over the age of 60 (Figure 2.18).
2. Name three continents which, in 2025, will have most or all of their countries with more than 20% aged over 60 (Figure 2.19).
3. What are the governments of Mexico and Thailand doing to try to reduce the growth of their populations?
4. Copy and finish off these pictograms:

A quarter of the world's population lives in MEDCs. People in MEDCs eat half of the world's food.

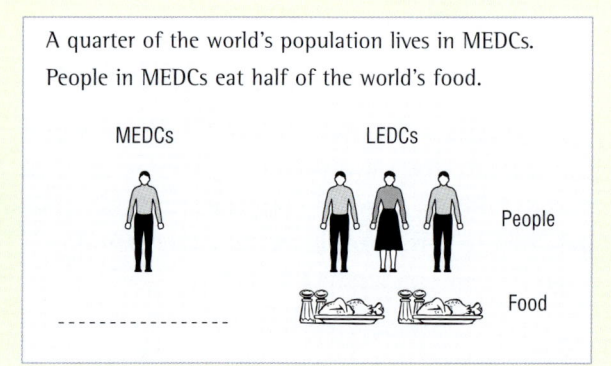

MEDCs   LEDCs   People
                          Food

A quarter of the world's population lives in MEDCs. People in MEDCs use four-fifths of the world's energy.

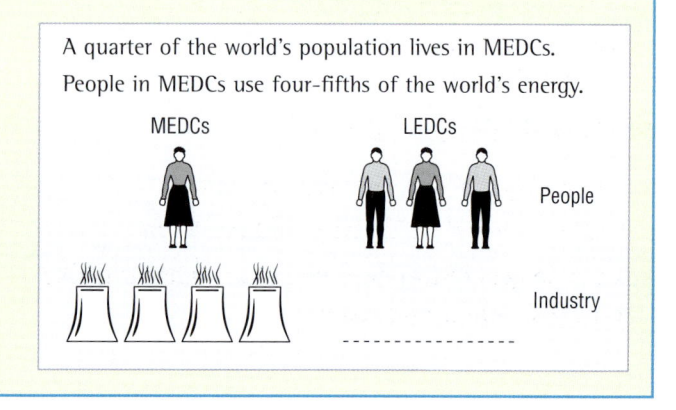

MEDCs   LEDCs   People
                          Industry

FAMILY PLANNING IN CHINA

> **SUMMARY** China made it the law to have no more than one child in each family. This has slowed down the increase in China's population, but caused other problems.

At one time, China wanted more workers. Families were encouraged to have many children. Then the Chinese Government realised it would not be possible to feed and look after all the people if the population continued to grow.

In 1975, the average Chinese family had three children. If nothing was done, there would be 2 billion Chinese by 2075. The Chinese Government decided in 1979 that there should be one child per family. Any couple who broke the law would be fined and lose benefits. Women who became pregnant with a second child were made to have an abortion and be sterilised. There were rewards for agreeing only to have one child.

Date	Birth rate	Death rate	Pop. change	Population (m)
1950	44	25	1.9	554 760
1960	38	17	2.1	657 492
1970	31	9	2.2	830 675
1980	19	7	1.2	996 134
1990	20	8	1.2	1 155 305
2000	17	7	1.0	1 300 000

Figure 2.22 Population change in China

The policy worked better in the cities than in the countryside. On farms, children could help with the work, as well as look after their parents in old age. Many parents wanted a boy to keep the farm and the family going. Some girl babies were killed so that their parents could try for a boy. The Chinese Government decided to allow a second child if the first was a girl.

Now people are worried that:

- China may not have enough workers
- The population of China could go down
- A whole generation does not know what it is like to have brothers and sisters.

TASKS

1. Look at Figure 2.22.
   a. Copy this graph frame.
   b. Plot the points for the birth rate. Two are done for you.
   c. Join them with a blue line.
   d. Now plot the death rate.
   e. Join them with a red line.
   f. Think what your graph shows, then write its title.
   g. Add a key to the colours.
2. If the birth rate and death rate are getting closer to each other, is the population growing faster or slower?
3. Draw a star diagram to show how China has made family planning happen. You can try using search engines to find more information on the internet.
4. Not everyone agrees with China's policy. If you were a top Chinese politician faced with the problems of China's increasing population, what other policies would you consider?

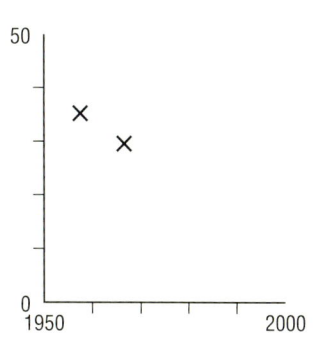

two — People and Places to Live

Population

MIGRATION

> **SUMMARY** Sometimes people move to another country to find work. Some stay for a short time. Others make their home in their new country. Many are willing to do jobs which it is hard to find workers for.

International migration is when people move from one country to another. **Emigrants** are people who leave a country. **Immigrants** arrive to live in another country.

People emigrate for a better life. Many choose to move so they can earn more money. These people usually move to a country they have links with, such as West Indians who moved to the UK. Other people are forced to leave their country by wars. These people are refugees; for example, Albanians from Kosovo. Many MEDCs welcome immigrants because they are short of workers. Immigrants take many of the low-paid jobs, such as cleaners, but they can also provide highly valued skills, such as doctors.

Guestworkers in Germany

Germany attracted immigrants from Eastern Europe (after the Second World War) and from Southern Europe (after the Berlin Wall was built) – see Figure 2.23. Originally, the immigrants were not expected to stay for long before returning to their home country, so they were called **guestworkers**. In fact, many have decided to stay in Germany. Less attractive jobs are done by people from poorer countries, such as Turkey. These are jobs which may be boring or dirty or have unattractive hours, like night shifts.

Immigration in the UK

In the 1950s, the UK was short of workers. Unemployment was high in the West Indies. Many West Indians had British passports, and some businesses, such as London Transport and the National Health Service, went to the West Indies to attract workers. Some British people were unhappy about immigration. They thought immigrants were taking jobs away. The Government passed laws to limit the number of immigrants and to protect and support them.

UK	110 000
USA	110 000
Poland	230 000
Italy	600 000
Turkey	2 000 000
Yugoslavia	800 000
Greece	360 000
Portugal	125 000
Spain	130 000

Figure 2.23 Origin of Germany's guestworkers

Country	1990
European Union	66 000
Australia/New Zealand/Canada	57 000
South Asia (India, Pakistan)	22 000
Caribbean	7 000
USA	29 000
South Africa	6 000
Middle East	10 000
Others	70 000

Figure 2.24 Migration into the UK

Migration 79

FIGURE 2.25

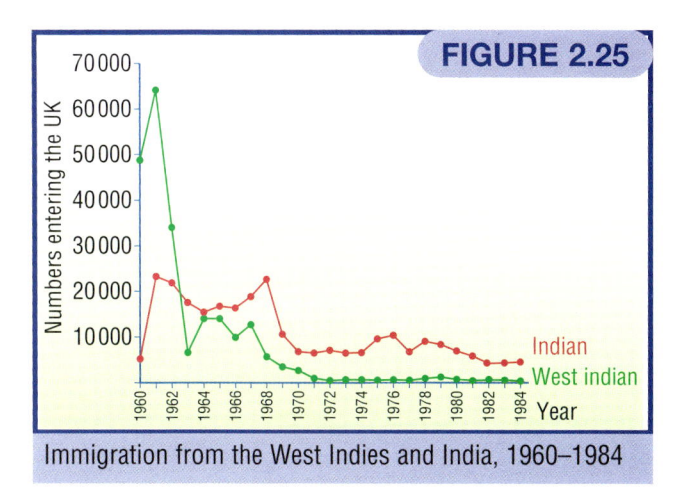

Immigration from the West Indies and India, 1960–1984

A **refugee** is someone who leaves their country because they are afraid. This might be because of war or a disaster such as a drought. They usually flee to the nearest safe country. Some then move on to another friendly country, such as the UK. Until a country accepts a refugee, he or she is known as an **asylum seeker**.

People also migrate from one MEDC to another MEDC, such as from the UK to Australia. They want a better life, perhaps a new start, or they may have to move with their jobs.

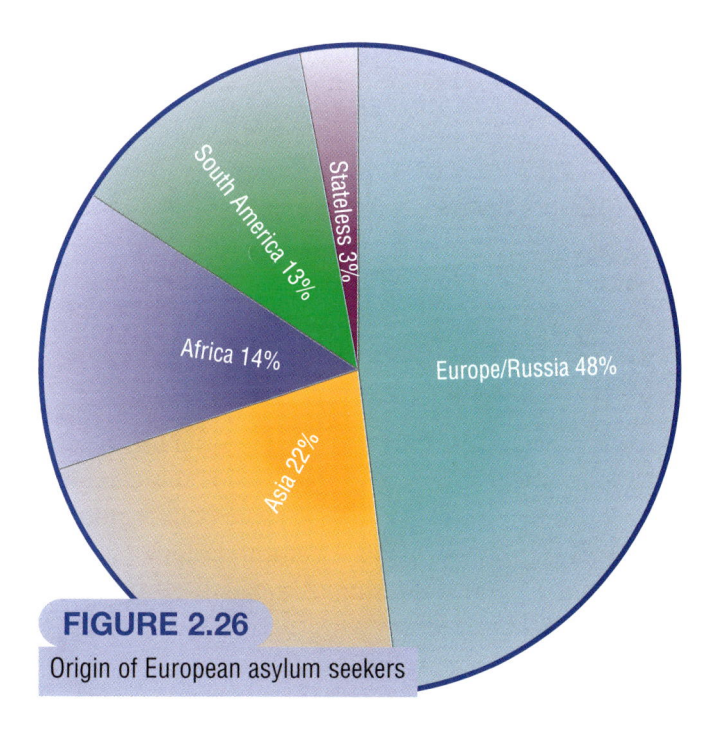

FIGURE 2.26
Origin of European asylum seekers

- Europe/Russia 48%
- Asia 22%
- Africa 14%
- South America 13%
- Stateless 3%

Country	1994
UK	10 300
New Zealand	10 200
China	7 200
India	4 900
SE Asia	10 500
Yugoslavia	3 000
Russia	2 300
USA	4 500
Africa	2 300
North Europe	1 400
South Europe	520
Others	23 400

Figure 2.27 Origin of immigrants to Australia, 1994

TASKS

1. What is the difference between an immigrant and an emigrant?

2. Make a list of all the reasons why people move to live in another country.

3. Look at Figures 2.23, 2.24 and 2.25. Copy this out and fill in the spaces.

   In Germany, immigrants who come to find work are called _____. The country which provides the most is _____. This is a much poorer country than Germany.

   The UK in 1990 received 66,000 immigrants from the _____ _____ and _____ immigrants from Australia/New Zealand/Canada. These are all MEDCs. Only 7,000 came from _____ because laws limited immigration, after its peak in 19__.

4. a Look at Figure 2.27. On an outline map of the world, draw arrows to Australia from each of the areas in the list except 'Others'.

   b Make the stick of each arrow 1 mm wide for every 1 000 people (so your arrow from UK to Australia will be 10 mm wide).

   c Use page 130 to decide whether each area is LEDC or MEDC. Colour the arrows, using red for LEDC and green for MEDC.

   d Are most of Australia's immigrants from LEDCs or MEDCs?

two — People and Places to Live

Population

MEXICANS TO THE USA

SUMMARY Villages in Mexico are losing their brightest young people. The USA pays better wages than Mexicans can earn at home. These are the jobs, though, that Americans do not want to do. Many migrants get into the USA illegally.

Encouragement to leave

	USA	Mexico
Births per 1 000 population	15	27
Years for population to double	116	32
Infant mortality	7	34
Percentage of population under age 15	22	36
Percentage using modern contraception	68	56
GNP per person in dollars	26 980	3 320

Figure 2.28

Mexico is an LEDC and the USA is an MEDC. The birth rate in Mexico is almost double that of the USA. More than one third of Mexicans are under 15 years old and have not had families yet, so the population is likely to double in only 32 years. Already there are problems with providing everyone with enough food. Farmers are now trying to grow crops on land they used to consider too poor for agriculture. Increasingly, there is not enough land to farm. It is a **push factor**, encouraging people to leave.

FIGURE 2.29
Mexicans provide cheap labour for low-skill jobs in California

Life in the countryside is hard. 80% have no clean water supply. About half of the children leave school by the age of 11. Most are unable to read and write.

The attraction of the USA

From a very early age, Mexicans have a glamorous idea of life in the USA – the 'Coca-Cola' image. Los Angeles, just 250 km across the border, is known as the 'City of Opportunity'. The wealth and bright lights image of the USA are **pull factors**.

For years, a few of the men from villages near the USA border have gone to California to work in the fruit and vegetable industries, or to Texas to pick cotton. There they can earn as much in a few months as in a whole year in Mexico. The USA needs the extra workers at harvest time. They are given work permits, so they are legal migrants.

Many more Mexicans would like to work in the USA. There may be 2 million attempts to cross the border illegally each year. The border is very long, the same distance as from the UK to Egypt! Despite 5 500 Border Patrol agents, tracker dogs and helicopters, one attempt in every seven is successful. Those who are caught are sent back to Mexico – and they try again on the next night.

Almost half go to California. Most migrants head for places where they have relatives or someone from the same village. These people help the new arrivals to find work and accommodation. They live in the poorest housing. Almost all of the neighbourhood is from Mexico. They work long hours in unpleasant, dirty, dangerous or boring jobs. It is hard to find Californians willing to do these jobs, but many Californians do not like the immigrants from Mexico. They fear they will work their way up and, one day, take better jobs, as Asian immigrants have done.

Maquiladora developments

In the last 20 years, more than 2 000 new factories have been built just inside Mexico for American firms. They are called **maquiladora** developments. The attractions are:

- Mexicans are willing to work for lower wages than Americans.
- Production costs are lower because there are fewer environmental controls in Mexico so waste can be dumped cheaply.
- Being close to the border, goods can easily be taken to the USA for sale.

These new factories, however, have encouraged migration from the Mexican countryside and provided some experience of working in industry. These people then become more likely to make the short journey across the border into the USA, in search of a better life.

Mexico's loss

Most of those who leave Mexico can read and write. They have skills. Mexico is losing some of its most trained and best-educated people. The poorest people are left in the villages.

FIGURE 2.30 Maquiladora factories pollute and encourage migration

TASKS

1. Study the information in Figure 2.28.
   a At the present rate of increase, in which year will the population of the USA be double what it is now?
   b In which year will Mexico's population be double what it is now?
   c Use all the information in the table to suggest reasons for Mexico's population increase.
2. In two columns, list the *Push Factors* from Mexico and the *Pull Factors* to the USA.
3. Describe what life is like in California for workers from Mexico. Write about:
   - the areas they live in
   - the work they do
   - the attitude of many Californians to them.
4. a What are maquiladora developments?
   b Write three reasons why American companies like them.
5. Imagine you live in a Mexican village.
   a You will soon be leaving school. Will you try to migrate to California? Why?
   b Will it be good or bad for the village? Why?

two
People and Places to Live
Settlement

WHAT IS URBANISATION?

> **SUMMARY** Urbanisation is when the proportion of people living in cities goes up over time. It has happened in MEDCs, such as the UK, over the last 200 years. It is happening now in LEDCs. Cities are getting larger. Places where more than 10 million people live are called megacities.

Urbanisation is when the percentage of people living in cities goes up. The urban population of the world has grown rapidly over the last 200 years:

World urbanisation

Year	% population living in urban areas
1800	3
1950	29
2006 (est.)	50

A country is urbanised when over 50% of people live in towns and cities. This happened first in countries such as Germany and the UK. Figure 2.31 shows the percentage of people living in urban areas across the world. MEDC cities, such as London, grew quite slowly. Many LEDC cities have grown very quickly over the last 50 years. Figure 2.32 shows how the world's urban population has changed.

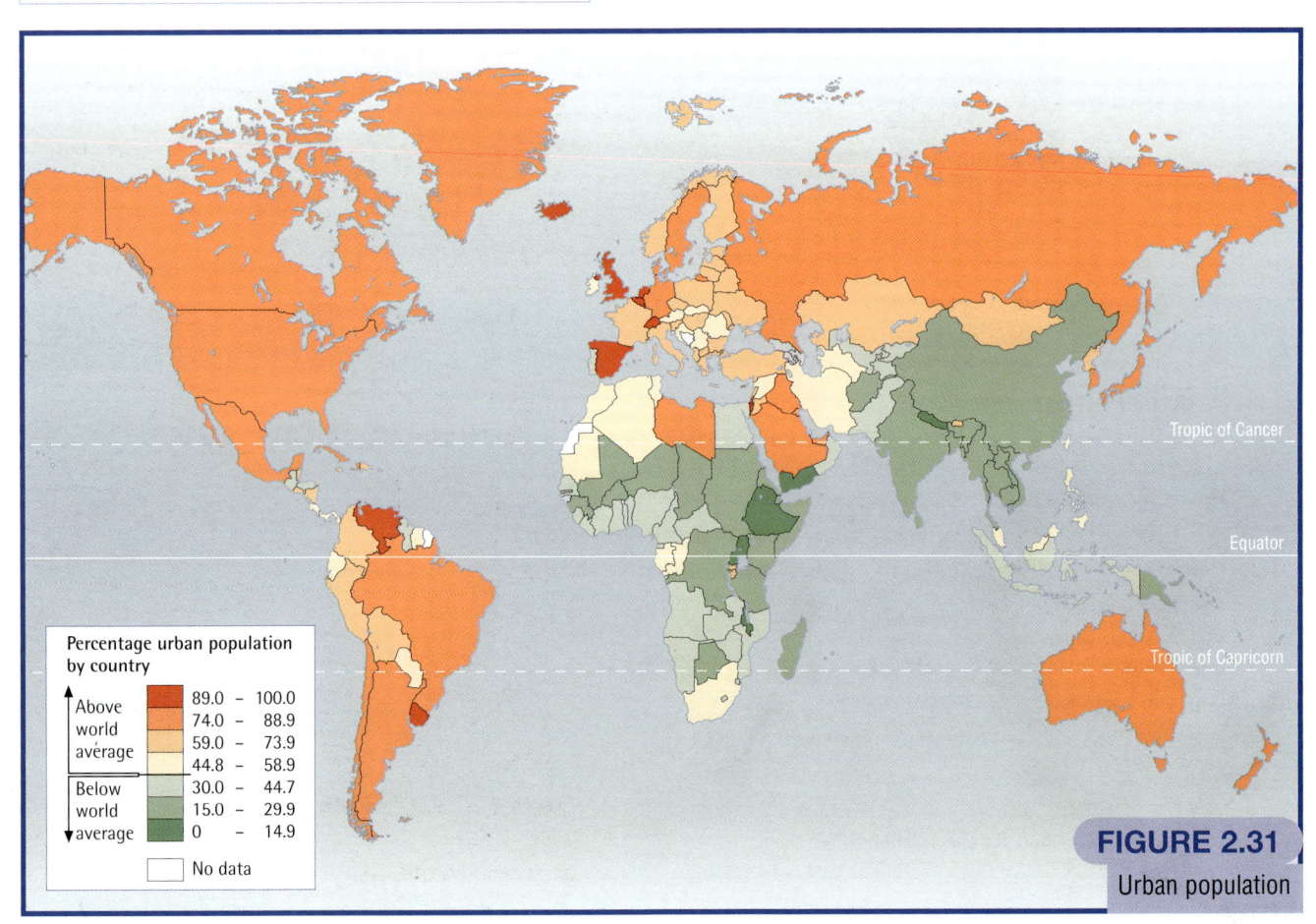

FIGURE 2.31 Urban population

Percentage urban population by country:
- Above world average: 89.0 – 100.0; 74.0 – 88.9; 59.0 – 73.9; 44.8 – 58.9
- Below world average: 30.0 – 44.7; 15.0 – 29.9; 0 – 14.9
- No data

Megacities

MEGACITIES

Many cities are getting larger. In 1900, London and Paris were the only two cities with more than 1 million people living there (**millionaire cities**). Today there are over 300 millionaire cities. **Megacities** have at least 10 million people living there. By 2015 there will be 27 megacities; 22 of these will be in LEDCs, especially in Latin America and Asia. Smaller cities are growing very quickly too.

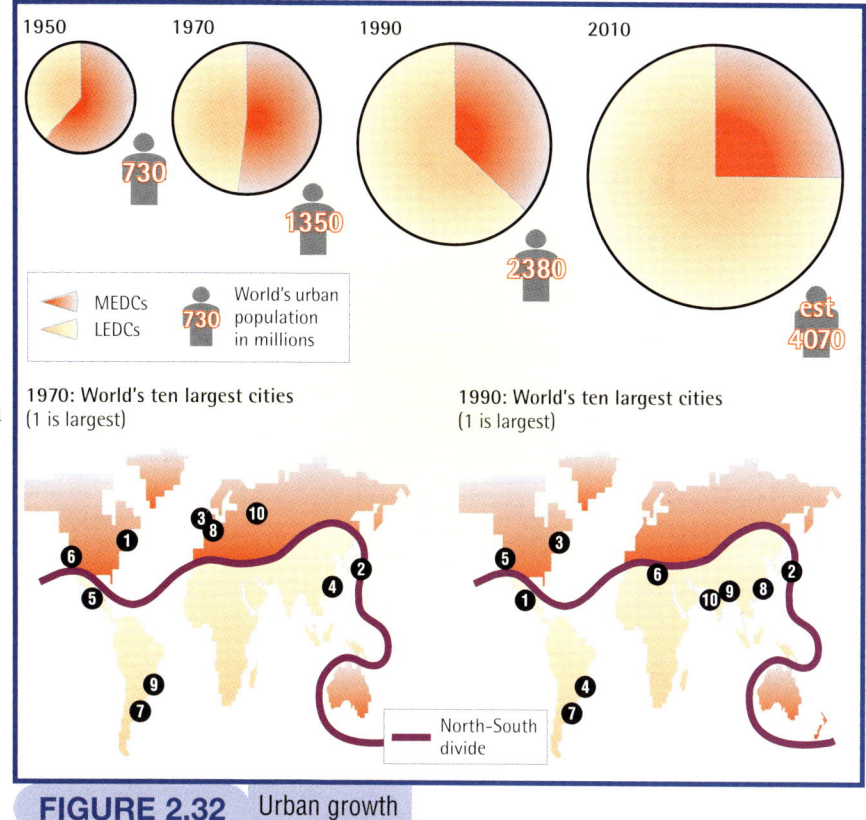

FIGURE 2.32 Urban growth

TASKS

1. Read pages 82–83 and look at Figure 2.33. Copy and complete the following:

   In 1800, ____ % of the world's urban population lived in towns and cities. By 2006 it may be over ____ %. An example of a millionaire city is _____. An example of a megacity is _____. By _____ there will be 27 megacities.

2. Look at Figure 2.31.
   a. List ten countries which have an urban population of above 74%. (Use an atlas to help you.)
   b. List ten countries which have an urban population of below world average.

3. Look at Figure 2.32. Read the sentences below. Copy out the true statements.
   - In 1950, the world's urban population was 730 million.
   - The world's urban population is decreasing.
   - By 1990, most of the world's ten largest cities were south of the North–South divide.
   - By 1970, the world's urban population was 2 380 million.
   - The percentage of the world's urban population living in LEDCs is increasing.
   - The majority of people living in cities today live in LEDCs.

4. a. Copy the axes below and draw a bar graph to show the information in Figure 2.33. 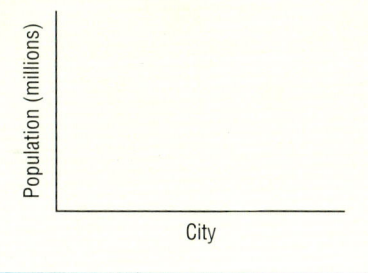
   b. Give your graph a title.
   c. Colour in MEDCs in one colour and LEDCs in another colour. Add a key.
   d. Write at least two sentences to describe what your graph shows.

		(pop. in millions)
1	Tokyo, Japan	28.7
2	Mumbai, India	27.4
3	Lagos, Nigeria	24.4
4	Shanghai, China	23.4
5	Jakarta, Indonesia	21.2
6	São Paulo, Brazil	20.8
7	Karachi, Pakistan	20.6
8	Beijing, China	19.4
9	Dhaka, Bangladesh	19.0
10	Mexico City, Mexico	18.8
11	New York, USA	17.6
12	Calcutta, India	17.6
13	Delhi, India	17.6
14	Tianjin, China	14.7
15	Metro Manila, Philippines	14.7

Figure 2.33 Projected 15 largest cities in the world, 2015

Source: United Nations 1995

People and Places to Live

Settlement

RURAL TO URBAN MIGRATION IN LEDCS

SUMMARY People are moving away from the countryside to cities in LEDCs. This is called rural–urban migration. It happens because of push factors and pull factors. There are many problems in cities such as squatter housing.

Cities in LEDCs are growing quickly for two reasons:

1. People are moving from the countryside to the cities (**rural–urban migration**).
2. Birth rates are high in cities (people who have moved to cities looking for jobs are often childbearing age).

People migrate to cities because of push factors and pull factors.

- **Push factors** = bad things which push people away from where they live.
- **Pull factors** = good things which attract people to move to a new location.

Improved employment opportunities, jobs in factories pay more than farming

Improved quality of life and standard of living to migrants who not only want a better quality of life for themselves but are determined that their children should have the chance of a good education to benefit from the chances that this might bring them

Pull

Expectations of improved housing with services such as electricity and water

Availability of schools, hospitals and entertainment

Access to education is very important

FIGURE 2.34 Push and pull factors

Push

Pressure on the land. Not enough for people to live on

Large families mean that there is not enough land for each child

Poor quality of life – hard work, long hours, little pay for farmers

Poor-quality housing

Increasing use of machinery reduces job opportunities in farming

Lack of infrastructure e.g. electricity, water and sewerage services

Overpopulation due to high birth rates

Starvation

Natural disasters e.g. drought, hurricanes, floods and volcanic eruptions, crop failure, fire, pests

Workers do not own the land and feel powerless

Lack of education, health and welfare facilities

Lack of investment from the government

Push and pull factors are shown in Figure 2.34. For example, farmers in rural Brazil may be pushed away from the countryside by drought and poverty and pulled into a city like São Paulo by jobs and a chance for their children to go to school and have a better quality of life.

Direction	Migrants per 1 000 of the population	
	1995	1996
Rural to rural	11.32	10.72
Rural to urban	7.8	8.3
Urban to rural	0.87	0.83
Urban to urban	21.29	31.36

Figure 2.35 Movement of migrants in Bangladesh

Migrants may live with friends and relatives who have already moved to the city when they first arrive. They may never have visited the city before they move there. Sometimes people move from the countryside to larger villages and towns. This is called **step migration**. When young workers leave the countryside and move to cities, villages may suffer and go into a spiral of decline.

PROBLEMS OF CITIES IN LEDCS

Lots of migrants find life in cities much harder than they expected. Many people arrive in cities

	Rural	Urban
Infant mortality rate	76/1 000	50/1 000
Life expectancy (age)	58.2	61.2
Adult literacy rate (%)	38.6	64.4
Calorie intake (kcal)	2 283	2 240
Access to toilet (%)	6.2	32.1
Access to safe drinking water (%)	95.8	99.4

Figure 2.36 Urban and rural contrasts in the quality of life in Bangladesh, 1996

everyday and this has led to a serious housing shortage. Migrants often build their own shacks on land they do not own or rent. This is called **squatter housing**. There are different names for areas of squatter housing – 'favelas' in Brazil, 'bustees' in India and 'shanties' in Africa. Squatter housing is often:

- built from waste wood, corrugated metal, cardboard, plastic and oil drums
- built illegally
- built on unwanted land (such as steep slopes, waste sites and swamps), near factories and alongside railway lines and roads – these sites can be polluted and unsafe
- overcrowded – large families often share one room to live, eat, wash and sleep in
- close to other squatter houses – strong communities can develop.

TASKS

1 Why are LEDC cities growing?
2 What is a push factor?
3 What is a pull factor?
4 Copy and complete the table by putting each push or pull factor from below into the correct column.

Push factors	Pull factors

natural disasters, jobs available in factories, no hospitals, no electricity, workers do not own land, chance to go to school, houses may not have running water, higher wages

5 Look at Figure 2.35 which shows the movement of migrants in Bangladesh. Which two directions have increased since 1995?
6 Look at Figure 2.36. Write a paragraph to explain why people move from rural to urban areas in Bangladesh. Include at least four numbers from the table in your paragraph.
7 Read the case study of flooding in Bangladesh on pages 36–39. Use search engines to find relevant information on the internet.

   How can flooding be a push factor which encourages people to leave the countryside?
8 How is migration in MEDCs such as the UK different to migration within an LEDC such as Bangladesh?

two
People and Places to Live
Settlement

Lack of basic amenities

The government and city authorities cannot keep up with how quickly many LEDC cities are growing. Many squatter houses do not have electricity, gas, running water or a toilet. Raw sewage may run in open streams and pollute drinking water. Every year 4 million people in urban areas die from diseases spread by polluted water. Litter is often not collected from squatter settlements which encourages rats and disease. There is a lot of competition for jobs. Migrants from the countryside may not have the qualifications or skills needed for factory work.

They work in the informal sector instead. This is when they try to make a living from things like selling fruit by the side of the road. Problems in LEDC cities include:

- poor quality and overcrowded housing
- homelessness, especially for abandoned children
- crime and vandalism
- competition for jobs
- poor environmental quality (such as polluted water).

Many LEDC cities are also at risk from hazards such as flooding, landslips and earthquakes.

BBC News

Friday, August 20, 1999 Published at 17:13 GMT 18:13 UK

Deathtrap cities keep growing

By Environment Correspondent Alex Kirby

One of the causes of the enormous loss of life in disasters in our modern age is the growth of modern cities. One hundred years ago, London headed the list of the world's ten largest metropolitan areas with 6.5 million inhabitants. But the UK capital does not even appear on the list of the ten largest cities on earth in the year 2000. Most of the world's biggest cities are in countries far poorer than the UK – places like Bombay, São Paulo and Lagos. Many cities are poor at the best of times. They are so jam-packed that, for millions of their people, day-to-day life is already lived wretchedly on the margins. A recent report from the Worldwatch Institute, *Reinventing Cities for People and Planet*, gave an outline. 'At least 220 million people in cities of the developing world lack clean drinking water, and 420 million do not have access to the simplest latrines. Six hundred million do not have adequate shelter, and 1.1 billion choke on unhealthy air.'

When chronic poverty erupts in natural or man-made disaster – earthquake, tidal wave, fire, storm or any other horror – the numbers of people in modern cities force casualties off the scale. The pace of urbanisation means conditions in the cities are getting worse much more quickly than governments can act. Between 1990 and 1995, Worldwatch says, 'the cities of the developing world grew by 263 million people – the equivalent of another Los Angeles or Shanghai forming every three months'. With almost half the people in the world living in cities today, the problem is already upon us.

In an ideal world, buildings would be constructed to survive earthquakes. The technology is there, but the money and the will are not. Probably the best we can hope for is not protection, but more preparedness. Next year marks the end of the UN's international decade for natural disaster reduction.

It exhorts all countries by 2000 to have comprehensive national assessments of risks from natural hazards integrated into development plans to address long-term disaster prevention, preparedness and awareness, ready access to global, regional, national and local warning systems.

Perhaps the simplest warning system might be to advise intending urban migrants they would often be safer staying put in the countryside.

Problems of cities in LEDCs

BBC News
Thursday, July 1, 1999 Published at 09:42 GMT 10:42 UK

Bangladesh struggles to cope

Overcrowded cities as many Bangladeshis leave their villages

By David Chazan in Dhaka

Zaynab Begum, her husband and three children live in a tiny bamboo and corrugated hut in a Dhaka slum. Their living space is smaller than six square metres. They have no electricity, running water or toilet, and an open sewer runs outside the hut. 'It's difficult to live here because it's cramped and uncomfortable,' she said. 'But my husband is a rickshaw-puller. We can't afford anything else.'

Zaynab Begum's family are among millions of Bangladeshis who have migrated to the cities in search of work. Fifty years ago, only about 4% of the population lived in urban areas. Now more than 25% are city dwellers. Overcrowding and malnutrition are worst among the urban poor, but the urban population is likely to continue to increase as people without land or jobs are driven into cities.

Strain on resources

Bangladesh is the world's ninth most populous country, with about 123 million people according to official estimates. The Ministry of Health and Family Welfare says the population is expected to grow to about 210 million by the year 2020.

Despite the relative success of family planning programmes which have brought the population growth rate to between 1.6% and 1.8% a year, already overcrowded Bangladesh will inevitably suffer further strain on its limited resources and land.

The population is expected to stabilise at about a quarter of a billion by 2050, if family planning programmes continue to reduce the birth rate.

But Bangladesh is already one of the world's most densely-populated countries, and its low per capita income is unlikely to increase.

'In a small country like Bangladesh, it will be a really big problem to accommodate such a huge population,' said Mizanur Rahman of the Family Planning Association of Bangladesh.

Millions migrate to cities in search of work. Malnutrition levels are already high. At least half of Bangladesh's people live below the poverty line. They eat only about half of the amount of food that would be considered normal elsewhere in the world.

Bangladesh is already unable to provide jobs, housing and food for all its people, and some analysts fear that there may be an increase in crime and violence as increasing numbers of people have to compete for resources.

TASKS

1. Read the BBC news articles 'Deathtrap cities keep growing' and 'Bangladesh struggles to cope'. What problems are being created by urbanisation?

2. Imagine you are a migrant who has just moved from the countryside to the city in Bangladesh to start a new life. Write a letter to your friends back home and describe your house, job, living conditions and the problems you face.

3. Explore the website about the city of Santiago, Chile:
   http://edcwww.cr.usgs.gov/earthshots/slow/tableofcontents
   Summarise how the city has changed and what problems there are. Include at least one photograph or image in your work.

two — People and Places to Live

Settlement

SQUATTER SETTLEMENTS

Squatter settlements often have extreme problems. There are many possible answers to these problems, which include:

- **bulldozing them** and encouraging people to return to the countryside
- **site and service schemes** – the authorities provide a site and basic materials such as breeze blocks and water tanks so people can build their own homes
- **improving areas** by digging drains, providing water taps and toilets and collecting litter – for example, the Metropolitan Development Authority was set up in Calcutta, India to improve living conditions
- **building houses elsewhere** – in Cairo, Egypt, satellite towns have been built away from the city.

Some squatter settlements are now more than 40 years old. Over time, people work hard to improve their houses. As they get better jobs, they can transform their shack into a house with facilities such as electricity and running water. Strong communities can develop as people work together.

FIGURE 2.37
Squatter settlement problems

TASKS

1. Read the newspaper article 'Measures to rehabilitate slum dwellers'. What is being done in Bangladesh to tackle slum problems?
2. Read the article 'World Bank criticises slum clearance'. Why does the World Bank think that bulldozing slums is not a good idea?
3. Copy and complete the table below:

Responses to squatter settlement problems		
Response	Advantage	Disadvantage
Bulldoze		
Site and service schemes		
Improve areas		
Build houses elsewhere		

4. Which response do you think is the best solution to the problems of squatter settlements? Explain your answer.

Squatter settlements

Daily Star Bangladesh — August 19, 1999

Measures to rehabilitate slum dwellers

Prime Minister Sheikh Hasina yesterday announced a series of measures for rehabilitation of the slum dwellers in their respective village homes, report agencies.

Each family intending to return to their village will be provided with travel expenses, three months' free food support under VGF programme and micro credit facilities through various institutions and agencies of the government.

The Prime Minister announced the programmes while addressing the first meeting of the recently constituted Slum Dwellers Rehabilitation Committee.

The Prime Minister referred to the government's massive programme for providing shelter and employment in the rural areas and said, 'We are working to ensure homes for the homeless and better living for the people.'

The slum dwellers are leading a subhuman life in the city slums and are being exploited by a section of people, she said, adding that some people are using the city slums as a haven for crimes.

The Prime Minister said the government is running the Asrayan Project for the homeless, a housing project for low-income group people, Adarsha Gram (ideal village) project and providing loan and training for the rehabilitation of the poor.

'We have provided homes to over 7 500 families through the Asrayan project, about 12 000 families through Adarsha Gram project and taken a new programme for providing homes to the low-income group people through the housing project,' she said.

'The Krishi Bank is running a project to provide loans and shelter to the people who are returning back to the village', she said, adding that under this programme 'Ghare Fera' (back to home), already 2 000 families have returned to the village and the programme is going on.

She said government has also taken steps to strengthen the rural economy and local government bodies through decentralisation of administration. She also mentioned other programmes for increasing facilities in the rural areas.

FIGURE 2.38
Improved squatter housing

BBC News
Sunday, August 29, 1999
Published at 04:31 GMT 05:31 UK
World: South Asia

WORLD BANK CRITICISES SLUM CLEARANCE

By Kamal Ahmed in Dhaka

THE WORLD BANK'S SENIOR OFFICIAL IN BANGLADESH, Fredrick Temple, has criticised a recent slum eviction drive ordered by the government.

'Bulldozing slums was not a solution to the problems of urban life,' Mr Temple said.

'Forcible eviction without relocation simply shifted poor people from one set of slums to another,' he added. The World Bank director called for a national urban strategy to cope with the pressures of urbanisation, which he said was a result of economic growth centred around city life.

POLICY CRITICISED

Mr Temple's comments are the most explicit criticism so far from the donor community of the controversial slum demolition drive, which made at least 50,000 people homeless.

The World Bank is one of Bangladesh's largest foreign aid donors, providing about $1bn last year.

He said that, in general, the clearance programme — carried out because the government said some slum areas in Dhaka and its outskirts were centres of crime — did not constitute a full urban settlement or shelter policy.

'The experience of other countries indicates that it is neither possible, nor affordable, for cities with large areas of slums to relocate the inhabitants' he added.

MIGRATION

Quoting the latest Bank study, Mr Temple said that, while four out of five Bangladeshis live in the countryside at present, in two decades every other Bangladeshi would live in cities.

The World Bank director said he shared the concerns of the Bangladesh government on urban law and order. But the forcible eviction of slum dwellers undermined the Bank's efforts, in conjunction with the Bangladeshi government, to provide education, health-care, job-training and micro-credit to the poor.

Police launched the slum clearance operation earlier this month, saying it constituted a crackdown on crime.

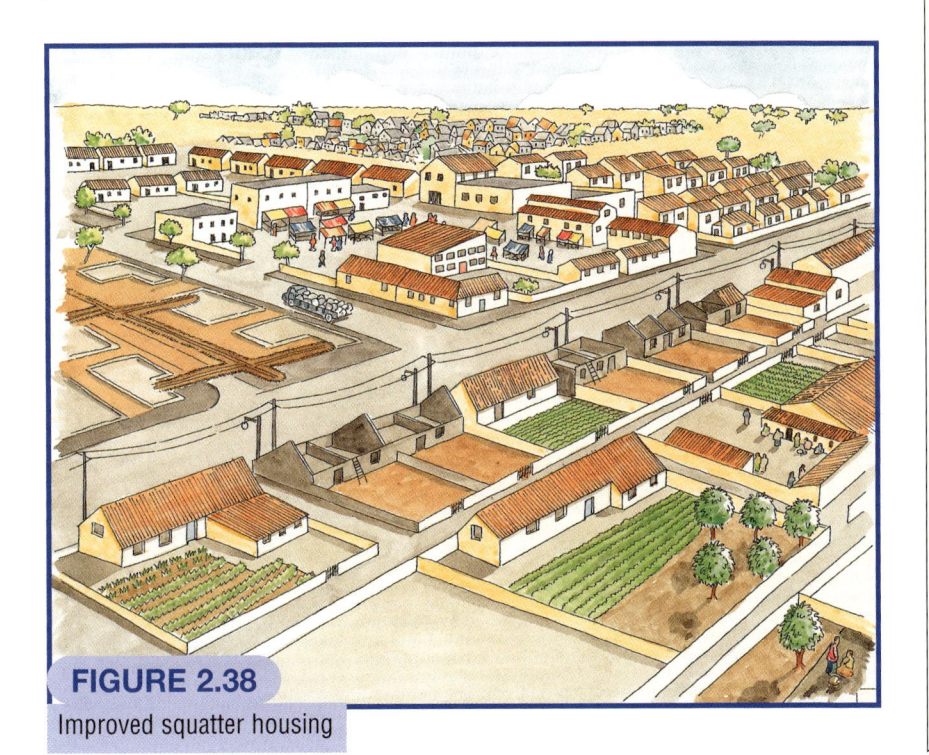

two People and Places to Live

Settlement

THE CENTRAL BUSINESS DISTRICT

> **SUMMARY** The Central Business District (CBD) is the part of the city which has many shops, offices and entertainment venues. It is very accessible.

The **Central Business District (CBD)** is a small area but it is very **accessible** (easy to get to). Roads and bus routes run into the CBD. Many shopkeepers and businesses want to locate in the CBD so the cost of land (the **bid price**) is high. The best location for a shop has the highest bid price – this is the **peak land value point (PLVP)**. It is often used by a chain store such as Marks and Spencer. Buildings in the CBD are often tall because land is expensive. It is hard to find room for car parks, bus stations and open space. Land in the CBD is too expensive for homes and factories.

Some things such as banks and places for entertainment may cluster together. Many people walk from place to place within the CBD. Some businesses locate on cheaper land at the edge of the CBD where more space is available.

TASKS

1. Define the following:
   - CBD
   - accessible
   - bid price
   - PLVP.
2. Why is it good for a shopkeeper to have an accessible site?
3. Explain two reasons why buildings are tall in the CBD.
4. Within the CBD, why do people often walk rather than drive or use public transport?

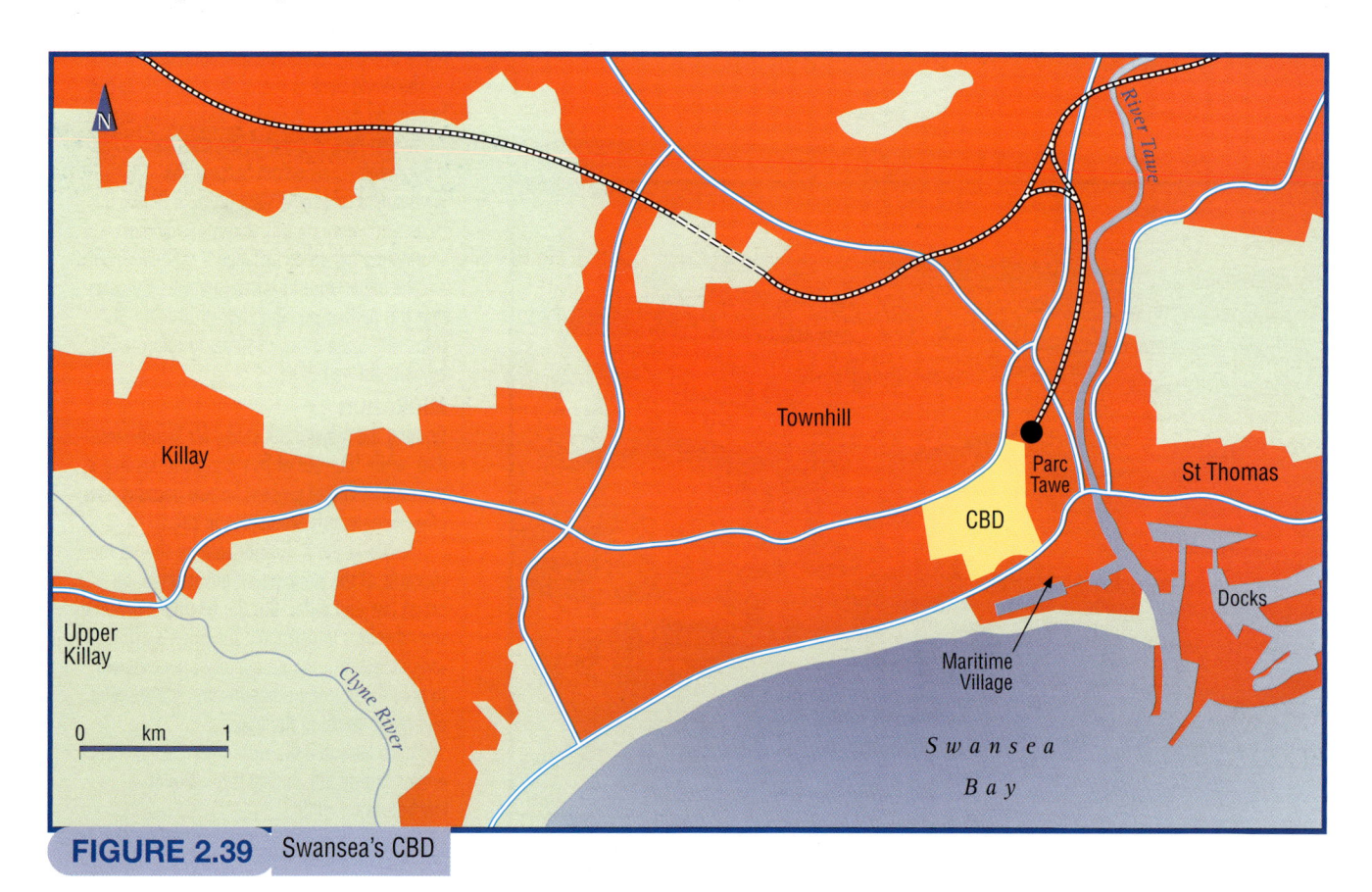

FIGURE 2.39 Swansea's CBD

The central business district

Swansea's CBD

The CBD of Swansea contains about 450 shops. Shoppers visit from the whole of south-west Wales. **High order goods** are expensive things which people do not buy often (such as fridges). Some high order goods cannot be bought anywhere else within 50 km. The oldest shopping area in Swansea is the High Street. The largest shops are to the west of this. Lots of this area is **pedestrianised** (no traffic allowed). It includes the Quadrant Centre – an undercover shopping centre opened in 1979 with a multi-storey car park.

FIGURE 2.40 Swansea's pedestrianised CBD

Llansamlet Retail Park is 4 km north of the CBD. The copper works here closed in 1980 leaving pollution and unemployment. The government made the area an **Enterprise Zone** (an area where businesses do not need to wait for planning permission and do not pay rates for ten years). There are now 40 large stores here. It is easy and free to park.

One third of the money spent by shoppers in the UK is now at out-of-town shopping centres rather than in the CBD. Some shops in the CBD have closed and been replaced by charity and second-hand shops. Swansea's CBD is fighting back with traffic-free streets, and housing is being built in the city centre.

FIGURE 2.41 Out-of-town shopping at Llansamlet

TASKS

5. Look at the two photographs on this page. Describe two advantages for shops trading at Llansamlet rather than in the CBD.
6. What is meant by:
   a. high order goods?
   b. enterprise zones?
7. What can a CBD do to fight back against the competition from out-of-town shopping?
8. Swansea's planners are encouraging people to live around the edge of the CBD and above shops. What would you like and dislike about living in a CBD?

two

■ People and Places to Live

Settement

FIGURE 2.42
St Thomas, Swansea

THE INNER ZONE

SUMMARY The inner zone contains factories, terraced houses and flats. This area has seen lots of changes.

Before the Industrial Revolution, Swansea was a port on the River Tawe. Just 6 000 people lived there. As Swansea became a major producer of copper, lots of people moved there for jobs. Many houses were built in areas such as St Thomas, close to the new industries and docks. Most of these terraced houses are now old with little or no front garden. Many have been improved by adding an inside toilet and bathroom. Some were demolished and replaced by high-rise flats.

FIGURE 2.43
Flats in Swansea

The inner zone

FIGURE 2.44 Maritime Village from the air

Building high-rise flats has created problems.

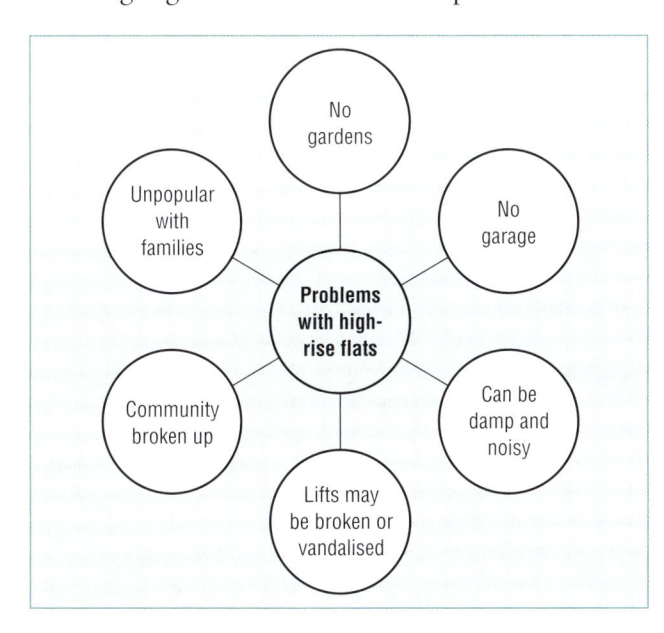

Problems with high-rise flats:
- No gardens
- No garage
- Can be damp and noisy
- Lifts may be broken or vandalised
- Community broken up
- Unpopular with families

Two areas of Swansea's inner zone have been changed:

1 **Parc Tawe** (shown in the background of Figure 2.42). This area is between the CBD and the river. It is now a shopping and leisure complex.

2 **South Dock**. This area is between the CBD and the beach. 100 years ago it was a successful area of warehouses and ships. Swansea council bought the dock when it closed. £500 million was spent on building the Maritime Village (Figure 2.44) with 1 500 homes, a yachting marina, Maritime Museum, shops and restaurants.

TASKS

1 Why were houses originally built close to industry?
2 Use Figure 2.42 to describe a typical inner zone house.
3 Look at Figure 2.43. What are the advantages and disadvantages of living in high-rise flats for:
   a a family with young children?
   b a young single person?
4 Describe how South Dock has changed.
5 Explain how building the Maritime Village has been good for Swansea.

two — People and Places to Live

Settlement

SUBURBS

SUMMARY The suburbs are on the edge of the city. There are many semi-detached and detached houses with gardens.

Half of the UK's population lives in suburbs. Many semi-detached houses were built in the 1920s and 1930s at the edge of the city. These houses were better than the inner-zone slums as they had inside toilets and bathrooms. People travelled to the docks and industries of the inner zone by bus.

Townhill is a Swansea suburb. Problems include:

- 45% long-term unemployment
- high crime rates
- school truancy
- many people rely on benefits
- there are few places for children to play.

£9 million is being spent on Townhill. Half of this is from the European Union. It is being used for:

- **The Greening Programme**. Local community groups set up an environmental project.
- **Traffic schemes**. Improvements include speed humps and new pedestrian crossings.
- **Employment projects**. Local colleges offer training and crêches and there are grants for businesses.

FIGURE 2.45
Townhill shops

Suburbs 95

behind it. This is called **ribbon development**. The government has set up **green belts** around the suburbs to stop cities growing. Segments of green belt are called **green wedges**. Building is not usually allowed in these areas. This encourages people to rebuild the inner zone.

Some suburbs have become run-down, houses are in poor condition and shops are shutting (or moving out of town) as more people own cars and drive elsewhere. Neighbourhood communities suffer because they have fewer facilities. Some people are leaving to move to the countryside. This is called **de-suburbanisation**.

FIGURE 2.46
Semi-detached Killay

Some suburbs are newer than Townhill. Killay was once a separate village. Most houses are privately owned with garages and gardens. Upper Killay has a line of houses alongside the road with farmland

TASKS

1 Copy and complete:

   Many suburbs were built in the 19__s and 19__s and were a great improvement on the slums of the _____ _____. People travelled to work by ___. Some shops and facilities are closing in the suburbs because ....

2 Define:
   - ribbon development
   - green belt
   - green wedge
   - de-suburbanisation.

3 Describe the photograph in Figure 2.45 of Townhill. Include at least one advantage and one disadvantage of living there.

4 Explain how Townhill is being improved.

5 Before planners stopped ribbon development, why did people want to build alongside main roads?

6 Do you think that green belts are a good idea? Explain your answer.

People and Places to Live

Settlement

TRAFFIC IN AN URBAN AREA

SUMMARY — Traffic problems have increased in many cities. There are lots of ways to reduce congestion, such as improving public transport.

Towns and cities grew in accessible places so goods could be bought and sold. Glasgow in Scotland grew where routes crossed the River Clyde at the lowest bridging point. Ships no longer come up the river to the city centre but roads are very busy. **Congestion** causes delays, air and noise pollution and accidents.

In the past, new roads and better junctions were built to help traffic flow. However, this encouraged more traffic and fewer people used buses or walked. Glasgow has tried to promote public transport and travelling on foot or by bicycle. Eighteen routes into Glasgow have a bus every 10 minutes. Some 'bendibuses' carry 120 passengers each and traffic lights change to green as buses approach. Areas such as Maryhill Road (Figure 2.49) have been improved by a Route Action Plan with **bus lanes**, information screens on bus stops and **bus gates** (junctions that only buses are allowed to use).

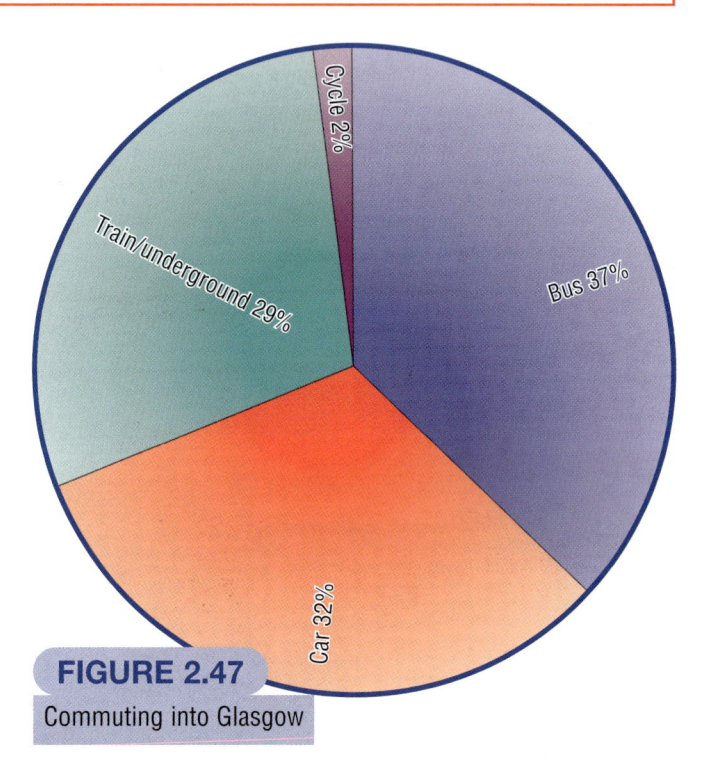

FIGURE 2.47
Commuting into Glasgow

- Bus 37%
- Car 32%
- Train/underground 29%
- Cycle 2%

FIGURE 2.48
Bus gates speeding up public transport

Traffic in an urban area

Integrated public transport

Buses and trains link together in Glasgow. Glasgow has many railway lines and new stations have been opened. There are plans to build a new line to Glasgow airport. The aim is to have every part of the city within 500 m of a station. Timetables and tickets will also be integrated (linked together). **Park and ride** schemes encourage people to park their cars for free and travel into Glasgow by train (Figure 2.50). **Kiss and ride** is when a commuter is dropped off at the station.

FIGURE 2.49
Maryhill Road bus lane

FIGURE 2.50
Park and ride rail station

two

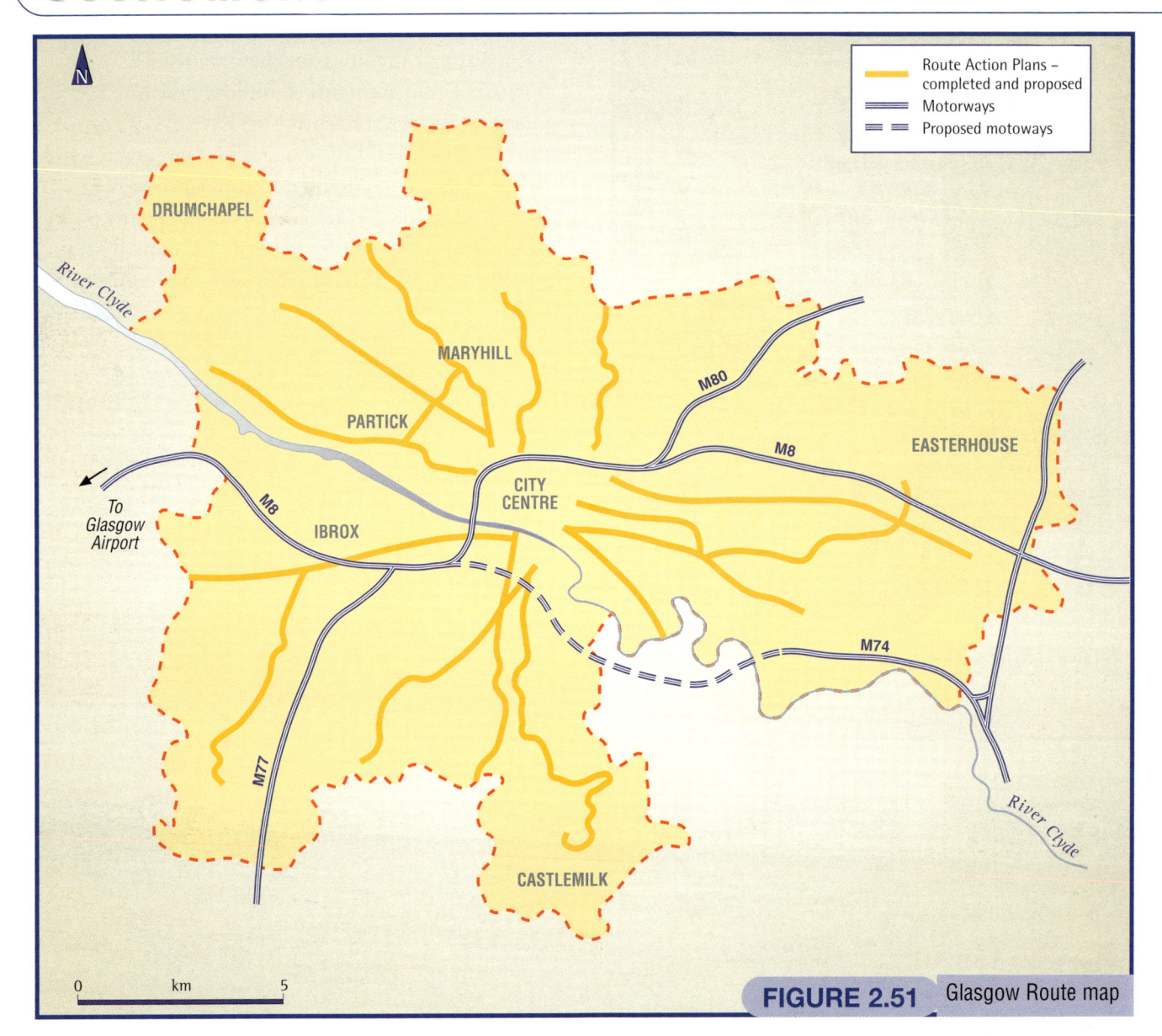

People and Places to Live

Settlement

FIGURE 2.51 Glasgow Route map

Paying to park

In Glasgow, the cost of parking has increased significantly over the last 20 years. This has put people off commuting by car into the city centre, although some park just outside the CBD and walk in. People who live in the inner zone now have to buy permits to park outside their homes.

Encouraging cycling

Glasgow's cycle network is 100 km long. People can cycle along routes such as closed railways. Cycling is expected to quadruple by 2012. Cycles can be taken on trains and there are many bike lockers. Cycling reduces traffic and keeps people fit.

Moving goods

97% of Glasgow's freight travels by road. However, deliveries are not allowed in the city centre during the working day. There are also restrictions on main roads into the city to reduce congestion during peak times.

More roads

The M8 motorway was built as part of the redevelopment of Glasgow's inner city in the 1960s. This is a fast route into the city centre. One proposal is to extend motorways to completely circle Glasgow.

Traffic in an urban area

FIGURE 2.52
The busiest bridge in Britain, Kingston Bridge, carries the M8 motorway over the River Clyde in Glasgow

TASKS

1 Which two methods of transport made Glasgow a good site to develop?
2 Why does building more roads sometimes make the problem worse?
3 Look at the pie chart in Figure 2.47.
   a What is the most popular way to commute into Glasgow?
   b How has Glasgow encouraged people to use this method of transport?
4 Make a large copy of the diagram opposite and add a sentence about each scheme.
5 Design a poster to encourage people to commute to work by bus or train.
6 Explain why some people do not like using public transport.
7 Do you think building more motorways is a good idea? Why?
8 How could traffic problems be improved in the area where you live?

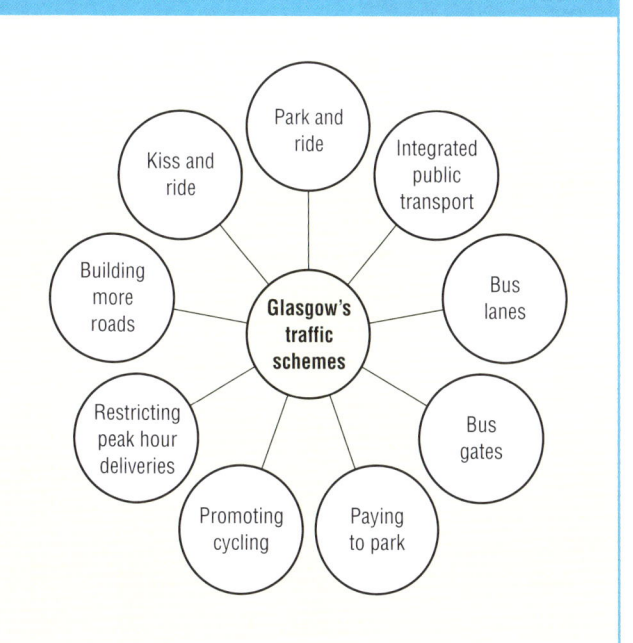

Glasgow's traffic schemes:
- Park and ride
- Integrated public transport
- Bus lanes
- Bus gates
- Paying to park
- Promoting cycling
- Restricting peak hour deliveries
- Building more roads
- Kiss and ride

two
■ People and Places to Live

Settlement

THE PROVISION OF SERVICES

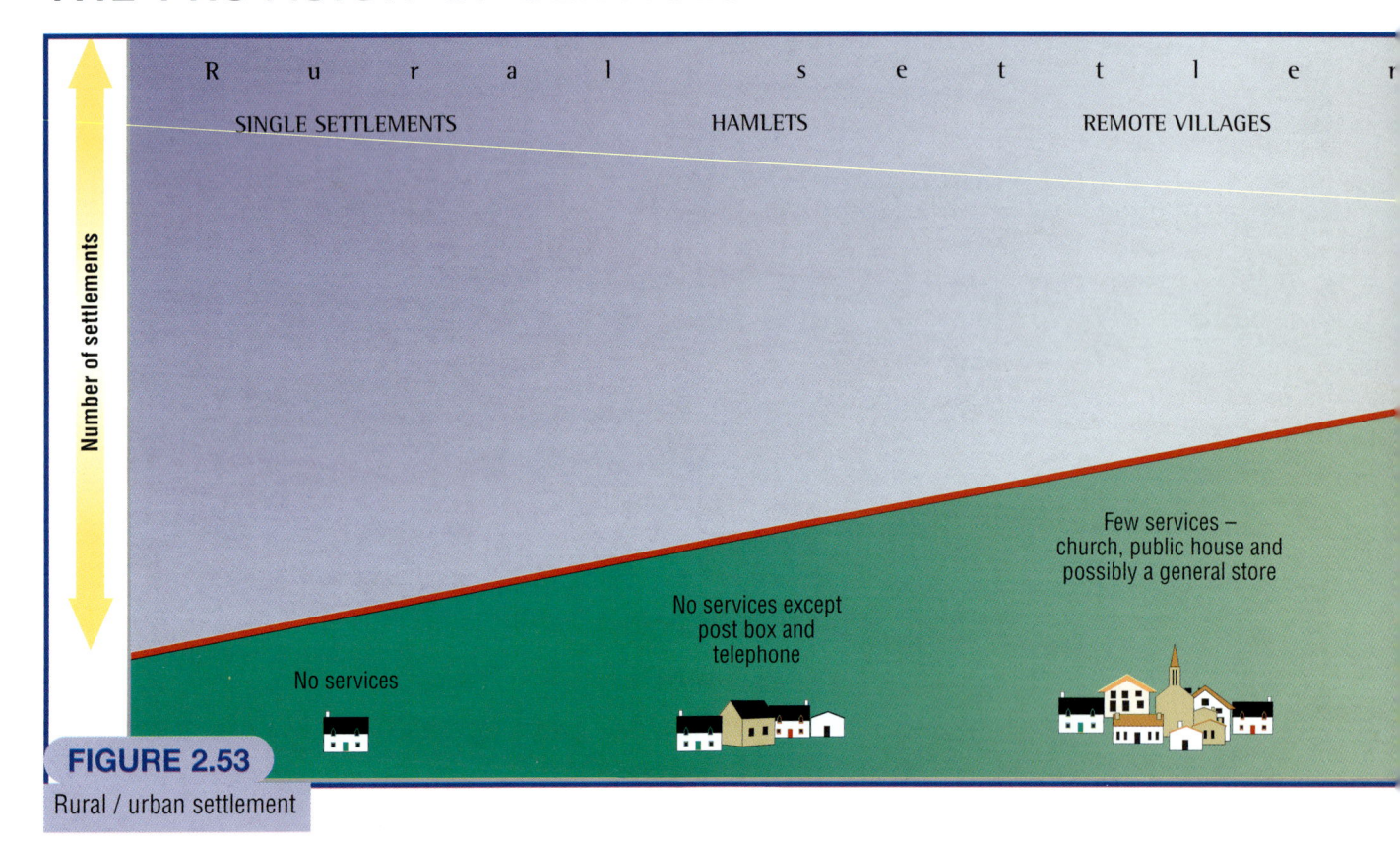

Rural settle...

SINGLE SETTLEMENTS · HAMLETS · REMOTE VILLAGES

Number of settlements

No services

No services except post box and telephone

Few services – church, public house and possibly a general store

FIGURE 2.53
Rural / urban settlement

SUMMARY Settlements vary in size and importance, from hamlets with no services to cities with lots of services. A settlement will change over time. The population may go up or down. Shops and services may open up or close down.

The hierarchy of settlements

Some people live away from other houses. These are **single settlements** such as farms. When a few homes are close together but there are no services such as shops, this is a **hamlet**. A larger place with more people and services is a **village**. Many villages near to towns and cities are growing because people can **commute** to work. Often services such as dental surgeries and electrical shops are only found in **towns** and **cities**. This is because they need lots of people nearby to stay in business. The number of people needed for a particular service to survive is called the **threshold population**.

Towns and cities – too successful?

Places grew because they were accessible for trade. As people moved there, the price of land rose. Cities became expensive and congestion got worse. Out-of-town shopping has grown where land is cheaper and easy to get to, such as by a motorway junction. Town centres and local shops have suffered as people use large hypermarkets out of town.

Rural services fight back

ACCESSIBLE VILLAGES — **TOWN** — **CITY**

Urban settlement

Limited range of services, e.g. small supermarket, butcher, hairdresser

Wider range of services, e.g. some specialist shops, library, dentist, bank, leisure centre, cinema

Wide choice of shops, chain stores, many specialist shops, regional offices, TV studio, airport

Range of services

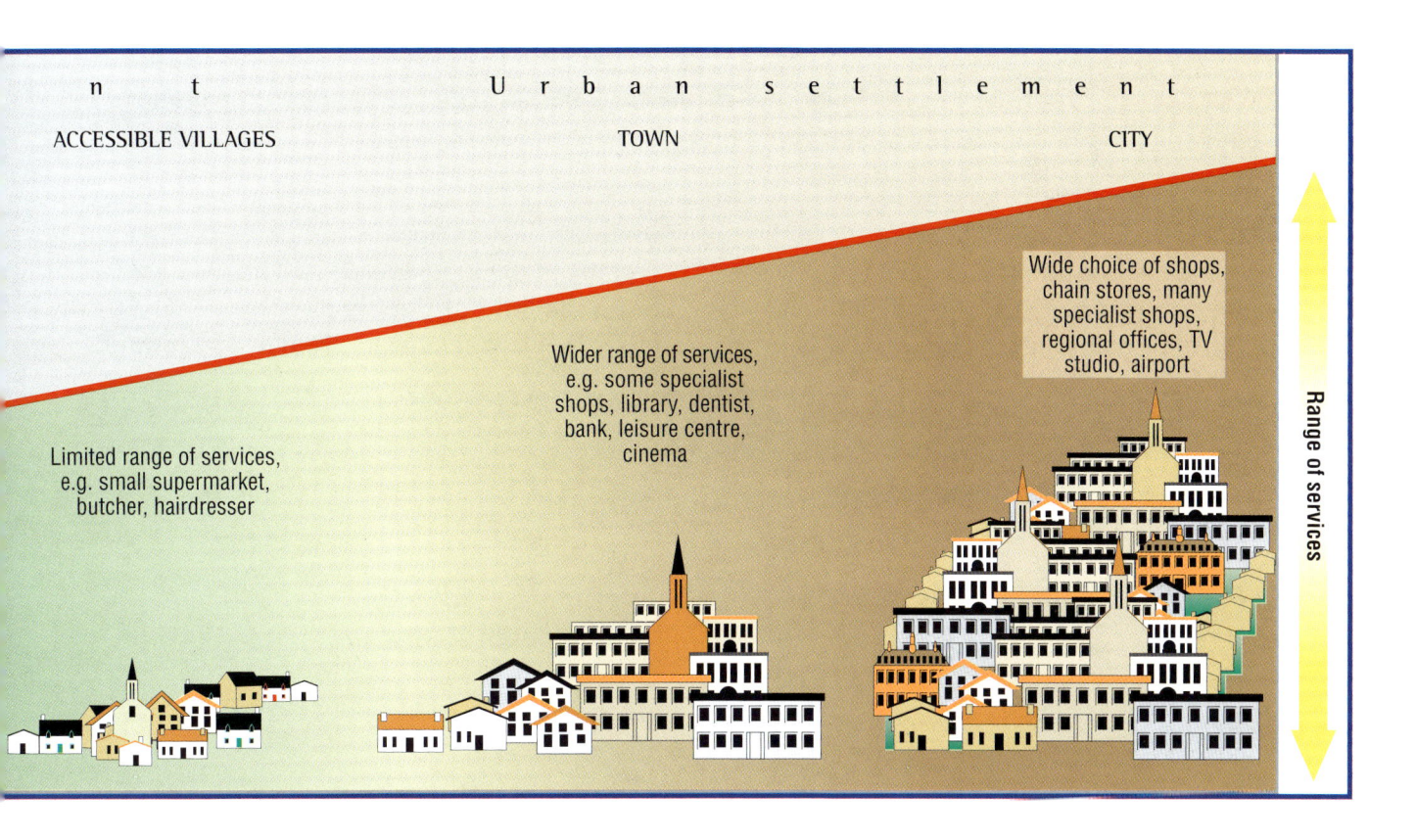

RURAL SERVICES FIGHT BACK

One in four people in the UK lives in the countryside and this number is growing. Rural services are trying to reverse their decline. For example:

- Village shops
  - sell lottery tickets
  - post offices offer many services such as travel insurance
  - some councils help by charging lower rates and offering loans.

- Public transport
  - schemes such as 'dial a ride' and 'post buses' (Royal Mail minibuses used by locals)
  - some stations are reopening.

- Community facilities
  - pubs and village halls are being improved.

- Mobile services
  - library vans and mobile banks can visit villages.

TASKS

1. a Copy the diagram and write the correct settlement type in each layer. Choose from these options:

   remote village, hamlet, city, town, accessible village, single settlement

   Increasing population and services ↑   ↑ Decreasing number of settlements

   b Add an example for each type (name real places).

2. Describe at least four ideas that rural shops and services are using to reverse their decline.

two
People and Places to Live
Settlement

NORTH WORCESTERSHIRE, A CASE STUDY

SUMMARY Areas such as North Worcestershire have been affected by counterurbanisation and commuting. Around many towns and cities, green belts have been set up.

Cookley is a village in North Worcestershire. 2 500 people live there. Most people commute to work and shop in nearby towns such as Kidderminster. Cookley has low-order shops (Figure 2.54). Many people use them to 'top up' but do most of their shopping in town supermarkets. The shop used most is the fish and chip shop. There are three pubs – people visit Cookley from nearby towns.

TASKS

1. Why do you think that the fish and chip shop is used most?
2. Look at the Ordnance Survey map opposite.
   a. Give the 6-figure grid reference for the centre of Cookley.
   b. Name the river which is closest to Cookley.
3. Using map evidence, list the services and land uses in
   a. Cookley
   b. Kidderminster.
4. Copy and complete the table using the map. Think about size and services.

Settlement type	Example of place (from map)	Map evidence
Town		
Village		
Hamlet		
Single settlement		

FIGURE 2.54 Cookley village

North Worcestershire, a Case Study

FIGURE 2.55
OS Landranger map of Kidderminster

two

- People and Places to Live

Settlement

As more people in Cookley now own cars, bus services have declined as there are too few passengers. One of the two primary schools has closed because the children of the families who moved into the new houses 40 years ago have now grown up. Older people support other services. The Parish Hall is doing well with activities such as barn dances, and the doctor's surgery is being extended.

In the 1960s and 1970s, new houses were built in Cookley. Most of the new residents travelled to the nearby town of Kidderminster for shops and services. Kidderminster has services such as estate agents as there are enough customers to make this profitable.

Within towns, there are clusters of shops away from the CBD. These **neighbourhood centres**, such as in the part of Kidderminster called Offmore (Figure 2.56), provide everyday goods such as bread and milk for local people. For high order goods, people travel to the CBD. For the highest order goods, Kidderminster's population travels to larger settlements such as Worcester or Birmingham.

FIGURE 2.56
Offmore neighbourhood centre in Kidderminster

Merry Hill is 14 km from Kidderminster. This out-of-town shopping centre provides many facilities, such as free parking for 10 000 cars, restaurants and entertainment, indoor shopping malls and a range of shops. Merry Hill needs to attract lots of shoppers for its high order shops to have enough customers. 4.5 million people live within its sphere of influence. With fewer people shopping in Kidderminster, some high order shops have closed down.

TASKS

5. Look at the OS map on page 103. Kidderminster is a route centre. How many main roads meet there?

6. a Which grid square do you think is Kidderminster's CBD? (Give a 4-figure grid reference.)
   b Why did you choose that square?

7. Look at Figure 2.56.
   a List three things that can be bought at neighbourhood shops such as these.
   b List three things which probably cannot be bought here.

8. Design a poster to advertise an out-of-town shopping centre such as Merry Hill. Think about all of the advantages of shopping there.

9. Why do some people think that no more large, modern out-of-town shopping centres should be built?

10. Think of a town you know well. What has been done to make it an attractive place to shop? How could it be made even better?

URBAN TO RURAL MIGRATION

FIGURE 2.57
Sheep for neighbours in Cutnall Green

Since the Industrial Revolution, UK towns have grown (especially those near coalfields). People moved from the countryside to towns to get jobs. There was rapid **urbanisation**. This is happening now in LEDCs (pages 82–83).

Since the 1960s, the population of UK towns and cities has been falling. More people are leaving cities than moving into them. This is **counterurbanisation**.

Causes

Counterurbanisation happens because of push and pull factors. Push factors are bad things such as traffic congestion and crime which make people leave cities. Pull factors are good things about the countryside which attract people, such as clean air and the image of friendly and safe village life. There are several reasons why counterurbanisation has happened. Some people can work from home using technology such as the Internet. Transport improvements have encouraged people to **commute**. Some people move to the countryside to retire.

People and Places to Live

Settlement

The consequences of urban to rural migration

Some villages near to cities have become **dormitory settlements** (the daytime population is much less than at night). Some villages have grown. With an increased population, there can be shops and supermarkets, offices and light industry. People and businesses are attracted to a pleasant environment where land is cheap. However, there can be tensions when newcomers move into a village and the close-knit community feeling can be lost.

The countryside around the UK's cities is protected by **green belts** (page 95). It is difficult to get permission to build new houses so labourers' cottages and farm barns are converted into luxury homes. Most young locals cannot afford these and leave the village to find cheaper houses in towns.

North Worcestershire

Many villages of North Worcestershire are expanding. They are less than an hour's journey from Birmingham, and many other towns and cities such as Kidderminster and Worcester can be reached in less time. House prices are also cheaper than in areas such as Solihull or Sutton Coldfield which are within the West Midlands conurbation.

> **TASKS**
>
> 1. Define:
>   - commuting
>   - counterurbanisation.
> 2. Divide your page into two. Put the title 'rural' on one side and 'urban' on the other. Draw pictures and add labels to show what it is like to live in rural areas and urban areas. Think about what is good and bad about living in each type of place. (You could use images from the Internet or cliparts.)
> 3. Explain two reasons why villages in North Worcestershire are growing.
> 4. Look at Figure 2.58. Describe the advantages and disadvantages of living there.
> 5. Suggest why house prices are cheaper in North Worcestershire than in Solihull.

FIGURE 2.58 A second home by the River Severn

Urban to rural migration

Some people who buy houses in North Worcestershire are buying a second home (Figure 2.58). As these houses are often empty, the owners contribute little to local villages. Some villages have a high proportion of older people who have moved there to retire. Young people may leave the villages. A two-bedroom starter home in Kidderminster is at least 20% cheaper than a two-bedroom cottage in a village.

New housing estates have been allowed to be built in some villages. When villages grow quickly it can cause problems.

Here is some information about the village of Cutnall Green:

- 10 km south-east of Kidderminster, 4 km from Droitwich (a town with many shops)
- population was 322 until the Brookfields estate added an extra 100 people in 1997
- population increase has not increased trade in the village shop and post office very much
- many of the newcomers commute to towns
- 30% of Cutnall Green's population is aged 45–59 (the England average is 17%). This shows that **gentrification** has happened.

FIGURE 2.59
The Chequers Pub, Cutnall Green

FIGURE 2.60
Where workers from Cutnall Green work

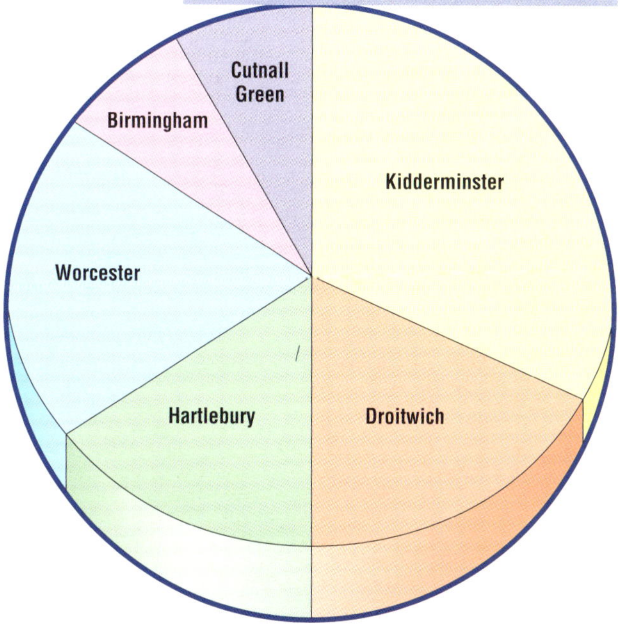

TASKS

6 Look at Figure 2.57. What is good about living in one of these houses?

7 Look at Figure 2.60. Estimate the percentage of people who work in
   a Cutnall Green
   b Kidderminster
   c Worcester.

8 Do you think it was a good idea to build new houses in Cutnall Green? Why?

two

People and Places to Live

Advice

COURSEWORK FOR SETTLEMENT

Many people choose to do coursework based on the settlement section of the course. There are many opportunities to investigate geography patterns and issues in your local area. It is easy to collect data nearby and local knowledge can be useful. If you live in a small village you may need to compare it to another village to get enough data. If you live in a large city you may need to focus on one part of the city or pick several sites.

CBD studies

The CBD is always changing. In larger towns and cities it is important to pick either one part of the CBD or one theme to study.

Suggested titles

- What is the sphere of influence of the CBD of town A?
- What are the characteristics of the CBD of town B?
- What changes occur as you move from the core to the edge of the CBD in city C?
- How and why have land uses changed in the CBD of city D?
- An investigation into the traffic problems and attempted solutions in town E.
- Where is the core of the CBD in city F?

FIGURE 2.61

London's Oxford Street – which characteristics typical of a CBD can be seen?

Coursework advice – Settlement

Characteristic of the CBD	Method of data collection
1. Land use Land uses are dominated by commercial activities such as shops, offices, eating places and entertainments – but not houses.	Land use survey noting observations on a large-scale map or plan using a simple land use classification (Figure 2.63).
2. Shops The CBD has the largest shops, the widest variety of types of shops, and the shops with the largest threshold (needing large numbers of customers to be profitable).	Land use survey as above but concentrating only on the shops (mainly A–F in Figure 2.63). Also – measure the size of shop frontages by pacing, record the number of storeys in use, count the number of customers going in and out of different shops.
3. Sphere of influence People will travel long distances to use the shops and services of the CBD. The larger the settlement, the greater the distance people will travel.	Design a questionnaire for shoppers. You need to find out where they live, frequency of visit, mode of transport, shops visited, type of goods bought, etc. You can work out distance travelled and draw a desire line map for the sphere of influence (Figure 2.64).
4. Core and periphery A central area (core) is busier and looks more prosperous than the outer area (periphery), in which shopping quality and street appearance decline. There is a decrease in numbers of pedestrians.	Land use surveys (as above) with smaller shops, offices and public buildings expected in the periphery. Do an environmental quality survey using factors such as litter, care of the pavements, street furniture, traffic and noise. Conduct pedestrian counts.
5. Change This is a zone of constant change – in land uses, redevelopment of shops and offices, traffic schemes and pedestrianisation.	Compare current land uses with those shown on Goad maps from previous years. Compare old plans showing the layout of buildings and streets with present-day observations.

Figure 2.62 Investigating the CBD

Letter	Description of land use
A	Department stores and chain stores selling a variety of goods
B	Clothing and shoe shops
C	Specialist shops, e.g. books, sports goods, jewellers, florists
D	Convenience shops, e.g. food (bakers, butchers, sweets, etc.), newsagents
E	Furniture and carpets
F	Personal services, e.g. hairdresser, travel agent, dry cleaner, TV rental
G	Catering and entertainment, e.g. eating places, pubs, hotels, cinemas
H	Offices and professional services, e.g. bank, building society, estate agent
J	Public offices and buildings, e.g. town hall, library, main post office, job centre
K	Transport, e.g. bus and rail stations, car parks
L	Change, e.g. vacant premises, building sites
M	Others, e.g. residential, industrial

Figure 2.63 A simple land use classification for CBD studies

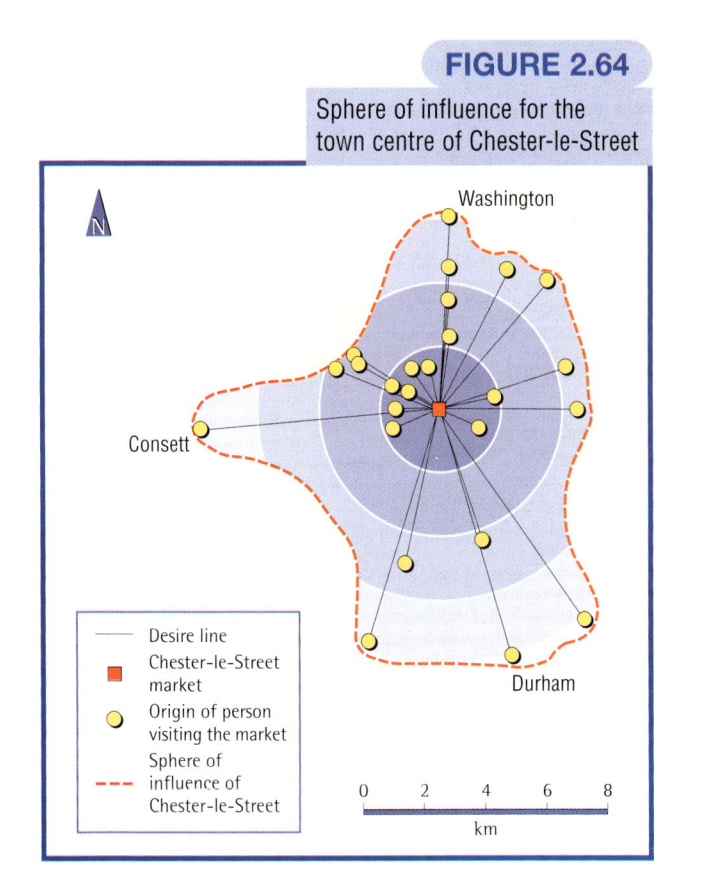

FIGURE 2.64

Sphere of influence for the town centre of Chester-le-Street

two
People and Places to Live
Advice

Other urban zones

For very small settlements, the whole area can be studied. For larger settlements, a transect from the centre to the edge can be investigated. Measurements could be taken at regular intervals (e.g. every 20 paces) and may focus on just one side of the road.

Suggested titles

- How and why do land uses change along road X between the centre and edge of town?
- Test the hypothesis 'The quality of the environment increases with distance from the centre'.
- Test the hypothesis 'Pedestrian (or traffic) density decreases with distance from the centre'.
- Does the type, size, quality and cost of housing increase towards the edge of the built up area?
- Does town Y fit the Burgess land use model?

Land use coursework

1. Find out about land use models from textbooks.
2. Choose a classification scheme (an example is shown above). This uses a number and a letter to classify areas. The number describes the land use (such as housing) and the letter provides more detail (such as the type of housing).
3. Choose a transect on a map.
4. Draw the streets and property blocks along your transect using a large-scale map.

AN URBAN LAND USE CLASSIFICATION SCHEME

Code number	Code letter
1 Housing	T = Terraced S = Semi-detached D = Detached F = Flats B = Bungalow
2 Shops and services	S = Shop B = Bank or Building Society O = Office G = Garage
3 Industrial	F = Factory W = Warehouse B = Builder's yard
4 Public buildings	S = School C = Church L = Library E = Other Educational such as a College
5 Entertainment	H = Hotel P = Pub E = Eating place L = Leisure Centre A = Arcade C = Cinema
6 Open space	CP = Car Park P = Park C = Cemetery S = Sports ground F = Farmland G = Gardens and allotments
7 Unused land	D = Derelict or empty building W = Waste land V = Vacant land being developed

FIGURE 2.65

Suburban shopping centre. Is the land use classification above adequate, or do other land uses need to be added?

Coursework advice – Settlement

> **Advice**
>
> Design your own land use classification or adapt one from a book to suit your study area.

5 Use a classification scheme to label land uses along the transect.

6 Mark on where the CBD, inner city, suburbs and green belt begin.

7 Explain why you chose to mark the boundaries in each place.

8 Compare with land use models and explain similarities and differences.

Housing surveys

House types, ages, prices and quality can be investigated to look for and explain patterns. Comparing two or more housing areas within the town or city can work well. It is important that the study areas are identified on maps and their locations are described in the Introduction and Analysis sections.

Data to collect:

- **Observations** (house type, environmental quality survey, if there are gardens and garages)
- **Photographs** and labelled **sketches**
- **House price survey** – collect evidence from estate agents or newspapers
- **Traffic counts** and **environmental quality surveys**
- **Questionnaire survey** – find out about the residents of your study areas (age group, occupation, car ownership, etc.)
- **Secondary data** – use census data to explain patterns.

> **Advice**
>
> - Locate study area(s) on a map of the urban area.
> - Use theory words such as suburbs.
> - Use data (e.g. calculate mean average house prices for particular areas).

FIGURE 2.66
What suggests this is part of the inner zone?

two

People and Places to Live

Advice

Quality		Good	5	4	3	2	1	Poor
1	Housing layout and design	Varied and interesting / Well spaced out						Poor and unimaginative / High density
2	Building materials	Attractive						Drab and uninteresting
3	House maintenance	Well maintained, e.g. fresh paint, new doors and windows						Poor maintenance, e.g. peeling paint, broken pipes and gutters
4	Other features	Trees, grass and flowers improve the appearance						No trees, grass and flowers
5	Open space	Is present and there are safe play areas for children						Absent with nowhere for children to play
6	Gardens	Present and well looked after						No gardens or poorly maintained
7	Car parking	Parking mainly off the roads						Parking mainly on the roads
8	Road crossing	Little traffic, slow moving, easy and safe to cross						Busy roads, difficult and dangerous to cross
9	Litter	No litter visible						Heavily littered
10	Vandalism	No obvious signs						Graffiti, signs of damage and abuse

Figure 2.67 Measuring environmental quality of housing areas

Many students use environmental quality surveys. Figure 2.67 is an example. If something is good, a high number is ticked. You should design your own or adapt one to suit your title.

Advice

Environmental quality surveys are based on your own opinions. You could give an example by including a photograph and your score for that place in your method section.

Use Figure 2.67 to give a total score for the areas in Figure 2.66 and 2.68. Compare your answer with your friends' answers.

FIGURE 2.68

Housing area – what is it worth for environmental quality out of 50?

Surveys of shops and services

Unless you are studying an out-of-town shopping centre or a CBD, it is usually best to compare two shopping centres to describe and explain the similarities and differences between them. You could study certain types of shops at different locations such as the CBD and an out-of-town shopping centre.

1 Complete a tally chart to show the number of high, medium and low order shops.
2 At several sites, complete an environmental quality survey.
3 Take photographs or complete labelled sketches.
4 Carry out a questionnaire survey of the public (or people you know). Find out where they are from so that you can map the sphere of influence.

FIGURE 2.69

Many new out-of-town shopping centres, which are privately owned, do not allow fieldwork without their permission

Shopping centres can be arranged in order of size and importance. This is called a hierarchy and is shown in Figure 2.70.

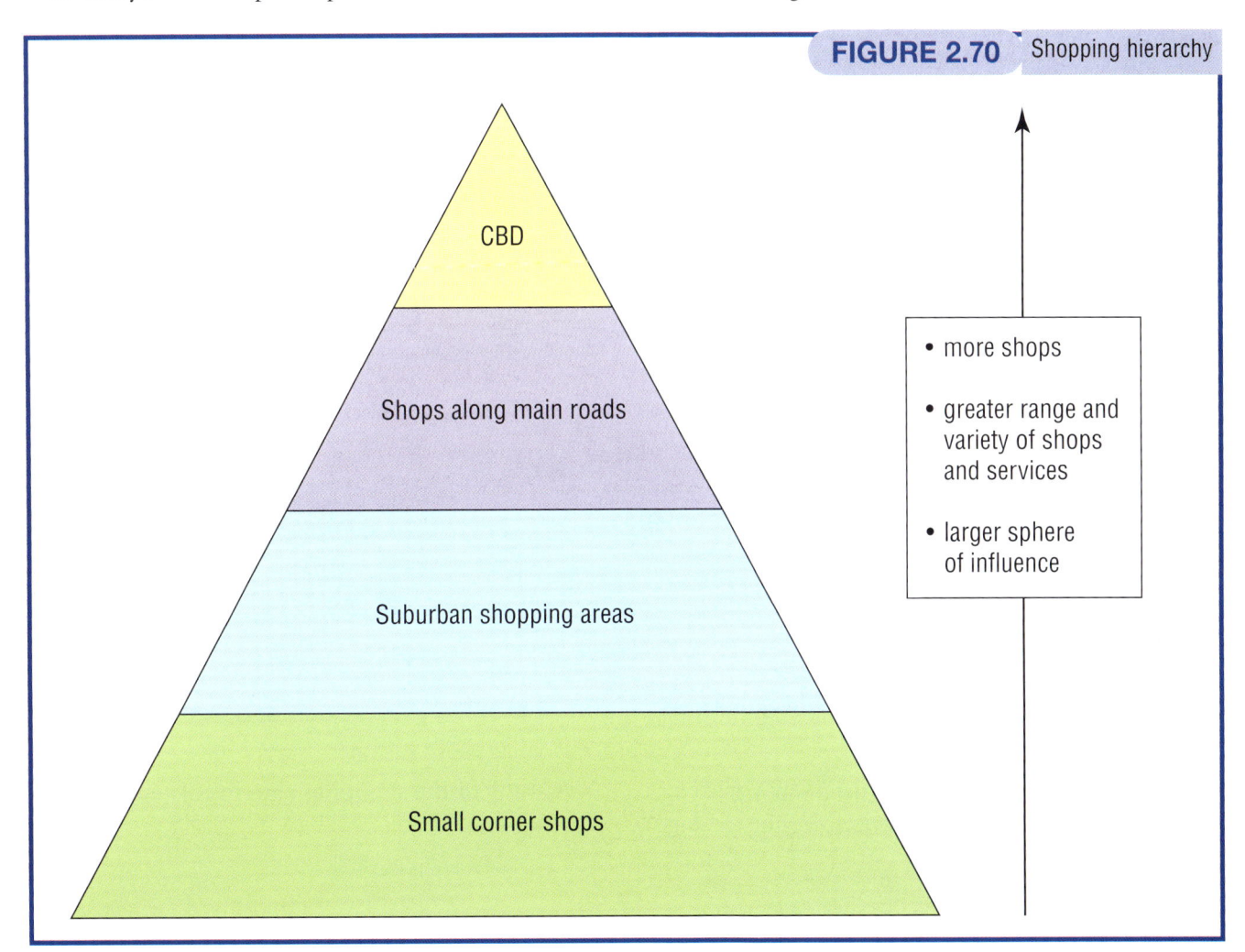

FIGURE 2.70 Shopping hierarchy

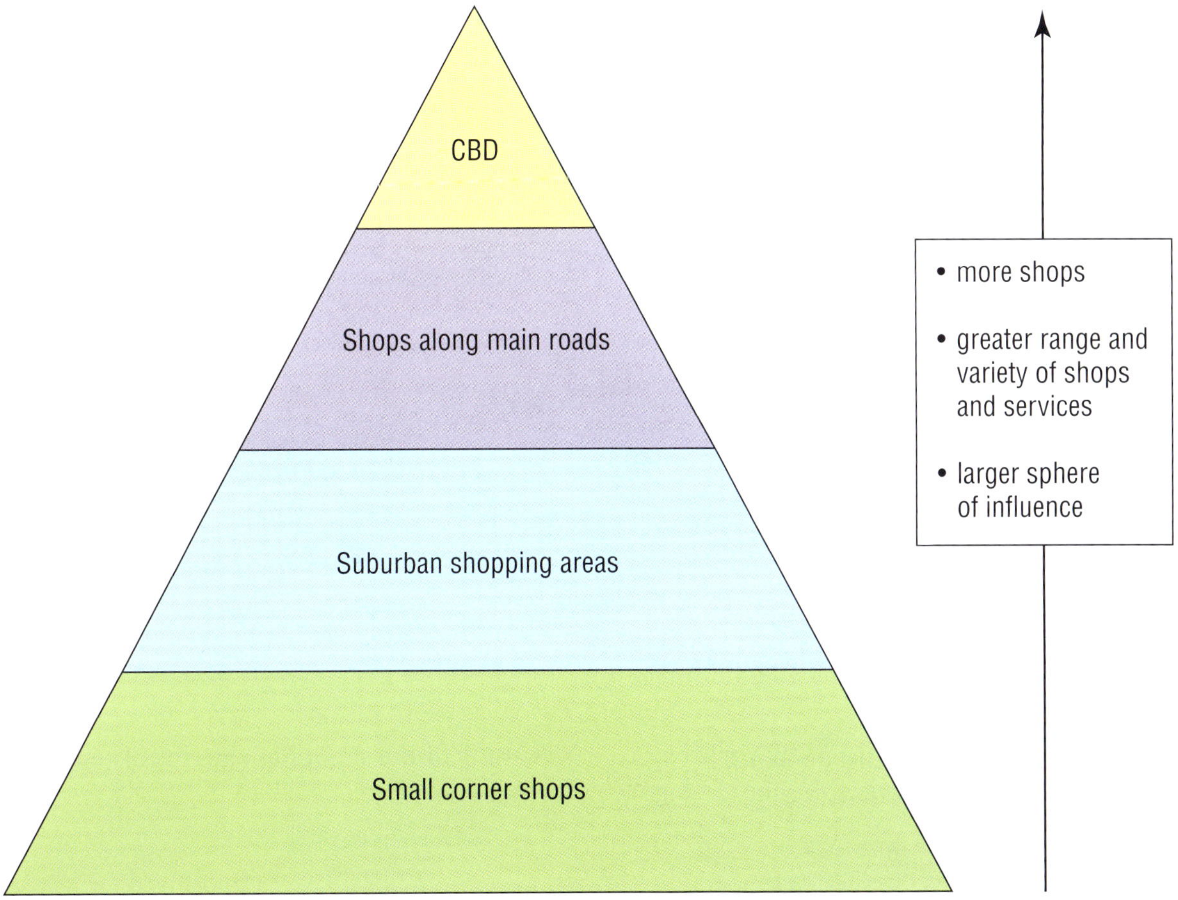
CBD
Shops along main roads
Suburban shopping areas
Small corner shops
• more shops
• greater range and variety of shops and services
• larger sphere of influence

two ■ People and Places to Live

Advice

Village studies

Villages can be studied to find out how and why they are changing. New developments in rural areas near towns (**the rural–urban fringe**) could be investigated. For example, there may be a bypass or an out-of-town shopping centre.

Suggested titles

- Does village A need a bypass?
- How and why is village B changing?
- Has village C become a commuter village?
- What are the similarities and differences between village D and E?

FIGURE 2.71
Entrance from the bypass into the village. What fieldwork possibilities lie ahead?

Possibilities

A Has the village grown or declined? For example, have new housing estates been built or have old industries closed down?

B Is there a local issue? Some villages may need a bypass or local shops and services may be closing.

- How are the old and new parts of the village different?
- Is village F in decline?
- A study of the shopping patterns of residents of village G.

Coursework advice – Settlement

Data sources for village studies

Primary data

Observation — land use survey (houses, services, etc.)
— environmental quality survey

Questionnaire — to all the different types of residents

Count — traffic counts on different days at different times

Secondary data

- old maps and photographs
- parish records
- census data
- newspapers

It is important that you can collect data which you can map and draw graphs from and use to link to your title.

Advice

- Try to get primary data such as questionnaire survey results.
- Use *relevant* secondary data (not too much historical information).
- Focus on the village today.
- Avoid a general village study – choose a theme such as whether the village is in decline.

FIGURE 2.73

A star diagram showing where commuters from the village work – a presentation technique likely to be useful in many village studies

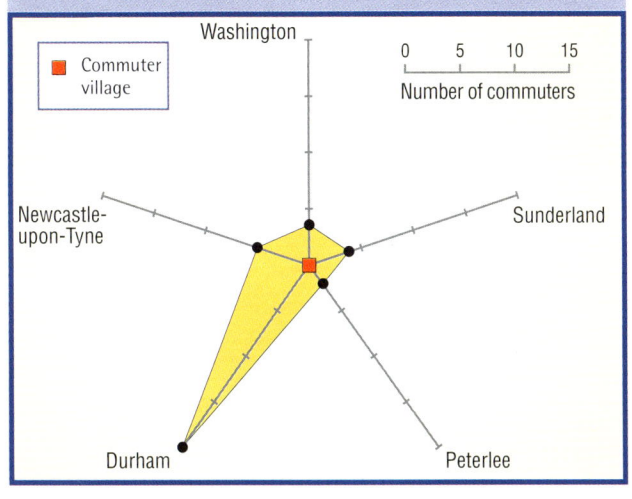

Title 'Does my home village need a bypass?'

DATA COLLECTION PLAN

- Measurement along the main road through the village.
- Do traffic counts at different times of the day for one week.
- Measure noise pollution along the road using a sound meter.

OBSERVATION

- Do an environmental quality survey along the main road.
- Compare the results with surveys along other streets off the road.

QUESTIONNAIRE

- To 20 people living along the sides of the main road.
- To 20 people in other parts of the village selected randomly.
- A separate questionnaire to the shopkeepers and garage owner.

OTHERS

- Looking for articles in the local newspaper from the library.
- Visit the Parish Councillor.

Figure 2.72 Student's plan for a village study

two — People and Places to Live

Advice

EXAMINATION TECHNIQUE – UNIT 2

At the end of your geography course, you will take two examination papers. Both papers could include questions about **Population** and **Settlement**. Do not assume that if you answer a Settlement question in the first paper there will not be another in the second paper. It is a major section, covering a lot of geography and different topics can be tested in the two papers.

Distribution is an important idea in geography. This word is included in the glossary on page 239. The questions to be examined first in this section focus on the map (Figure 2.74) which shows population distribution.

Notice that the question is about **high** population density. Do not make the mistake of writing about low population density. You can score two marks for this question. A short answer is required but it must be precise. To focus your answer on 'distribution', think about the following questions:

- Where are the areas of high population density?
- Are these areas near together or spread out?

Distribution does not mean give a list of the different locations which have a high population density. The other clues provided on the map are the four lines of latitude which can be used to describe distribution.

The answer below scores two marks:

> Most of the areas of high population density are north of the Equator (or north of the Tropic of Cancer). These areas are spread out unevenly (or scattered around the world).

Do not write 'above the equator', it is a poor geographical description. Always use compass points when describing distribution.

1 (a) Study Figure 2.74 which shows the distribution of population densities around the world.

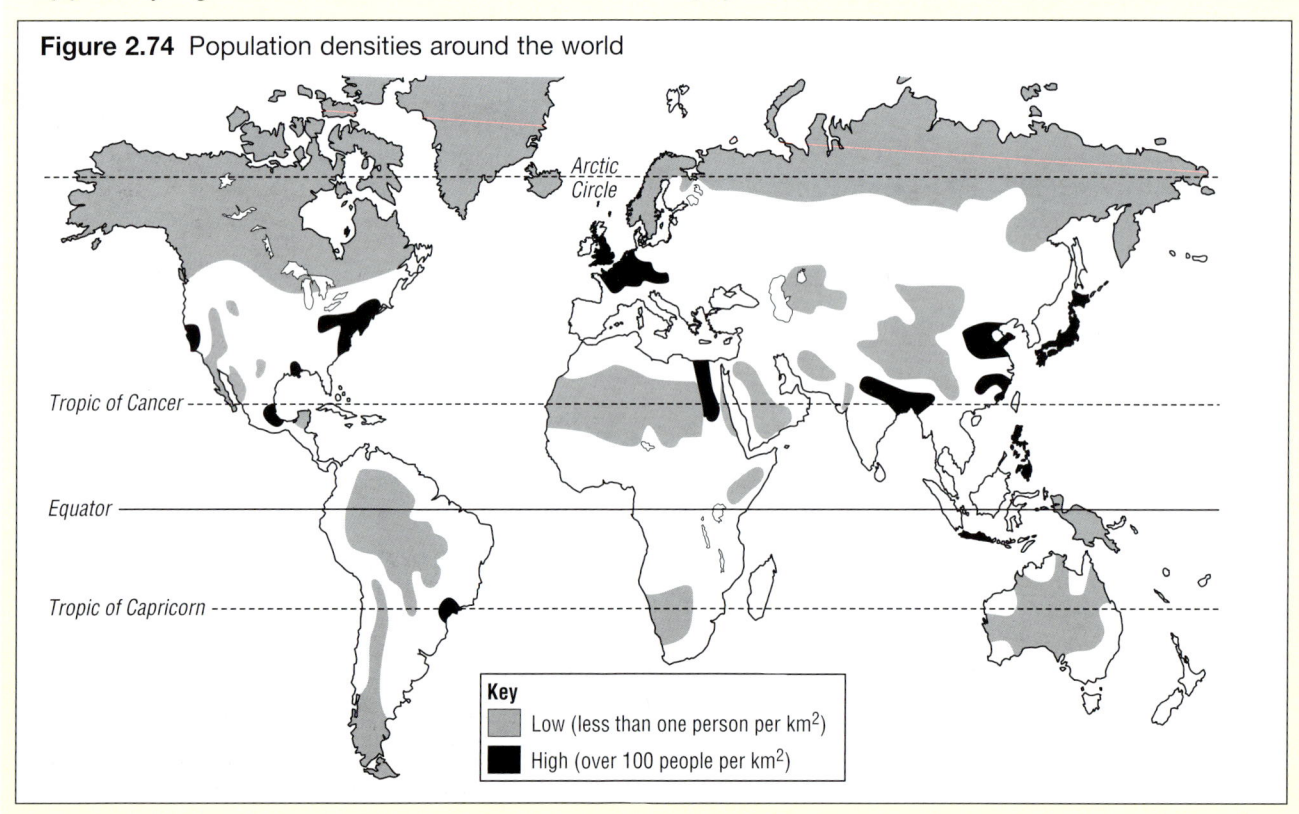

Figure 2.74 Population densities around the world

Key
- Low (less than one person per km²)
- High (over 100 people per km²)

Describe the world distribution of the areas of high population density (over 100 people per sq. km.) [2]

Examination advice – Unit 2

The next question goes into more detail about areas of high population density.

(b) Give three reasons why some parts of the world are densely populated. [3]

Below are four answers from different candidates. Their marks varied from 0 to 3. With a partner, work out which candidates scored 0, 1, 2 or 3 marks. Then explain why the candidates scored different marks.

Answer from candidate 1

1. People migrate there in the hope of a better life.
2. The birth rate is higher than the death rate so the population increases.
3. Because they can't afford good health care.

Answer from candidate 2

1. Not enough jobs.
2. Not enough food and water. No schools.
3. The area is very dry and so it is difficult to grow food.

Answer from candidate 3

1. More money because of more jobs.
2. Better weather may appeal to some people.
3. Better health care means higher life expectancy.

Answer from candidate 4

1. The land is flat and easy to build on.
2. Climate is not too cold or hot or dry.
3. Lots of raw materials for industries.

Examiner's comment

The answers were marked as follows:

Marks	Candidate
0	2
1	3
2	1
3	4

The **theme** of this question now changes from high population density to low population density.

(c) Many areas have few people living there. Name an area which you have studied and explain why there are not many people living there. [5]

The question is another opportunity to use a **case study**. Answers will be marked in 'levels' and to achieve Level 3 you must give specific information about your chosen area. The answers below show how three candidates have tackled this question. Try to work out what makes the answers good or bad before you read the examiner's comments.

Answer from candidate 1

Name of area: Sahara Desert

Reasons why not many people live there:

The climate is far too hot for people to be comfortable. The ground makes it difficult to build on, and to farm on. There are no water resources to make crops grow, except in the land around the River Nile. The desert land is also very inaccessible and it is difficult to build roads on.

Examiner's comment

The candidate names an area correctly. This makes it possible to achieve Level 3 (5 marks maximum). In the reasons there is a mixture of Level 1 and Level 2 ideas. At Level 1 there is a simple statement: 'The climate is far too hot for people to be comfortable.' The Level 2 statements are more specific about the Sahara: 'There are no water resources to make crops grow, except in the land around the River Nile' and 'The desert land is also very inaccessible and it is difficult to build roads on.'

The candidate therefore scores Level 3 (5 marks).

Answer from candidate 2

Name of area: Amazon, Brazil

Reasons why not many people live there:

Many people don't live there because it is a rainforest. A human cannot survive there because of the weather (hot, rain). There won't be enough food to eat if other farmers are taking it to sell. Also there will be a lot of wildlife in the forest.

People and Places to Live

Advice

Examiner's comment

The candidate correctly names an area where few people live. There is one Level 2 statement: 'Many people don't live there because it is a rainforest. A human cannot survive there because of the weather (hot, rain).' The rest of the answer is quite vague and could refer to lots of different types of area. The candidate therefore scores Level 2 (3 marks).

Answer from candidate 3

> Name of area: Skelton
>
> People don't live there because of many reasons such as there are not enough shops and facilities, there are no job opportunities and it isn't very close to a main road.

Examiner's comment

The candidate correctly names a local village but the reasons are very simple statements which could be about any village, e.g. 'there are not enough shops', 'there are no job opportunities'. The candidate therefore scores Level 1 (2 marks).

The next questions are about 'squatter settlements'.

2 (a) Many of the people who migrate to cities in LEDCs live in squatter settlements.

Figure 2.75 Part of a squatter settlement

(i) Write down two things that are likely to cause problems to the people living in the squatter settlement. [2]

(ii) For each one, explain why it will cause problems for the people who live in the squatter settlement. [2]

There are lots of possible problems shown in the diagram such as:

- buildings are not very strong
- rubbish in the street
- houses are small
- houses are close to each other
- houses are close to industrial areas
- air pollution from factory
- sewage and waste in the stream
- no piped water, it must be got from the standpipe.

Having chosen two problems you need to explain why each is a problem. Below there are some examples of candidates' answers. Some were marked correct but others were marked incorrect. With a partner, work out why some statements were given a tick while others were given a cross.

Answers which were correct	Answers which were wrong
The fumes from the factory would affect people's health.	Unwanted rubbish polluting the area.
The waste in the river means it would not provide a clean supply of water.	Houses might fall down.
Water from the tap can cause germs and is unhygienic.	People that need to wash clothes could get hurt by the pollution.
The houses are not properly built and might fall down in a thunderstorm.	Factories cause pollution.

Examination advice – Unit 2

Finally, the case study question:

> **(b)** For a named city which you have studied in an LEDC, describe what is being done to improve the living conditions in squatter settlements. **[5]**

Having written about the problems of living in a squatter settlement, the case study instructs the candidate to describe what improvements are being made. The usual case study 'rule' applies. To get a high mark you must write about improvements which are being made in your named example.

See how the following candidates score marks at different levels.

Answer from candidate 1

> Name of LEDC city: São Paulo in Brazil
>
> What is being done to improve living conditions:
>
> Many of the houses in these favelas (shanty towns) are made from corrugated iron, wood, cardboard, etc. **(Level 3)** The city council are now trying to rebuild these houses with bricks and with working toilets. **(Level 2)** The houses are being wired up with electricity so they are safe for families. **(Level 2)** More industries are being set up which creates jobs for the local people. **(Level 1)**

Examiner's comment

The city is well known for its squatter settlements which, as the candidate knows, are called 'favelas'. The answer contains a simple Level 1 statement and three specific Level 2 statements. The answer also contains the Level 3 statement and scored 5 marks.

Answer from candidate 2

> Name of LEDC city: Rio de Janeiro
>
> What is being done to improve living conditions:
>
> People living in the squatter settlement are being paid to collect rubbish. **(Level 2)** Sewage systems have been built so that the sewage doesn't go down the street. **(Level 2)** Electricity is being connected to peoples' homes for cooking and watching television. **(Level 2)** Schools have been built to develop education for the children. **(Level 2)**

Examiner's comment

The answer includes four ideas which have all been developed into Level 2 statements. The only weakness with this answer is that it could be about a squatter settlement in any city in the world. There is nothing to link it to Rio de Janeiro which would make the answer Level 3. The answer scored 4 marks.

Answer from candidate 3

> Name of LEDC city: Brazil
>
> What is being done to improve living conditions:
>
> The government and authorities for the city are helping to build better houses for the people to live in. **(Level 1)** They are providing better water facilities **(Level 1)** and are improving the jobs available to these people. **(Level 1)**

Examiner's comment

Brazil is not a city and the candidate struggles to score marks. There are three simple Level 1 statements but none of them is sufficiently developed to reach Level 2. The answer scored 2 marks.

The following questions use the OS map extract on page 122.

> **3 (a)** The CBD (Central Business District) of St Helens is in and around grid square 5195. Use map evidence to identify one building in the CBD of St Helens. **[1]**

This first question is testing whether you can find a grid square by using a 4-figure grid reference. Then you must know how to recognise the CBD and use the map key to identify a building such as the Town Hall.

> **(b)** What building is at 523940? **[1]**

two
People and Places to Live

Advice

This question is more difficult because you must work out a 6-figure grid reference. If you find it difficult to use a 6-figure reference a useful tip is to underline the 4-figure reference (52<u>3</u>94<u>0</u>). Then look in this grid square for a building and check if it fits with the third and sixth figure of the grid reference.

(c) Use evidence from the OS map extract to suggest why Billinge (in and around grid square 5200) is a larger settlement than Houghwood (Grid Square 5100). [2]

The mark allocation suggests that two ideas are needed. Your answer must use map evidence (i.e. what you can see on the map). You will **not** gain any marks for an answer like the one below because there is no evidence of this on the map.

Answer from candidate 1

Billinge is bigger than Houghwood because there are more shops and there is an industrial estate where the people will work.

Examiner's comments

Also remember that to answer this question you must **compare** the two settlements. Therefore your answer must show this comparison, like the answer below.

Answer from candidate 2

There are many main roads running through or near to Billinge, but there is only one small road going to Houghwood so the transport is not as good. Also the land is flatter around Billinge than Houghwood, so farming would be easier there.

The following questions refer to five settlements located on the OS map. Information about their services is given in Figure 2.76 below.

Settlement	Grid Square	Population	Post Box	Church or Chapel	Public House	Post Office	Primary School	Hairdresser	Surgery/Health Ctr.	Dentist	Secondary School
Billinge	5200	9300	✓	✓	✓	✓	✓	✓	✓	✓	✗
Crank	5099	500	✓	✓	✓	✓	✗	✗	✗	✗	✗
Houghwood	5100	50	✗	✗	✗	✗	✗	✗	✗	✗	✗
Kings Moss	5001	150	✓	✗	✓	✗	✗	✗	✗	✗	✗
Rainford	4801	7100	✓	✓	✓	✓	✓	✓	✓	✓	✓

Key
✓ = Service present
✗ = Service absent

Figure 2.76

Now look at the questions which use the information in this table.

(d) (i) Compare the services available in Crank and Kings Moss. [2]

(ii) Describe the general relationship shown by the table between the number of people who live in a settlement and the services available. [1]

(iii) Suggest why settlements like Crank, Houghwood and Kings Moss do not have many services. [2]

The idea being tested is about what services there are in a rural area. The questions have three different commands:

- compare
- describe
- suggest why.

You must understand what each **command word** means. Page 232 will help you to do this.

Examination advice – Unit 2

The following questions concentrate on land use in a small area and use another type of resource – a large-scale street plan which shows more detail (Figure 2.77).

4 (a) (i) Housing is the main land use in area Y. Use map evidence only to give one other land use in this area. [1]

The question focuses on area Y (not area X). The example must come from the map. It cannot be a general land use like shops.

(ii) Use map evidence only to describe one difference in the road layout between areas X and Y. [1]

This question again requires map evidence and the answer must show the difference between the two areas. Therefore you must use words that show comparison in your answer. See page 232 for advice on how to answer this type of question.

(iii) Give three likely differences between the houses in areas X and Y. [3]

This question is also telling the candidate to focus on differences, therefore the answer must contain comparisons. Unlike part (ii) the answer cannot be taken directly from the map so you must use your knowledge and your understanding of how types of houses will vary between different areas of a town.

Figure 2.76 The western part of St Helens

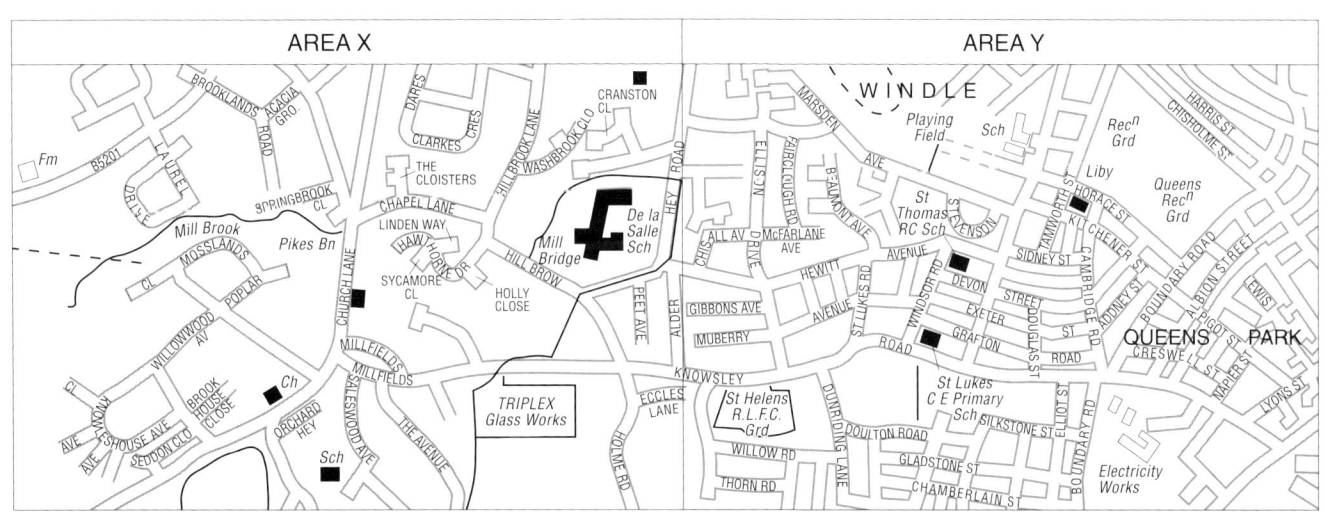

two

People and Places to Live

Advice

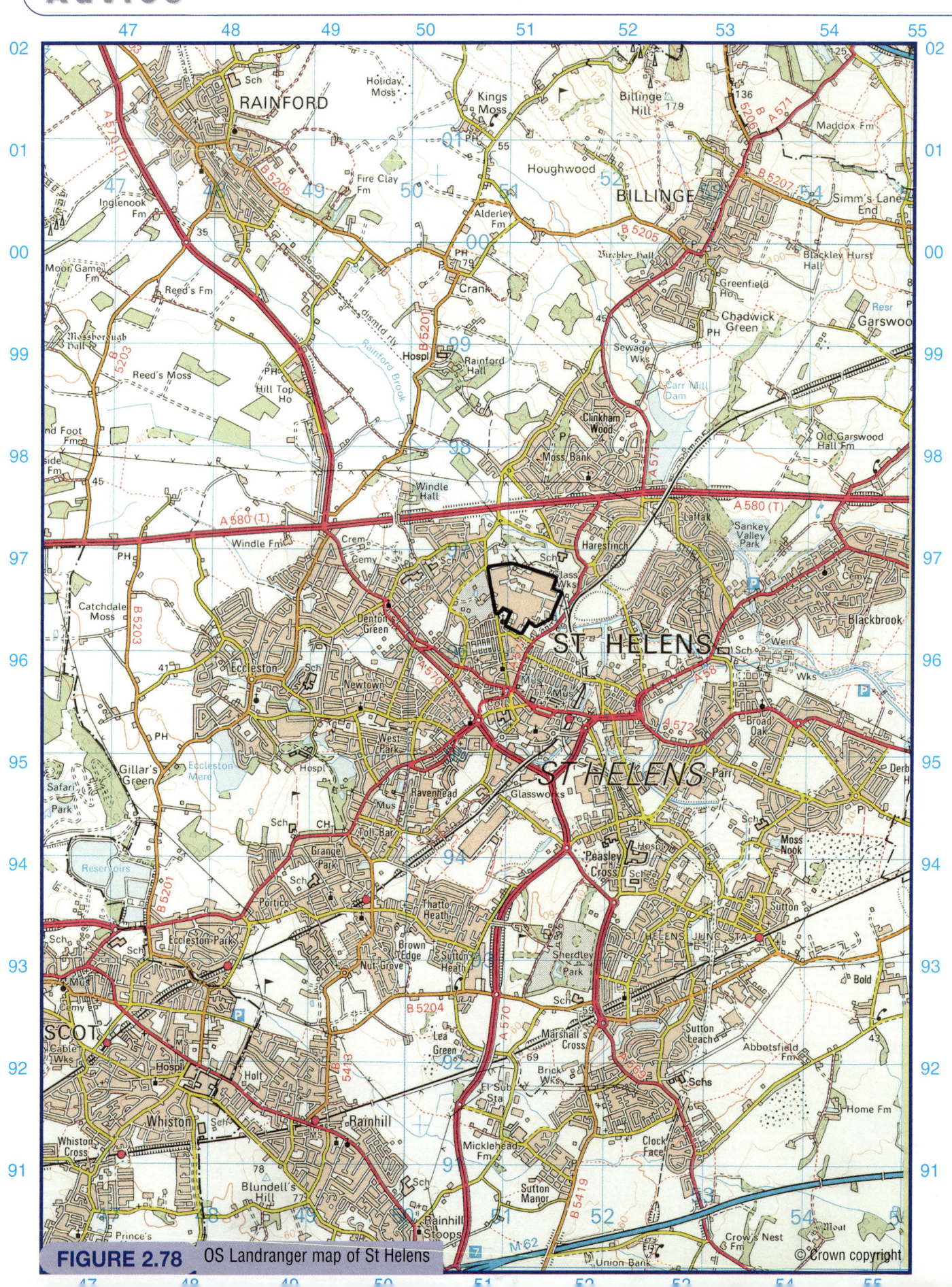

FIGURE 2.78 OS Landranger map of St Helens

Examination advice – Unit 2

ROADS AND PATHS   Not necessarily rights of way

- Motorway (dual carriageway)
- Motorway under construction
- Trunk road
- A 470 (T) Dual carriageway
- Main road
- Main road under construction
- Secondary road
- B 4518
- A 855 Bridge B 885
- Narrow road with passing places
- Road generally more than 4m wide
- Road generally less than 4m wide
- Path / Other road, drive or track
- Gradient: 20% (1 in 5) and steeper, 14% (1 in 7) to 20% (1 in 5)
- Gates / Road Tunnel
- Ferry P / Ferry V
- Ferry (passenger) / Ferry (vehicle)

Service area, Junction number, Elevated, M1, Unfenced, Footbridge

RAILWAYS

- Track multiple or single
- Station, (a) principal
- Track narrow gauge
- Freight line, siding or tramway
- Bridges / Footbridge
- Embankment
- Cutting
- Tunnel
- Viaduct / Level crossing (LC)

WATER FEATURES

Marsh or salting, Towpath, Lock, Cliff, Slopes, Shingle, Aqueduct, Canal, Ford, Beacon, Flat rock, Lighthouse, Lighthouse (in use), Weir, Normal tidal limit, Sand, Lighthouse (disused), Low water mark, Lake, Footbridge, Bridge, Dunes, Mud, High water mark, Canal (dry)

HEIGHTS   1 metre = 3·2808 feet

- 50 — Contours are at 10 metres vertical interval
- 144 — Heights are to the nearest metre above mean sea level

Heights shown close to a triangulation pillar refer to the ground at the base of the pillar and not necessarily to the summit.

ROCK FEATURES

Outcrop, Cliff, Scree

PUBLIC RIGHTS OF WAY

Not shown on maps of Scotland

- Footpath
- Road used as a public path
- Bridleway
- Byway open to all traffic

The symbols show the defined route so far as the scale of mapping will allow.

The representation on this map of any other road, track or path is no evidence of the existence of a right of way

Danger Area — Firing and Test Ranges in the area. Danger! Observe warning notices.

OTHER PUBLIC ACCESS

- Other route with public access (not normally shown in urban areas). Alignments are based on the best information available. These routes are not shown on maps of Scotland.
- National/Regional Cycle Network
- Surfaced cycle route
- 4 National Cycle Network number
- 8 Regional Cycle Network number
- National Trail, Long Distance Route, selected Recreational Routes

ANTIQUITIES

- + Site of monument
- · o Stone monument
- ✕ Battlefield (with date)
- ☆ .... Visible earthwork
- VILLA Roman
- Castle Non-Roman

ABBREVIATIONS

- CG Coastguard
- CH Clubhouse
- MP Milepost
- MS Milestone
- P Post office
- PC Public convenience (in rural areas)
- PH Public house
- TH Town Hall, Guildhall or equivalent

LAND FEATURES

- Electricity transmission line (pylons shown at standard spacing)
- Pipe line (arrow indicates direction of flow)
- ruin
- Buildings
- Public building (selected)
- Bus or coach station
- Place of worship { with tower / with spire, minaret or dome / without such additions }
- Chimney or tower
- Glasshouse
- Heliport
- Triangulation pillar
- Radio or TV mast
- Windpump / wind generator
- Windmill with or without sails
- Graticule intersection at 5' intervals
- Quarry
- Spoil heap, refuse tip or dump
- Coniferous wood
- Non-coniferous wood
- Mixed wood
- Orchard
- Park or ornamental ground
- Forestry Commission access land
- National Trust-always open
- National Trust-limited access, observe local signs
- National Trust for Scotland

TOURIST INFORMATION

- Information centre, all year / seasonal
- Viewpoint
- Parking
- Picnic site
- Camp site
- Caravan site
- Selected places of tourist interest
- Telephone, public / motoring organisation
- Golf course or links
- Youth hostel

BOUNDARIES

- National
- District
- County, Unitary Authority, Metropolitan District or London Borough
- National Park or Forest Park

two
People and Places to Live
Advice

The following question again uses the OS map extract on page 122 (Figure 2.78).

> 5 The population of Rainford (in and around grid square 4801) has increased in recent years as people have moved from urban areas such as St Helens.
>
> Suggest any three attractions of living in Rainford. You should give evidence from the OS map extract in your answer. (3)

The following candidates have different amounts of success in answering this question.

Answer from candidate 1

> 1. Would be away from CBD containing factories.
> 2. Short drive to the main shopping town.
> 3. Small village in the countryside.

Examiner's comment

The candidate uses the OS map to give three reasons why Rainford is an attractive village to live in. Although the three statements have poor grammar, they do show that the candidate knows that the rural area has advantages, especially for people with cars.

Answer from candidate 2

> 1. Rainford has a school and a church and good facilities.
> 2. It is less crowded around Rainford than in St Helens.
> 3. There are not many roads near Rainford and less noise and pollution.

Examiner's comment

The candidate uses the OS map to identify services located in Rainford, but only one mark is allocated for these. The second point shows that the candidate understands that there is a lower population density in the countryside. The third idea is almost acceptable but the link between noise and the bypass is not really made.

Answer from candidate 3

> 1. No noise from traffic.
> 2. There will not be much pollution in the area.
> 3. There will be a lot more space around.

Examiner's comment

The candidate has some understanding of why Rainford may be an attractive place to live but none of the ideas is sufficiently explained. The candidate needed to explain:

- why there is no (or less) traffic noise
- the type of pollution and why it will be less
- the type of open space and why there will be more.

The following questions use a different street map. It is a map of part of Willerby on the rural–urban fringe of Hull (Figure 2.79).

Figure 2.79 Street map of part of Willerby, on the rural–urban fringe of Hull

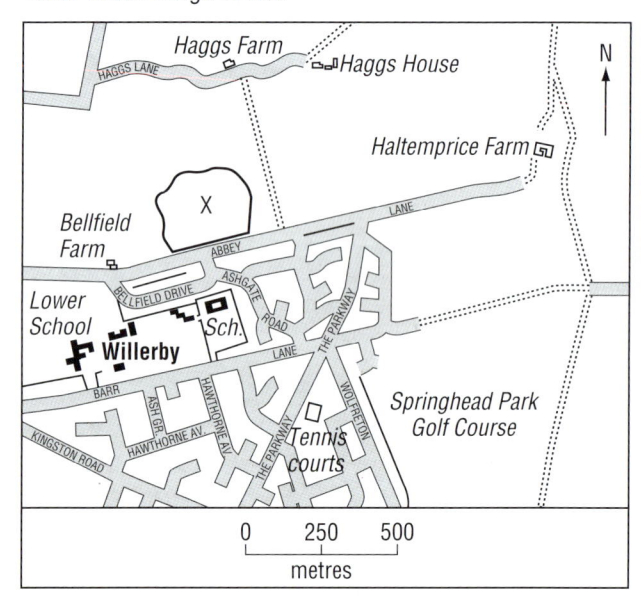

6 (a) What is meant by the rural–urban fringe of a city? [1]

Which of the following answers are correct explanations?

1. This is the edge of a city where countryside and a city (urban) meet.
2. Where the city and countryside come together.
3. Where there is a city and countryside near each other.

All of these answers are correct, although answer 1 is most accurate.

(b) Describe two main features of the housing in areas such as Willerby. [2]

Although there is no picture of the houses to help you, the map suggests that houses in the area will be large, spread out, detached, modern, and will have gardens around them

(c) The owner of Bellfield farm plans to sell some land for a housing estate to be built in the area marked X. What problems are likely to occur if this development goes ahead? [3]

The final question gives you the chance to give some ideas of your own about the possible new housing development. Below is one example of an answer which scored 3 marks, although many other ideas also scored marks.

Candidate's answer

When this development goes ahead a lot of noise pollution will take place, especially from big machines which will be used to build the housing estate. The place will be dusty with all the building and the road, Abbey Lane, may be congested due to more residents living next to it and using it to go to work.

Can you see where the candidate scored the three marks?

TASK

The following question is based on the street plan of St Helens (Figure 2.77) on page 121.

Give three likely differences between the housing in areas X and Y. [3]

Now you become an examiner. Study the answers below and decide how many marks each one scored in the examination.

Answer A
1. Smaller houses and gardens in Y.
2. Larger houses and gardens in X.
3. Homes in Y are dearer because of being so close to town.

Answer B
1. Area X will have more detached houses than area Y.
2. The houses will be older in area Y.
3. They will also be more expensive in area X.

Answer C
1. The houses in this area will be older.
2. They will be closer together.
3. They will probably be terraced.

Answer D
1. Housing in area Y will be mostly terraced housing.
2. Housing in area X will be more expensive.
3. Housing in area X will be bigger than Y.

Answer E
1. There will be small, terraced houses in Y and semi-detached in X.
2. The roads will be smaller in Y.
3. The houses will be cheaper in Y.

The actual marks scored were:

Answer A : 1   B : 3   C : 0   D : 2   E : 2

two
■ People and Places to Live

Advice

THE ENTRY LEVEL CERTIFICATE

Coursework tasks are a very important part of the Entry Level Certificate course. They are worth a total of 50% of the marks and you can work on the tasks at your own speed to improve your marks.

Coursework tasks can include some data collection. This means you can include some information that has been collected from the local area or from newspapers or surveys. You must also show that you can present work in a variety of ways. It could include maps, sketches, photos, tables of information or leaflets and newspaper cuttings which are about your work. The task should include a commentary where the work is described and explained in as much detail as possible.

Good examples of coursework tasks can include a piece of fieldwork. It provides evidence that you have actually visited, observed and collected information. It does not have to be a long trip to collect the information. It could be collected in the place where you live.

People and Places to Live – a coursework task

Settlements are places where people live, work and play. People live in many different types of settlements all over the world – cities, towns, villages, hamlets or in houses all on their own. The land inside settlements is used in many different ways, such as for shops, parks, factories and offices as well as houses.

In the UK, only 15% of the people live in rural areas – villages or hamlets in the countryside. 85% of the people live in urban areas – towns and cities. Here you will find a pattern for how the land is used. In the Central Business District (CBD) most of the buildings are shops and offices. There are very few places to live.

Most people live in the inner city or suburbs, in houses or flats or bungalows, away from the expensive centre of the settlement.

TASKS

Title – Places to Live

1. Make a copy of the table showing different sorts of buildings that people live in. For each one, write a sentence to describe it. The first has been done for you.

Type of home	What it is like
Bungalow	House with no upstairs

2. Why do few people live in the CBD?
3. Draw a pie graph or a bar graph to show the percentage of people living in urban and rural areas of the UK.
4. Why do so many people live in urban areas in the UK? What are the attractions?

Certificate advice

C

People live in many types of buildings in different parts of towns and cities. Photos A, B and C show three different types of housing – terraced housing, detached and semi-detached.

In many towns, the terraced housing is the oldest housing. It was built in rows of streets near to the CBD. There will often be small corner shops, schools and old factories all close together in an area known as the inner city. Newer semi-detached and detached housing is usually found near the edge of towns in estates in the suburbs. On some estates, there are very few shops and services at all.

TASKS

5. Draw a plan or sketch of two of the houses in the photos. Label them with information about the features of the houses, such as building materials, rooms and size.
   * **Fieldwork Tip** – As part of your coursework, you could sketch your own house and one different type of house in your area. Label them with information.
6. Look at the Heads and Tails. Sort them out to match up.

Heads	Tails
Line of houses joined together	Flat
One house not joined to any other	Terraced
Two houses joined together	Detached
Several homes in one building	Semi detached

People sometimes move from one part of a town to another at different times in their lives. For example, an elderly couple may move from a semi-detached house to a bungalow when they retire. Once their children grow up and leave home, they need less space. As they get older, they may not be as able to climb stairs so easily.

TASK

7. Explain why someone may move from a terraced house into a semi-detached or detached house, at some time in their life.

Some areas of the inner city are now over 100 years old. As a result, the houses may need to be repaired or modernised. Window frames may need replacing. The roof may need new tiles. Brickwork may need pointing. To make the houses more modern, some may need an inside toilet and bathroom or central heating added. In some areas, roads have been blocked off and play areas and small garden areas made where the street used to be. The back alleyways may be paved and street lights fitted to make people feel safer.

In many cities, the terraced housing was demolished and replaced by multi-storey flats. The flats were sometimes over twenty storeys high with balconies instead of back yards or gardens. The flats were fitted with lifts and parking and play areas were found at ground level.

TASKS

8. Think of different sorts of housing. Which would be best for:
   a an elderly couple in their 60s,
   b a middle-aged couple with a young child,
   c a group of students at college?
   Write down why you chose each one.
9. a Which type of housing would you prefer to live in?
   b Write down your reasons.

three

People and their Needs

The quality of life

WHAT IS QUALITY OF LIFE?

> **SUMMARY** The UK is a rich country. It has a high quality of life. People live a long time, few babies die and almost every adult can read and write. This is not true for many other countries.

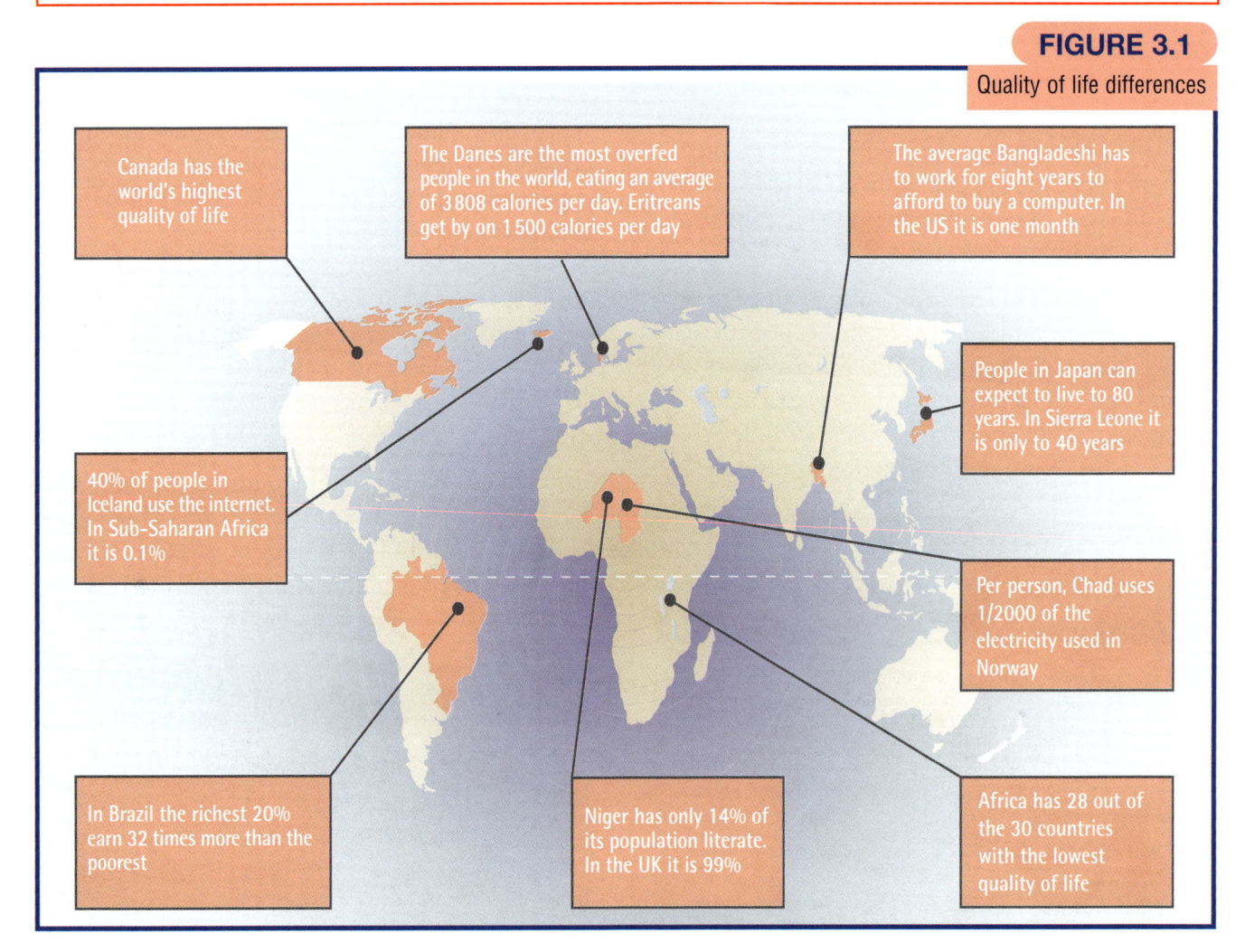

FIGURE 3.1 Quality of life differences

- Canada has the world's highest quality of life
- The Danes are the most overfed people in the world, eating an average of 3808 calories per day. Eritreans get by on 1500 calories per day
- The average Bangladeshi has to work for eight years to afford to buy a computer. In the US it is one month
- People in Japan can expect to live to 80 years. In Sierra Leone it is only to 40 years
- 40% of people in Iceland use the internet. In Sub-Saharan Africa it is 0.1%
- Per person, Chad uses 1/2000 of the electricity used in Norway
- In Brazil the richest 20% earn 32 times more than the poorest
- Niger has only 14% of its population literate. In the UK it is 99%
- Africa has 28 out of the 30 countries with the lowest quality of life

Indicators

There are many ways to show the **level of development** of a country. You can see some of them in Figure 3.1. Another is **Gross Domestic Product (GDP)**. This measures all the work done in a country. If we add in the money that the country earns abroad, it is called Gross National Product (GNP). It is hard to compare the GNP of a small country with a large one, so we look at GNP per person (Figure 3.2).

The problem with using an indicator like GNP per person is that it is an average. Everyone is not as well off as everyone else in the country.

What is quality of life?

Country	GNP $millions	GNP/person $	Popn. millions
Argentina	280 000	8 100	35
Australia	338 000	18 700	19
Bolivia	6 000	800	8
Burkina Faso	2 500	230	11
China	750 000	620	1 210
Egypt	45 600	790	63
France	1 451 000	25 000	58
India	319 000	340	980
Portugal	96 700	9 800	10
UK	1 095 000	18 700	58
USA	7 100 000	27 000	268
Zambia	3 600	400	9.5

Figure 3.2 GNP and population data for selected countries

Profiles and indexes

It is better to put together several indicators to measure the quality of life. The United Nations uses the Quality of Life Index (Figure 3.3). It combines life expectancy (how long a newly born baby is expected to live), infant mortality (a measure of how many babies die before they would be one year old) and adult literacy (the percentage of people over the age of 15 who can read and write).

TASKS

1. a Look at Figures 3.1 and 3.3. Which continent has the lowest quality of life?
   b Which continent has the highest quality of life?
2. How does the United Nations measure the quality of life of countries?
3. Make two columns, with headings 'High quality of life' and 'Low quality of life'. Copy the words from the word boxes in Figure 3.1 into the correct column. (For some word boxes, you will need to put some of the words in one column and the rest in the other column.)

FIGURE 3.3 Quality of Life Index

Quality of life by country as measured by the UN Quality of Life Index

- PQLI 90 or more
- PQLI 75 – 89 — Basic level for human need –75
- PQLI 55 – 74
- PQLI 54 or less

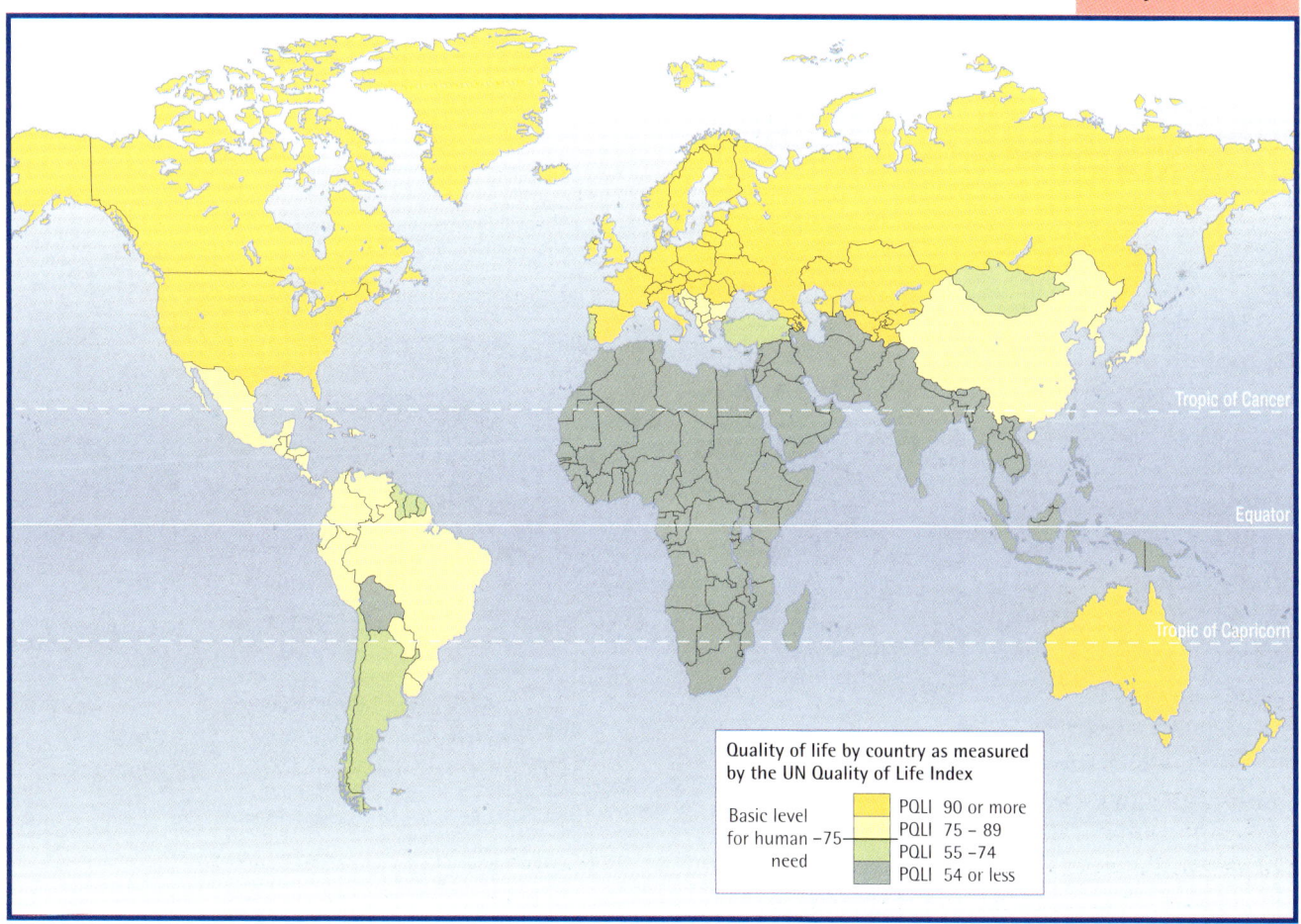

three
■ **People and their Needs**

The quality of life

Measuring development

SUMMARY When we look at the quality of life for every country in the world, we see most of the countries in the north have a high quality of life. We call them MEDCs. Most of those in the south are less well off. We call them LEDCs.

MEDC OVERALL
- ✔ Population — 1 175 000 000
- ✔ Infant mortality — 9 per 1000
- ✔ Maternal deaths — 10 per 1000
- ✔ Life expectancy — 71 years
- ✔ 80% of the world's wealth
- ✔ Majority have access to healthcare and education
- ✔ Access to safe reliable water supply

LEDC OVERALL
- ✘ Population — 4 666 000 000
- ✘ Infant mortality — 70 per 1000
- ✘ Maternal deaths — 64 per 1000
- ✘ Life expectancy — 62 years
- ✘ 20% of the world's wealth
- ✘ 50% have no chance of education
- ✘ Children start to work at a young age
- ✘ Over 20% experience hunger and malnutrition
- ✘ Average income is $1310

FIGURE 3.4 North–South divide

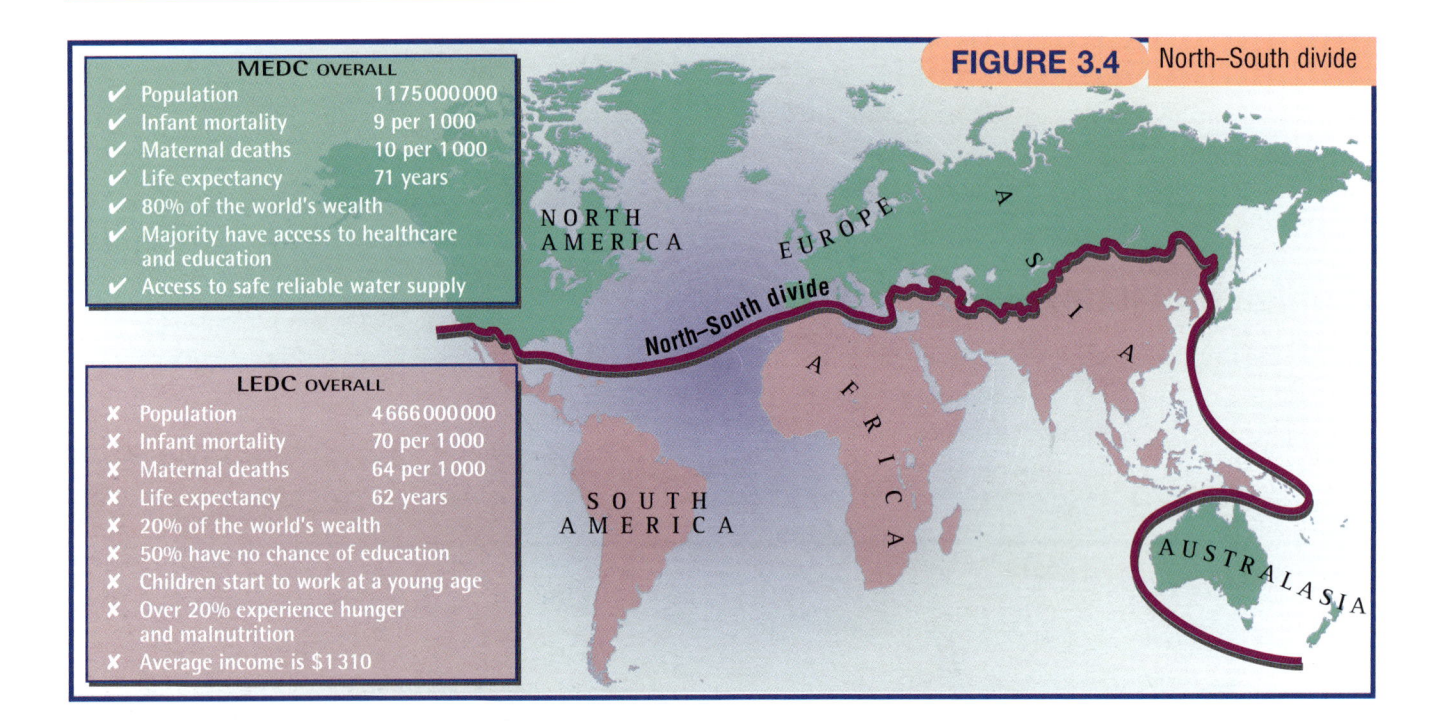

Figure 3.4 shows the pattern of development across the world. 80% of the world's wealth belongs to people in the green areas. These are the More Economically Developed Countries (MEDCs). A thick line on the map (the North–South divide) separates them from the Less Economically Developed Countries (LEDCs), which are south of the line. Note on which side of the divide Australia and New Zealand are.

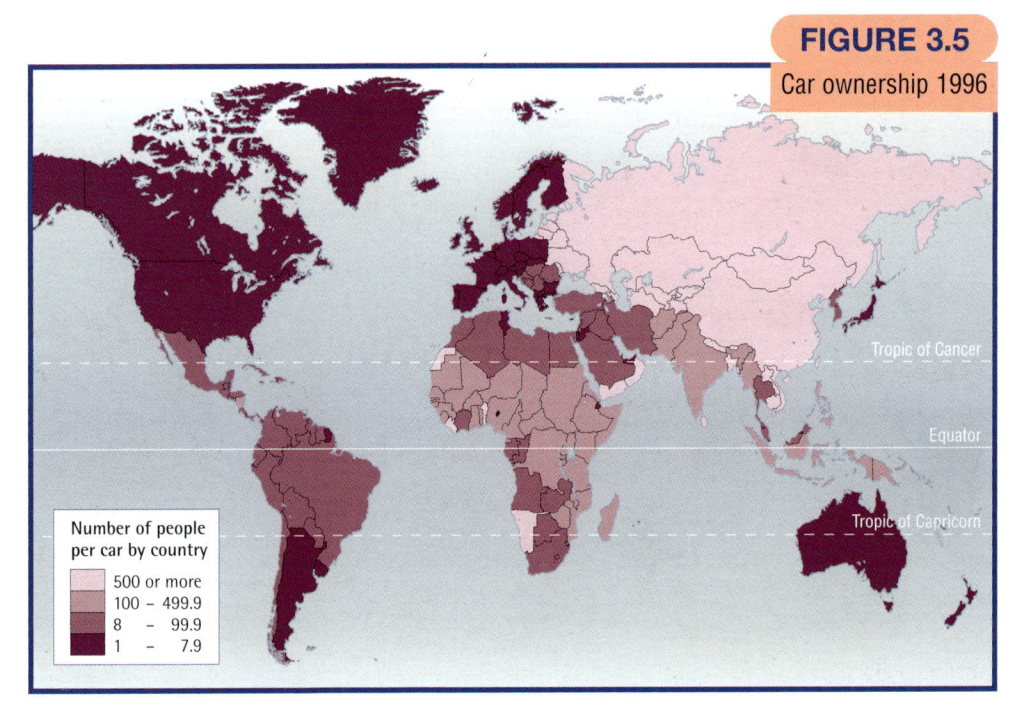

FIGURE 3.5 Car ownership 1996

Number of people per car by country
- 500 or more
- 100 – 499.9
- 8 – 99.9
- 1 – 7.9

What is quality of life?

There are many ways of indicating how developed a country is. Figure 3.5 shows the number of people per car. It uses a single colour. The darker the shading, the higher is the value. So there are many people rich enough to own cars in the countries shown in purple. Find in your atlas other maps like this. See how those indicators of development compare to car ownership. If the pattern is the same, there may be a **correlation** (that means, as one measure changes, it causes the other measure to change) between the indicators.

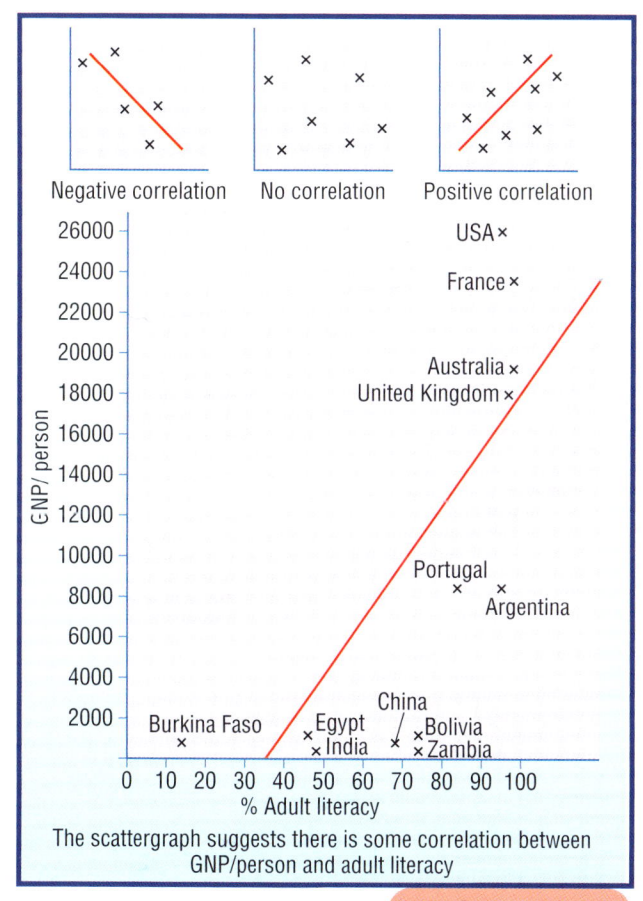

FIGURE 3.6 Scattergraph of adult literacy against GNP

A **scattergraph** helps you see if there is a link between two indicators of development. Look at Figure 3.6. For 12 countries it shows the GNP per person on the vertical axis and literacy on the horizontal axis. See how the cross for each country is plotted. The red line is called the 'best fit line'. It is a straight line, which comes close to many of the points on the graph. If there were an absolutely perfect relationship, it would join all the points together along the straight line. If the crosses are scattered, there is no relationship between the two indicators and no best fit line can be drawn. If the best fit line goes from top left to bottom right, there is a negative correlation. This means that as one indicator gets bigger, the other gets smaller.

Country	Life expectancy (years)	Access to safe water (%)
Argentina	75	79
Australia	80	99
Bolivia	64	52
Burkina Faso	48	42
China	72	67
Egypt	70	87
France	79	100
India	63	81
Portugal	76	82
UK	78	100
USA	77	100
Zambia	35	38

Figure 3.7 Correlation between access to clean water and life expectancy

TASKS

1. Look at Figure 3.4.
   a. Name two continents where all the countries are LEDCs.
   b. Name three continents where all the countries are MEDCs.
   c. Name one continent where some of the countries are LEDCs and some countries are MEDCs.

2. For the continent you identified for Task 1c,
   a. name one country that is an LEDC
   b. name one country that is an MEDC.

   Use an atlas to help you.

3. Look at the information about 'MEDC overall' and 'LEDC overall' in Figure 3.4. Copy this paragraph and fill in the gaps.

   There are not equal numbers of people living in MEDCs and LEDCs. Four times as many people live in _____ as _____. Life in MEDCs on average is _____ years longer than in LEDCs. Whereas only nine babies die in every 1 000 births, in LEDCs there are _____ babies who die.

4. Look at Figure 3.5. It does not show exactly the same pattern as Figure 3.4. Use an atlas to name one country where car ownership is much higher than you would expect.

5. Draw a scattergraph to show the correlation between life expectancy and access to clean water (Figure 3.7).

   Carefully draw onto your scattergraph the best fit line. Is it a negative or positive correlation?

three
People and their Needs

The quality of life

COMPARING THE UK WITH BURKINA FASO

SUMMARY Life in Burkina Faso is very different to the UK. It is one of the poorest countries in the world. The quality of life indicators contrast with the UK.

Burkina Faso is a country in West Africa with nearly 10 million people. It is landlocked. That means it has no borders with the sea, so no ports for trade or fishing. It is a dry country, on the edge of the world's largest desert.

- It is poor. The average income is only US$230 a year (about £3 a week). As prices go up, that buys less than it used to.
- Life is hard, especially for mothers and children. 17% of children die before the age of five. 30% of children are malnourished (not enough to eat). On average, each woman gives birth to seven children. 10% of mothers die during or as a result of childbirth.
- Life expectancy is only 48 years. Adult literacy is 18%. 36% of boys and 23% of girls attend school.
- Only 56% of the population have a supply of clean, reliable water and less than half have access to healthcare. 82% live in the countryside. There are no taps, no hospitals and few schools there.

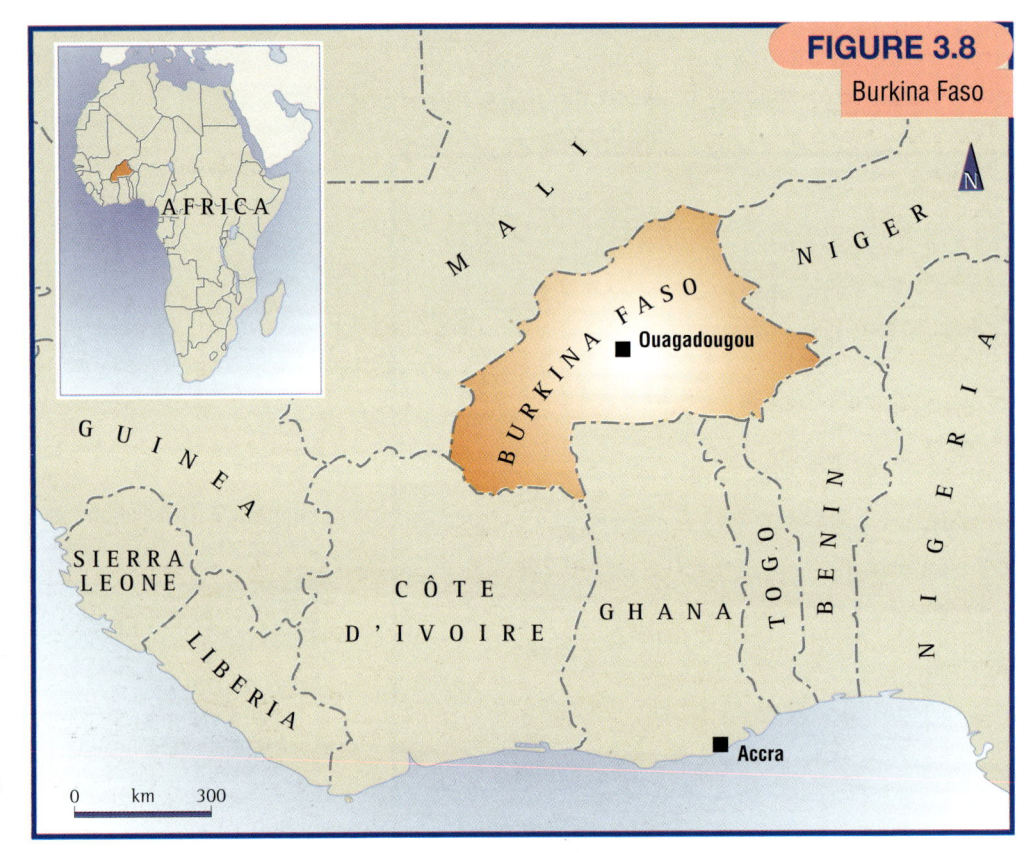

FIGURE 3.8 Burkina Faso

Burkina Faso is not in the news very often. It is a poor country, on the edge of the Sahara Desert in West Africa. What happens there may not affect us very much, but what the rich countries do can have an enormous effect on Burkina Faso.

Only 18% live in towns. Most people try to farm. When the rains come, the crops grow. When there is a drought, the country does not have the money to help the people who are suffering.

Poverty can be seen in the lack of cars. Even in a town of 3 000 people, there may not be even one private car. It's 100 miles from the capital city south to the border with Ghana and there is no petrol pump along the way.

The journey south has already been taken by a million people from Burkina Faso looking for work and a better life, mainly to Cote d'Ivoire. More will go as the population is expected to double in the next twenty years. Burkina Faso cannot feed, clothe or provide homes or work for all these people.

Figure 3.9 Looking for a road out of nowhere

Comparing the UK with Burkina Faso

Health	
Infant mortality	6 per 1 000 births
Malnourishment	2% of the population
Average calorie intake per day	3 317 calories
Maternal deaths	7 per 1 000 births
Fertility rate	1.7 children per women
Life expectancy	77 years
Birth rate	13 per 1 000
Death rate	11 per 1 000
Population doubling time	433 years
Access to healthcare	100%
Population per doctor	300 people
Social	
Adult literacy	99%
GDP spent on education	5.3%
Urban population	90%
Access to safe, reliable water	98%
Average income per year	$18 000

Figure 3.10 UK quality of life indicators

TASKS

1 Describe where Burkina Faso is.
2 Choose five quality of life indicators. Make a table to show them for Burkina Faso and the UK.
3 Look at Figures 3.9 and 3.11. Imagine you are visiting Burkina Faso. Write a postcard to your friends back home, describing what life is like. Use information from the photograph and the news article.

FIGURE 3.11
Market day, Burkina Faso

three
■ People and their Needs

The quality of life

ECONOMIC INDICATORS OF DEVELOPMENT

SUMMARY We can look at types of industry to see how developed a country is. LEDCs have a lot of primary jobs, like farming. MEDCs have a lot of tertiary jobs in services.

The employment structure of a country is another way of showing how developed a country is. Industry can be classified as primary, secondary or tertiary.

- **Primary industry.** This provides the raw materials used by people and industry, for example through farming, mining, fishing and forestry. Unprocessed goods are often of low value and include items such as hardwood, mineral ores, and agricultural products such as cotton.

- **Secondary (or manufacturing).** These industries use raw materials to make other products. This adds value to the raw materials. For example, iron ore is used to make steel for cars and wood is used to make furniture.

- **Tertiary (or services).** These industries do not produce raw materials or manufactured goods. Instead, they provide specialist services such as banking, administration, healthcare, education, transport and entertainment. As a country becomes more developed the proportion of people employed in each industrial sector changes. Figure 3.12 shows this for the USA and Egypt, and Figure 3.13 shows recent changes in the UK.

	USA			Egypt		
	primary	secondary	tertiary	primary	secondary	tertiary
1900	38	27	35	71	10	19
1920	28	33	39	65	11	22
1940	19	35	46	70	10	20
1960	7	39	54	57	12	31
1980	4	35	61	50	14	36
2000	3	25	72	42	21	37

Figure 3.12 Changes in occupational structure in USA and Egypt (per cent)

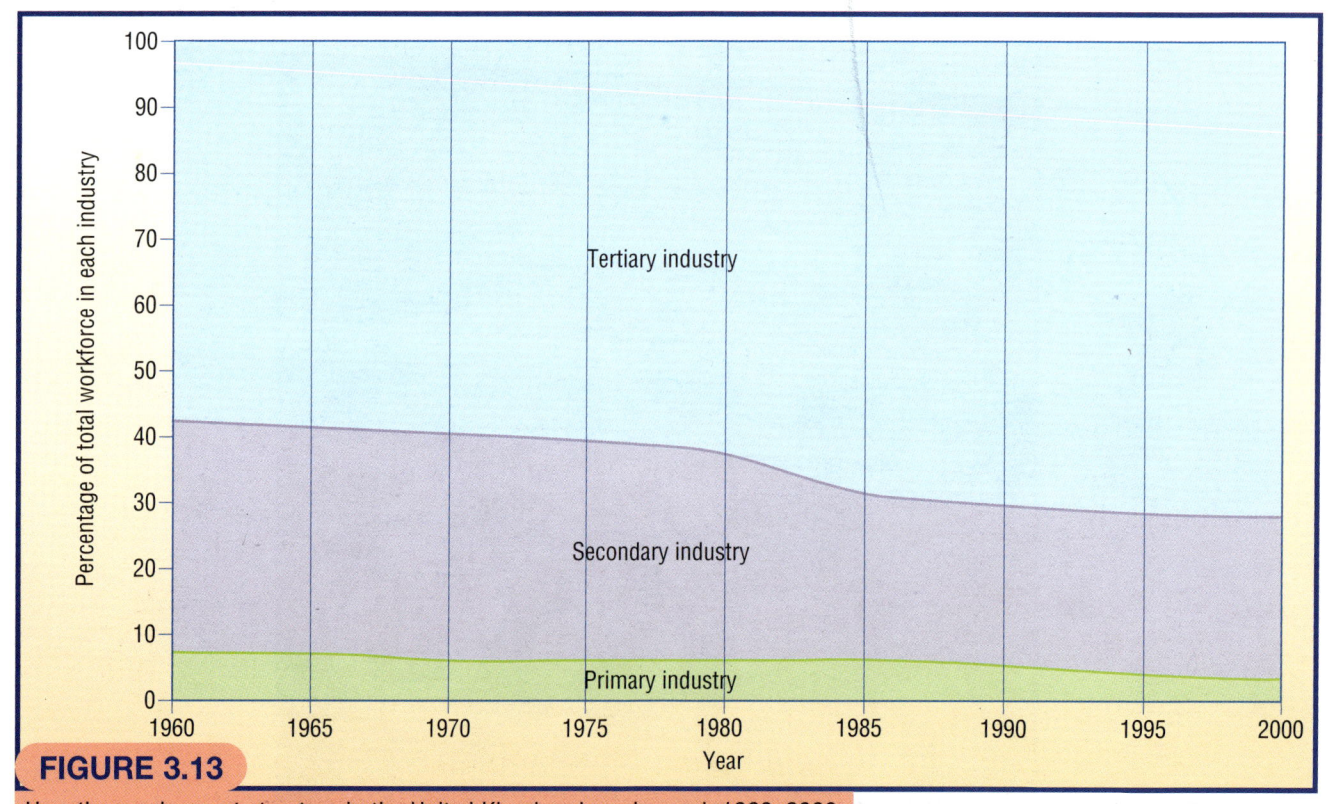

FIGURE 3.13

How the employment structure in the United Kingdom has changed, 1960–2000

Economic indicators of development

Country	Agriculture %	Industry %	Services %	Pop. growth	Income
Bangladesh	59	13	28	1.0	$240
Brazil	25	25	50	0.8	$3 640
Chad	83	5	12	2.5	$180
Egypt	42	21	37	2.6	$790
France	9	29	62	0.6	$20 580
Ghana	59	11	30	2.7	$390
India	62	11	27	2.5	$340
Italy	9	32	59	0.2	$19 020
Japan	7	34	59	0.3	$39 000
Sweden	3	28	69	0.7	$23 750
UK	2	28	70	0.3	$18 700

Figure 3.14 Occupational structure for selected countries

TASKS

1. a Do a survey among your teaching group. List and categorise the range of jobs found in students' families.
   b Copy the table below to list your results.

Primary	Secondary	Tertiary

   c Present your results as a bar chart.
   d Describe and suggest reasons for your results.

2. Look at Figure 3.12. For both countries:
   a What has happened to the percentage employed in primary jobs over the years?
   b What has happened to tertiary jobs?
   c Look carefully at the percentages. How can you tell that one country is an MEDC and the other is still an LEDC?

3. Figure 3.15 shows you how to draw a triangular graph.
   a Make a copy of the red, blue and green lines.
   b Add the dots and names for Bangladesh, Italy and Sweden.
   c Use the numbers in Figure 3.14 to add dots and country names for the other countries in the list.
   d Draw a ring round the dots near the bottom of the graph. Draw another ring round the dots in the top half of the graph. Label one ring 'MEDC' and the other ring 'LEDC'.

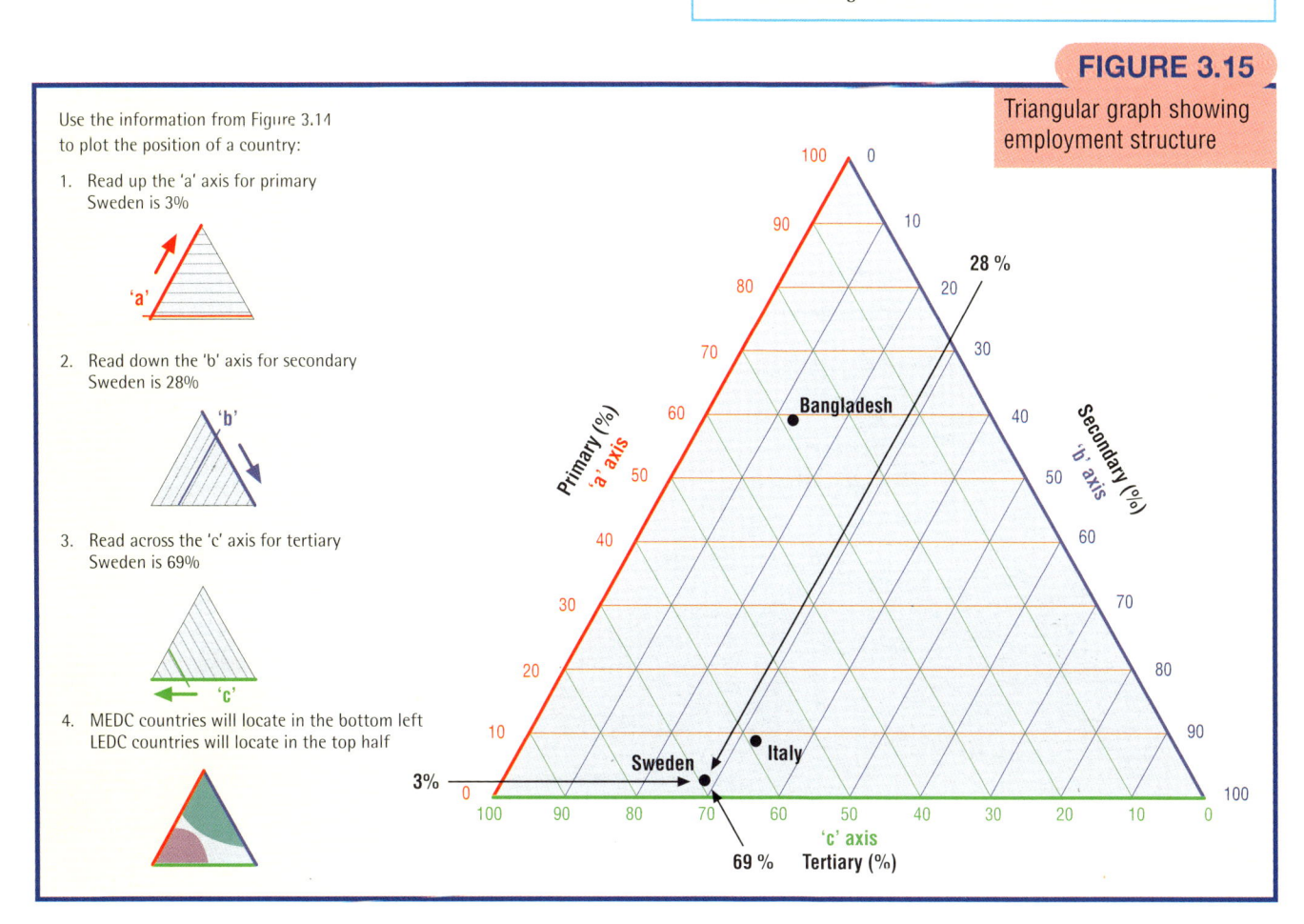

FIGURE 3.15

Triangular graph showing employment structure

Use the information from Figure 3.14 to plot the position of a country:

1. Read up the 'a' axis for primary
   Sweden is 3%

2. Read down the 'b' axis for secondary
   Sweden is 28%

3. Read across the 'c' axis for tertiary
   Sweden is 69%

4. MEDC countries will locate in the bottom left
   LEDC countries will locate in the top half

three
■ People and their Needs

The quality of life

INDUSTRIALISATION AND ECONOMIC GROWTH

SUMMARY In the UK, industries grew rapidly in the eighteenth and nineteenth centuries. Trade with other countries made people wealthy and improved the quality of life. In the last century, some Asian countries have developed their industries. They are called 'Tiger Economies'.

The UK was the first country in the world to improve its quality of life by developing manufacturing industry. Japan was the first Asian country to industrialise. It has been rapidly followed by Hong Kong (now part of China), Taiwan, South Korea and Singapore. We call them Tiger Economies (Figure 3.16). They are **newly industrialised countries (NICs)**.

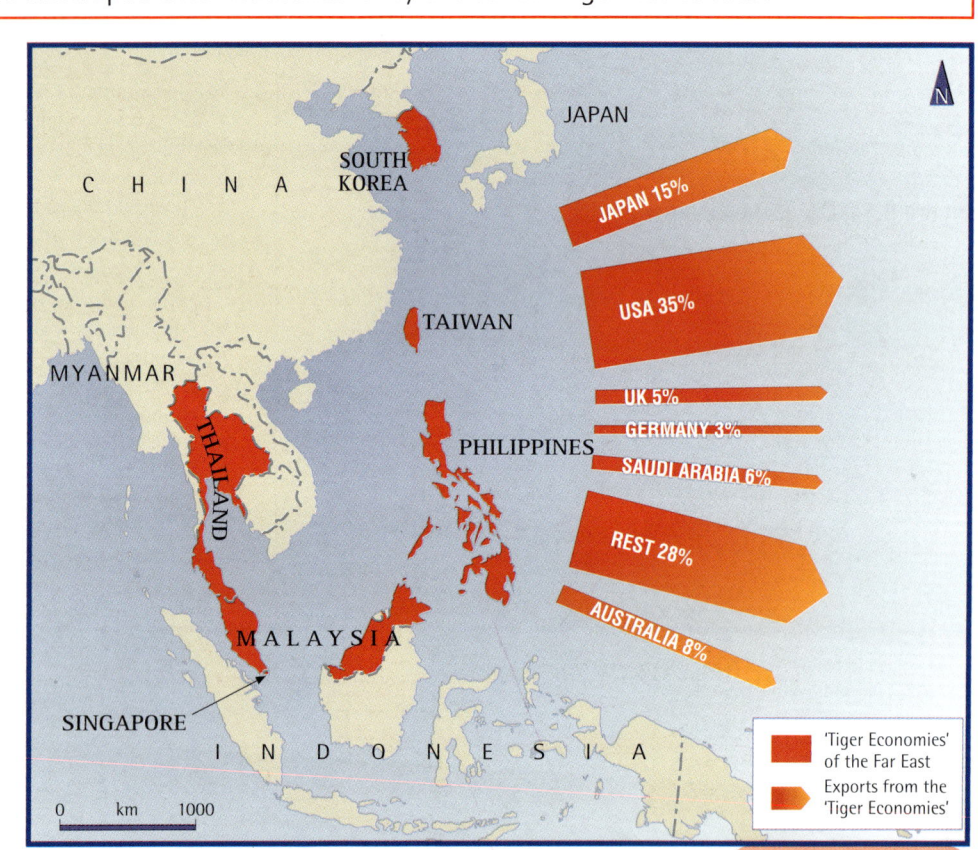

FIGURE 3.17 Changes in UK manufacturing, 1979–1998

Manufacturing jobs have shrunk…

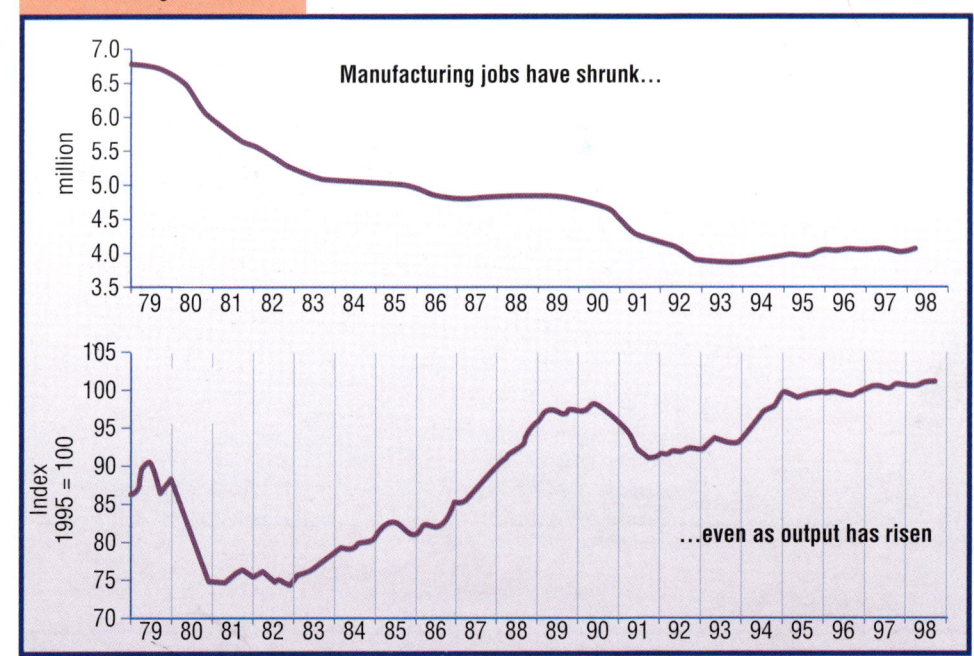

…even as output has risen

FIGURE 3.16 Asian economies

Exports from the 'Tiger Economies':
- JAPAN 15%
- USA 35%
- UK 5%
- GERMANY 3%
- SAUDI ARABIA 6%
- REST 28%
- AUSTRALIA 8%

Industrialisation and economic growth 137

The growth of NICs has made it harder for factories in the UK to compete. The UK's share of manufacturing has halved in the last 20 years, which has meant fewer jobs in this industry (Figure 3.17). The Tiger Economies now produce 15% of the world's goods.

There are six stages to becoming an industrialised country. They are shown in Figure 3.18. LEDCs at Stage 1 or 2 often lack the **infrastructure** (such as reliable power supplies, transport, a good education system) to develop to Stage 3. **Trans-national companies (TNCs)** are based in MEDCs and operate worldwide. They often invest in LEDCs, where wages are very low, but they are more likely to be interested in their own profits than developing the country.

FIGURE 3.18
Rostow model of economic growth

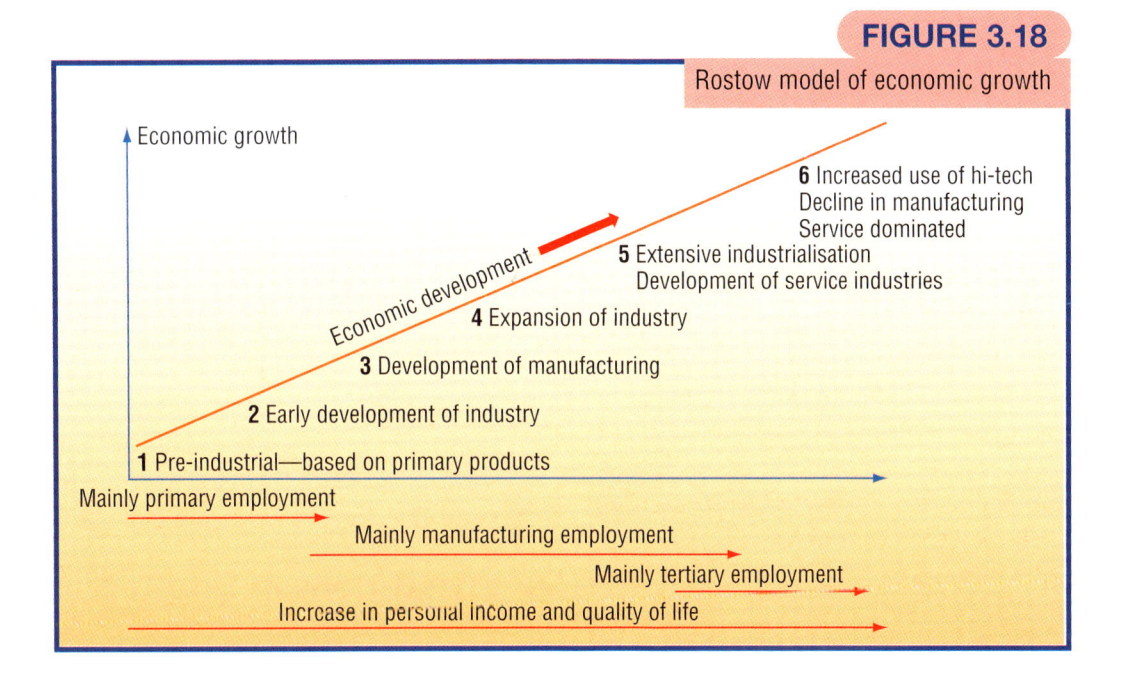

Stages:
1 Pre-industrial—based on primary products
2 Early development of industry
3 Development of manufacturing
4 Expansion of industry
5 Extensive industrialisation / Development of service industries
6 Increased use of hi-tech / Decline in manufacturing / Service dominated

- Mainly primary employment
- Mainly manufacturing employment
- Mainly tertiary employment
- Increase in personal income and quality of life

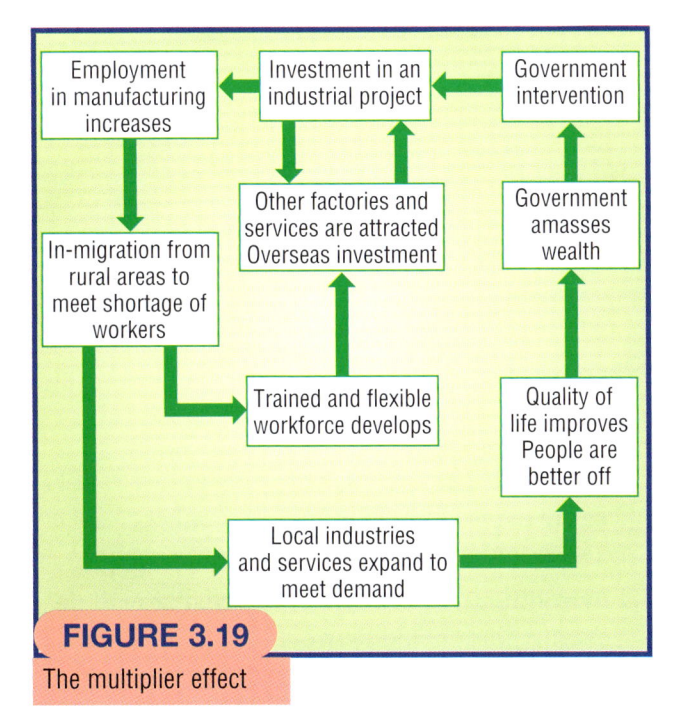

FIGURE 3.19 The multiplier effect

(Cycle: Investment in an industrial project → Employment in manufacturing increases → In-migration from rural areas to meet shortage of workers → Trained and flexible workforce develops → Other factories and services are attracted / Overseas investment → Government intervention → Government amasses wealth → Quality of life improves / People are better off → Local industries and services expand to meet demand)

In the Tiger Economies, the government controlled the development of industry. Profits were used for further investment. This spiral of growth is called the multiplier effect (Figure 3.19).

TASKS

1. Which countries are known as Tiger Economies?
2. Do a survey at home and in school to find out where things were made. Look for labels saying, 'Made in ...'. What goods have come from the Tiger Economies?
3. Look at the stages of economic growth (Figure 3.18). At which stage is
   a Burkina Faso (page 132)?
   b UK?
4. What attracts TNCs to having a factory in an LEDC?

three
■ People and their Needs

The quality of life

SOUTH KOREA

> **SUMMARY** In the last 50 years, South Korea has become an important industrial country. Although most raw materials have to be imported, it has low wages and plenty of workers. For the future, it needs to do more research and development to keep its products in demand.

South Korea, like the other Tiger Economies, has few natural resources, just a little coal and iron ore. It is a mountainous peninsula. Its real resource is its cheap and flexible workforce. In the last 50 years, the government has helped large companies to invest and trade. It has paid for research and runs the steelworks to provide cheap raw materials to South Korean factories. It also provided cheap loans to family businesses such as Daewoo, Samsung, Goldstar, Kia and Hyundai. It adds high taxes to goods that are imported, so that these are more expensive than goods made in South Korea. Seven million people have migrated from the countryside where incomes were even lower, so the expanding factories have plenty of cheap workers.

Steel industry

In 1971, South Korea made one million tonnes of steel. In 2000, it was 50 million tonnes. Coal, oil and iron ore have to be imported from Australia, the USA and Canada.

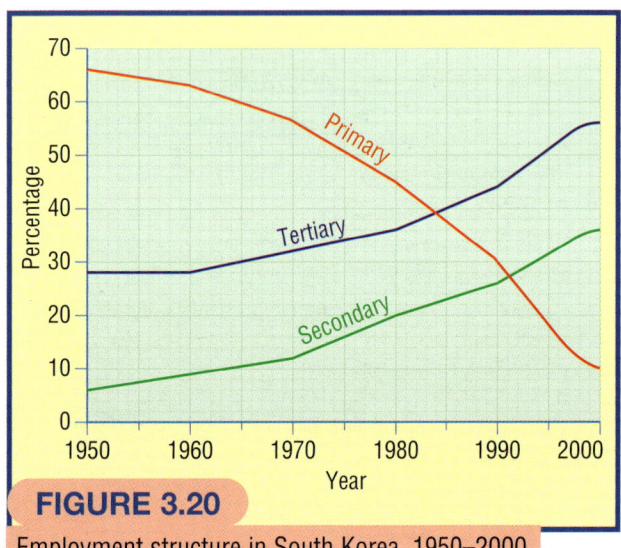

FIGURE 3.20
Employment structure in South Korea, 1950–2000

Shipbuilding

One-third of the world's ships are now built in South Korea. It is the world's leading producer of oil tankers. Its shipyards are modern and efficient. Wages are low, but not as low as China, which is now winning more orders for new ships.

Cars

Thirty years ago, no cars were produced in South Korea. Then Hyundai, Kia and Daewoo linked up with Japanese and American companies. Now South Korea exports cars, particularly to LEDCs.

Investment in South Korea

TNCs, like Sony which is based in Japan, set up factories in South Korea. TNCs were originally attracted by

▸ low wages
▸ no trade unions
▸ being close to China, where goods could be sold.

Now South Korea has its own TNCs, like Samsung, with factories in the USA and Europe (Figure 3.21).

Problems

Rapid growth has had some bad effects:

▸ **Social problems**. Women are only paid 75% of what men get. Immigrant workers only get 50%. It causes unrest.
▸ **Environmental problems**. Industrial growth has caused pollution and destroyed natural habitats.

South Korea

- **Lack of investment in research and development.** At first Japan shared its research with South Korea. Now it is less willing to. South Korea, though, does not do enough research on its own.

- **World trade.** The country relies on people in other countries wanting – and being able to afford – to buy their goods. That depends on conditions outside the control of South Korea, such as the price of oil.

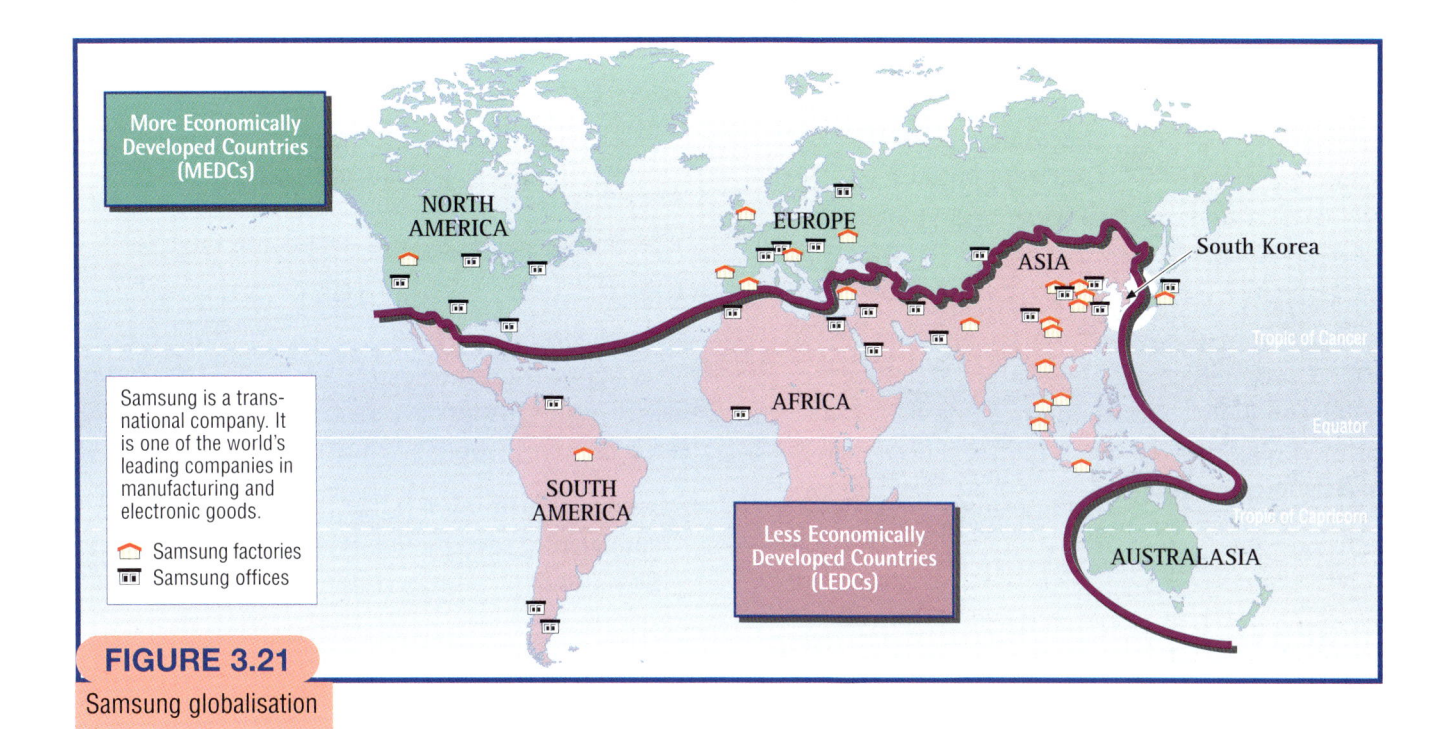

FIGURE 3.21 Samsung globalisation

Samsung is a trans-national company. It is one of the world's leading companies in manufacturing and electronic goods.

	1970	1995	
	Number produced	Number produced	World share 1995
Televisions	114 000	17 102 000	12.7% 2nd
Tyres	900 000	53 472 000	5.9% 5th
Ships	0	5 000	33% 2nd
Cars	13 000	2 000 000	5.6% 5th
Commercial vehicles	15 000	510 000	3.3% 5th
Steel	480 000 tonnes	36 million tonnes	4.9% 6th
Energy use	1.37 tonnes per person	3.77 tonnes per person	
GNP per person	$4000	$9700	

Figure 3.22 South Korea: economic growth

TASKS

1. Describe the location of South Korea.
2. Explain how each of these factors helped South Korean companies develop:
   a. cheap, flexible workforce
   b. government support with high import taxes
   c. low cost of living for the workers.
3. Give three examples of South Korean companies. List some of their products you can buy in the UK.
4. Look at Figure 3.20. What percentage of workers were in primary, secondary and tertiary industry in
   a. 1950?
   b. 2000?
5. Copy this paragraph and fill in the gaps.

   Korea built no ships in _____ but by 1995 it was the second most important shipbuilding country in the _____. It is also the second most important country for producing _____.
   Industrialisation has made people better off as _____ has more than doubled since 1970.

three
People and their Needs
Economic activities

FARMING SYSTEMS

> **SUMMARY** Farming operates as a system with inputs, processes and outputs. There are different types of farm such as arable and pastoral.

In MEDCs, such as the UK, farmers grow crops and rear animals for sale to make a profit. This is called **commercial farming**. In LEDCs there are some commercial farms, but many farmers only grow enough to feed their families. This is called **subsistence farming**. Most farming is **sedentary** (farmers stay in one place). **Nomadic** farming is when farmers move from place to place.

Types of farm

- **Arable farm** – grows crops
- **Pastoral farm** – rears animals
- **Mixed farm** – grows crops and rears animals.

A farm works as a system. **Inputs** are what goes into the farm (such as seed and rain). **Processes** are what happens on the farm (such as planting and harvesting). **Outputs** are the products of the farm (such as crops, wool and meat).

- **Extensive farming** is when the farm size is large compared to the amount of money spent on it or the number of people working there (low inputs and low outputs).
- **Intensive farming** is when the farm is small compared to the numbers working there or the amount of money spent on it (high inputs and high outputs).

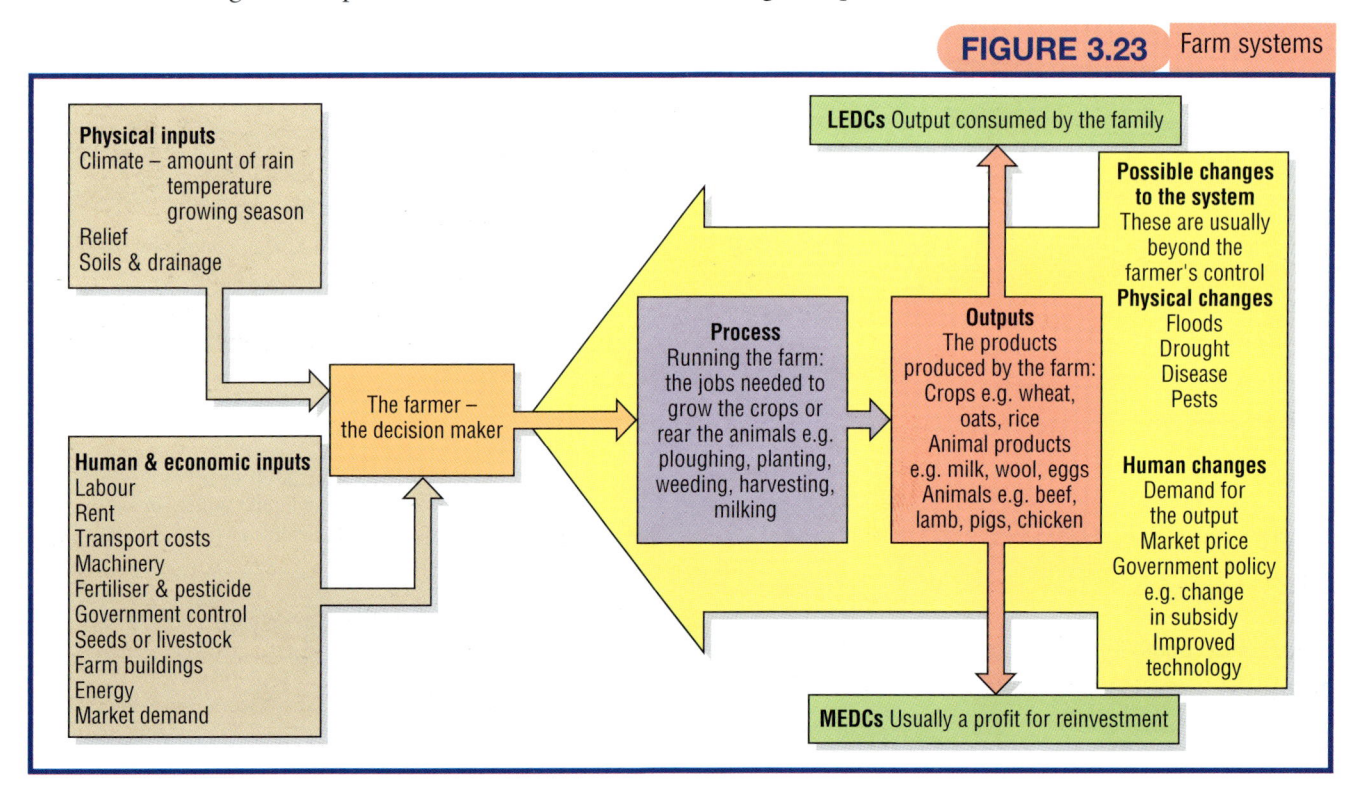

FIGURE 3.23 Farm systems

Physical inputs
Climate – amount of rain
temperature
growing season
Relief
Soils & drainage

Human & economic inputs
Labour
Rent
Transport costs
Machinery
Fertiliser & pesticide
Government control
Seeds or livestock
Farm buildings
Energy
Market demand

The farmer – the decision maker

Process
Running the farm: the jobs needed to grow the crops or rear the animals e.g. ploughing, planting, weeding, harvesting, milking

Outputs
The products produced by the farm:
Crops e.g. wheat, oats, rice
Animal products e.g. milk, wool, eggs
Animals e.g. beef, lamb, pigs, chicken

LEDCs Output consumed by the family

Possible changes to the system
These are usually beyond the farmer's control

Physical changes
Floods
Drought
Disease
Pests

Human changes
Demand for the output
Market price
Government policy e.g. change in subsidy
Improved technology

MEDCs Usually a profit for reinvestment

A commercial farm in an MEDC 141

TASKS

1. On a whole page, design and illustrate a mini-dictionary of farming words. Include these words and their definitions:

   arable, pastoral, mixed farming, commercial, subsistence, sedentary, nomadic, inputs, processes, outputs, intensive, extensive.

2. Look at this website: http://www.nfu.org.uk/
   a. Choose two different farm case studies and describe each one.
   b. How are these farms different?

3. Look at Figure 3.23. Every farm is different. Make two copies of the diagram below and fill in the boxes for *either* your two farms from task 2 *or* a subsistence farm in an LEDC and an arable farm in an MEDC.

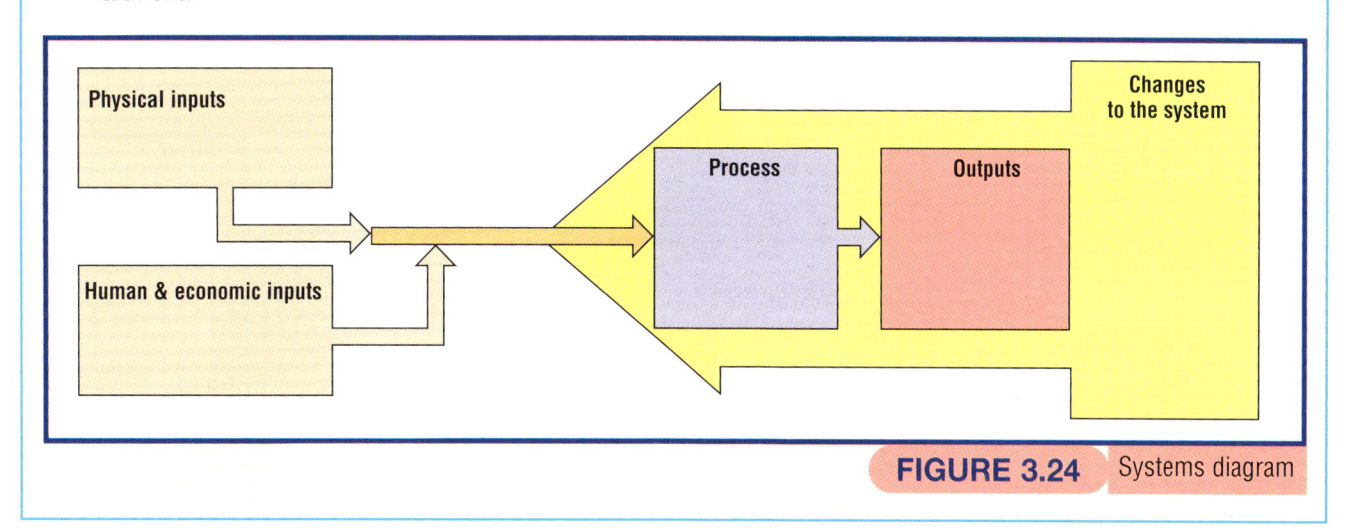

FIGURE 3.24 Systems diagram

A COMMERCIAL FARM IN AN MEDC

FIGURE 3.25 Thorn Park Farm

Dairy farming at Thorn Park Farm, North Yorkshire

Thorn Park is a dairy farm in a valley. The hills around it provide shelter from the winds which blow off the North Sea. The Wilson family run the farm and also employ one other person. They rent the land from Scarborough Borough Council. Each of their 110 cows produces an average of 7 000 litres of milk in a year.

three
■ People and their Needs

Economic activities

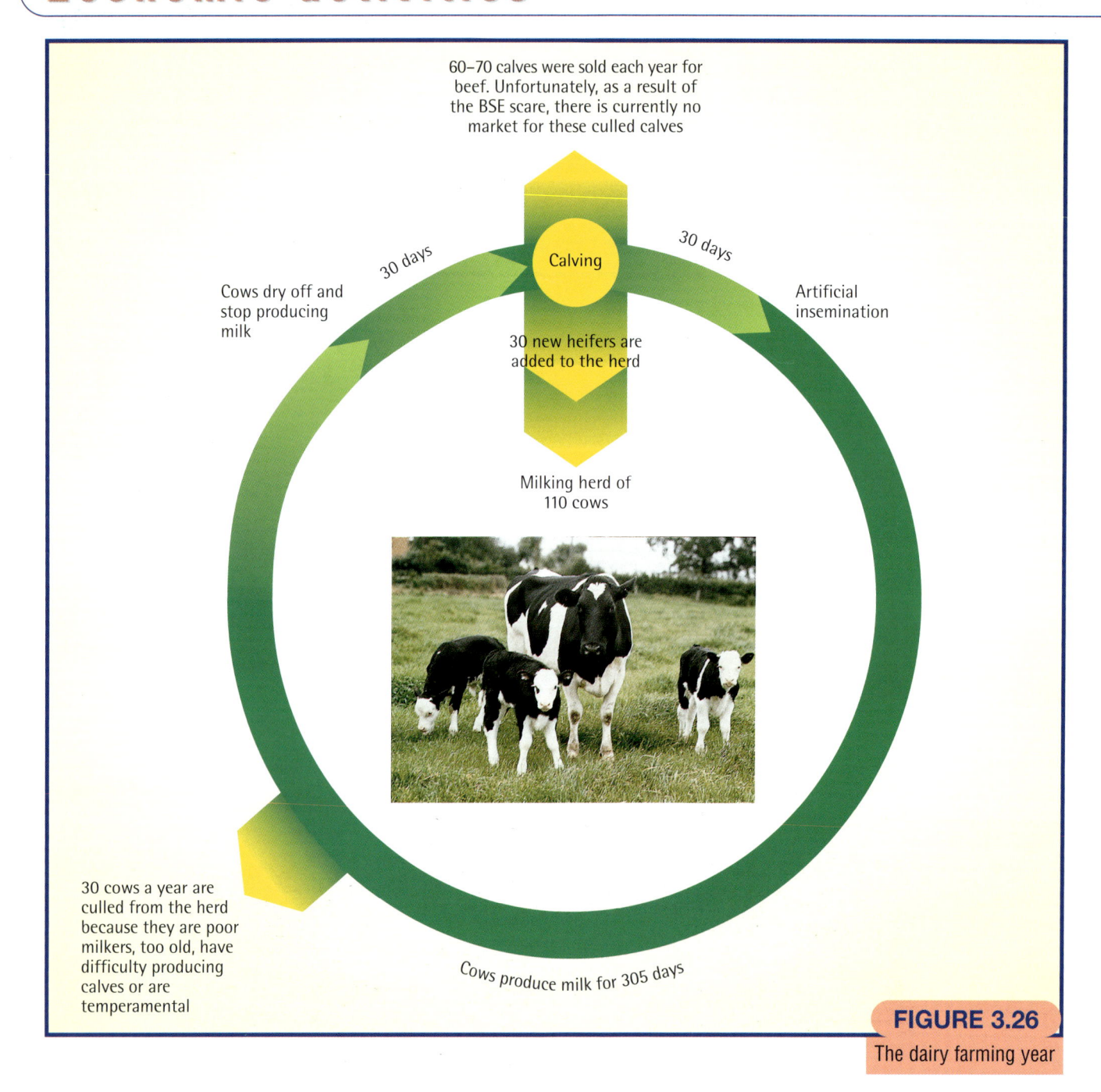

FIGURE 3.26 The dairy farming year

- 60–70 calves were sold each year for beef. Unfortunately, as a result of the BSE scare, there is currently no market for these culled calves
- 30 days — Cows dry off and stop producing milk
- Calving
- 30 days — Artificial insemination
- 30 new heifers are added to the herd
- Milking herd of 110 cows
- Cows produce milk for 305 days
- 30 cows a year are culled from the herd because they are poor milkers, too old, have difficulty producing calves or are temperamental

Thorn Park Farm is a good site for dairying. The farm is too small, the climate is too wet and the soils are too heavy to grow crops. Grass grows easily here. Running a dairy farm is hard work. Milking is done at 0600 and 1700 hours every day of the year and takes up to 2 hours. A tanker collects the milk from refrigerated tanks every morning. From April to November, the cattle graze in the fields. Some grass is cut for silage and stored as winter feed. This increases profit as the farmer does not need to buy in feed. In the autumn, cows also eat kale (a kind of cabbage). The cows are kept in barns and eat silage during the winter. All year round the farmer has to keep records about each cow and make sure that they are healthy. Outputs of the farm include milk and calves. Manure is spread on the fields as fertiliser.

A commercial farm in an MEDC

Changes at Thorn Park Farm

The European Union introduced milk **quotas** in 1984. A quota is the maximum amount of milk allowed to be produced by each farm. The aim is to reduce overproduction.

The price of beef has fallen due to a disease called BSE. In 3 years, the price for calves has fallen by 90%, the price for culled cows by 50% and the price for milk by 37%. Costs of inputs have either gone up or stayed the same.

What should the Wilson family do?

They have three options:

- Sell up. They would get very little money for their cows and they only rent the land.

- Diversify (do other things such as set up a caravan site). The farm is in the North York Moors National Park which attracts tourists. However, planning rules are very strict.

- Stick it out. As other farmers go bankrupt, a shortage of milk will increase prices. They could increase their herd to 160 cows and make a profit. The Wilson family chose this option.

TASKS

1. List the inputs, processes and outputs for Thorn Park Farm.
2. Imagine you are a member of the Wilson family. Write a diary entry for a typical day at Thorn Park Farm.
3. What are quotas?
4. Why has the price of beef fallen?
5. Look at the Wilson family's three options. Which would you have chosen and why?
6. Look at the Ordnance Survey map on pages 44–45. Thorn Park Farm is marked on with a thick black line.
   a. Give the 4-figure grid reference for each square in which the farm has land.
   b. Estimate approximately how much land Thorn Park Farm covers.
   c. Name and give the 6-figure grid reference for the next nearest farm.
   d. Imagine you were walking from Suffield Ings (982893) to Osborne Lodge (987870). Describe what you would see and when you would be walking uphill or downhill.

FIGURE 3.27
Cutting grass for silage on Thorn Park Farm

three
People and their Needs
Economic activities

SUBSISTENCE RICE FARMING IN INDIA, AN LEDC

> **SUMMARY** Farming in LEDCs is changing. Changes include using machinery and technology, irrigation (adding water), and land reform schemes.

The importance of rice

Rice is a major world crop which feeds one-third of the world's population. It needs very moist soils. The main rice areas are in South East Asia on small subsistence farms. Rice farming is often **labour intensive** (lots of workers but little machinery). Water buffaloes prepare the paddy fields and the manure fertilises the soil.

Rice growing in India

- India is the world's second largest producer of rice.
- Rice is 90% of India's total diet.
- 70% of India's workforce is employed in farming.

In the 1960s, people worried that it would not be possible to grow enough food to feed the world's growing population. The **Green Revolution** is the name used for changes in LEDC farming in the last 50 years when technology has been used to grow more food. Technology includes machinery such as tractors and chemicals such as pesticides.

High yield varieties

High Yield Varieties (HYVs) of rice, wheat and maize were developed by MEDCs such as the UK. Rice yields grew by 300%, an extra crop could be grown each year and crops were more resistant to disease, wind and rain. Farmers who can afford to buy HYVs have grown a surplus to sell in the cities. They can afford machinery and have improved their quality of life.

Problems caused by HYVs:

- Rich farmers have become richer and poor farmers have become poorer.
- Some farmers borrowed money to buy HYVs and are now in debt.
- HYVs need lots of fertilisers and insecticides (expensive and cause pollution).
- Soil erosion is increasing.

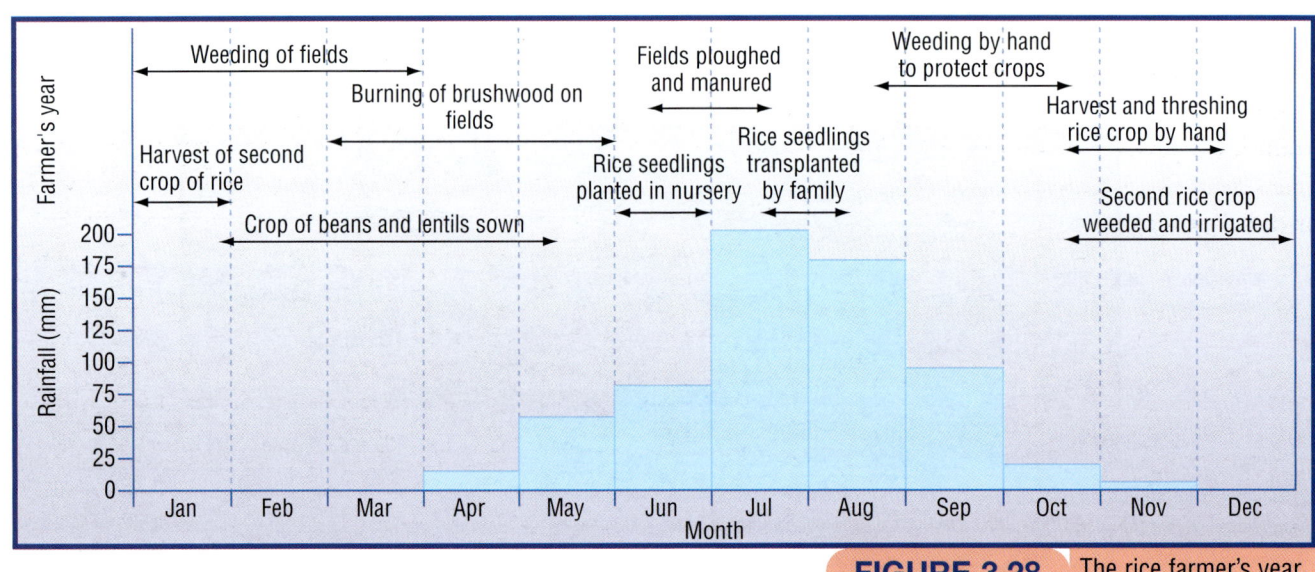

FIGURE 3.28 The rice farmer's year

THE GREEN REVOLUTION

FIGURE 3.29 The growing requirements of rice

Labels on figure:
- Dry sunny weather for ripening and harvest
- Temperatures: 18° C for growth for 3 months; 24° C for ripening
- Flat land which will stop water draining away, allowing the rice to grow in it
- Lots of labour
- Plenty of moisture for growth
- Growing season: only 90 days for quick maturing varieties. Most take 120 days or more

Mechanisation

In LEDCs, richer farmers with larger farms have imported tractors and ploughs from MEDCs. This has increased rural inequalities.

Irrigation

HYV seeds need more water than traditional rice. About 45 million ha of land is irrigated in India. Traditionally, wells are dug in the Ganges Valley. The Green Revolution has seen farms use electric or diesel water pumps.

TASKS

1 Define the Green Revolution.

2 Write a paragraph about rice farming. Include the following words:

   arable, labour, Green Revolution, HYVs, yields, mechanisation, irrigation

3 Copy and complete the table:

The Green Revolution	
Advantages	Disadvantages

4 Look at Figure 3.29. Explain why this is a good place to grow rice.

5 Compare the photographs in Figures 3.29 and 3.27. How are these farms different?

three
People and their Needs
Economic activities

> **Irrigation case study – Narmada River Project, India**
>
> - 30 dams provide hydro-electricity.
> - 2 million ha of land is irrigated.
> - 100 000 ha of forest and farmland has been flooded.
> - Soil can become waterlogged and salty.

Land reform

Many farms in LEDCs are very small. The majority of farmland is owned by a few wealthy landowners. These rich farmers can afford HYV varieties and buy land from poorer farmers who run into debt from buying HYV seed and fertilisers. India has tried to introduce **land reform** to increase average farm size by limiting the size of large farms and giving land to the landless.

Appropriate technology

The Green Revolution has meant that technology used in MEDCs has been introduced to LEDCs. This has caused some problems such as increasing the gap between rich and poor farmers and it has affected the environment. Now **appropriate technology** (or intermediate technology) is an alternative way to help LEDCs develop. Appropriate technology is technology that is affordable and can be used by ordinary men and women without causing long-term damage to the environment. Examples of appropriate technology schemes are training for animal first-aid workers and building improved fishing boats. These schemes do not rely on high technology machinery imported from MEDCs and can improve quality of life for people.

TASKS

1. Some farms in LEDCs are very small. What problems does this cause?
2. What is land reform?
3. What is appropriate technology?
4. Describe three advantages of using appropriate technology in LEDCs.
5. Read the article on page 147 about problems in rice production in the future.
   a. Write out the facts which include these numbers:
      - 90%
      - 520m tonnes
      - 770m tonnes
      - 400m ha
      - 47m ha
   b. Match and copy out these 'heads and tails':

Hybrid rice	has increased annual rice output by more than 3%.
New plant type	has yields up to 20% higher than other HYVs.
Green Revolution technology	is also called 'super rice'.

Rice crisis looms in Asia

Green Revolution technologies are 'almost exhausted' of any further productivity gains

By 2025, average rice yields must almost double, using less land, less water, less labour and fewer chemical inputs. Rice is the life-line of Asia. More than 90% of the world's rice total crop – currently some 520 million tonnes – is produced there, providing the region's 3100 million people more than a third of their total calories. With Asia's population growing by some 56 million a year, domestic demand for rice is expected to top 770 million tonnes by the year 2025.

How that increase will be achieved is the subject of growing concern among rice scientists and policymakers alike. If present trends continue, within 20 years most countries will no longer be self-sufficient in rice and Asia's legendary rice bowl will be filled increasingly by grain imports.

At the latest session of the International Rice Commission, held in Cairo this month, rice experts were describing the challenges ahead as 'mind-boggling' and even 'frightening'. To meet rice demand over the next 30 years, the yield of irrigated rice in Asia will need to increase to about 6 tonnes/ha, nearly twice the current level. And this will have to be achieved using less land, less water, less labour and fewer chemical inputs, particularly pesticides.

Green Revolution technologies, which spurred increases in annual rice output of more than 3% – and probably saved millions from the threat of famine – are now considered 'almost exhausted' of any further productivity gains.

The size of Asia's rice lands is shrinking, under pressure from industrialisation and urbanisation. In China, the area under rice fell from 37 million ha in 1976 to 31 million ha in 1996. Further, soil salinisation, waterlogging and other degradation associated with intensive rice cropping may lead to a net drop in Asia's total irrigated area. Land suitable for further expansion of rice is also disappearing: water and wind erosion are estimated to affect some 400 million ha of the region's farm land, while another 47 million are subject to chemical and physical degradation. Over the next 25 years, uncropped land will be halved in South Asia and reduced by one-third in East Asia. The quantity and quality of water available for rice growing is also expected to decline.

Last, but not least, production will also be affected by the 'greying' of Asia's rice farming population. The average age of farmers is increasing in almost every country, in parallel with its rate of industrialisation. In Korea, the number of rice farmers fell by two-thirds between 1965 and 1995. Urbanisation and industrialisation will further reduce the labour force, push up farm wages, increase farm size, and increase pressure for mechanisation.

Conclusion: even if the current level of productivity is sustained, it cannot match the food needs of Asia's expanding population. Some rice scientists say that only aggressive research aimed at breaking through present yield ceilings and establishing a new, stable yield plateau can 'help prevent a disaster'.

Hybrids and 'super rice'

The future research scenario will probably focus on hybrid rice and what is known as the New Plant Type (NPT), or 'super rice'. Hybrid rice is the only genetic yield-enhancing technology to have emerged since the Green Revolution. With yields up to 20% higher than those of conventional HYVs, hybrids have been widely adopted in China, where they now cover more than 50% of the total rice-planted area and account for about two-thirds of national production. However, transferring Chinese hybrid technology to other Asian countries has proven difficult, mainly due to the technical problems and costs involved in producing hybrid seeds. FAO and IRRI have now created a task force to promote development and use of hybrids in 12 other Asian countries. Meanwhile, work on 'super rice' is virtually complete at IRRI, and the plant promises to increase land productivity significantly. However, further intensive research will be needed to realize NPT's full potential of 15 tonnes/ha, and improve its disease and insect-pest resistance.

Biotechnology can also help, improving resistance to major pests and diseases, and transferring genes to rice from wild and unrelated species.

Finally, to be effective, strategies to increase Asian rice production must be supported by sound government policies and will depend heavily on adequate information on genetic resources, land use, water availability and irrigation potential.

Source: FAO: AG21: Magazine: Spotlight: Rice

http://www.fao.org/WAICENT/FAOINFO/AGRICULT/magazine/9809/spot1.htm

People and their Needs
Economic activities

CHANGES IN FARMING IN AN MEDC

SUMMARY Farming in Britain has changed lots over the last 50 years. The Common Agricultural Policy of the European Union has affected farms with laws, grants and subsidies.

During the Second World War, Britain was faced with being starved into defeat. After the war, new laws aimed to make Britain able to produce all the food that it needed.

In 1973, Britain joined the Common Market (now called the European Union) and adopted the **Common Agricultural Policy (CAP)**. The CAP aimed to:

- produce more food
- increase average field and farm sizes and farmers' incomes
- restrict imports from outside the EU
- create a single market in which agricultural products could move freely within the EU.

The CAP pays **guaranteed fixed prices** for products. Farmers receive extra payments called **subsidies**. By the 1980s, the CAP had led to **surpluses** (unwanted extras – cereal, butter and beef mountains and milk and wine lakes). Milk **quotas** (limits on how much can be produced) were introduced to reduce overproduction of milk.

In 1992, the CAP was revised because of the costs, environmental problems and surpluses which it had made. **Set aside** was introduced, where farmers are paid not to farm parts of their land for five years. Land can be left **fallow**, trees can be planted or land can be used for non-farming purposes. The CAP has used subsidies to encourage farmers to grow some crops such as oil seed rape because of a shortage of vegetable oil.

Agribusiness is when farms are large and industrialised, with larger fields, more machinery and fewer workers. Wetlands have been drained and hedges removed to make more profit.

FIGURE 3.30
Oil seed rape

Changes in farming in an MEDC 149

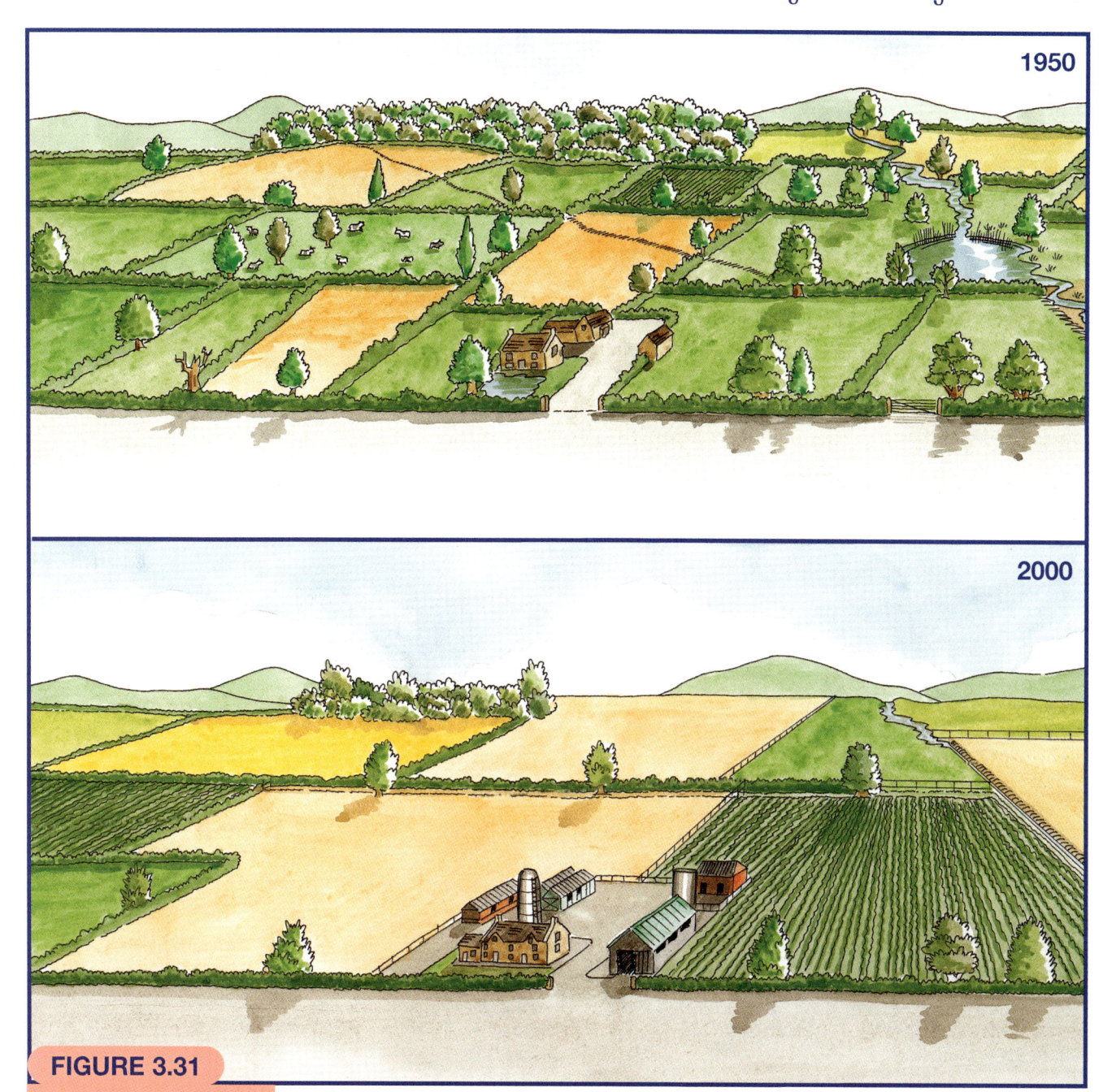

1950

2000

FIGURE 3.31
A farm in 1950 and in 2000

TASKS

1 Why did UK farming start to change 50 years ago?
2 Define:
   - CAP
   - guaranteed prices
   - subsidies
   - surpluses.
3 Look at the sketches in Figure 3.31.
   a On a whole page, sketch the year 2000 picture.
   b Use arrows and labels to answer the following questions:
      - What changed between 1950 and 2000?
      - Why did these changes happen?
4 What problems did the CAP create?
5 Explain what quotas and set aside aim to do.
6 What is agribusiness?

three — People and their Needs
Economic activities

THE ENVIRONMENTAL IMPACT OF FARMING

Removal of hedgerows

Between 1945 and 1990, 380 000 km of hedgerows (nearly 50% of the UK's total) were removed. Large machines can be used in bigger fields, so space is created by removing hedges.

Maintaining hedges is also expensive and they provide a home to harmful insects and pests. However, hedges are windbreaks to protect soil from erosion and they are also home to lots of wildlife.

BBC News Online — Thursday, August 12, 1999 Published at 11:10 GMT 12:10 UK

Farmland birds in crisis

By Environment Correspondent Alex Kirby

A team of British researchers is calling for reform of Europe's agricultural policy to allow birds and other wild creatures a greater chance of survival. The team estimates that, in Britain alone, loss of biodiversity has meant the disappearance of 10 million breeding individuals of 10 farmland bird species in the past two decades. They say: 'Parallel changes have taken place in many other European countries.'

History repeats itself
In all, 116 species of farmland birds — one-fifth of European avifauna — are now of conservation concern. Intensification of agriculture 'is about making as great a proportion of primary production as possible available for human consumption. To the extent that this is achieved, the rest of nature is bound to suffer.'

They identify some key changes in British farming over the last 30 years:

- land drainage
- hedgerow removal
- introduction of new crop types
- increased use of agrochemicals, and a move towards monoculture
- a change from spring to autumn sowing
- the harvesting of grass for silage
- a reduction in the traditional rotation of crops.

The researchers say most of the evidence that farming is to blame for what is happening to the birds 'is by association, but in sum total it is damning'. Annual BTO censuses of 42 species of breeding birds show that 13 species living exclusively in farmland, such as the skylark and corn bunting, declined by an average of 30% between 1968 and 1995. 'Yet 29 species of habitat generalists, such as the carrion crow and the wren, have increased by an average of 23%.'

The researchers say there are agricultural schemes in the UK that could help biodiversity.

But there is 'no magic bullet with which to reverse the declines of a large suite of species … the most general prescription is to reverse the intensification of agriculture'.

Areas for research they recommend include the effects of introducing more variety into farming.

Chemical pollution

Pollutants are washed from fields by rainwater, and silage and slurry (animal waste) can pollute water. Farming led to 13% of recorded pollution incidents in England and Wales in 1994. The effects of pollution include:

- less variety of species in fresh water, with an increase in a few species such as algae
- wildlife is poisoned by pesticides
- chemicals may affect human health.

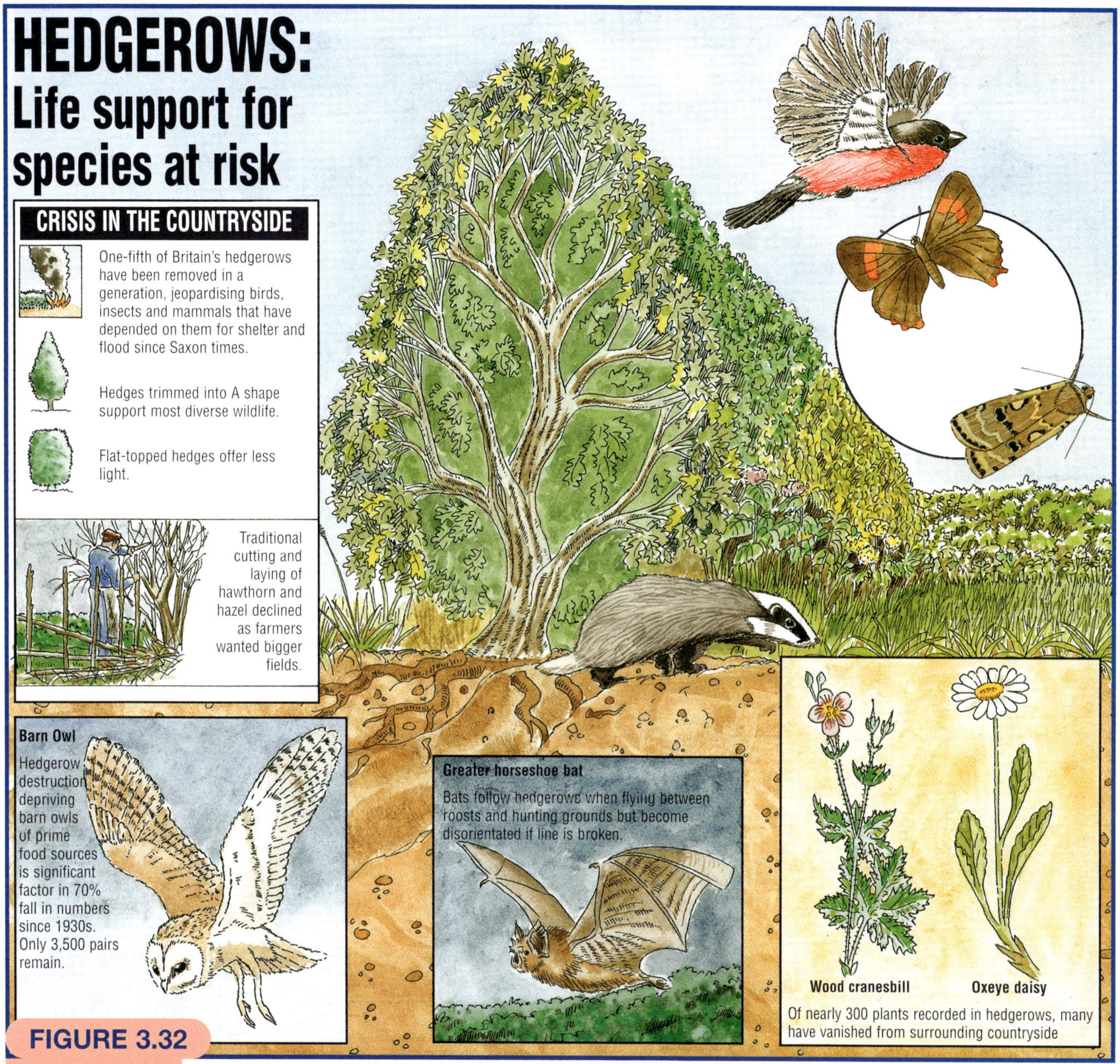

The environmental impact of farming

HEDGEROWS: Life support for species at risk

CRISIS IN THE COUNTRYSIDE

One-fifth of Britain's hedgerows have been removed in a generation, jeopardising birds, insects and mammals that have depended on them for shelter and flood since Saxon times.

Hedges trimmed into A shape support most diverse wildlife.

Flat-topped hedges offer less light.

Traditional cutting and laying of hawthorn and hazel declined as farmers wanted bigger fields.

Barn Owl
Hedgerow destruction depriving barn owls of prime food sources is significant factor in 70% fall in numbers since 1930s. Only 3,500 pairs remain.

Greater horseshoe bat
Bats follow hedgerows when flying between roosts and hunting grounds but become disorientated if line is broken.

Wood cranesbill   Oxeye daisy
Of nearly 300 plants recorded in hedgerows, many have vanished from surrounding countryside

FIGURE 3.32
Hedgerows at risk

FIGURE 3.33
Farmland birds are in crisis

TASKS

1. a List all of the ways that modern farming changes the natural environment.
   b How could farmers cause less damage to the environment?
2. Look at Figure 3.32. Design a poster to 'Save our hedgerows'. Include evidence about why hedgerows are important.
3. Read the newspaper article on page 150 and look at Figure 3.33. Why are people concerned about farmland birds?
4. How does farming result in chemical pollution?
5. What are the effects of chemical pollution?

three
People and their Needs
Economic activities

THE LOCATION OF INDUSTRY

SUMMARY The location of industry is affected by factors such as transport, raw materials, markets, labour and power supply.

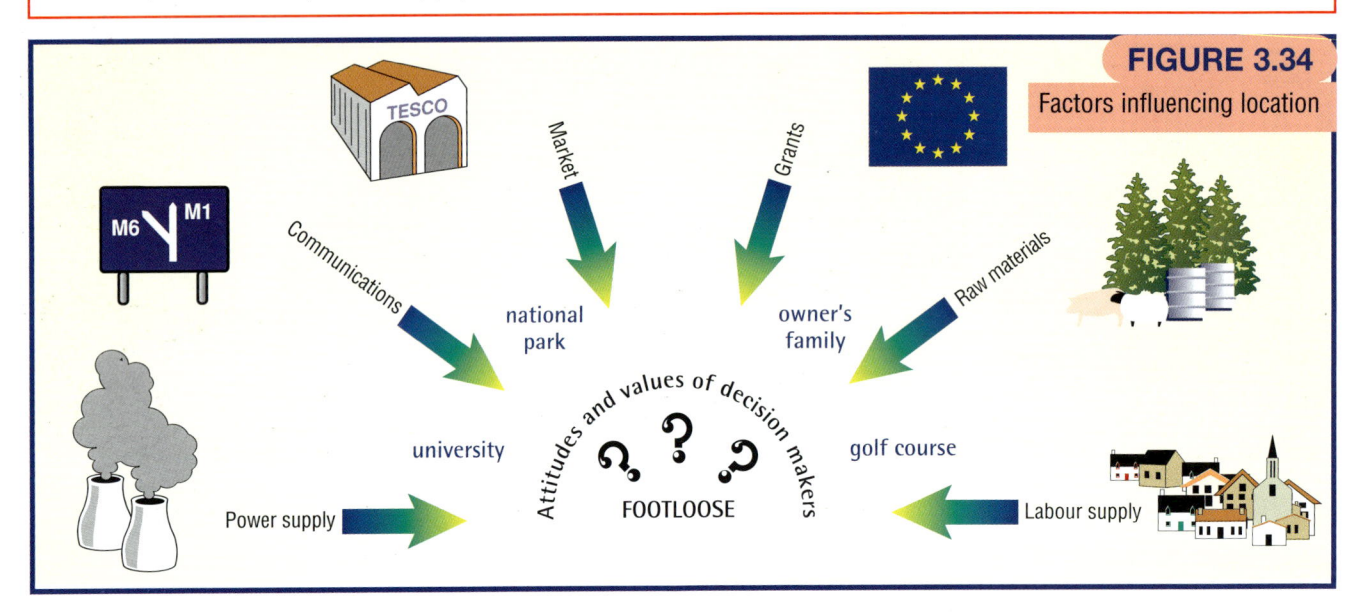

FIGURE 3.34 Factors influencing location

There are many things which affect where a new factory is built. Some of these are shown in Figure 3.34. Sometimes one factor is particularly important. For example, a frozen peas factory needs to be close to where the peas are grown so they are fresh. The natural things needed to make products are called **raw materials**.

Labour supply (workforce) may be the most important factor. In Birmingham's Jewellery Quarter, special skills are needed. Being near to an **energy** source is important for industries such as aluminium smelting. Locating near to the **market** (customers) can be important if the factory is making fresh items such as bread, or beer which is heavy and expensive to transport.

Transport is very important. Motorway junctions are accessible places and popular industrial locations. Before cars and lorries existed, industry located by canals so coal could be delivered. Some factories have stayed alongside canals, although they now use electricity and road and rail transport. Staying in a location when the original factor no longer applies is called **industrial inertia**.

Some industries today can locate almost anywhere – they are **footloose**. Where managers want to live can influence the location chosen. **Grants** and help from the Government or the European Union can help businesses to decide where to locate.

TASKS

1. Write a sentence to explain how each of the following affects where factories locate:
   - raw materials
   - labour supply
   - energy source
   - transport
   - market
   - grants.

2. Name a factory near where you live. Suggest why it is located there.

3. Match up the key word and definition and copy out:

Footloose	means 'factories stay in original location'.
Accessible	means 'can locate anywhere'.
Industrial inertia	means 'easy to get to'.

ARGOS DISTRIBUTION WAREHOUSE, STAFFORD

FIGURE 3.35
Argos, Acton Gate, Stafford

This warehouse was built in 1998 to supply goods to regional bases throughout Britain. The location was chosen for several reasons:

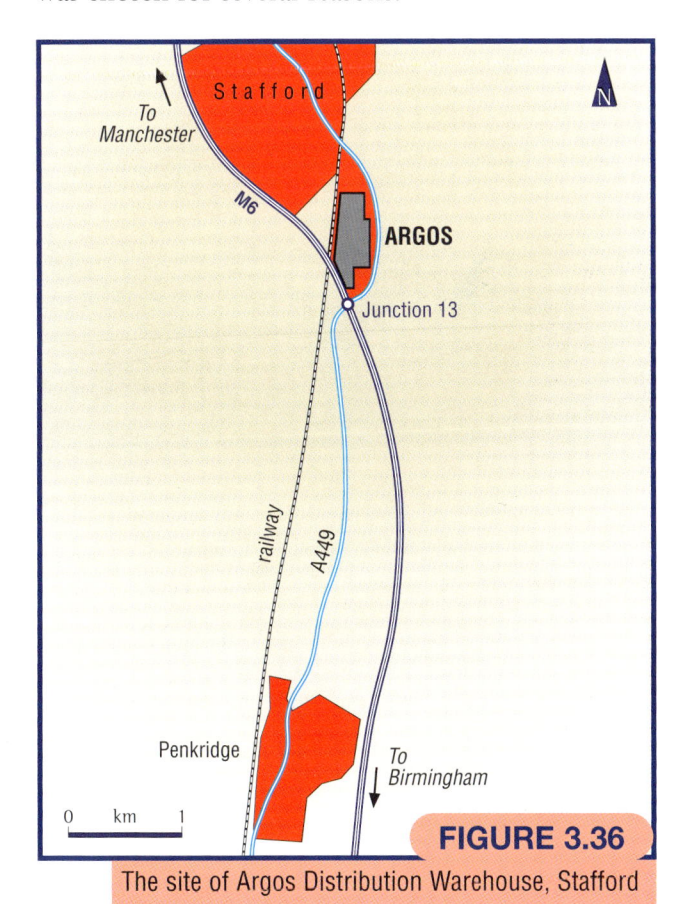

Transport	The M6 crosses the A449 at this junction.
	It is in central England so deliveries can be made to many places.
Labour	The town of Stafford is nearby.
	Many workers used to work at the smaller warehouse nearby before this warehouse was built.
Flat site	The land was easy to build on.
Greenfield site	The land had not been used before.

However, the site is too small and there is no room to expand.

FIGURE 3.36
The site of Argos Distribution Warehouse, Stafford

TASKS

Look at the photograph (Figure 3.35) and map (Figure 3.36).
1 Describe the photograph.
2 Use the map and photograph evidence to explain why this location was chosen.
3 Use the map and photograph to work out which direction the camera was pointing towards.
4 a Planners did not allow this building to be taller. Suggest why.
   b What else stops Argos from expanding this site?

People and their Needs
Economic activities

ALCAN SMELTER, LYNEMOUTH

FIGURE 3.37
The Lynemouth smelter

Aluminium is a metal used for many things from making turkey foil to aircraft wings. It is made from bauxite (a rock found in places such as Jamaica). Aluminium is produced in the Northumberland village of Lynemouth even though there is no bauxite nearby. There are many reasons why this location was chosen:

- The smelter has its own power station and coal mine to provide power.
- The Government gave a grant of £28 million to create jobs here.
- Many former coal miners now work there.
- There was a large area of flat land available.
- Aluminium is supplied to firms in the UK, Ireland and the rest of Europe.
- Alumina powder (refined bauxite) is imported to produce aluminium. There is a direct railway line to the port where raw materials are brought in.

Alcan smelter, Lynemouth

TASKS

1 Draw a sketch of Figure 3.37. Label:
   a the aluminium smelter
   b the power station
   c the coal mine
   d the railway
   e the North Sea.

2 Look at Figure 3.37. Use Figure 3.38 to work out which direction the camera was pointing towards.

3 Look at Figure 3.38.
   a Name four settlements within 5 km of the Alcan smelter.
   b How far is it by rail from the smelter to where alumina is imported?

4 Write a paragraph to explain why this location was chosen. Include and underline these words:
   - power supply
   - labour
   - grant
   - market
   - transport
   - flat land.

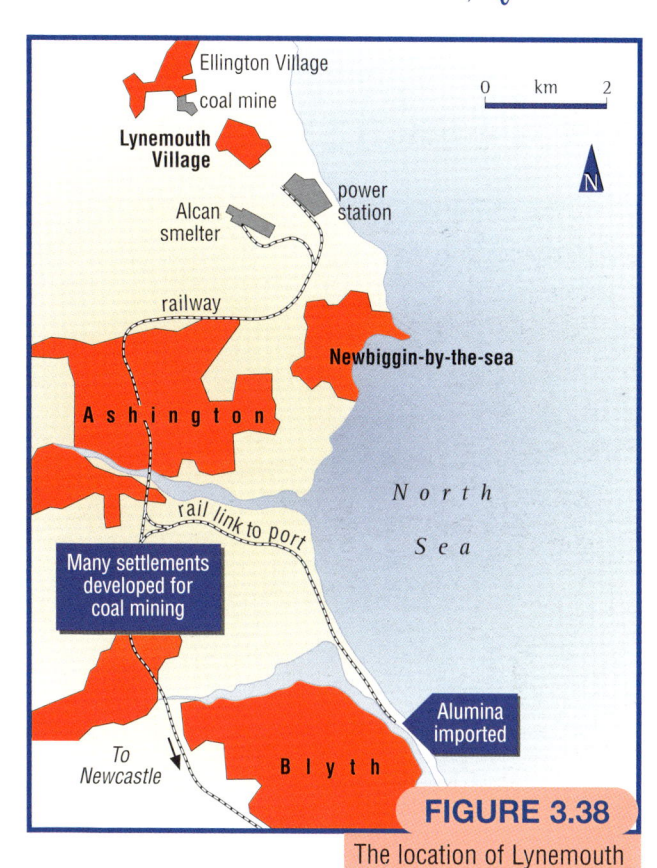

FIGURE 3.38 The location of Lynemouth

FIGURE 3.39 Ellington Colliery

three
■ People and their Needs

Economic activities

THE EFFECTS OF TOURISM – MENORCA

FIGURE 3.40
Menorca holiday photo

SUMMARY Tourism has grown rapidly. It brings benefits and problems.

Menorca is one of the Spanish Balearic islands in the Mediterranean Sea. It is only 19 km from north to south and 48 km from east to west with a population of 69 000. Over the last 50 years, tourism has developed and become the largest employer in Menorca. Before tourism grew, many young people, especially men, left the island to look for work. Now the population is rising by a thousand people a year. Some are foreigners moving there to retire.

Three-quarters of visitors to Menorca are British. Most of the rest are German or Scandinavian.

Figure 3.41 shows that many fishing villages have been built up with hotels, shops and apartments. Tourism has benefits. Jobs have been created in hotels as well as for people making things such as crafts and ice creams. This spiral of growth is the **multiplier effect**.

FIGURE 3.41
Development in Menorca

The effects of tourism – Menorca

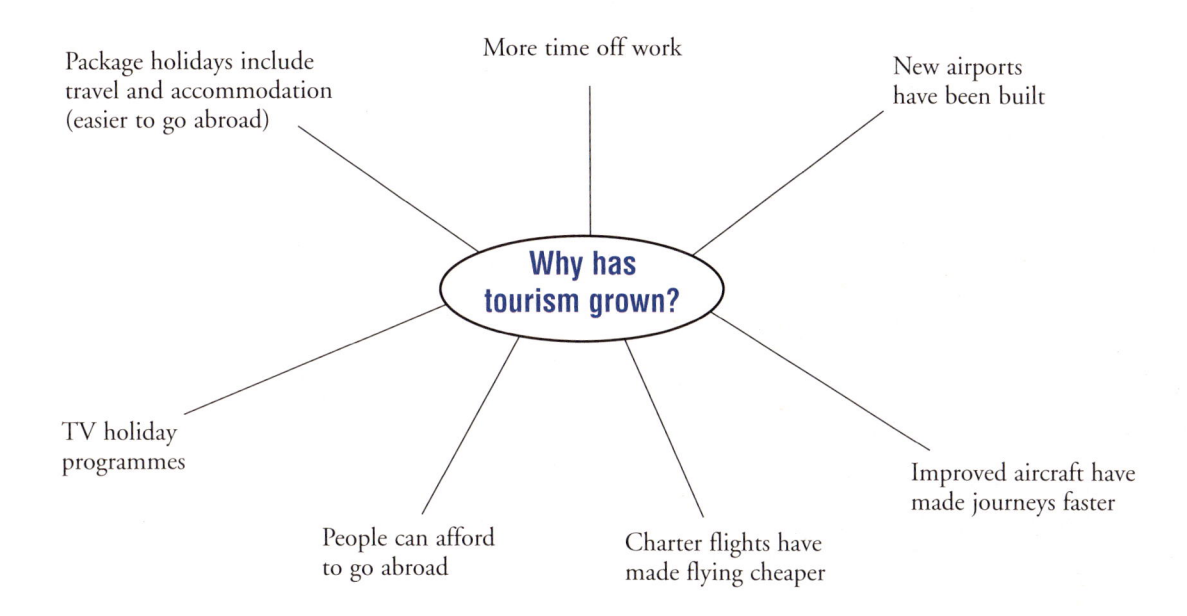

Why has tourism grown?
- Package holidays include travel and accommodation (easier to go abroad)
- More time off work
- New airports have been built
- TV holiday programmes
- People can afford to go abroad
- Charter flights have made flying cheaper
- Improved aircraft have made journeys faster

Tourism in Menorca is **seasonal**. There are few tourists between November and April when it is wet. The government provides *paro* (money for tourism workers who are unemployed during winter). The government is trying to preserve the island's traditional language (Menorqui) with laws and fines.

Some of the oldest hotels are eyesores. Today, rules say that new buildings within 250 m of the coast cannot be higher than two storeys. Undeveloped areas are protected. Many Menorcans believe that enough development has taken place.

FIGURE 3.42 Menorca's climate

TASKS

1. Look at Figure 3.40. List the pull factors (good things) which attract tourists to Menorca.
2. Suggest five different jobs in the tourism industry.
3. What is the multiplier effect?
4. Use Figure 3.42 to describe how temperature and rainfall vary in Menorca. Include actual months and numbers in your answer.
5. Copy the diagram 'Why has tourism grown?'
6. Suggest five problems caused by tourism.
7. a Find out more about Menorca on the internet. Use search engines to find relevant sites.
   b Design a page of a holiday brochure for a holiday to Menorca. You could use photographs and information from the internet and produce it using ICT.

three
People and their Needs
Economic activities

THE EFFECTS OF TOURISM – KENYA

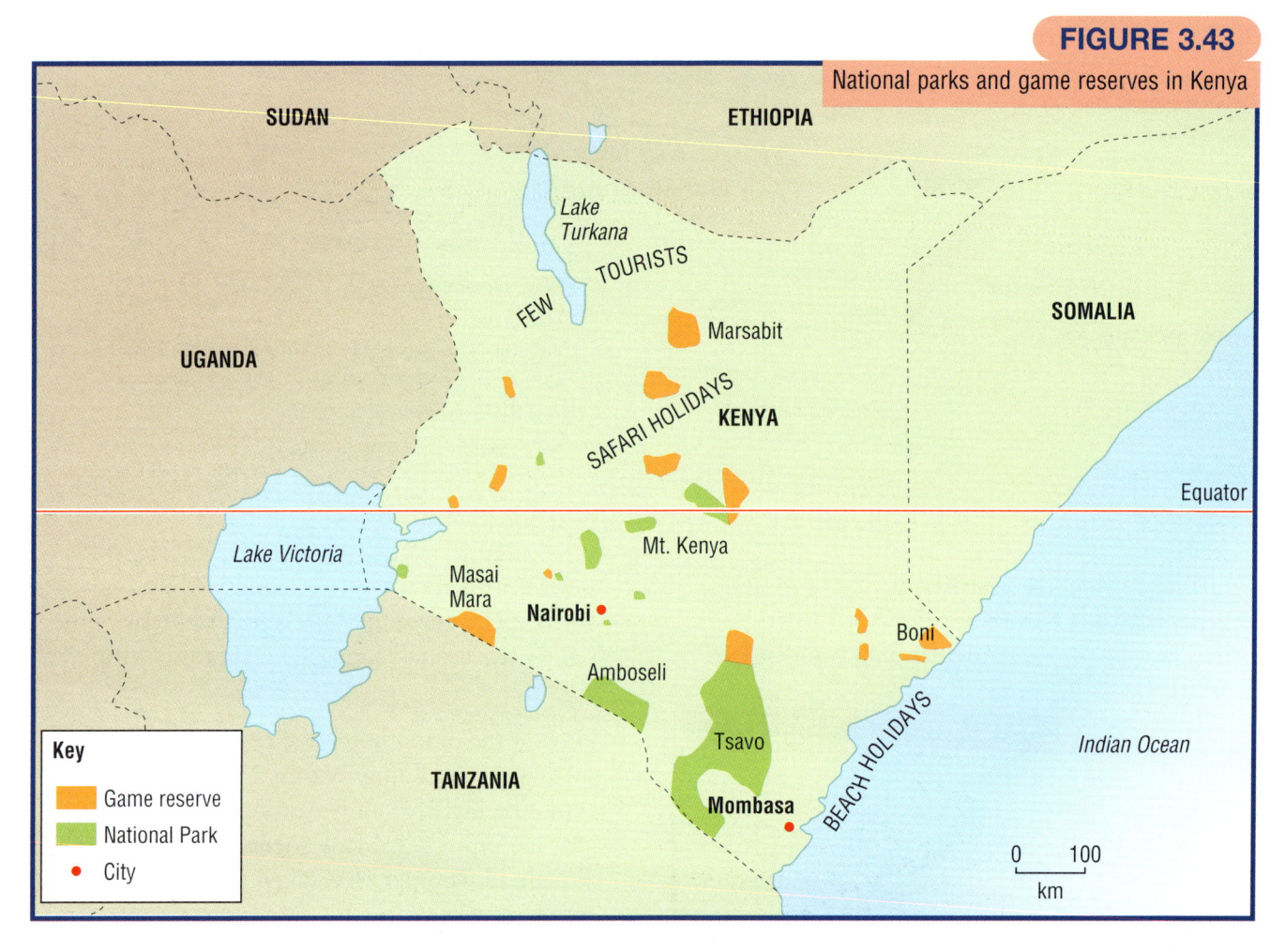

FIGURE 3.43
National parks and game reserves in Kenya

Why did tourism grow in Kenya?

Mass tourism came to Kenya 30 years later than Menorca. Larger aircraft could fly further and many people were looking for a different type of holiday. Television programmes promoted things like safari holidays. It is hot and sunny in Kenya all year round. Kenya has beach resorts, national parks and game reserves.

FIGURE 3.44
A Kenyan beach holiday

The effects of tourism – Kenya

Benefits

- Jobs have been created.
- Tourism became Kenya's biggest earner.
- Airports and roads have been improved.
- Water supply has improved in places such as Mombasa.

Problems

- Some parts of Kenya have not attracted tourists.
- Most new jobs are in cities. People migrate to cities and live in shanty towns.
- Many jobs are unskilled and poorly paid.
- Travel companies, airlines and hotels are often foreign owned. More than half of the money paid for holidays never comes to Kenya.
- Environmental problems include sewage in the sea.
- Some people who used to live in the national parks have been forced out.
- Traditional ways of life are being threatened.
- Drugs and crime have increased.
- Since the 1990s, the number of visitors to Kenya from the UK has decreased. People are worried about safety.

TASKS

1. What attracts tourists to Kenya?
2. Look at Figure 3.43. Name one game reserve, one city and one national park in Kenya.
3. Explain two benefits and two problems caused by tourism in Kenya.
4. Design a poster including words and pictures to encourage more people to go to Kenya on holiday. Websites such as http://www.kenyaweb.com/ provide useful information.

FIGURE 3.45
Safari traffic jam when a lion is sighted

three

People and their Needs

Energy

CHANGING ENERGY USE IN THE UK

SUMMARY Coal used to be the most important fuel in the UK. Now nearly all of the coal mines have closed. Gas and oil provide most of our energy.

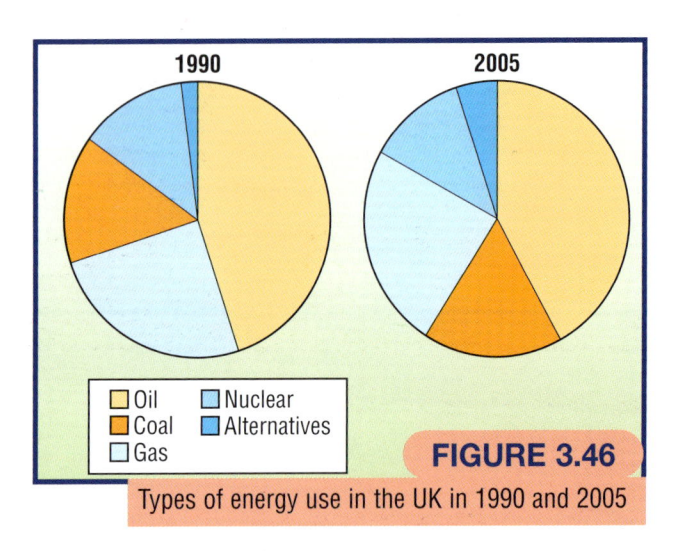

FIGURE 3.46 Types of energy use in the UK in 1990 and 2005

- Oil
- Nuclear
- Coal
- Alternatives
- Gas

FIGURE 3.47 UK coalfields

Coalfields: Central Scotland, Ayrshire, Northumberland, Durham, Lancashire, North Wales, Yorkshire, Staffordshire, Notts/Derby, Leicestershire, South Wales, Kent

The coal industry

The source of our energy continues to change. Our Industrial Revolution was based on coal. Factories were built and towns grew where coal could be easily dug (Figure 3.47). But the coal industry has been in decline since the 1920s. Only a few 'super pits' now survive in the UK and one-third of UK-produced coal comes from open-cast mines, such as in north-east Derbyshire (Figure 3.51). It is cheaper to buy coal from other countries.

Most coal is sold to power stations to make electricity, and the electricity companies save money by importing coal. They have also built new power stations that burn natural gas (Figure 3.52) as it is cheaper than coal. Some coal-fired power stations were converted to burn gas too. Gas produces less pollution, such as acid rain. When coal is burned, it gives off CO_2 and SO_4. Some coal-fired power stations have had expensive filters fitted to reduce pollution, but that has put up the cost of electricity. Alternative, cleaner energy sources are now being developed, such as wind power.

Year	Amount of coal mined (m tonnes)	No. of mines	No. of miners	Average amount coal produced per miner (tonnes)
1950	220	901	688 000	320
1960	197	698	588 000	335
1970	145	292	286 000	507
1980	126	211	230 000	548
1990	81	73	65 000	1 462
2000	43	13	7 000	6 143

Figure 3.48 The British coal mining industry

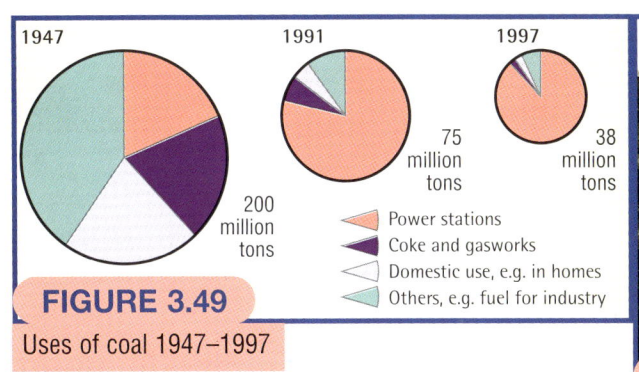

Changing energy use in the UK

FIGURE 3.49 Uses of coal 1947–1997

(1947: 200 million tons; 1991: 75 million tons; 1997: 38 million tons)

- Power stations
- Coke and gasworks
- Domestic use, e.g. in homes
- Others, e.g. fuel for industry

FIGURE 3.51 Open-cast site in Derbyshire

FIGURE 3.52 A modern gas-fired power station at Sutton Bridge, Lincolnshire

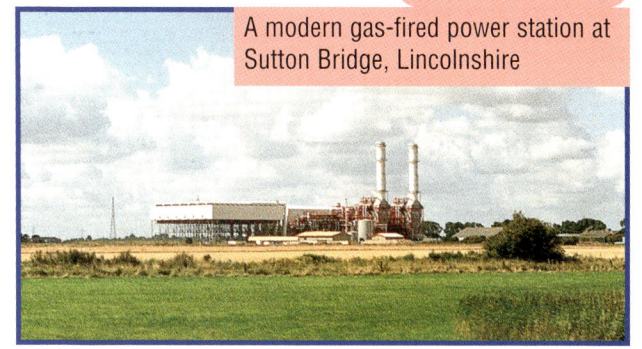

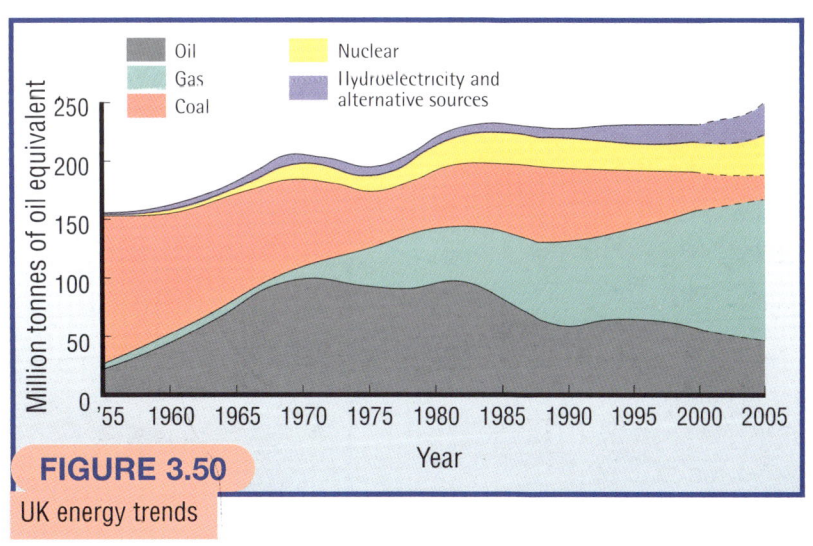

Oil and gas

The UK has oilfields under the North Sea and Irish Sea. A lot of gas has been extracted from under the North Sea too. These have reduced the amount of energy that needs importing, and taken over from coal as the UK's main energy sources. Gas now provides one-third of all the energy used in the UK. In the 1990s, it was chosen for most new power stations. This became known as 'the dash for gas'. It is a cleaner fuel than coal and the new power stations helped the Government meet international pollution agreements.

FIGURE 3.50 UK energy trends

(Oil, Gas, Coal, Nuclear, Hydroelectricity and alternative sources; Million tonnes of oil equivalent, 1955–2005)

TASKS

1. Look at Figure 3.46. Which is the most important type of energy in the UK today?

2. a Draw the axes for a line graph. The horizontal axis goes from 1950 to 2000. The vertical axis goes from 0 to 1 600.
   b Use the information in Figure 3.48 to plot the points for a line graph of the number of coal mines. Choose a colour for the line that joins up the points. Use the same colour for labelling the line, 'Coal mines'.
   c Onto the same graph, plot the points for another line to show 'Coal produced per miner'. Use a different colour.
   d Give your graph a title, 'Fewer but more productive coal mines'.

3. Open-cast coal mining has become more important. Use Figure 3.51 to describe how it affects an area.

4. a What was the dash for gas?
   b What happens now as the gas under the North Sea runs out?

three
People and their Needs
Energy

MEETING FUTURE ENERGY DEMANDS

SUMMARY Alternative energy sources are producing more of the UK's energy. Many people are worried about the safety of nuclear power. Some people object to wind power. They do not like the sight or sound of wind turbines.

The government wants 4% of the UK's energy to come from alternative energy sources, such as wind and hydro-electric power. At present, it is less than 1%.

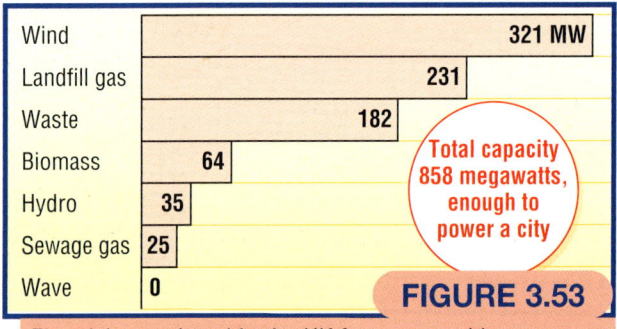

Wind	321 MW
Landfill gas	231
Waste	182
Biomass	64
Hydro	35
Sewage gas	25
Wave	0

Total capacity 858 megawatts, enough to power a city

FIGURE 3.53
Electricity produced in the UK from renewable resources

Nuclear power

Nuclear power provides 28% of the UK's needs, but there are concerns over safety. The fuel is a radioactive rock called uranium. Heat is produced from nuclear fission. The heat turns water into steam. The steam is used to drive the turbines that generate the electricity. Nuclear power stations tend to be located on flat, coastal sites. They use vast amounts of sea water for cooling.

In 1986, an explosion at Chernobyl nuclear power station in the Ukraine killed 31 people. A large area was contaminated. Radiation blew as far as the UK and polluted rain made soil radioactive in parts of Wales and Scotland. Some farmers in Wales still have a ban on the sale of their sheep. As well as the safety of the power stations, there is concern about nuclear waste. The Irish Sea has been polluted by waste from Sellafield in Cumbria. Nuclear fuel waste must be stored in a safe environment. It stays radioactive for thousands of years.

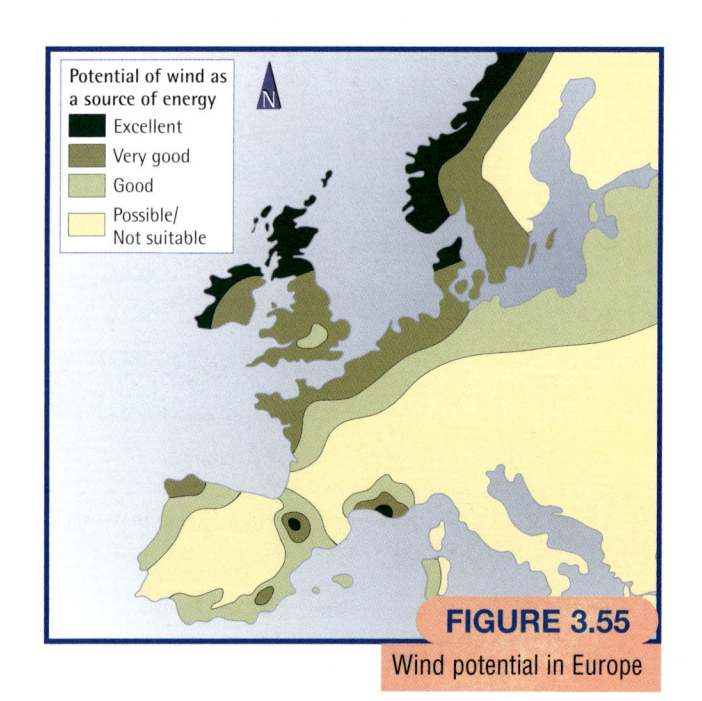

FIGURE 3.54
UK nuclear power stations

Wind power

Wind power is safer but there is still opposition. Britain has nearly half of Europe's wind potential (Figure 3.55).

FIGURE 3.55
Wind potential in Europe

Meeting future energy demands 163

Electricity is generated by large blades turning a turbine. To be worthwhile, several wind turbines need to be located together on a **wind farm**. They only work when the wind blows and, if it is too strong, they have to be shut down. The energy they produce causes no air pollution and they use very little land. Most are on high land in the west of Britain (Figure 3.56). Protesters say they produce very little energy and spoil remote places. The buzz can be heard up to 10 km away.

FIGURE 3.57
A wind farm in mid-Wales

FIGURE 3.56
Wind power stations in England and Wales

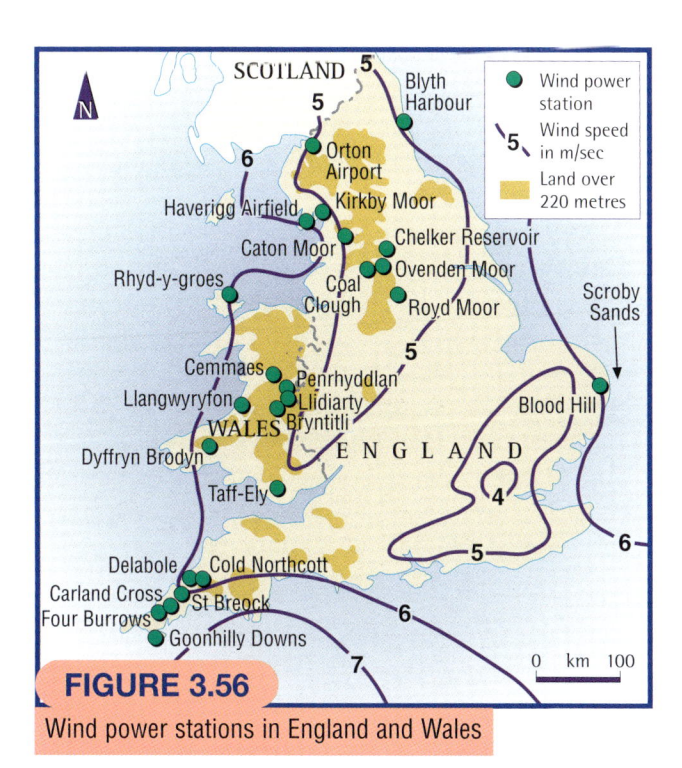

There is a plan to build a wind farm with 25 turbines off the Norfolk coast on Scroby Sandbank, near Great Yarmouth (Figure 3.56). Despite being away from people, there are concerns for seabirds and basking seals.

TASKS

1 Describe the location of UK nuclear power stations. What do most of these sites have in common?
2 What are the advantages of nuclear power over fossil fuels?
3 Why are people concerned about nuclear power?
4 Study Figure 3.55. Identify the parts of Britain which have the best potential for wind farms.
5 Study Figure 3.56. Describe the location of the UK wind farms. How many are located in beautiful areas, like national parks?
6 Explain why four out of five people support wind power, yet there is considerable opposition to wind farms.

three
People and their Needs
Energy

HOLMEWOOD

SUMMARY Holmewood is a village built for coal miners. When the mine closed in 1970, unemployment went up and local shops closed. Now an enterprise zone has attracted new industry.

Holmewood was built about 100 years ago, on the North Derbyshire coalfield, when a new coal mine was dug. The mine closed in 1970 and 2 299 mining jobs were lost. Some of Holmewood's miners took jobs at other mines, but every Derbyshire mine has now closed. By 1987, unemployment in Holmewood was 18%, nearly twice the national average. People have less money to spend, and some of the local shops and services have had to close down.

Holmewood found it hard to attract new industry. Its houses were old and many were in poor condition. The environment had been spoiled by the waste from mining. There was subsidence where the land had sunk after the coal underneath had been removed and there were pollution problems. Some families moved away to look for work. Many who stayed saw their community decline. More people suffered stress and poor diet. They stopped believing in themselves.

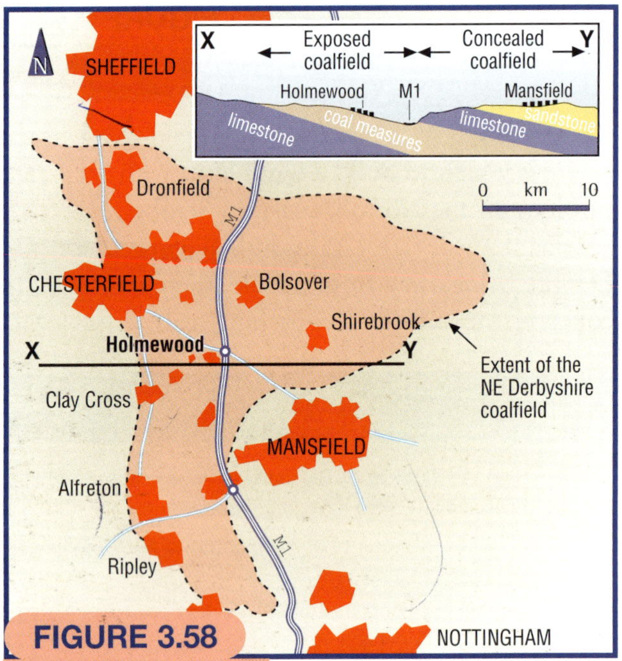

FIGURE 3.58 Location of Holmewood

Holmewood pit closure is to be brought forward

Geological faults in the main coal seam have brought forward the closure date. The life of the pit, which employs 800 men, was very limited, the spokesman said, because of the near exhaustion of workable coal reserves.

A closure date is to be announced within the next few weeks, but the men would be offered jobs at other North Derbyshire collieries, he said.

Holmewood Colliery, which produces about 6,500 tons a week, was said three years ago to be a short-life pit, due for closure by 1970.

The last coal face in the main seam will be worked out by the end of September, leaving only the Three-Quarter Seam, which is uneconomic and difficult to mine.

Figure 3.59 Newspaper extract (based on the *Sheffield Telegraph* report, 1968)

Holmewood

The local council set about improving the area, reclaiming the waste land and setting up an **enterprise zone**. It attracted new industry, promising there would be no rates to pay for ten years. It is close to the M1 motorway for good transport links.

New jobs have been created, but only 23% of the workers at Holmewood Enterprise Zone come from Holmewood. Unemployment in the village is still high. Some new housing has been built, but most people in these houses commute to Sheffield, Chesterfield or Nottingham.

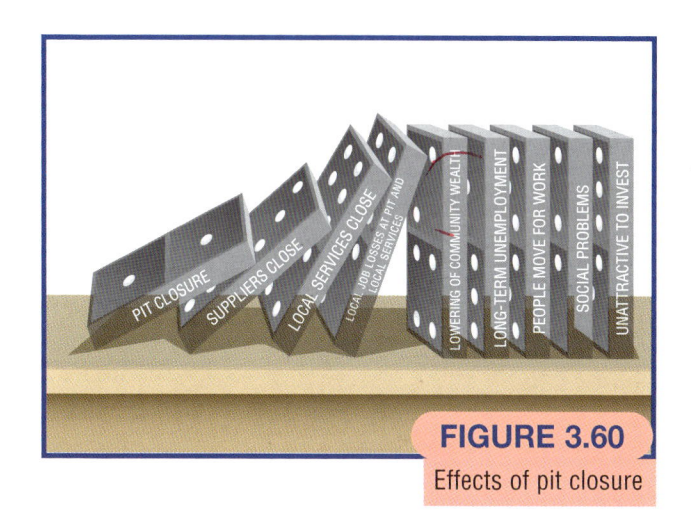

FIGURE 3.60 Effects of pit closure

TASKS

1. Why did some of the shops in Holmewood close down when the mine closed?
2. Look at Figure 3.60. Use it to explain why the closure of coal mines has a 'domino effect' on an area.
3. a What has been done to try to give Holmewood a future?
   b How successful has it been so far?
4. Describe the buildings in Holmewood Enterprise Zone (Figure 3.61).

FIGURE 3.61 New industry in Holmewood Enterprise Zone

three
■ People and their Needs

Energy

CONSETT AFTER COAL AND STEEL

> **SUMMARY** Consett once had lots of jobs at Britain's largest ironworks. After it closed in 1980, unemployment was very high. Project Genesis was a plan to bring new jobs to Consett.

FIGURE 3.62
Consett's improved transport infrastructure

Consett is a town of 25 000 people, high on the edge of the Pennines in north-east Durham. In 1841, it was a village community of only 145, but about to become a boom town. Below ground was coal and ironstone. Nearby was limestone. These were the three ingredients needed for blast furnaces to produce iron and steel. Thousands of migrants came to find work. The iron company looked after its workers, providing houses, a hospital, schools and a library. It did not have to pay high prices for coal as it owned 37 coal mines, so it could make iron at a good price. In less than 30 years, it became the largest ironworks in Britain.

As early as 1852, local ironstone was running out. It was cheaper to bring it from the Cleveland Hills in Yorkshire. Later it came from Kiruna in Sweden. This was the first sign of industrial inertia (page 152).

A report in 1970 identified the best locations for making iron and steel as large, flat sites at the coast next to deep-water ports. Consett's future was to change as rapidly as it had done 140 years earlier. In 1980, the steelworks closed and 3 715 people lost their jobs. As well as the steelworks, thousands more jobs were lost in other businesses such as transport and local shops. This is the multiplier effect.

By 1981, Consett's unemployment was the worst in England. Many young people moved away looking for work. The need was to make Consett attractive to new industry. The government improved the road network, the local environment and services. In 1992, Project Genesis was announced.

Consett after coal and steel

FIGURE 3.63
Pleasant surroundings for making Phileas Fogg crisps

Project Genesis

The first stage was to reclaim the massive site – as big as 280 football pitches. Not all is for new industry; some is being used for recreation and some has gone back to agriculture. There is public open space and land for horseriding. Large areas are set aside for new factories in parkland setting. Firms that are now established in Consett make crisps, caravans and Christmas decorations!

Project Genesis proposed a hotel to boost tourism, new shops to enlarge the town centre, and an extension to the bypass to make pedestrianisation possible. To the south of town, land was identified for a wind farm and a power station burning forest waste.

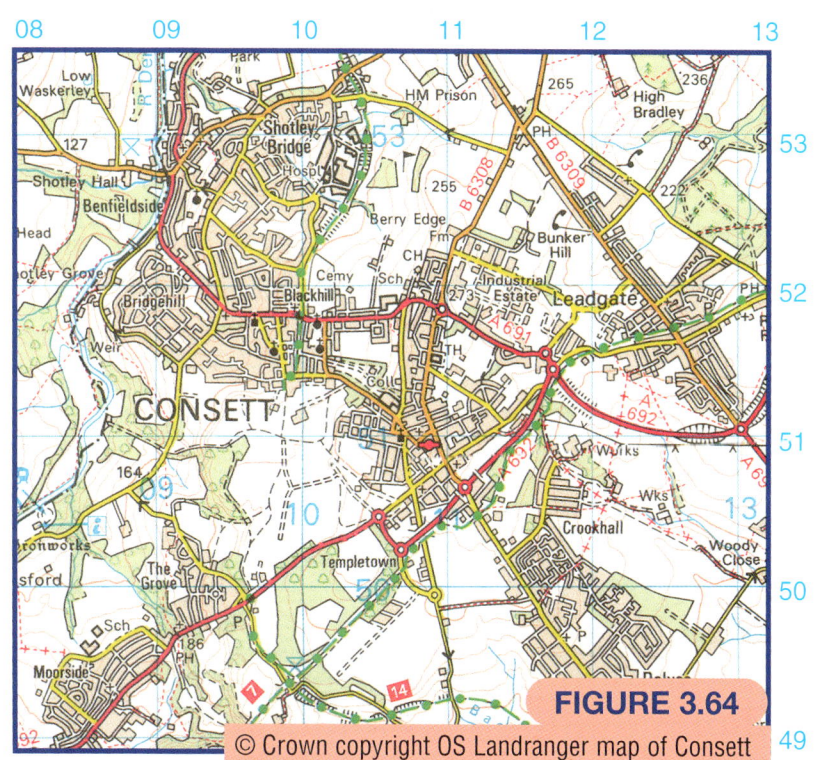

FIGURE 3.64
© Crown copyright OS Landranger map of Consett

TASKS

1. Find Consett in the atlas.
   a. What direction and distance is Consett from Newcastle?
   b. Use the atlas to describe the situation of Consett.
2. List the reasons why Consett became an important iron and steel town.
3. Write the story of Consett with a sentence for each of these dates: 1841, 1852, 1870, 1970, 1980, 1981, 1992.
4. How did the multiplier effect work in Consett?
5. a. Look at the Ordnance Survey map (Figure 3.64). Part of the steelworks was in the Templetown area of Consett. What is the land now used for?
   b. Figure 3.62 was taken from grid reference 111506 looking towards the north-east. What is the number of this road?
   c. This new road has been built along the route of an old railway which used to bring coal and iron ore to Consett. Most of the routes of old railways here are now shown with a green symbol. Use the key to an OS Landranger map to find out what this means (page 123).
   d. What map evidence is there that tourism is being developed in this area?
6. What are the advantages of having a wide variety of industries in a town, rather than most employment being at a single large employer?
7. How has the quality of life been improved in Consett?
8. Who should pay for schemes like Project Genesis?

three

■ People and their Needs

Advice

COURSEWORK FOR ECONOMIC ACTIVITIES

Farming

Farm-based coursework is difficult, unless you live on a farm, as contacts are needed. A single farm study works best if it is a farm which has different physical areas, such as a valley floor and hill tops. Two or more farms could be compared. This can provide more data and allow the similarities and differences to be described and explained.

1. Collect measurements and observations about the weather, soil and vegetation.
2. Produce a sketch map of the farm and label it.
3. Take photographs or draw sketches to annotate.
4. Interview the farmer to find out how and why the farm has changed.

FIGURE 3.65
Lake District Farm. If only sheep could be interviewed to increase primary data collection from farm studies!

Manufacturing industry

It can be difficult to get replies from letters to companies. Sometimes the information received does not help to investigate geography patterns and changes. It may be better to base your study upon observation.

Possible titles:

▸ An investigation into the distribution of industry in town A.

A Inner-city canalside location

B City-edge location near a motorway

FIGURE 3.66
Two industrial locations suitable for a comparative study

▸ A comparison of the old industrial area and the new industrial estates in town B.
▸ What are the advantages of the new industrial areas in town C?

Industrial areas can be identified on a map. Environmental quality surveys can be backed up with observations about things such as age of buildings, room for expansion and access to major roads. Photographs can be taken and traffic counts can be used to compare areas. It is important to try to explain *why* industry locates in particular places, and to use geographical terms such as accessibility and inner cities.

Coursework advice – Economic Activities

Tourism

Tourism and leisure are popular topics for coursework. Many studies are based in coastal resorts. Examples are shown in the table below.

Enquiry idea	Fieldwork possibilities	Secondary sources
The distribution of tourist attractions and facilities and the reasons for the distribution.	Observation of the physical attractions e.g. beach, cliffs and the human facilities.	Map the locations with the help of a large-scale map or plan.
How popular are the different attractions? Why are some more popular than others?	Do people counts. Give out questionnaires asking people where they have visited and why. Do an environmental quality survey. Examine ease of access e.g. car parks and public transport.	Visitor figures from the Council or Tourist Information Office. Local bus routes and timetables.
Comparison of spheres of influence between two beaches or two or more attractions.	Observation of their physical / human attractions. Questionnaires to visitors handed out at the attractions.	Leaflets about them and publicity. Use maps and timetables to study accessibility.

Advice

- Try not to just *describe* a tourist attraction or leisure centre.
- You need to collect data to investigate geographical ideas such as the sphere of influence.
- Think about comparing attractions.
- Plan ahead to make sure that you will be able to draw maps and graphs.

Leisure and tourism studies can also be based on inland areas. Parks, leisure centres and tourist attractions can be studied to find out where people have come from and the impact of visitors on places.

1 Map the attractions for visitors and take photographs as evidence.
2 Find information from tourist information centres, local councils and attractions. Try to find out how the number of visitors varies during the year.
3 Carry out a questionnaire survey. Do a draft version and pilot it by trying it with a few people. Figure 3.68 is an example of a questionnaire. It is important to design your own to fit your title.

FIGURE 3.67

Signpost outside York Minster to some of the other tourist attractions

VISITOR QUESTIONNAIRE
1. In which town (in the UK) or country (foreign visitor) do you live?
2. How have you travelled here (from within the UK)?
   Car   Bus   Train   Cycle   Other
3. How long are you staying?
   Less than 1 day   2–3 days   5–7 days   1–2 weeks   Longer
4. In what type of accommodation are you staying?
   Hotel   Guest house/BB   Friends/Relatives   Camping/caravan   Other
5. Rate the following on a scale of 1–5 (1= poor, 3 = average, 5 = good)

	1	2	3	4	5
York Minster					
Jorvik Museum					
The Walls					
The Shambles					
The Castle Museum					
Shopping					
Eating					
Parking					
Entertainment					
Service by the local people					
Tidiness					

FIGURE 3.68

Visitor questionnaire used in York

three ● People and their Needs

Advice

EXAMINATION TECHNIQUE – UNIT 3

Unit 3 is about how people live in different areas of the world and what they need to carry on their lives. You will have studied topics on farming, industry, tourism and energy in LEDCs and MEDCs. The examination advice from this unit focuses on how to improve case study answers. For many candidates, the case studies from this unit are the most difficult in which to score high marks. The questions from Paper 3 will concentrate on graphs.

The **case study** is usually the final section of a question and is worth 5 marks on Paper 1. Remember, the case study is marked by the examiner in 'levels'. The three levels are worth different marks. The level you are awarded depends on the quality of your answer. This is shown below:

- **Level 1**: worth 1 or 2 marks
  Simple statements (often they are vague or general)
- **Level 2**: worth 3 or 4 marks
  More specific statements (they are more precise and contain some detail)
- **Level 3**: worth 5 marks
  Detailed and accurate place-specific statements with a named example (as well as being precise, they refer to the named case study).

Throughout this book you will be learning about case studies. A case study is just a real-world example of the idea you are studying. See pages 233 and 238 for some examples of the different ways in which case study questions can be set out in the examination paper.

In case study questions you need to name the example which you are going to use. This may be a city, an area, or even an industry in your local town. You must then try to focus your answer on the example you have given. The examiner will be looking for facts about the example, not vague statements that might describe any industry or farm in any part of the world. The 'secret' to writing a Level 3 answer is to learn your notes and remember the details about why people grow rice in Bangladesh, or how tourism is spoiling the environment in the Yorkshire Dales National Park.

This first example of a case study question focuses on farming in an area of the UK.

> **1** Name and locate an example of farming in an area of the UK. Describe how farming has changed. [5]
>
> Type of farming: _____
>
> Area of the UK: _____
>
> How farming has changed:
> _____

First you must decide your example and location. Be careful that you do not get mixed up between the UK and the EU – you may have an example of both. The question is then straightforward but pay attention to the following instructions.

The **command word** is 'describe' (see page 232 for details about command words).

The focus of the question is to describe how farming has *changed*, not just what farming is like. Your answer must, therefore, describe the new developments which have happened.

The following answers show how two candidates attempted this question.

Answer from candidate 1

> **Type of farming:** Crops
>
> **Area of the UK:** England
>
> **How farming has changed:**
>
> Use of more machinery such as tractors to harvest more crops.
>
> Healthier crops due to better irrigation.
>
> More fertilisers are used to help the soil regain nutrients faster.

Examination advice – Unit 3

Examiner's comment

The farming changes which are described could apply to many areas of the UK but they are all important developments in farming. For each change the answer is developed by describing its results. The only weak part of this answer is that it does not say which crops are grown. The answer gets into Level 2.

Answer from candidate 2

> Type of farming: Growing wheat
>
> Area of the UK: East Anglia
>
> How farming has changed:
>
> New types of wheat can be grown every year. This is more profitable than leaving fields empty.
>
> The new crops are better because they resist disease.
>
> Hedges have been removed so that big machines can be used.
>
> Agribusiness has replaced old farms. A new farm is run by a manager who makes it into a profitable business.

Examiner's comment

This is a better answer. It includes four changes which are all about wheat growing in East Anglia. It is a good Level 3 answer.

Case study questions do not usually need any kind of **resource** in the examination paper. However, the following question does contain some information for you to read before you begin to use your case study knowledge.

2
- Town devastated as factory is closed
- New quarry to be developed at local site
- Large company plans to open new store in town
- END OF AN INDUSTRIAL ERA AS LAST MINE IS CLOSED DOWN

Name an area you have studied and describe how **one** of these developments will affect the local people. [5]

Name of area: _____

Development you have chosen: _____

Effects on local people: _____

The command word is 'describe', but the instruction is also to choose one type of development as your example.

Think about how the two answers below are different. One candidate makes a good attempt by focusing on the case study, while the other candidate jumps around from one idea to another.

Answer from candidate 1

> Name of area: Cotgrave, Nottinghamshire
>
> Development you have chosen: Mine closes down
>
> Effects on local people:
> Cotgrave was once a small mining town but the coal mines have closed down because there is no more coal left to dig up. After they closed the mines many people were left unemployed. Many of the unemployed had to move to other cities to look for jobs. Local shopkeepers also suffered as people spent less money on buying new things. A café near to the mine was also shut as miners stopped going into it.

Examiner's comment

The candidate chose a local example of industrial change and described three effects on local people.

These are caused by the mine closing down:

- People lost their jobs and moved to other cities to look for new jobs.
- People had less money to spend in the local shops.
- A café was closed because there were too few customers.

People and their Needs

Advice

Answer from candidate 2

> Name of area: York
>
> Development you have chosen:
>
> Effects on local people:
> Development such as these cause a lot of pollution. When industries like mines are abandoned they make the environment ugly. Also when factories are closed it sometimes causes financial loss and in some cases unemployment. A new store creates more jobs but more traffic congestion.

Examiner's comment

The answer is not about York and is too general. Pollution, for example, is not explained. The other ideas are vague, they could apply to any town. The candidate does not follow the instruction to choose one development. The answer does contain some appropriate ideas but they need to be developed.

The following question is about a manufacturing industry and the **command word** is 'explain'.

> **3** Name and locate an example of a manufacturing industry or factory which you have studied in the UK. Explain why the industry or factory was located there. [5]

Read the following three answers and examiner comments. They show how candidates' work is marked at different levels.

Answer from candidate 1

> Factory or manufacturing industry: Toyota car company
>
> Location: Derby
>
> Reasons why the industry or factory was located there:
> There was good road accessibility with the M6 so transport such as importing components was easily done. Near main cities such as Birmingham and Manchester so that there were buyers and nearby markets as well. Government had advised Toyota to use a brownfield site as it was cheaper land. Derby is a large area so there will be many skilled people to work in the factory.

Examiner's comment

This is a Level 3 answer.

Good points:

- The industry is precisely named and located.
- The roads are identified, but a better description would be '…with the A50 which leads to the M6 and the A38 which leads to the M1'.
- The main cities are named (although they won't be the only markets).
- Correct reference to cheap 'brownfield' site.
- Workers in the area are described as skilled.
- All points refer to this particular car factory.

Answer from candidate 2

> Factory or manufacturing industry: Science Park
>
> Location:
>
> Reasons why the industry or factory was located there:
> Main roads right next to the Park so easy to transport goods. Near to built up areas so workers are easy to find. Located on a large flat area of land so good to build on with lots of parking. Easy to get to other cities to sell goods.

Examiner's comment

This is a Level 2 answer.

Weak points:

- There is no named or located industry.
- The roads are not identified.
- The built-up areas (or towns) are not named.
- No other cities are named as being possible markets.
- The answer could be about any large factory.

Good points:

- The link is made between roads and transport of goods.
- The idea about why it is important to have flat land is specific.

Examination advice – Unit 3

Answer from candidate 3

Factory or manufacturing industry: Honda cars

Location: UK

Reasons why the industry or factory was located there:
They have been located there because it is near to the motorway. This is good because people can get there easily because the roads go there. They can also travel there on a railway. There was a lot of open land.

Examiner's comment

This is a Level 1 answer.

Weak points:

- The factory is not accurately located in the UK.
- The motorway is not identified.
- There is no information about the railway.
- No reason is given why open land is important.

Good points:

- The car company is named.

Along with maps, graphs are the most popular type of resource used in the examination papers. Also, like maps, there are different types of graph which can be used in a variety of ways. You may be required to complete a bar graph, line graph, pie chart, divided bar graph, scatter graph or triangular graph. You may have to describe or use information contained within the graph. Whatever the question, accuracy is important when dealing with graphs. If you are completing or getting information from any type of graph you must use the scale carefully and give a precise answer. Vague or incorrect measurements do not score marks.

The first two questions focus on a bar graph. The questions show how this kind of graph is used. The first question is a straightforward graph completion exercise.

4 Study Figure 3.69

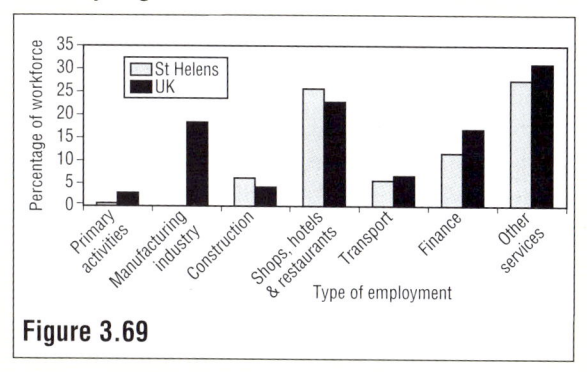

Figure 3.69

(a) Complete Figure 3.69 by using the following information:

25% of the workforce of St Helens is employed in manufacturing industry. [1]

Remember, you must be accurate in drawing the bar to the correct percentage. Also remember that straight lines in the bar graph must be drawn with a ruler.

(b) How important is employment in finance industry in St Helens compared with the UK as a whole? You should support your answer with figures. [2]

This question is an example of using information in the graph. Notice that in this question you only need to use the information about the finance industry. To gain the second mark, figures must be read accurately from the graph.

The following questions use a line graph.

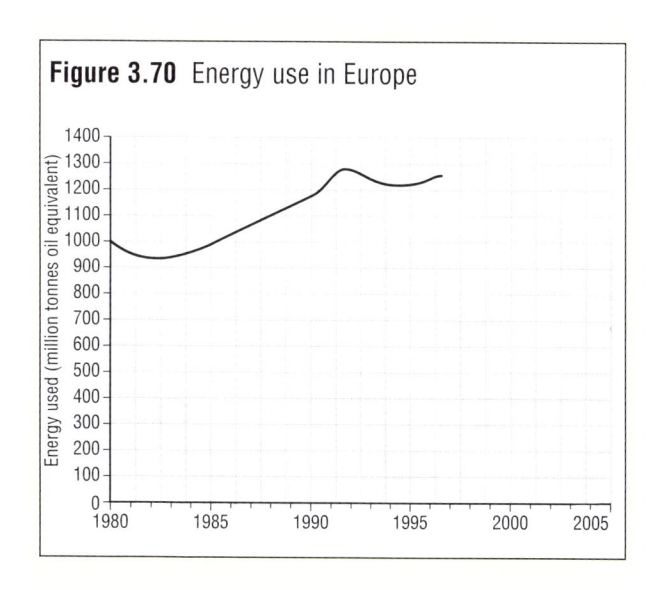

Figure 3.70 Energy use in Europe

three People and their Needs

Advice

There are three questions which focus on this graph.

> **5 (a)** How much energy was used in 1990? [1]
>
> _____ million tonnes oil equivalent

You must read the figures off the graph.

> **(b)** It has been estimated that the amount of energy used in 2005 will be 1400 million tonnes of oil equivalent. Use this information to complete the graph. [1]

You must complete the graph accurately.

> **(c)** Describe the changes in the amount of energy used between 1985 and 1995. Support your answer with figures and dates. [3]

You must describe the changes over time and use both energy figures and dates.

A good answer will be detailed and accurate as shown in the example below.

Candidate's answer

> It has increased. The amount of energy used in 1985 was 1 000 million tonnes oil equivalent whereas in 1995 it was 1220 million tonnes.
> There was a definite increase in use between 1985 and 1990, then there was a terrific rise in 1991–1992, then a fall until 1995.

Examiner's comment

There were three marks allocated to this question:
1 mark: describe the general increase in use
1 mark: recognise that the increase is not constant
1 mark: use figures and dates from the graph in the answer.
This candidate does all three tasks well.

A common way to show percentage information is in a pie chart. This is shown below in a question which continues the focus on energy use.

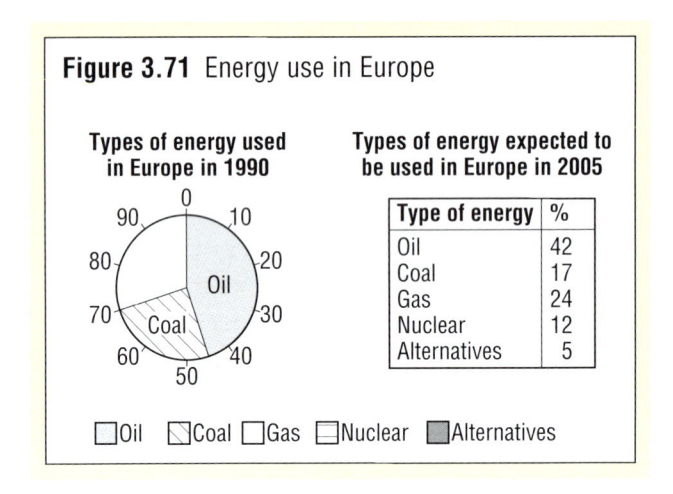

Figure 3.71 Energy use in Europe

Types of energy used in Europe in 1990

Types of energy expected to be used in Europe in 2005

Type of energy	%
Oil	42
Coal	17
Gas	24
Nuclear	12
Alternatives	5

☐Oil ☒Coal ☐Gas ☐Nuclear ■Alternatives

The data for 2005 is presented as a table rather than another pie chart.

> **6 (a)** Complete the pie chart by using the following figures:
>
> | Type of energy | Percentage |
> |---|---|
> | Gas | 15 |
> | Nuclear | 13 |
> | Alternatives | 2 |
>
> [2]

1 mark for correctly dividing the chart, 1 mark for shading or labelling.

> **(b)** Which type of energy was used most in 1990? [1]

Read from the pie chart.

> **(c)** In 1990 what percentage of Europe's energy was obtained from coal? [1]

Read from the pie chart.

> **(d)** Describe what is likely to happen to the percentage of coal used between 1990 and 2005. [1]

Read from the pie chart and table.

(e) Which two types of energy are likely to increase in importance between 1990 and 2005? [1]

Read from the pie chart and table.

(f) Suggest why the importance of different types of energy may change by 2005. [4]

You need to know some ideas about change in the use of energy. Question 6f is quite hard and is testing the understanding of candidates about changes in the use of energy over the last few years. One advantage of this type of question is that it deals with a topic where many different ideas can be used. The answers below show how three candidates answered this question.

Answer from candidate 1

This may happen as governments realise that oil and coal cause massive amounts of air pollution and that nuclear power is dangerous. Oil and coal may rise in price as they are non-renewable fuels.

Examiner's comment

The candidate understands that governments influence energy production and use. However, the candidate does not say how government policy may affect energy use. The candidate also recognises two other issues to do with fossil fuels (such as coal and oil) – pollution and cost.

Answer from candidate 2

People are more worried about the environment each year. Also coal and oil resources are expected to run out in around 200 years so people are looking for a non-polluting, renewable source of energy.

Examination advice – Unit 3 — 175

Examiner's comment

The candidate deals with the two main issues about energy production – pollution of the environment and exhaustion. The answer shows some understanding of the contrast between fossil fuels and alternative energy sources.

Answer from candidate 3

We are using different types of technology and so we don't really need coal, and we are trying to cut down on the pollution that we create.

Examiner's comment

The candidate does not describe *what* types of new technology. Also the candidate does not explain that pollution is connected to fossil fuels. There is room to improve this answer.

TASKS

1. The following are important topics in the People and their Needs unit. You need to know case studies for them. Make a check list of your case studies for these topics:
   a. Commercial farming in the UK or EU
   b. Subsistence farming in an LEDC
   c. Rapid industrial growth in an LEDC
   d. Location of a manufacturing industry in the UK
   e. Location of a distribution industry in the UK
   f. Effects of tourism in the EU
   g. Effects of tourism in an LEDC
   h. Consequences for a community in the UK or other MEDC of changes in energy production.

2. Here is another opportunity to become an examiner. You have seen three answers to the following question earlier in this chapter.

   On page 176 are three more answers to this question. Why do the candidates score different marks?

   Name and locate an example of a manufacturing industry or factory which you have studied in the UK. Explain why the industry or factory was located there.
   [5]

People and their Needs

Advice

TASKS

Candidate 1: a Level 3 answer

Factory or manufacturing industry: Samsung

Location: Northampton

Reasons why the industry or factory was located there:
The same reasons mostly why most large industries are located where they are, good access to and from major roads such as the M1 for parts and to move finished goods. It is situated on a large industrial estate with no residential area nearby because noise could be made by heavy machinery. Easy access for employees from Northampton, also near to a train line, although the station was a mile or so away.

Candidate 2: a Level 2 answer

Factory or manufacturing industry: Alberton industrial estate

Location: Alberton, Middlesex

Reasons why the industry or factory was located there:
Good access to the estate is available as it is close to the motorway. It isn't that far from the inner city which means to import and export materials isn't much of a problem. Residential buildings and houses are close by which means employees wont have to travel far to work if they live close by.

Candidate 3: a Level 1 answer

Factory or manufacturing industry: Leaflet company

Location: North London

Reasons why the industry or factory was located there:
The factory is located there because it has easy access to the whole country via main roads and motorways. It can send a lorry anywhere in the country or there is access to railways which can also transport goods.

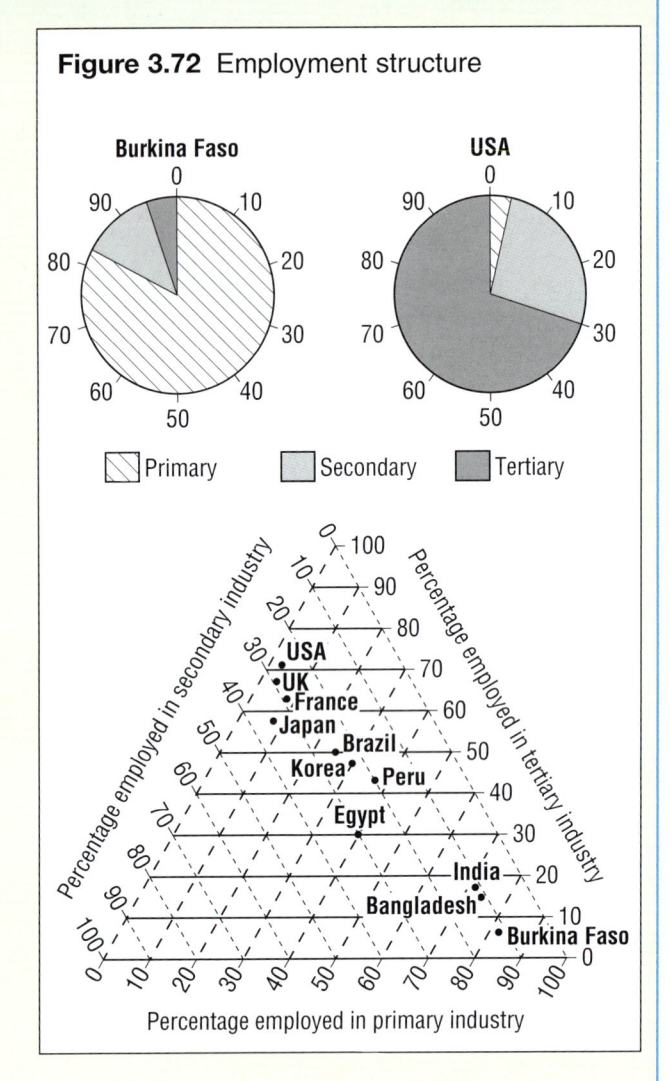

Figure 3.72 Employment structure

3   The two sets of graphs above show employment structure in a number of countries. You will be familiar with pie charts but may not have used a triangular graph before.

With a partner answer the following.

a   What does employment structure mean?

b   What unit is used to measure employment in both graphs?

c   Use the table below to work out how to read data from a triangular graph. Copy out the table and fill in the gaps.

Country	Percentage employment		
	Primary	Secondary	Tertiary
Burkina Faso	82	12	6
	8	29	63
Bangladesh	74		15
USA			70

Examination advice – Unit 3

TASKS

d Give **two** differences between the employment structure of Burkina Faso and USA.

e Suggest a reason for each difference you have identified.

4 Study the scatter graph below.

Figure 3.73 Life expectancy and GDP

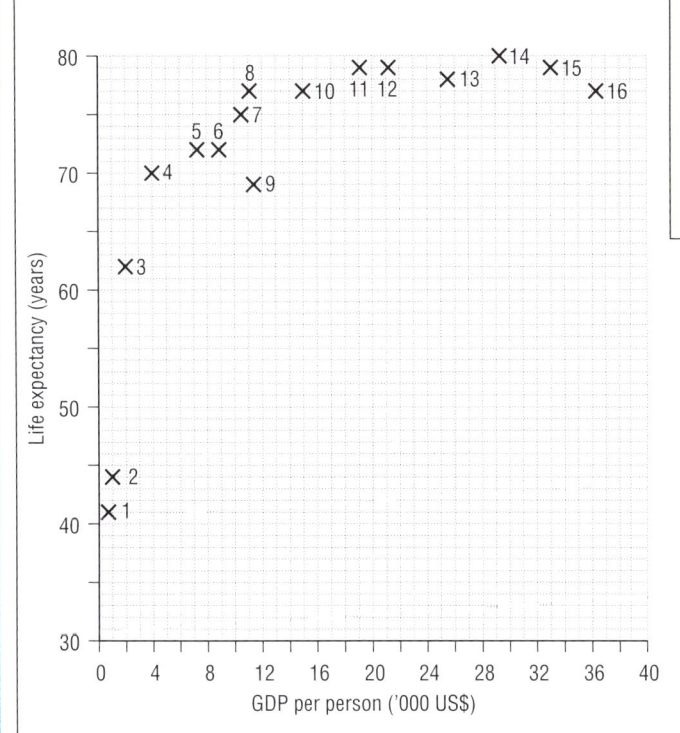

GDP is a way of measuring how rich a country is.

Answer the following questions.

a What does life expectancy mean?

b What is the average life expectancy in years in Saudi Arabia?

c In which country is average life expectancy highest?

d In which country is GDP $15 000 and average life expectancy 77 years?

e Describe the general relationship between GDP and average life expectancy.

f Explain why this relationship occurs.

g Give two reasons, other than GDP, why average life expectancy varies between countries.

Reference number	Country
1	Ethiopia
2	Burkina Faso
3	Pakistan
4	Egypt
5	Turkey
6	Mexico
7	Argentina
8	Puerto Rico
9	Saudi Arabia
10	Cyprus
11	Greece
12	Spain
13	UK
14	Canada
15	Norway
16	USA

People and their Needs

Advice

THE ENTRY LEVEL CERTIFICATE

The Oral accounts for 20% of the marks for the Entry Level Certificate. Near the end of the course, you will be given some information on one of the topics you have studied. It could be a map or photo or a graph or a newspaper article. Your teacher will ask you some questions about the topic and record the Oral on tape.

Your teacher will arrange a time to meet and will find a room – possibly your classroom or an office – to record your interview on tape. No other pupils will be there, so you will be able to show what you know and understand. There is nothing to write down. Just talk about the resources you are looking at and be prepared to use your knowledge of real examples (case studies).

Here is an example of a case study which you may need to use in an Oral.

People and their Needs – Industry

CASE STUDY: Changing jobs in Stoke on Trent

Jobs are changing today in towns and cities across the country. Stoke on Trent, as well as having many jobs in pottery factories (secondary), used to have many jobs in coal-mining (primary). Hem Heath coal mine was one of the most efficient mines in the country. Photo A shows the entrance to the mine today – it has closed and there are now no working coal mines in the area. Many people still work in the pottery industry making cups, plates and ornaments. There are a number of other secondary jobs on industrial estates too. Photo B shows a factory on Newstead Industrial Estate on the edge of the city. Across the road is a new business park, Trentham Lakes. Photo C shows the entrance and the new Worldgate offices. All this is on the land that used to be Hem Heath coal mine. In just a few years, the types of jobs for people in this area of Stoke on Trent have changed a great deal.

TASKS

1. What happened to Hem Heath coal mine?
2. What changes do the photos show for primary and secondary jobs?
3. a What are industrial estates?
   b What are the advantages of having many factories all in one area?

   Fieldwork Tip – As part of your coursework, you could find out about a business park or industrial estate near you. Map it. Make a note of all the factories or offices on the site and find out what they do. Describe its location and work out how many offer jobs in primary, secondary or tertiary work.

PHOTO A

Certificate advice

PHOTO B

Oral task

a) Introduction

▶ General conversation with questions about work.
Have you got a part-time job?
What do you have to do?

Where are you going on work experience?
What will you have to do?

What job do you want to do in the future?
What will you have to do?

▶ Look at the three photos. They show three types of work.

One of them was primary work. Which photo is it?

Can you tell me how these three types of job differ?

(*Can the student identify primary, secondary and tertiary activities?*)

b) Describing and explaining

▶ Referring to the local area.

Can you name three jobs in our local area from each sector of industry?

Can you name a factory or other place of work for each example you give?

▶ Imagine you were going to open a factory making _____ (*use local example*).

What things would you need to make the factory successful?

(*Can the student identify the factors of production – labour, etc?*)

c) Case Study

▶ Referring to the local area.

Name a local factory.

What do they make?

Why do you think the factory was located where it is?

If you were setting up a new factory near here, where would be the best place for it?

Why would you locate it there?

How is that location better than the other factory you were talking about?

▶ The best Orals end up more like a conversation, than a question and answer session. Your teacher will have some questions but they are only a 'guide' to help get the best out of you.

PHOTO C

People and the Environment

Local environments

LIMESTONE

SUMMARY Limestone is an important raw material in cement, roads and construction. Much of it is in national parks, such as the Peak District in Derbyshire. Quarrying damages the landscape but provides local jobs.

The extraction of raw materials by mining or quarrying

Limestone is a hard rock that produces attractive scenery. Many limestone areas are in national parks. It is the main raw material in cement and, because it is hard, it is used for roads and construction.

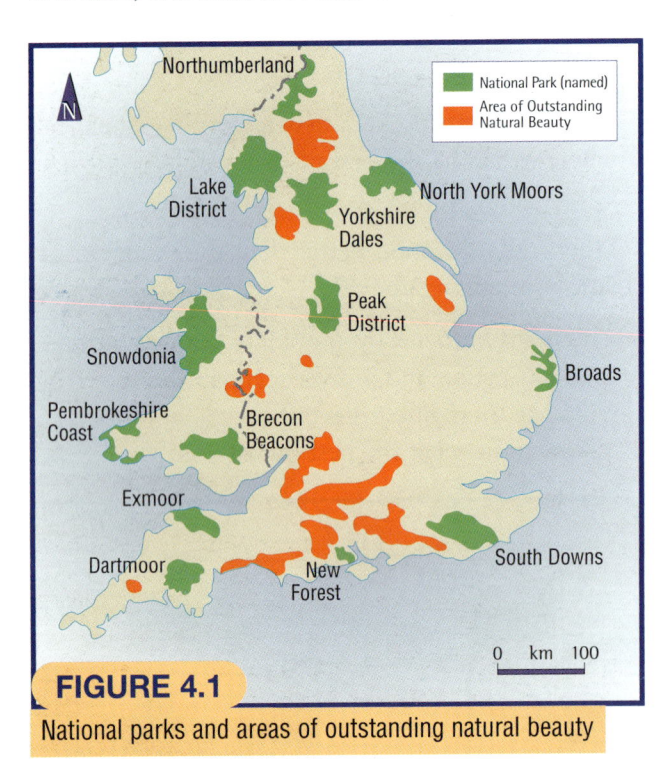

FIGURE 4.1
National parks and areas of outstanding natural beauty

FIGURE 4.2
Uses of limestone (1996)

- construction 41%
- roadstone 38%
- cement 10%
- others 5%
- iron and steel 3%
- agriculture 2%
- building stone 1%

FIGURE 4.3
Origin of limestone in the UK

Percentage of limestone by county:
- 16 or more
- 11 – 15
- 6 – 10
- 2 – 5

MG MID GLAMORGAN
SY SOUTH YORKSHIRE
WG WEST YORKSHIRE

Quarrying in Derbyshire

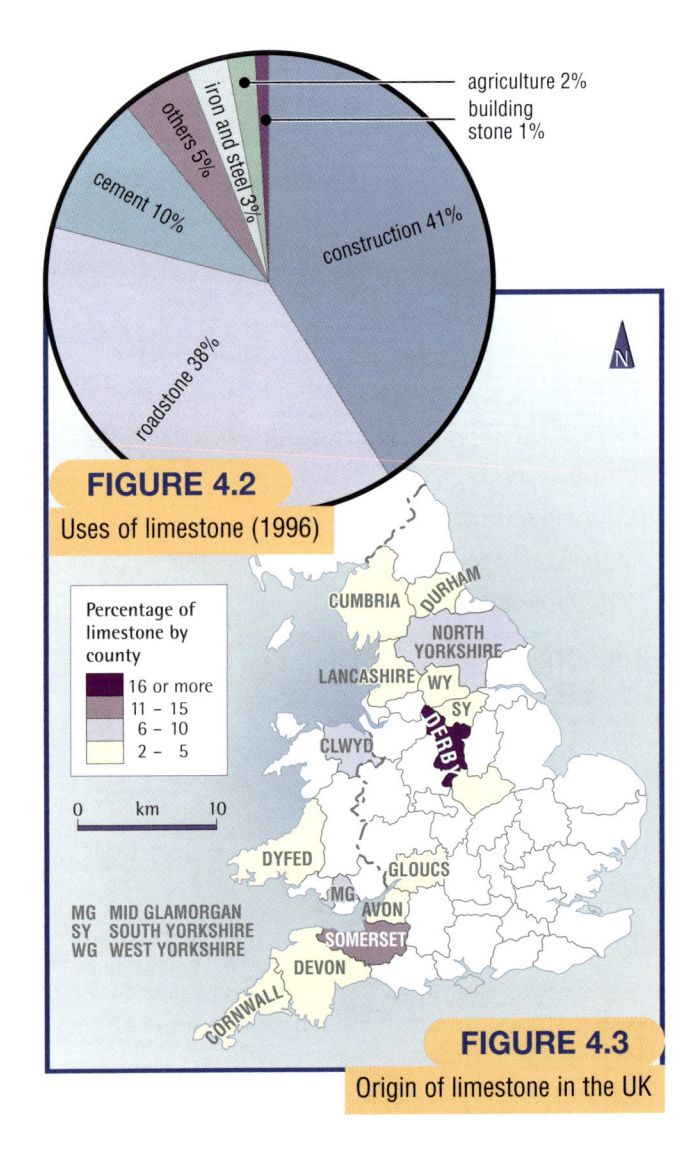

Derbyshire is the UK's largest area of limestone quarrying and several quarries are within the Peak District National Park. By law, the park authorities have to look after natural areas and wildlife, but also support the jobs of local people. That makes life difficult, because in the Derbyshire Dales and High Peak areas, quarrying is a major employer (Figures 4.4 and 4.5).

	Primary	Secondary	Tertiary
Derby City	5	32	63
Derbyshire Dales	17	16	67
High Peak	15	24	61
SE Derbyshire	25	17	58
County average	11	28	61

Figure 4.4 Employment in Derbyshire (%)

	1981	1991	1996
Amber Valley	14	12	10
Bolsover	46	29	8
Chesterfield	18	12	2
Derby City	5	5	2
Derbyshire Dales	11	12	12
Erewash	5	1	1
High Peak	19	14	13
NE Derbyshire	21	8	2
SE Derbyshire	29	22	14

Figure 4.5 Mineral and metal extraction employment, 1981–96 (%)

Environmental impact

Limestone quarries have a massive impact on the environment (Figure 4.6). Earth mounds are used to reduce the noise of explosions and of machinery. Water sprays are used to keep the dust down. However, quarrying can be heard and seen over a wide area. There are large white scars on the landscape. Although trains are used where possible, much limestone goes by road. There are problems with lorries along narrow roads and through villages, already busy with tourist traffic.

FIGURE 4.6
Limestone quarry, Wirksworth, Derbyshire

TASKS

1. Look at Figure 4.2. What are the three main uses of limestone?
2. Compare Figures 4.1 and 4.3. Suggest which national parks are affected by limestone quarrying.
3. What problems are the result of quarrying limestone in the Peak District National Park? Write about:
   - the effect on the scenery
   - noise
   - air pollution
   - traffic.
4. Why are many local people in favour of quarrying?
5. Look at the OS map on page 230.
   a. Use a piece of tracing paper to trace the area of the quarry (in grid squares 1581 and 1681), the works area (in grid square 1682), the railway siding from the works to the main line at 172842, the main-line railway, and the villages of Hope, Castleton and Bradwell. Name all of these on your tracing paper.
   b. The scale is 4 cm = 1 km (or 4 mm = 100 m). How long is the railway siding from the works to the main line?
   c. On another small piece of tracing paper, draw a grid of 4 mm squares, large enough to cover the quarry. Each square is one hectare. Use it to work out the size of the quarry in hectares.
   d. Now look at the photograph on page 229. Use the map to work out which village is at the bottom of the photograph.
   e. Write down the likely opinions of different people in the village to the quarry and cement works. Include someone about to leave school who is looking for a job, and someone who lives in Sheffield who has a holiday home here.

four
People and the Environment
Local environments

TROPICAL RAINFORESTS

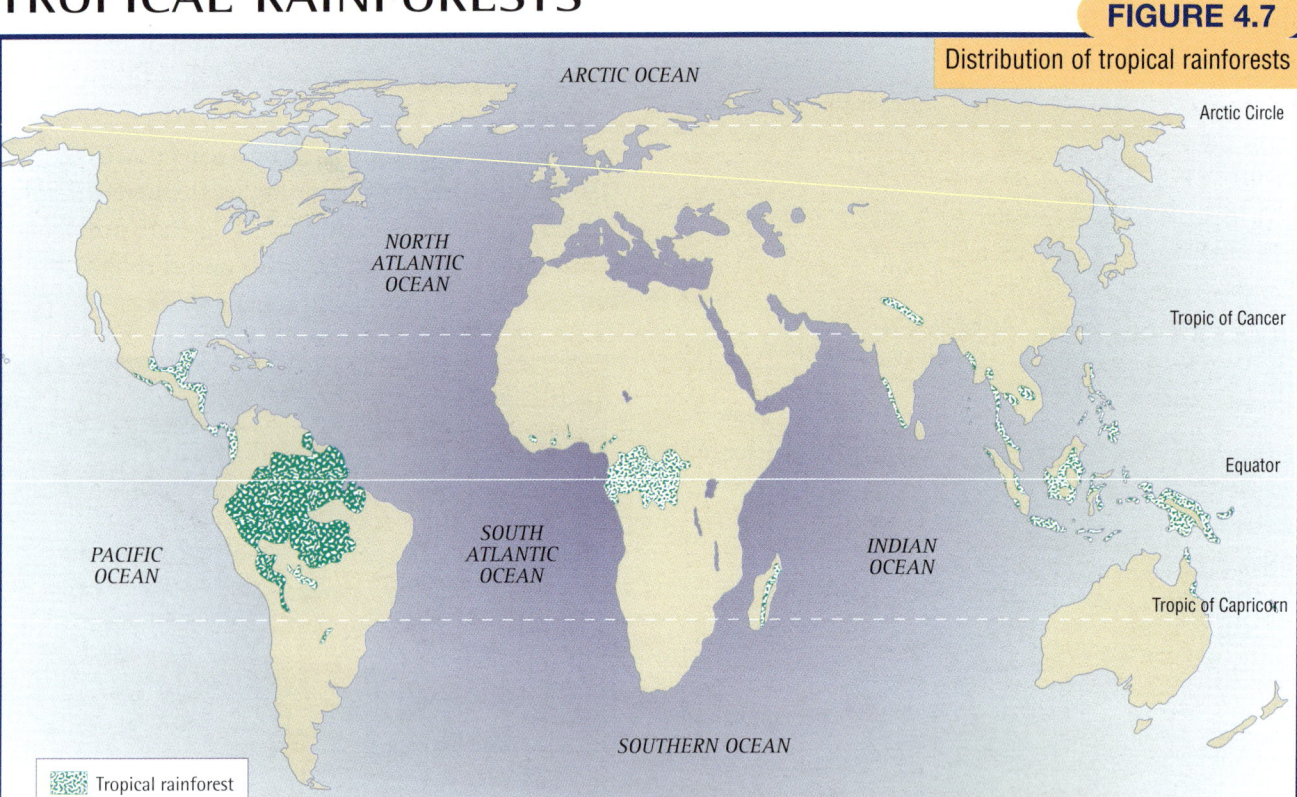

FIGURE 4.7
Distribution of tropical rainforests

> **SUMMARY** More than half of the world's plant and animal species live in tropical rainforests. The climate is hot and wet all through the year. The vegetation is well adapted to these conditions.

Tropical rainforests are the most productive ecosystem in the world. More than one-third of all the trees in the world grow there. The rainforest affects the whole world's climate and the content of the atmosphere.

The tropical rainforest climate has no seasons. Every day:

- The temperature rises to 32ºC and falls to about 22ºC in the evening.
- The morning is sunny, evaporating yesterday's rain.
- Clouds build up during the afternoon, until it pours down, often with a thunderstorm. This is **convection rainfall**.

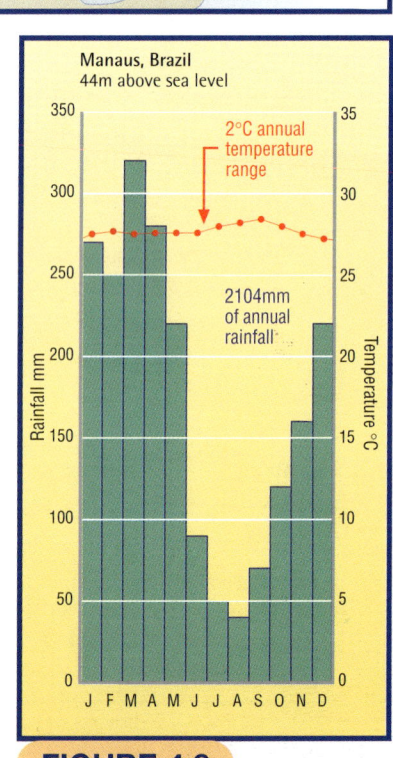

FIGURE 4.8
Climate graph for Manaus

Tropical rainforests

Much of the rain falls on leaves and never reaches the ground. The dense vegetation is protecting the soil from erosion. The soil has a rich humus layer from decomposing leaves, providing minerals for plant growth. So there are two cycles at work, the water cycle and the nutrient cycle (Figure 4.9).

Rainforest vegetation is a vast tangle of climbing plants and creepers, but it is very well ordered. Plants have adapted to local conditions. Leaves have developed drip tips to get rid of heavy raindrops and trees have large buttress roots to support them (Figure 4.10).

Water cycle Much of the rainfall is intercepted by the vegetation and then next day evaporated into the atmosphere to provide the following day's rainfall

Heavy daily convectional rainfall intercepted by tree canopy

Ground is protected from the heavy rainfall

Nutrient cycle Rapid decomposition takes place in wet, hot conditions. This provides minerals for future plant growth

Leaves provide humus

Tree roots are shallow to allow them to take up nutrients quickly

FIGURE 4.9
Water cycle and nutrient cycle in the rainforest

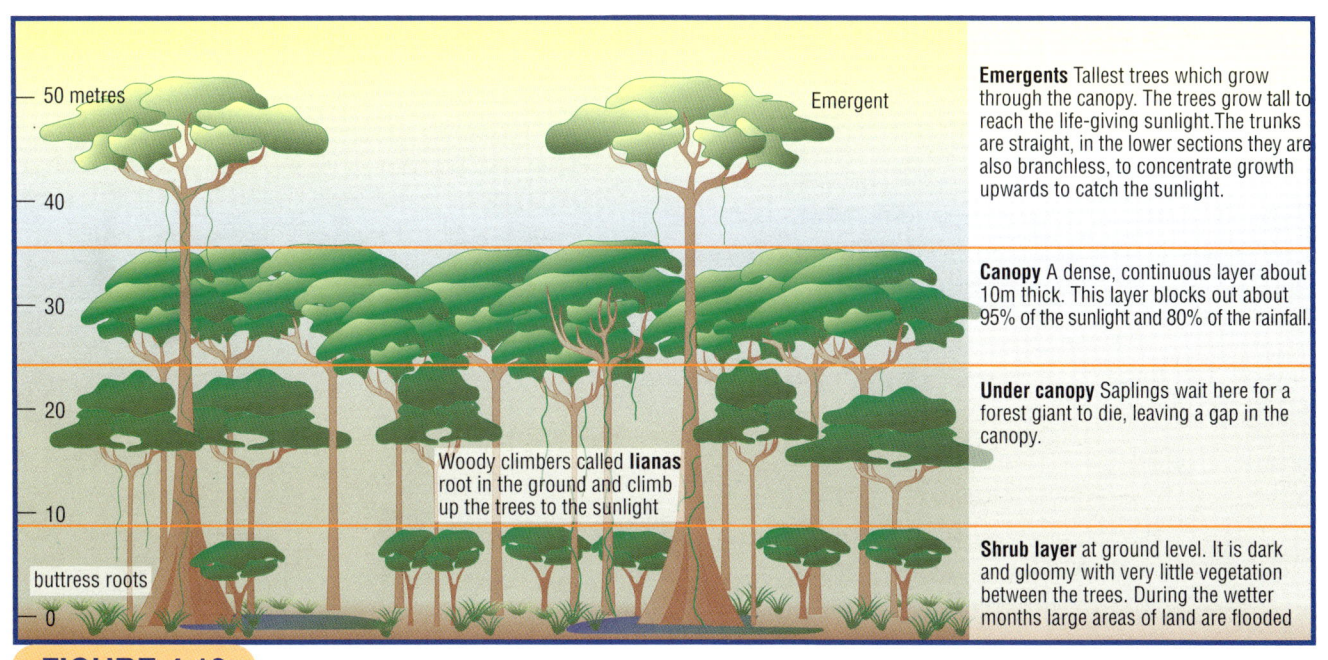

TASKS

1. a Use Figure 4.7 to describe where in the world there are tropical rainforests.
   b Most of the rainforest is in just three countries. Use an atlas to name them.
2. Imagine you spent 24 hours in Manaus in the Amazon Rainforest in Brazil (Figure 4.8). Write about the weather at different times of day and night.
3. Produce a poster to show why rainforests should be looked after carefully. You can get information from CD-ROMs and the internet.

   Useful websites:

   http://www.ran.org/

   http://www.rainforest-alliance.org/

Emergents Tallest trees which grow through the canopy. The trees grow tall to reach the life-giving sunlight. The trunks are straight, in the lower sections they are also branchless, to concentrate growth upwards to catch the sunlight.

Canopy A dense, continuous layer about 10m thick. This layer blocks out about 95% of the sunlight and 80% of the rainfall.

Under canopy Saplings wait here for a forest giant to die, leaving a gap in the canopy.

Woody climbers called **lianas** root in the ground and climb up the trees to the sunlight

Shrub layer at ground level. It is dark and gloomy with very little vegetation between the trees. During the wetter months large areas of land are flooded

buttress roots

FIGURE 4.10
Vegetation in the tropical rainforest

four — People and the Environment
Local environments

DEVELOPMENT PROJECTS IN THE AMAZON

SUMMARY The Amazon Rainforest is changing. Brazil needs to use more of its resources to improve its economic development. It has set up some big schemes, but many involve deforestation.

Brazil's population is growing rapidly. More land is needed for people to live on and farm. Brazil has enormous debts and needs to pay them. Big schemes in Amazonia were attractive to the government.

Transport
Most of the plans needed the rainforest to be accessible. Over 12 000 km of new roads were built, including the Trans-Amazonian Highway which is 5 300 km long (the same distance as London to Baghdad in Iraq). New roads meant that people could move into the rainforest and resources could be brought out.

Small-scale farming
People from poor farming areas were offered land in the rainforest. Thousands of families moved, especially from north-east Brazil where droughts are common.

Commercial cattle ranching
Large ranches, run by trans-national companies, use a quarter of the area cleared of forest after the trees have been burnt off.

Forestry
Tropical hardwoods like ebony and mahogany get good prices in MEDCs, but the areas that the trees came from are often not replanted.

Minerals
Under the rainforest are iron ore, bauxite, manganese, diamonds, silver and gold. The largest iron ore reserve in the world, 18 billion tonnes, is at Carajas (Figure 4.11). It will take 300 years to extract it. The EU and the World Bank paid for the mine and 13.6 million tonnes a year goes to Europe at a bargain price.

Hydro-electric power
More than 125 dams are being built, but vast reservoirs will flood areas of rainforest.

Settlement
Large areas of forest have been cleared for new settlements. In 1960, 2 million people lived in Amazonia. Now it is more than 30 million.

TASKS
1. Brazil wants to be better off by developing the Amazon Rainforest. Take each of the seven headings on this page and write a good point and a bad point about it.
2. If you were Brazil's Minister for Development, what schemes would you allow and encourage?

Development projects in the Amazon 185

FIGURE 4.11
Carajas – the world's largest iron ore mine

FIGURE 4.12
Cattle ranching in Para State, Brazil

FIGURE 4.13
New road through partly deforested land, Amazonia

FIGURE 4.14
Itaipu hydroelectric dam

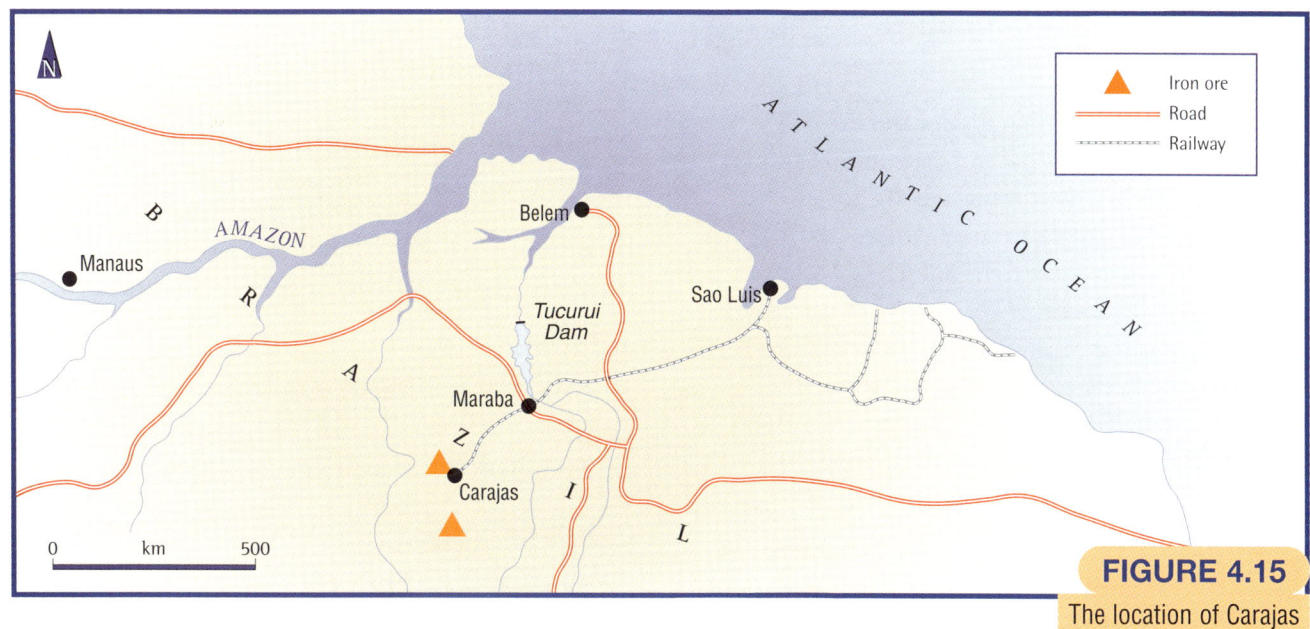

FIGURE 4.15
The location of Carajas

four — People and the Environment

Local environments

ENVIRONMENTAL CONSEQUENCES

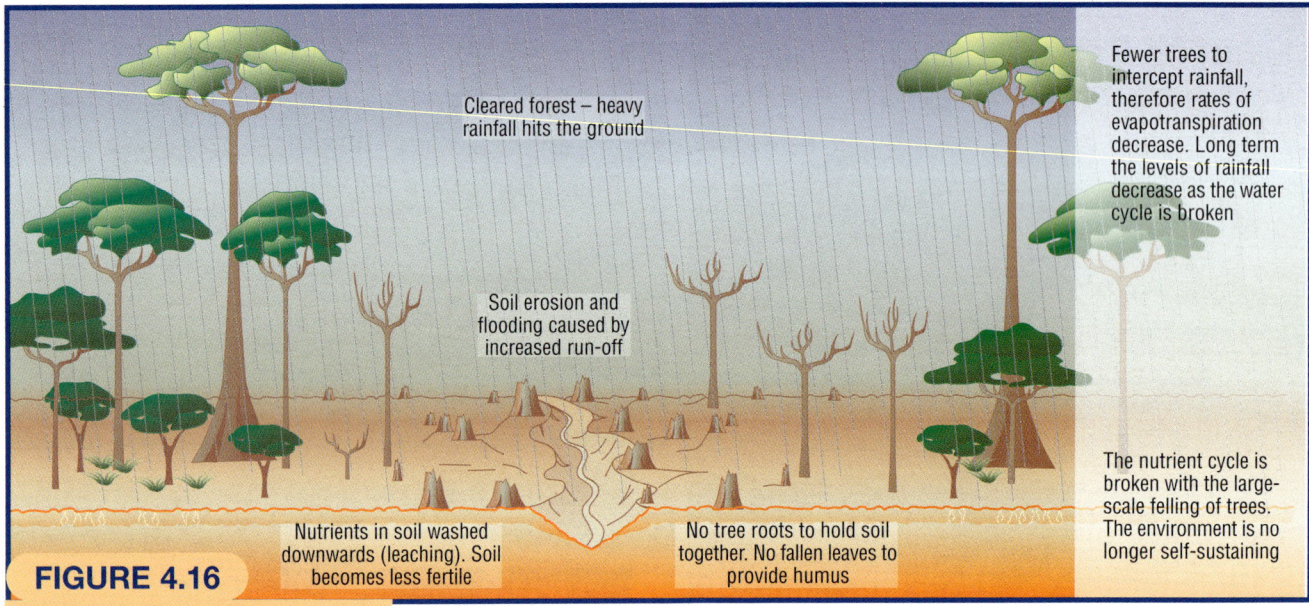

FIGURE 4.16 The consequences of deforestation

Labels on figure:
- Cleared forest – heavy rainfall hits the ground
- Soil erosion and flooding caused by increased run-off
- Fewer trees to intercept rainfall, therefore rates of evapotranspiration decrease. Long term the levels of rainfall decrease as the water cycle is broken
- Nutrients in soil washed downwards (leaching). Soil becomes less fertile
- No tree roots to hold soil together. No fallen leaves to provide humus
- The nutrient cycle is broken with the large-scale felling of trees. The environment is no longer self-sustaining

---

SUMMARY Developing the rainforest damages the environment. Many of the plants and animals that live there cannot cope with the changes. Some become extinct. Deforestation is also changing the climate – it is speeding up global warming. Some areas that were rainforest are becoming deserts.

Some LEDCs with rainforests, such as Brazil, need to use their resources to make them better off. However, the rainforest is damaged by the changes (Figure 4.16).

Rainforests cover less than 2% of the earth's surface, yet they are home to between 40% and 50% of all life forms. It is a finely balanced ecosystem. If the trees are cut down or burned, animals and insects lose their habitats. Without branches and leaves above, the heavy rain hits the ground. The soil is washed away and there is flooding. The cycle of evapotranspiration and rainfall is altered. The climate changes. Less rain falls. In the end, the area becomes desert.

Trees take in carbon dioxide and give off oxygen. Without trees, the earth's atmosphere contains more carbon dioxide and this increases global warming. Burning down the trees also pollutes the atmosphere, increasing carbon dioxide even more.

The Amazon is home to 30 million species of plants, animals and insects. From them we produce everything from chocolate to medicine. More than half of our medicines come from rainforests – and scientists keep discovering new ones. There may be cures for diseases such as cancer and AIDS waiting to be discovered – unless we destroy the rainforest first.

Global rates of destruction

1 ha per second: equivalent to two US football fields

= 60 ha per minute

= 86 000 ha per day: an area larger than New York City

= 31 million ha per year: an area larger than Poland

Species extinction

Distinguished scientists estimate that an average of 137 species of life forms are driven into extinction every day. That is 50 000 species each year.

Wednesday, April 14, 1999 Published at 20:36 GMT 21:36 UK — BBC Online News

Amazon forest loss estimates double

Logging's damage is less obvious than forest clearance, but no less real

By Environment Correspondent, Alex Kirby

The true extent of rainforest damage in the Amazon is more than twice as great as present estimates suggest, researchers say. Daniel Nepstad: 'The degradation will continue'. The team says field surveys of logging and burning show far more deforestation than satellite monitoring has revealed.

The researchers interviewed 1393 wood mill operators, representing more than half the mills in 75 Amazonian logging centres. As well, they interviewed 202 landlords, whose properties covered 9200 sq. km.

They found that logging crews annually cause severe damage to between 10 000 and 15 000 sq. km of forest that are not included in current deforestation estimates.

Insidious damage

They also discovered that fires burning on the surface consume large areas of forest which again are not recorded. The researchers say the failure so far to register the much greater loss rate they have discovered is because the loggers reduce tree cover, but do not eliminate it. By contrast, ranchers and farmers deforest land in preparation for pasture and crops by clear-cutting it, and by burning whole areas. The more the forest burns, the more vulnerable to fire it becomes. And where logging and fires have caused damage, they say, the vegetation will grow back fast enough to dupe a satellite.

The only reliable way to find out what is happening is by field surveys. Logging and surface fires seldom kill all the trees. But they help to make them more vulnerable. Logging increases the flammability of the forest by reducing leaf canopy coverage by up to 50 per cent. This lets the sunlight strike through to the forest floor, where it dries out the organic debris created by the logging.

Satellites not enough

But they found that only about a tenth of the area classified as forest actually supported undisturbed forest. The researchers say: 'Satellite-based deforestation monitoring is an essential tool in studies of human effects on tropical forests, because it documents the most extreme form of land use, over large areas, and at low cost.' But this monitoring needs to be expanded to include forests affected by logging and surface fire if it is to accurately reflect the full magnitude of human influences on tropical forests.

TASKS

1. Put these statements into the correct order. Include an arrow from each sentence to the next.
   - Drier climate, not enough rain to grow crops
   - Rainforest vegetation gets heavy rain every day
   - Rain can now reach the ground
   - Forest cut down
   - Soil erosion increases
   - Less evaporation and transpiration to form clouds.
2. Why are medical experts worried about developments in rainforests?
3. The United States Geological Survey's website, Earthshots, investigates environmental change through the use of satellite imagery. One of its case studies examines the impact of deforestation in the Rondônia area of the Amazon rainforest. If you have access to the internet, visit this case study at the following web address:

   http://edcwww.cr.usgs.gov/earthshots/slow/tableofcontentstext

   Download the satellite images of the case study area in Rondônia for 1975 and 1992. Copy and paste the images into a desktop publishing programme and, using the software tools, label the changes that have occurred in the area.

People and the Environment

Local environments

STEWARDSHIP AND SUSTAINABLE DEVELOPMENT

SUMMARY The rainforest must be developed carefully if the ecosystem is not to be damaged. It provides many products, including important medicines. Ecotourism could become a major industry. If its resources are wasted, local people will not become better off and the whole world will suffer.

LEDCs with areas of rainforest know they have resources that can make the country richer. They want to sell more of these resources to other countries and use some in their own new industries.

They also know that 'get rich quick' schemes will damage the rainforest. It will affect environments and climates all over the world if rainforests are destroyed.

What is needed is **sustainable development** with careful planning and help from richer countries to ensure that development conserves the rainforest. Most important is the attitude of the government. Brazil is now keen to keep the rainforest alive, rather than let loggers take all the trees out of an area. It is backing schemes which improve the quality of life for the 30 million people who live in Amazonia.

Rubber tapping

Tapping rubber trees to get the sap to make rubber has been part of the way of life in Amazonia for more than 100 years. It does not damage the forest. Trees are not cut down to get the latex out. The Brazilian government has protected about 1% of the rainforest from development, where 63 000 families make their living getting rubber in the traditional way. The rubber tappers would like 10% to be protected. At present, they only produce one-seventieth of the rubber that Brazil needs.

FIGURE 4.17
Harvesting the rainforest, Brazil

Stewardship and sustainable development

Non-timber forest products

For many years, people have harvested the forest without destroying it. They collect fibres, fruits, seeds, nuts and honey.

- Collecting Brazil nuts is the main source of income for many tribes.
- One palm tree can produce as much as 20 kg of fruit each year.
- A plant called camu-camu produces more Vitamin C than any other fruit known today. It is sold to the USA for making vitamin pills.
- More than two-thirds of all mass-produced medicines come from plants. About 650 species are traded from Amazonia.

Ecotourism

There is very little tourism at present, but it could be developed in ways that protect the environment. This is called **ecotourism**. Local people could provide the accommodation and work as guides, so communities would become better off. There are plenty of opportunities for adventure, such as trekking, rafting, diving, cruising, birdwatching and looking at other wildlife. On page 190 there is the 'mission statement' of an ecotourism company. It wants to provide for more tourists in Amazonia in a sustainable way.

Sustainable logging

The Amazon rainforest is the greatest reserve of commercial timber in the world. Less than 1%, however, is logged in a sustainable way. Good forest management is only used in a small area (see the news articles on page 191). It does not damage the ecosystem. The great variety of plants and animal life is hardly affected.

FIGURE 4.18
Panning for gold, Venezuela

four People and the Environment

Local environments

'Lagamar Expeditions is a company specializing in adventure travel in the environmentally rich areas of the Amazon region of Brazil. Our mission is to help spread the understanding of our environment and importance of our environment's biodiversity, by sharing secrets and mysteries surrounding us and our world. We are committed to rainforest conservation and furthering the empowerment of the peoples of the Amazon to become full participants in natural resource decision making.

Lagamar Expeditions' objective is to provide sustainable tourism in natural areas that interpret the local environment and culture, further the tourist's understanding of them, foster conservation, and add to the well-being of the local people. Tourism is based on a guest/host relationship. It is vital for the guest (tourist) to respect the ownership, rights, and wishes of local people and communities, tread lightly on the environment, and contribute to the local economy rather than exploit it.'

The 'mission statement' of Lagamar Expeditions, as shown on their website

Lagamar Expeditions

Amazon • Pantanal • Galapagos • Paddling Programs • Brazil • Ecuador • Peru • Chile • Costa Rica

RECOMMENDED BY
BRITANNICA
INTERNET GUIDE
by ENCYCLOPAEDIA BRITANNICA
www.ebig.com

- Safari Guide
- Multi Media
- The Habitat
- Booking Info
- About Us
- Books

Exploring the Amazon & Pantanal regions of South America

We outfit special interest expeditions for birdwatchers, botanist, photographers, etc.

BEST OF Buy IT OnLine

Rare Trips for the Adventurous

Got a burning desire to explore Amazon's deepest jungles, trek the Inca Trail to magical Machu Picchu, paddle the wild waters of Chile's Rio Futalehfu, participate on a Photo Safari in the Amazon & Pantanal?

- Then you've landed at the right place -

Lagamar Expeditions provides responsible adventure tourism in the Amazon, Pantanal, and other regions of Latin America. See our Safari Guide for program details.

For further program information please call: 1-800-823-8531.
E-mail address: WebMaster@lagamar.com

FIGURE 4.19 Lagamar Expeditions website

Stewardship and sustainable development

BBC Online News
Monday, April 19, 1999 Published at 12:38 GMT 13:38 UK

Amazon logging deal agreed
An area the size of Belgium was cleared in 1998

Brazil has lifted a ban on new logging permits in the Amazon Rainforest after landowners and loggers agreed to slow their rates of forest destruction. However, the country's environment ministry says any new permits for felling trees will be subject to strict guidelines. Some conservationists, who doubt whether any new controls can be effectively enforced, have questioned the wisdom of issuing permits. Brazil's authorities refused to issue new logging permits in February after they discovered more than 15 500 square kilometres (6 000 square miles) – an area the size of Belgium – was cleared in 1998. This was a rise of nearly a third on the previous year's clearing rates.

New commitment

The new guidelines limit local farmers to clearing just three hectares a year. Logging firms signing up to the agreement have also pledged to make better use of areas which have been partially logged, and to limit their use of fire in clearing forest. Antonio Prado, a spokesman for IBAMA – Brazil's environment protection agency – says the agreement marks the first time such a commitment has been reached between government, loggers and environmental groups.

Mr Prado said convincing Brazilian loggers to accept sustainable practices will also require financial incentives, and he said he will be seeking economic support from Western countries to help IBAMA enforce its new rainforest guidelines.

Effective enforcement

The environmental campaign group, Friends of the Earth, says the agreement is a welcome step. But its spokesman, Tony Juniper, believes IBAMA will have to overcome a history of failing to enforce conservation laws if the rainforest agreement is to succeed. If the new measures succeed, they could make a significant difference in preserving one of the world's most important natural resources.

BBC Online News
Friday, December 5, 1997
Published at 17:48 GMT
Sue Branford

Eduardo Martins, head of Brazil's main environmental body, IBAMA, has announced a new plan to conserve the Amazon rainforest. Mr Martins, who is in London with the Brazilian president, Fernando Henrique Cardoso, said Brazil had decided to accept the request, made recently by Prince Philip, the president of the World Wide Fund for Nature, that every country in the world should conserve 10% of its forest cover.

The announcement, made in London by Eduardo Martins, took environmentalists by surprise. Mr Martins said that the Brazilian government had decided to respond positively to the appeal made by Prince Philip.

Brazil, he said, would increase the percentage of its forest that is protected from the current level, of less than 4%, to 10%. The new commitment will mean that the government will create new ecological reserves, covering four million hectares. Mr Martins said that just as important was another new measure. The government, he said, will be creating wide ecological corridors between all the existing reserves. These will allow birds and animals to move freely between the protected areas, greatly increasing their efficiency in protecting biodiversity. These conservation measures are to be paid for by the Group of Seven industrialised countries, who are giving Brazil $250m for Amazon conservation.

TASKS

1. What is meant by 'sustainable development'?
2. Write down two reasons why the government of Brazil should encourage more rubber tapping.
3. Why are health experts in the UK interested in how the rainforest is developed?
4. Explain how ecotourism is different from other tourism.
5. Produce a poster to advertise the activities which an ecotourism company could provide to attract visitors to Amazonia.
6. What is the Brazilian government doing to stop the logging companies ruining the rainforest?

four People and the Environment

Local environments

LAND USE CONFLICTS IN NATIONAL PARKS

SUMMARY National parks were set up to look after large areas of beautiful countryside. However, they are not owned by the nation. Most of the land is still privately owned. Careful planning is needed to cope with all the visitors.

In the 1950s, the first ten national parks were set up to

- look after the natural beauty and wildlife of the area
- encourage people to understand and enjoy the countryside
- protect the jobs and communities within the national park.

A National Park Authority runs each national park, but they only own about 3% of the land. Two-thirds of the land is privately owned by farmers, the rest by organisations such as the National Trust, Forestry Commission, the water companies and the Ministry of Defence.

The main challenge facing National Park Authorities is planning for more visitors. Already the national parks receive more than 100 million 'visitor days' a year. People have

- more money to spend on leisure
- more time for holidays, especially short breaks
- better transport links from the cities.

Visitors tend to forget that the national parks are home to 300 000 people. At busy times, there is traffic congestion and not enough parking. Visitors expect toilets, picnic areas, litter collection and tourist shops. In some national parks, house prices are high because rich people from cities have paid more for their second home than most local people can afford. Some villages have many retired people who have moved in, which changes the community.

FIGURE 4.20
Wild pony in Dartmoor National Park

TASKS

1 Copy these sentences and write 'True' or 'False':
   a Farming is not allowed in national parks.
   b People now have more time and spare money to enjoy visits to national parks.
   c Two-thirds of the land is owned by the National Park Authorities.
   d Rich people from cities buy second homes or retire to national parks, which pushes house prices up, so some local people cannot afford to live there.
2 Which of the three aims that were set out in the 1950s makes the other two aims more difficult?

Land use conflicts in national parks

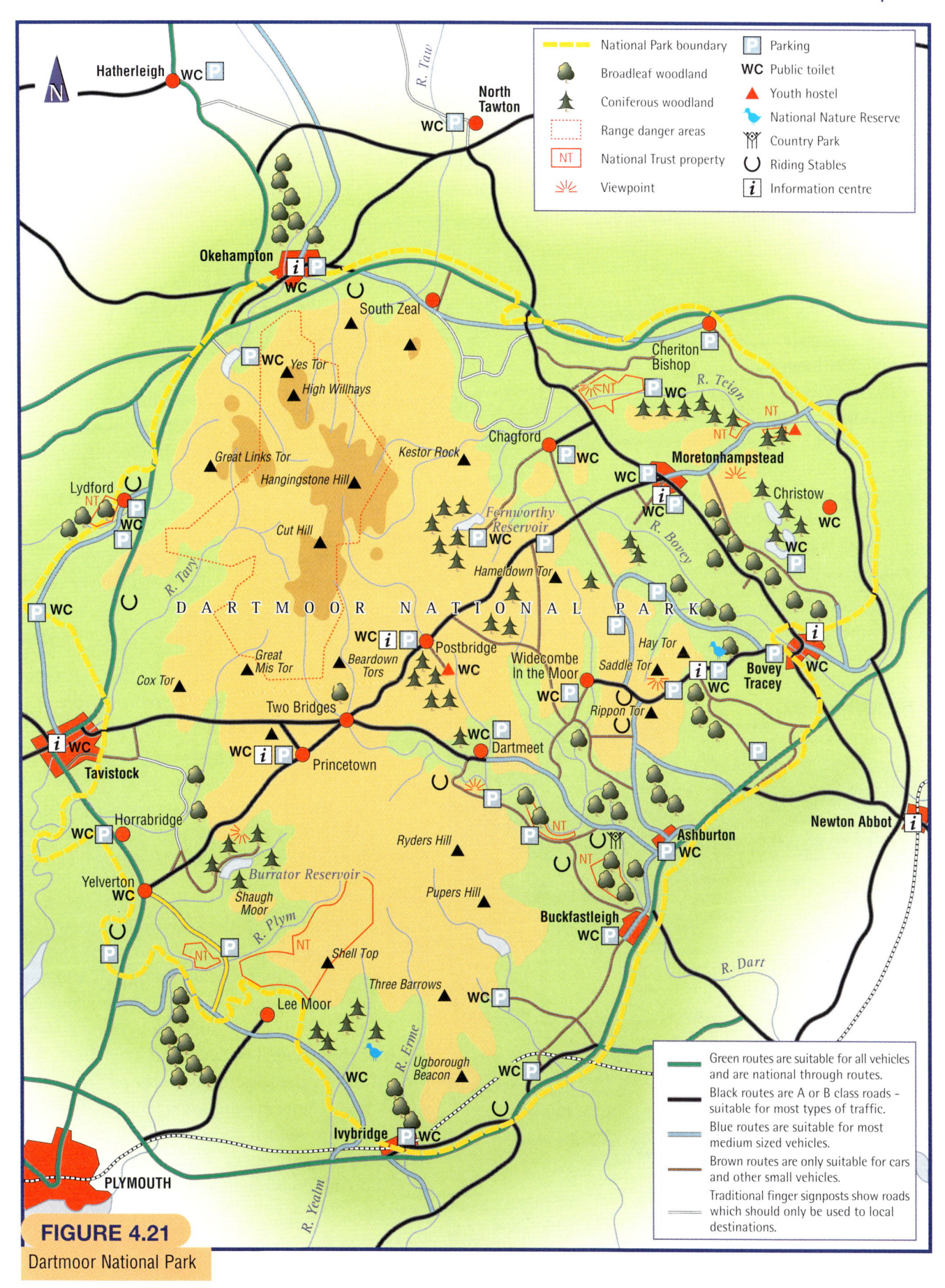

FIGURE 4.21
Dartmoor National Park

four — People and the Environment

Local environments

DARTMOOR

SUMMARY Dartmoor is a national park that gets many visitors. Some of the park, however, is closed to visitors. It is used for training by the army. Other areas are mined for china clay. Although some valleys have been flooded for reservoirs, visitors find them attractive.

Erosion

Dartmoor is the largest and wildest area of open country in the south of England. Two-thirds is granite moorland, with tors which provide spectacular views. The most accessible are **honeypots** (very popular) to visitors. Hay Tor, for example, is only 300 m from a car park (Figure 4.23). Too many feet trample the vegetation here. Heavy rain has washed away the exposed soil. In some areas, vehicles have been driven onto open land, causing more erosion, and horseriding has damaged the granite tramway at Hay Tor.

The National Park Authority's strategy is to turf or re-seed the most eroded parts. A new path at Hay Tor has been created and temporary fences used to divert horses and walkers away from the worst areas. Grass banks and blocks of granite are used to keep vehicles off open land.

Military training

14% of Dartmoor is used by the Ministry of Defence for training. Large areas of high moorland in North Dartmoor are closed to the public when live ammunition is in use and there has been damage to ancient monuments and wildlife. The area used is now only about half of what the army had when Dartmoor became a national park. The National Park Authority would like to see the end of all military training on the moor.

Water supply

Dartmoor has no natural lakes but there are eight reservoirs, such as Burrator Reservoir (Figure 4.22), where valleys have been flooded to store water for Devon's towns and cities. Summer water shortages are common in the towns, but rainfall is high on the moor. The wettest parts average more than 2 000 mm a year. (For comparison, London receives 610 mm.)

China clay

The granite that forms the high moorland and the tors also weathers into kaolin or china clay. It is used to make paper shiny. Mining it is a major industry on Dartmoor and china clay is exported all over the world. There are large amounts in the south of the national park around Lee Moor. Here is one of the largest china clay pits in the world, over 90 m deep. However, vast quantities of waste are produced and dumped in large heaps near the open-cast mine. Important areas for recreation and wildlife have been under threat.

FIGURE 4.22 Burrator Reservoir

Dartmoor 195

FIGURE 4.23
National Park warden picking up litter at Hay Tor car park

Conserving the environment

The wettest areas are permanently waterlogged, where sphagnum moss grows. These are Sites of Special Scientific Interest (SSSIs). Where it is less wet, there are heather and grass moors. In winter, patches of old heather are burnt off to encourage new growth and grazing for animals. Some areas have too many animals and the environment is suffering.

TASKS

1. What is meant by a honeypot?
2. Copy this sentence and choose the correct ending:
   Dartmoor is a good place for reservoirs because, compared to London, it gets *half/twice/more than three times as much rain*.
3. Photocopy the map on page 193 into the middle of an A3 sheet. In the white space round the map, write notes about Dartmoor's land uses.
4. Look at Figure 4.22. Do you think the reservoir spoils or enhances the landscape? Write down your reasons.
5. Using the information in this book together with the website below, produce a desktop published leaflet outlining the land use issues facing Dartmoor National Park. You can find out more detailed information on the Council for National Parks' website:

   http://www.dartmoor-npa.gov.uk/

four — People and the Environment
Local environments

WATER POLLUTION

> **SUMMARY** Sewage works, factories, farms and power stations can pollute rivers, lakes or the sea. Pollution interferes with ecosystems.

Sources of water pollution

- **Sewage**. In MEDCs, drains carry sewage to treatment works. Some drains are old and leak sewage into rivers.
- **Manufacturing industry**. Many factories use water for cooling. It goes back into the river as warm water. Some factories also let dirty water get into a river, accidentally or deliberately.
- **Agriculture**. Farmers use chemicals to kill weeds and pests. They put nitrates on their land as fertiliser. Some chemicals are washed off into rivers and lakes. Sometimes cattle slurry (manure) and silage (fermented grass for fodder) leak into streams.
- **Energy**. Oil spills happen in ports and at sea from oil tankers. Power stations use water for cooling. Warm water then goes back into rivers. If they burn coal or oil, power stations also produce the pollution that becomes acid rain (pages 202–205).

The effects of sewage pollution

- Bacteria break down sewage into ammonia but use up oxygen from the water in the process. The lack of oxygen means a smaller range of creatures can live in the water.
- Other bacteria break down the ammonia into nitrates, which leads to eutrophication (fast growth of algae).
- As the plant life encouraged by eutrophication grows, dies and is broken down by bacteria, more oxygen is used up.

The effects of nitrate pollution

- Nitrates are plant food, and too much of them will encourage the growth of green plants which use up oxygen and block out light. This reduces the range of creatures which can live in the water.
- There is a health threat from too much nitrate in drinking water.

TASKS

1. What is eutrophication?
2. Read about the pollution incidents below.

   Amoco Cadiz 1978. This oil tanker ran aground off the Brittany coast, France, and leaked crude oil.

   Sandoz 1986. A fire at this chemical factory in Basle, Switzerland, caused chemicals to be washed into the River Rhine when firefighters fought the blaze with hoses. The pollution flowed downstream and into the North Sea.

   Bulmer's 1994. This Hereford cider manufacturer admitted polluting the River Wye with an accidental leak of liquid glucose which caused a loss of salmon stock.

   River Stour, East Anglia. Nitrate levels rose steadily from 1940 to 1980 towards the EU limit.

   Southern North Sea 1989. A toxic algae plague was reported off Britain's coast. It was blamed on eutrophication due to pollution from farms and sewage works and it seriously damaged fish stocks.

   Copy each case study. At the end of each:
   a. write what caused it (write either 'Sewage', 'Agriculture', 'Industry' or 'Energy')
   b. write what the pollution affected (write either 'Lake', 'River' or 'Sea').

SPANISH SLUDGE SPILL, APRIL 1998

SUMMARY Waste water from mines at Aznalcóllar in Spain rushed down the Guadiamar River when a dam burst. It polluted farmland, killed fish and wildlife, and affected the health of local people. It will be many years before the damage is put right.

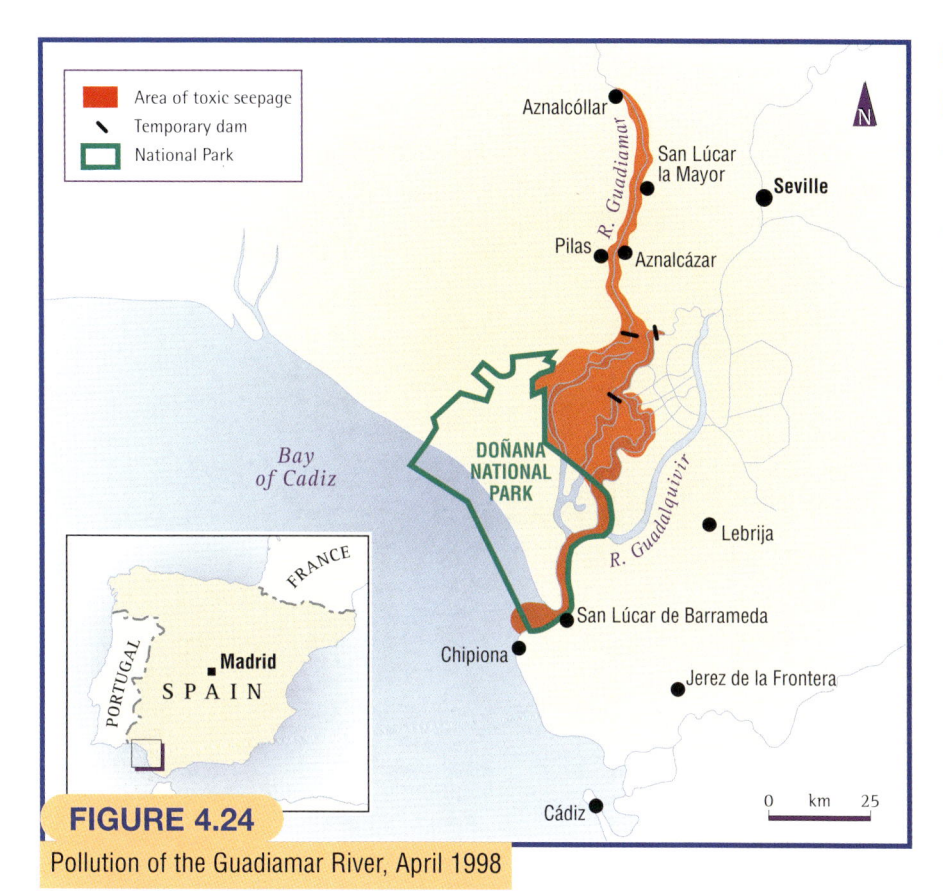

FIGURE 4.24
Pollution of the Guadiamar River, April 1998

Causes of the pollution

On 25 April 1998, a dam burst at Los Frailes zinc and lead mines in Spain (Figure 4.25). Sludge containing poisonous lead, arsenic, zinc and mercury flowed into the Guadiamar River (Figure 4.24).

FIGURE 4.25
The broken dam which released the toxic mining waste

People and the Environment

Local environments

Short-term effects of the pollution

- Sludge flowed down the Guadiamar River for 40 km.
- The poisonous sludge polluted farmland, killing olive trees, orchards and vegetables.
- Many fish died (Figure 4.26) and other creatures in the food chain, such as birds and animals, were poisoned.
- 400 families had their water supply polluted.
- Some homes were flooded with polluted water.
- People near the river suffered health problems.
- Near the river mouth is Doñana National Park. It is Europe's largest wild bird sanctuary. A quarter of a million birds were in danger.

FIGURE 4.26
Fish die in the toxic sludge

Longer-term effects

- The mining company removed 7 million tonnes of polluted top soil from the river bank.
- The mine engineers pumped more waste into the river as they worked on repairing the dam.
- Local people were worried about the long-term effects on their health.
- The bed of the river was polluted. Species near the start of food chains feed and breed there.

FIGURE 4.27
Cleaning up the toxic sludge deposited in the Guadiamar valley

Spanish sludge spill, 1998   199

FIGURE 4.28
The area before the spill, 8.3.98

FIGURE 4.29
The area after the spill, 25.4.98

- Temporary dams were built to try to stop the pollution getting into Doñana National Park. But this meant the polluted water flowed down to the sea. Here, fishermen in 1 000 small boats worked, catching shrimps and eels.
- Hundreds of workers collected 20 tonnes of dead fish (Figure 4.26) to stop them being eaten by birds. National Park wardens scared birds away with guns.
- The delicate wetland ecosystem of the national park had a water shortage because water from the polluted river was stopped from flowing into it.
- Farmers cannot use the flooded land. It may be toxic for 25 years.

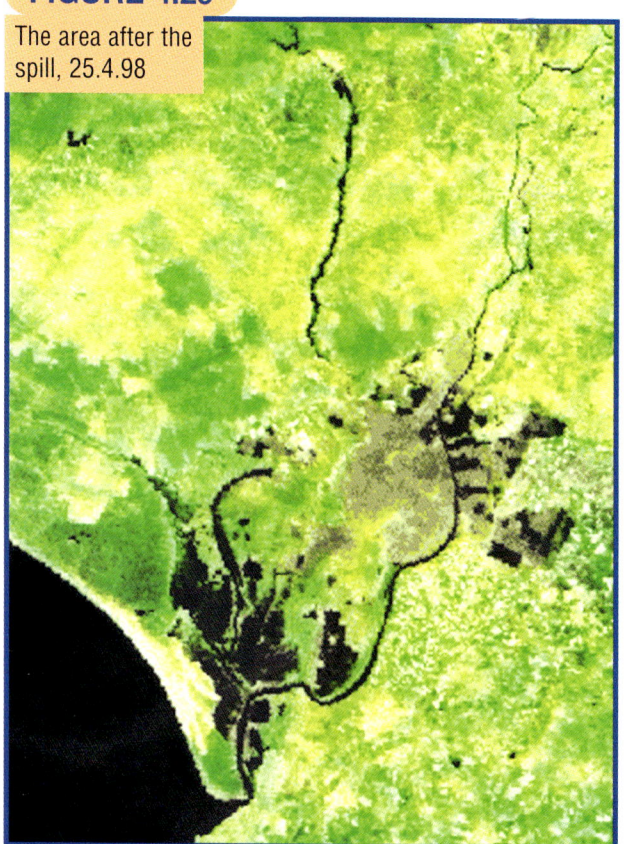

TASKS

1. a Trace the frame of the satellite image for 25 April (Figure 4.29). Then, using Figure 4.24 to guide you, trace the following features:
    - the coastline
    - the Guadalquivir River
    - the Guadiamar River.
   b Use colour shading to mark the following details onto your tracing:
    - the reservoir from which the toxic sludge originated
    - the area affected by toxic seepage
    - the area of the Doñana National Park
    - the urban area of Seville.
2. Write a newspaper report about what happened to the Guadiamar River on 25 April 1998. Include a map to show readers the area affected. Include interviews with a National Park warden and a local farmer.
3. Produce a poster warning people of the dangers soon after the dam burst.

People and the Environment

Local environments

PEMBROKESHIRE COAST OIL SPILL, WALES

SUMMARY When an oil tanker hit the rocks, pollution poisoned wildlife and cost the fishing industry and tourism millions of pounds.

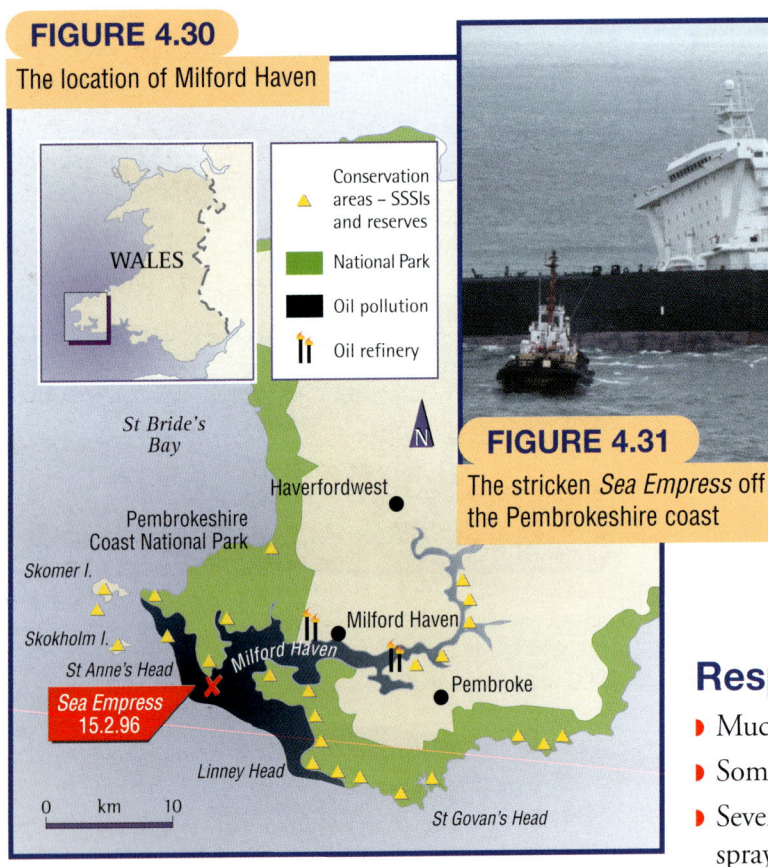

FIGURE 4.30 The location of Milford Haven

FIGURE 4.31 The stricken *Sea Empress* off the Pembrokeshire coast

tonnes of oil, half of its cargo, leaked into the sea. The oil was carried by winds, currents and tides.

- Oil was washed up on the coast, especially to the east.
- Some oil was washed northwards to Skomer Island.
- Balls of tar were blown as far as the North Devon coast and the coast of Ireland.

Responses to the oil spill

- Much of the oil evaporated into the atmosphere.
- Some was skimmed off the surface of the sea.
- Seven specially adapted aircraft were used to spray the oil with chemicals. These broke up the oil and made it sink, so it was less of a hazard to seals and seabirds. The chemicals, though, may have had bad effects on other wildlife.
- Tourist beaches had oil removed by blasting it with jets of water into trenches. Pumps then sucked it up into skips (Figure 4.33). The main beaches reopened for Easter.
- Quiet beaches were left for natural processes to work on the oil. Waves washed the oil from the pebbles and bacteria broke the oil down.

The *Sea Empress* oil spill

The *Sea Empress* was a 147 000 tonne supertanker. On 15 February 1996, the ship approached the Texaco oil refinery at Milford Haven in West Wales, loaded with oil from the North Sea. It was low tide and the ship hit the rocks off St Anne's Head (Figure 4.30). As the tide rose, the Sea Empress floated again, but 6 000 tonnes of oil had escaped through the damaged hull.

Over the next week, the salvage operation went wrong several times. The ship was allowed to run aground several more times. More than 70 000

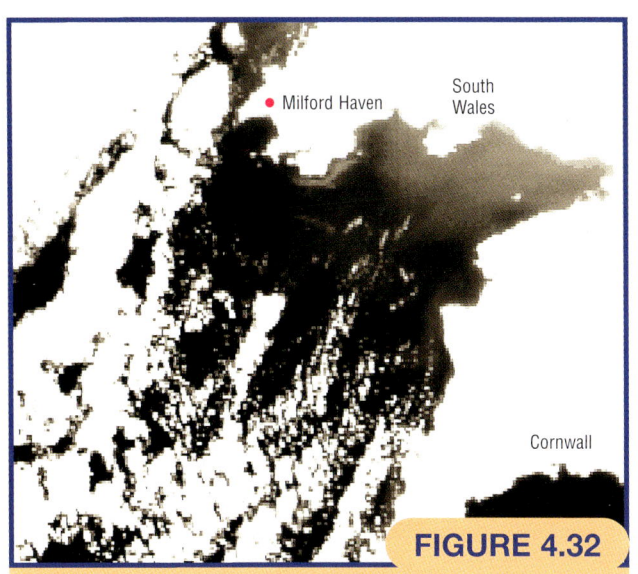

Pembrokeshire coast oil spill, Wales

FIGURE 4.32
Satellite image of south-west Wales taken at 08:08 on 21 February 1996, at the height of the pollution incident

FIGURE 4.33
Beach cleaning in progress

Effects of the oil spill

Wildlife
20 000 birds died. When they try to clean oil off their feathers, birds swallow it and are poisoned. Shellfish were badly affected. They feed by filtering seawater through their bodies. Half of all the limpets along this coast died. Hundreds of cockles and razor shells were washed up on beaches.

Fishing
As soon as the oil spill happened, fishing was banned. 1 000 people here worked in the fishing industry. The business was worth £3 million a year.

Tourism
There are many jobs in holiday accommodation, catering and leisure activities. Bookings went right down and losses may have been as much as £50 million.

Farming
Some farmers near the coast had a thin covering of oil blown onto their land. Experts decided it was not dangerous.

TASKS

1 Compile a case study revision map of the Pembrokeshire oil spill. You should draw an outline map of the coastline with plenty of space around it to make notes which should summarise the information on pages 200 and 201.

2 Write out the half sentences in column A, one at a time. Finish each one off with the correct words from column B.

A	B
The Sea Empress was	the coast around Milford Haven in Wales.
When it first hit the rocks	to spray the oil with chemicals.
Altogether, 70 000 tonnes of oil polluted	because few holiday makers came.
Special aircraft were used	6 000 tonnes of oil escaped into the sea.
Hotel owners lost money	a large oil tanker.
Many sea birds died	because they swallowed oil.

3 Put yourself in the position of each of the following Pembrokeshire people and write down no more than four short points to summarise the likely views of each person on the *Sea Empress* oil spill:

a Tenby hotel-owner, a wildlife trust volunteer, a commercial fisherman, a field study centre warden, a coastguard, an oil refinery worker

four
People and the Environment
The global environment

THE CAUSES OF ACID RAIN

> **SUMMARY** Air pollution from some electricity power stations and from road transport puts harmful gases into the atmosphere. They dissolve in clouds and fall as acid rain. It damages the environment, often very far away from where the pollution was produced.

Rain is normally slightly acidic. Gases in the atmosphere dissolve into it. When the pH value (Figure 4.34) is lower than 5.6, it is called **acid rain**. The extra acidity comes from:

- Power stations that burn fossil fuels containing sulphur. They give off **sulphur dioxide**.
- Road vehicles. **Nitrogen oxides** come out of exhaust pipes.

These polluting gases turn into **sulphuric acid** and **nitric acid** in the atmosphere. They may travel for more than 1 000 km, blown along by the **prevailing winds** (winds that regularly blow from a similar direction) before falling as rain. The acid rain lands on vegetation, soaks into the soil and enters rivers and lakes.

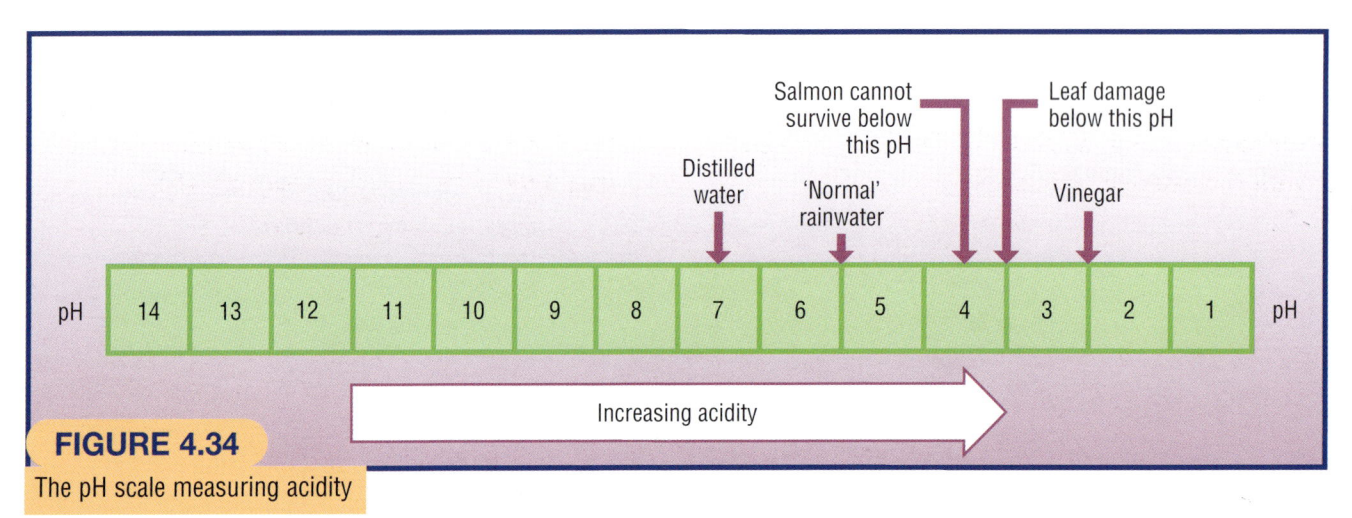

FIGURE 4.35
Emissions from Ironbridge Power Station, Shropshire

FIGURE 4.34
The pH scale measuring acidity

pH: 14 13 12 11 10 9 8 7 6 5 4 3 2 1

- Distilled water (pH 7)
- 'Normal' rainwater (pH 6)
- Salmon cannot survive below this pH (pH 4)
- Leaf damage below this pH (pH 3)
- Vinegar (pH 3)

Increasing acidity →

TASKS

1. a. Make a copy of Figure 4.36. It shows how much sulphur pollution went into the atmosphere (emission) and how much came down as acid rain (deposition). Work out the difference for each of the countries and fill in the column.
   - Where a country has more deposition than emission, your answer is a minus number. It is a net receiver of sulphur.
   - Where a country has more emission than deposition, your answer is a plus number. It is a net exporter of sulphur.

   b. Choose two colours. Colour the name of each country in your table. Use one colour for the countries that are net receivers and another colour for the net exporters.

   c. Use an atlas to see where the countries are. In which parts of Europe are the net exporters?

   d. In which parts of Europe are the net receivers?

   e. Which countries do you think most want to take action against acid rain – and why?

   f. Why do you think it is difficult for one country to blame another for being the source of acid rain?

Country	Total emission	Total deposition	Emission difference
Belgium	152	62	
Czech Republic	710	260	
Denmark	78	45	
Finland	60	106	
France	568	362	
Germany	1 948	803	
Italy	1 126	299	
Netherlands	84	71	
Norway	18	94	
Poland	1 362	822	
Sweden	50	161	
United Kingdom	1 597	430	

Figure 4.36 Sulphur emissions and depositions in Europe (2 tonnes of sulphur dioxide is equivalent to 1 tonne of sulphur) – figures are in 1 000 tonnes per year in 1994

THE EFFECTS OF ACID RAIN

- Acid rain increases the level of acidity in some rivers and lakes. Some species cannot survive and some lakes now have no living creatures in them. In Sweden, 20% of lakes have been seriously damaged by acid rain.

- Acid rain soaks into soil. Chemical reactions produce toxic metals, such as aluminium, in soil. These damage tree roots and, when the water drains into rivers, the toxic metals kill fish. This is called **acid-toxic stress**.

- Acid in the water supply rots pipes, tastes bad and has even turned hair green after washing. In some badly polluted parts of the Czech Republic, life expectancy has gone down by 10 years compared with the national average.

- Acid rain damages trees. In Germany, 1 in 12 is affected. Trees can also be damaged by fungus, drought and disease so it is difficult to blame acid rain entirely.

- Food crops may be affected by acid rain. In part of China, more than 1 000 ha of rice were killed.

- Acid rain damages buildings. Stonework is turned black and crumbles. The Acropolis, an ancient monument in Athens, has suffered as much in the last 20 years as in the previous 2 000 years.

- Damage from acid rain each year in Europe could cost as much as £1 billion.

- Concerns about acid rain have changed decisions about producing electricity. Less is being generated by power stations that burn coal. That has cut down the pollution that causes acid rain, but it has also killed many communities where coal mines have closed (pages 160–161).

People and the Environment

The global environment

TACKLING ACID RAIN

International co-operation

One country cannot prove that another country has caused its acid rain. Winds may blow the pollution around for days before it comes down with the rain. So the damage may be blamed, at least partly, on other causes.

- In Europe, countries are working together. In 1979, 31 countries agreed to share information and help each other with research, so that less sulphur dioxide is produced.
- The UN wants countries to reduce sulphur dioxide by 30%.
- Electricity companies and coal producers in the UK have worked with scientists in Norway and Sweden. They want to get a better understanding of what causes acid rain and how to tackle the problems.
- Less sulphur dioxide is now polluting Europe, but nitrogen oxide and carbon dioxide emissions have continued to increase.
- Some people say improvements are only because industry is using less energy, and because more gas is being burned to make electricity instead of using coal and oil.

FIGURE 4.37
Acid rain is blamed for tree damage in the Erzgebirge mountains, Czech Republic

TASKS

1   a   Print off, or trace from an atlas, a map of Europe to show the boundaries of the countries in the list below.

Country	Emission (tonnes/1 000 people/year)
Belgium	15
Czech Republic	69
Denmark	15
Finland	12
France	10
Germany	24
Italy	20
Netherlands	5
Norway	4
Poland	35
Sweden	6
United Kingdom	27

  b   Draw three small boxes for the key to your map. Label the boxes
- low sulphur emissions (0–15)
- medium sulphur emissions (16–30)
- high sulphur emissions (30+).

  c   Choose one coloured pencil and shade the first box, very lightly, for 'low'. Press harder to make the 'high' box dark. Then colour the 'medium' box a shade between the other two.

  d   Now colour the map of Europe according to the key.

  e   Copy this paragraph. Choose from these words to complete it.

Eastern, low, prevailing, Czech Republic, Poland, UK, acid

The countries which produce the most sulphur for every 1 000 people are _____ and _____. They are both in _____ Europe. The four countries of Scandinavia are _____ producers of sulphur, although they suffer badly from _____ rain. The _____ winds from the south west bring them pollution from other countries, such as _____.

Tackling acid rain

Reducing emissions from coal-fired power stations

- Up to 95% of sulphur dioxide emissions from coal-fired power stations can be stopped by using crushed limestone. A chemical reaction turns the limestone into gypsum, used for making plaster. The equipment, called 'scrubbers', is expensive. It has not been fitted to many UK coal-burning power stations.
- Coal with a high sulphur content is mixed with (more expensive) low sulphur coal. It is crushed and washed, which takes out 15% of the sulphur.
- Some power stations have low temperature burners. They produce less nitrogen oxide.

Other solutions to the problems of acid rain

- Lime can be added to lakes. Sweden has done this for many years. However, it does harm some animals and plants.
- Electricity can be produced without burning oil or coal. Nuclear energy produces no acid rain, but there are problems, such as the enormous cost of disposing of nuclear waste. Electricity from wind power can be increased.
- Garages now sell low sulphur diesel fuel.
- A lot of energy is wasted now. Better insulation, more efficient central heating boilers and designing new buildings for passive solar heating (by putting the windows where the sun can shine through them) all reduce the energy needed.
- Water jets are used to clean up buildings blackened by acid rain.

TASKS

1. Look at Figure 4.38. Acid rain is strongest inside the area marked pH 4.3. Use an atlas to name the countries in this area.
2. Draw a mind map for acid rain. Colour the bubbles with one colour for 'Causes', another colour for 'Effects', and a third colour for 'Solutions'.

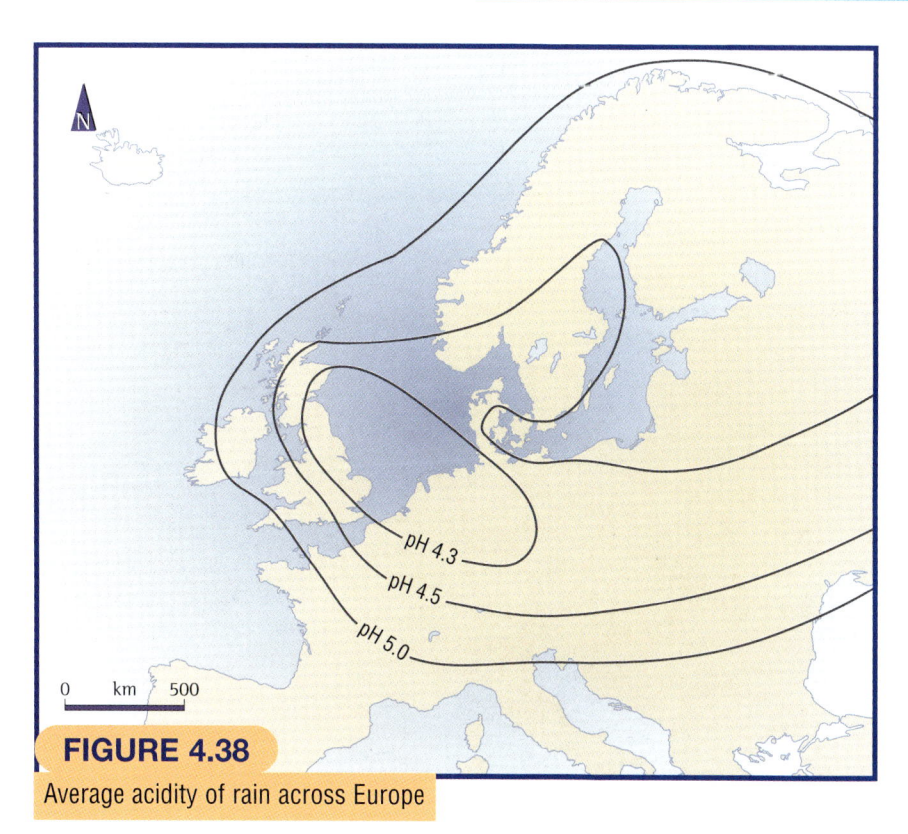

FIGURE 4.38
Average acidity of rain across Europe

four — People and the Environment

The global environment

GLOBAL WARMING

SUMMARY The earth is getting warmer. Greenhouse gases are stopping some heat escaping as radiation. As climates change, growing food becomes more difficult for some people. Sea levels are rising and there is more severe weather, like hurricanes. Countries need to work together to reduce the pollution that produces greenhouse gases.

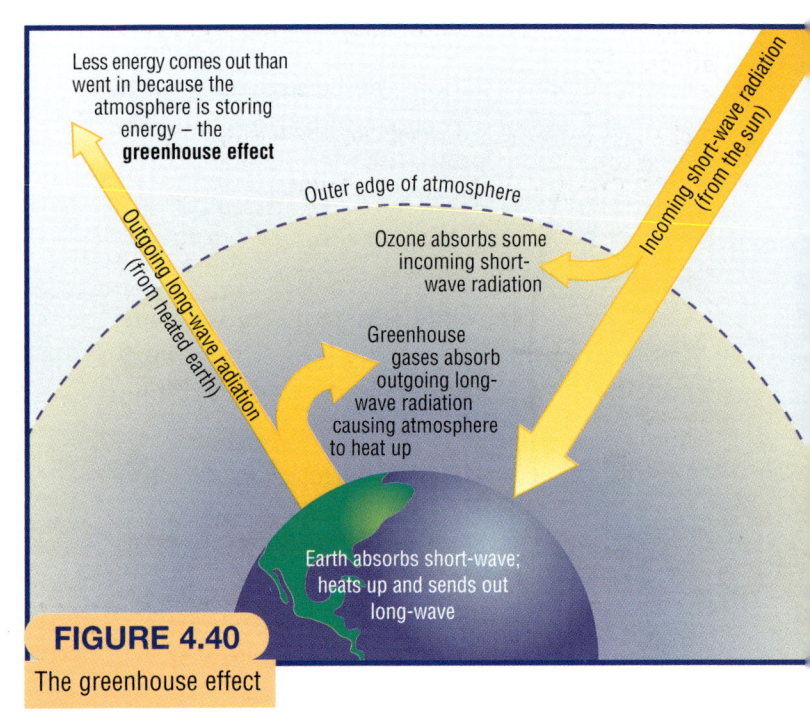

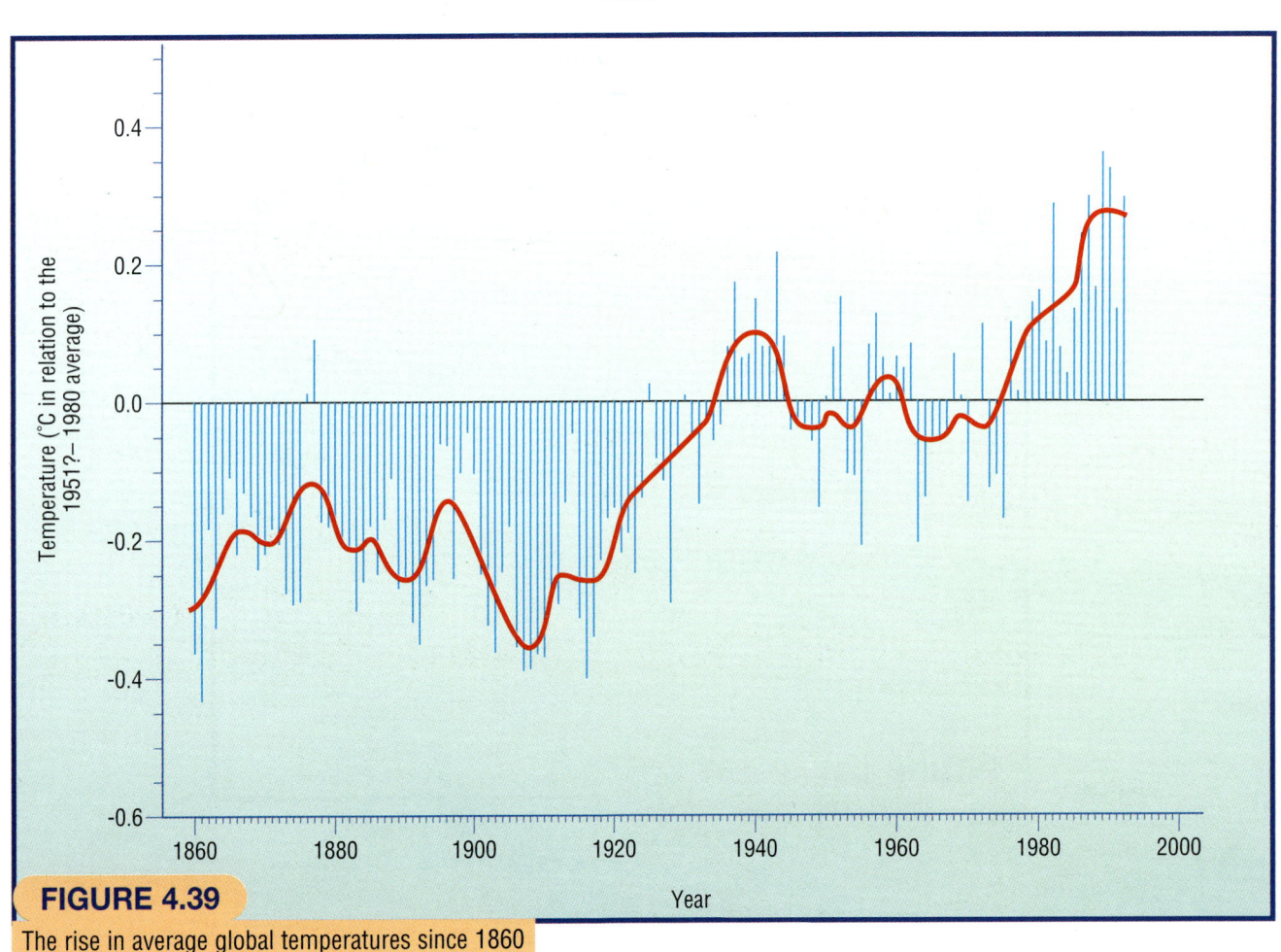

FIGURE 4.40 The greenhouse effect

- Less energy comes out than went in because the atmosphere is storing energy – the **greenhouse effect**
- Outer edge of atmosphere
- Outgoing long-wave radiation (from heated earth)
- Incoming short-wave radiation (from the sun)
- Ozone absorbs some incoming short-wave radiation
- Greenhouse gases absorb outgoing long-wave radiation causing atmosphere to heat up
- Earth absorbs short-wave; heats up and sends out long-wave

FIGURE 4.39 The rise in average global temperatures since 1860

(Graph: Temperature (°C in relation to the 1951?–1980 average) vs Year, from 1860 to 2000)

Global warming

Climate change

Average temperatures rose steadily through the twentieth century (Figure 4.39). Temperature is affected by

- changes in the amount of solar radiation
- the movement of the earth's plates
- changes in ocean currents
- changes in the gases in the atmosphere.

We do not know how much the rising temperature is due to natural events and how much is due to our use of resources.

The greenhouse effect and global warming

Most of the atmosphere is nitrogen and oxygen. There are also small amounts of gases that keep the heat in. We call them **greenhouse gases**. Figure 4.40 shows how the **greenhouse effect** works.

- Energy from the sun (short-wave radiation) passes through the atmosphere. Some harmful ultra-violet radiation is absorbed by a gas called ozone.
- The land and the surface of the sea warm up. They then radiate long-wave radiation back.
- Greenhouse gases absorb most of this long-wave radiation, which heats up the atmosphere.
- People use more energy, which creates more greenhouse gases, so temperatures rise even higher.

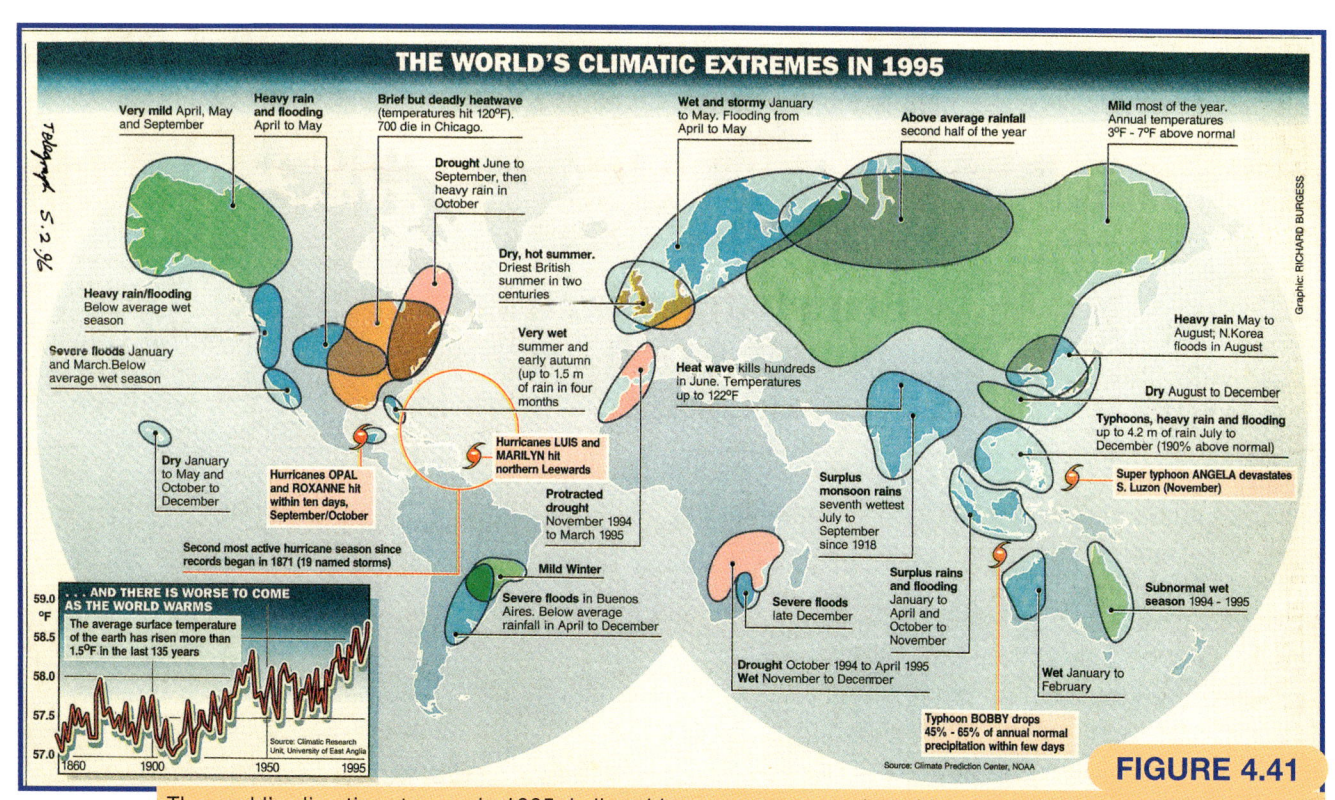

FIGURE 4.41 The world's climatic extremes in 1995, believed by some experts to be evidence of the effects of global warming

four People and the Environment

The global environment

THE POTENTIAL CONSEQUENCES OF GLOBAL WARMING

FIGURE 4.42
A crack appears because of melting in the Antarctic ice in 1998

- Tropical diseases could become common in new areas.
- Insurance companies are getting more claims for hurricane damage and flooding. Some farmers are having to pay to irrigate land, when not enough rain now falls.

- Glaciers and icecaps melt. More water in the oceans means sea levels rise. If it is a small rise of 50 cm over the next 100 years, it would flood 12% of Bangladesh.
- Water expands as it gets warmer. This is a second reason for sea levels rising.
- Climates could change. Severe weather is becoming more common, with droughts in Africa more often, and more powerful hurricanes in the Caribbean. This could be linked to El Niño, a warm current of water in the Pacific Ocean. Not everywhere is getting warmer, though. The UK could become much colder if changes in ocean currents divert the North Atlantic Drift. This is a flow of water across the Atlantic Ocean which keeps the UK warm.
- Less food could be grown in some areas, as present-day crops would not be well suited to the changed climate, especially if it were drier. In some countries, more people would be malnourished. If global warming warms the UK, vines would grow well and more wine could be produced.
- Plants and animals may not adapt quickly enough. One-third of the world's forests could be at risk. There could be more forest fires. The fires would put carbon dioxide into the atmosphere and make the greenhouse effect worse.
- Tourism often relies on the climate. Less snow on the Alps would mean fewer skiers – and that would mean fewer tourist jobs. Tourist developments in LEDCs may rely on beaches and coral reefs, but these may disappear with rising sea levels and changing water temperatures.

TASKS

1. Many people believe that greenhouse gases are causing global warming. Copy the pie chart below. Label and colour it to show the information in Figure 4.43.

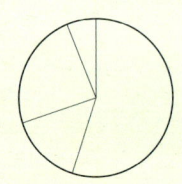

Greenhouse gas	Source	Estimated % contribution to global warming
Carbon dioxide	Burning fossil fuels to provide energy and burning vegetation, e.g. deforestation.	55
Methane	Produced by bacterial decay of organic material; released by swamps, paddy fields, the digestion of grazing animals and by mining (having been trapped in coal for millions of years).	15
Chloro-flouro-carbons (CFCs)	Synthetic chemicals used to propel aerosol sprays, manufacture plastic foam packaging and as a refrigerant.	24
Nitrous oxide	Released when farmers use artificial fertilisers and when fossil fuels are burned in power stations and vehicles.	6

Figure 4.43 Greenhouse gases

2. Write the script for a TV news item on global warming. Include in brackets what you want the film crew to show for each part of your script.

HOW TO DEAL WITH THE EFFECTS OF GLOBAL WARMING

International co-operation

One country on its own cannot tackle global warming. There must be international co-operation. The IPCC (Intergovernmental Panel on Climate Change) was set up so that countries could work together. The IPCC says there is now enough evidence that pollution is at least partly to blame for the earth heating up.

FIGURE 4.44
Protesters occupy a derelict petrol station in London during the Kyoto summit to protest about the world's high consumption of fossil fuels and consequent emission of greenhouse gases

The UN held a conference in 1997 at Kyoto in Japan (Figure 4.44). Targets were set to reduce pollution, but the USA, responsible for 25% of all pollution, has done very little to cut back. Global warming is linked to the development of industry in MEDCs, which has made them rich. Now LEDCs want to raise their standard of living, with more industry, but that will increase the pollution they produce. The challenge is to achieve equal emissions per person by the year 2050. That will allow an increase in LEDCs, but needs a big reduction in MEDCs.

Possible ways of reducing emissions

- Encouraging energy conservation. Cars with small engines, which use less fuel and produce less pollution, pay less road tax.
- No longer using CFCs to make the spray from aerosol cans.
- Ensuring old fridges containing CFCs can no longer be dumped. The CFCs have to be carefully removed.
- Producing more renewable energy. The government wants renewable sources to provide 10% of the UK's electricity by 2010 – compared with 2% in 1995.
- Encouraging more tree planting. Trees turn carbon dioxide into oxygen.
- Changing farming to reduce methane and nitrous oxide emissions.

TASKS

1. Make a list of ways of dealing with global warming. After each one, write in brackets who is, or should be, doing it. You might include the UN, the UK government, certain industries, yourself.
2. Find out more about global warming on the internet. Use:

   http://www.globalwarming.org/
   http://www.foe.co.uk/climatechange/index.html

   Produce a poster to tell people what individuals can do.

four
People and the Environment
Advice

COURSEWORK FOR THE ENVIRONMENTAL EFFECTS OF PEOPLE

Opportunities to study the effects of people on the environment depend on your local area. Many rivers that were polluted have been cleaned up. Issues such as proposed quarries or mines could be studied. National Parks in England and Wales attract many visitors. Conflicts of interest and the impact of tourism on the environment can be studied, especially in honeypot locations.

River pollution

Suitable sites need to be chosen. Readings could be taken above and below an outflow pipe or in fast- and slow-flowing sections of a stream.

1. Identify suitable sites and mark them on a map.
2. Complete a recording sheet such as the one shown in Figure 4.45. Pages 54–55 give information about taking measurements such as depth. Test acidity using pH paper. Record clarity (how clear the water is) by putting a white yoghurt carton on the end of a pole and lowering it into the water. Measure the depth at which the carton cannot be seen.
3. Survey water life by counting the number of species at each site (use Figure 4.46). Expect to find about 20 in non-polluted water. This survey could be done at different times of the year.

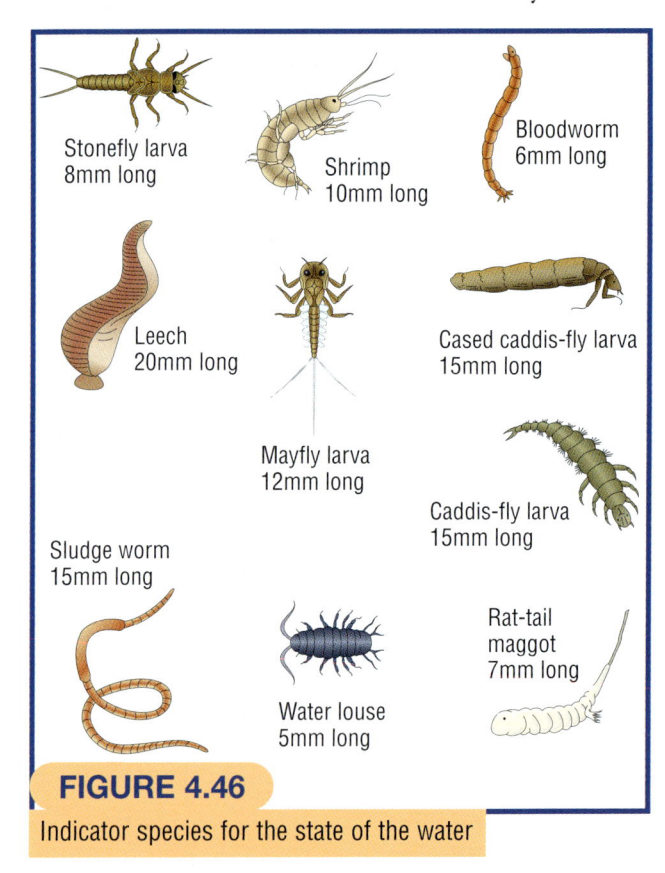

FIGURE 4.46 Indicator species for the state of the water

- Stonefly larva 8mm long
- Shrimp 10mm long
- Bloodworm 6mm long
- Leech 20mm long
- Mayfly larva 12mm long
- Cased caddis-fly larva 15mm long
- Sludge worm 15mm long
- Water louse 5mm long
- Caddis-fly larva 15mm long
- Rat-tail maggot 7mm long

River Pollution Booking Sheet			Overall score: 0-3 very clean 4-9 clean 10-15 fairly clean 16-21 doubtful 22+ badly polluted		
River, stream		Site Number		Grid reference	
Date		Weather		Depth of river (cm)	
Width (m)		Ave. surface velocity (m/sec)		Visibility using yoghurt carton (cm)	
Water temperature (°C)		pH			
Visual Survey (✓ tick)	**0 points**	**1 point**	**2 points**	**3 points**	**4 points**
Presence of suspended solids, e.g. sewage	Very clear	Clear	Fairly clear	Slightly murky	Murky
Colour	Very clear	Clear	Slightly brown	Dark brown	Black
Stones	Clean and bare	Clean	Lightly covered in brown fluffy matter	Coated with brown fluff	Coated with brown and grey deposits
Water weed	None	A little in shallows	Lots in shallows	Abundant	Chocked
Grey algae (sewage fungus)	None	None	A little	Present in patches	Plentiful
Scum/froth/oil	None	Odd bubbles	Noticeable foam islands	Large quantities	Covers whole river
Dumped rubbish	None	A few small items	A few large items	Large and small items	Many large, different items

FIGURE 4.45 Recording sheet for river pollution

Coursework advice – the environmental effects of people

Mining and quarrying

Mines and quarries provide jobs and money for many areas. However, they can be ugly and cause air, noise and water pollution. A coursework investigation needs to be balanced by finding the views of different groups of people. Figure 4.47 shows ideas for a mining or quarrying study.

National Parks

It can be useful to study one honeypot location. This could be a settlement or a scenic site.

- Describe the human and physical reasons why the place is popular.
- Carry out people, traffic, litter and parked car counts.
- A questionnaire survey may be useful (see page 169 for ideas).
- Look for evidence of overuse such as footpath erosion. One footpath could be studied. At regular intervals, measurements such as width can be recorded and evidence of management marked onto sketches.

To extend this study, data collection can be repeated at a different time (day or season).

TITLE OF THE STUDY
'What is the impact of open-cast mining on people and the environment?'

Observation
* Mapping the site and its workings including heaps of overburden and waste.
* Environmental survey of the site and surrounding area.
* Environmental survey of areas unaffected for comparison.

Measurement
* Vehicle counts during working hours.
* Noise levels recorded on a sound meter (around the site and further away).

Interview / Questionnaires
* Arrange an interview with the site manager to hear the company's view and gain details such as the number of workers and home locations, where the raw materials from the mine go to, the number of lorries and routes, and pollution precautions.
* Questionnaires to local residents and farmers about their opinions of the site. Ask people in different locations at different distances from the site.
* Interview owners of local shops and services - has the mine brought any extra income?

Secondary sources
* Geological maps
* Newspaper articles
* Open-cast mine applications and environmental reports

FIGURE 4.47
A student plan for data collection

FIGURE 4.48
Measuring footpath erosion in winter. Quadrats are useful for estimating the percentage of bare ground/vegetation cover from one side of the path to the other

four

People and the Environment

Advice

EXAMINATION TECHNIQUE – UNIT 4

In Unit 4 the link between people and the environment is emphasised. Examination questions investigate environmental issues at all scales, from local to global.

This relationship between people and the environment is important. People have different viewpoints or attitudes towards the environment. These can influence the way that they treat it.

To answer questions on environmental topics successfully you need to know the geographical issues and some case studies. You also need to understand how people may have different ideas about how to use the natural environment. The way people use the environment must be controlled in order to protect it.

The first question tests your understanding of a global environmental topic – acid rain. Figure 4.49 below shows the acid rain 'cycle'.

Figure 4.49

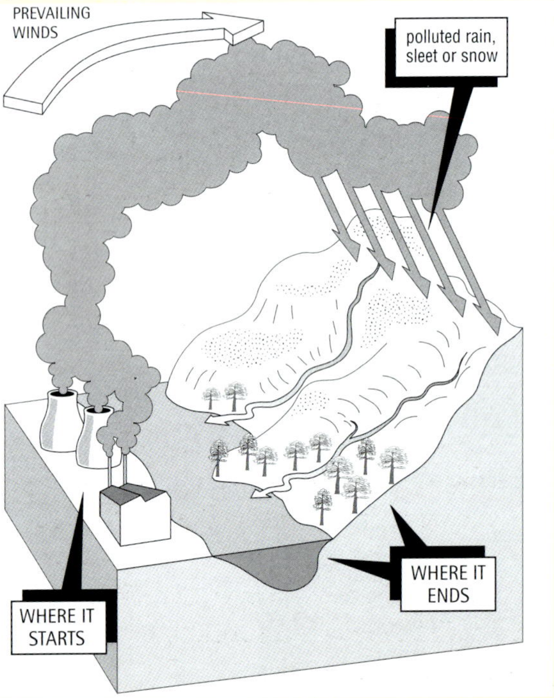

[Diagram showing prevailing winds carrying pollution from factories ("WHERE IT STARTS") across to produce polluted rain, sleet or snow falling on hills and forests ("WHERE IT ENDS").]

1 (a) Use the ideas in Figure 4.49 to explain why acid rain occurs. [3]

(b) Explain why countries need to work together to reduce acid rain. [3]

From this question you can see that when revising a geographical **concept** such as acid rain it is possible to break the topic down into three simple questions.

▸ How is the problem caused?
▸ How does it affect people and/or the environment?
▸ What can be done to reduce or manage the problem?

Before answering an examination question, read it carefully. Often you will not have to deal with all three of these questions.

The following example shows how such a revision plan would work in order to answer a question about global warming (or, as it is often called, the greenhouse effect). Like acid rain, global warming is an international or global issue. The answers to each question show how revision can result in high marks.

2 (a) Rainforest destruction is one cause of the greenhouse effect. Give two other causes. [2]

Revision question: How is the problem caused?

Answer from candidate 1

1. Factories giving out various gases.
2. Too many cars causing a lot of carbon dioxide to be released into the atmosphere.

Answer from candidate 2

1. Burning of fossil fuels through power stations.
2. Industries letting off carbon dioxide and other gases.

(b) Explain how the greenhouse effect causes temperatures to rise. You may include a labelled diagram. [3]

Revision question: How is the problem caused?

Examination advice – Unit 4

Answer from candidate 1

> The greenhouse effect is the building up of the carbon dioxide layer surrounding the earth. The sun's rays hit the earth and the earth radiates this heat out into space. The greenhouse effect is when this heat becomes trapped between the earth and the carbon dioxide layer.

Answer from candidate 2

> Sun's rays are sent out and are meant to reflect back off the earth's surface. But huge clouds of carbon dioxide pollution form in the atmosphere which trap the sun's rays. The causes the atmosphere to warm up as the heat cannot escape.

(c) Describe three ways that global warming might affect the lives of people. [3]

Revision question: How does it affect people?

You need examples of those effects. Note that this question does not ask about reducing or managing the problem.

Answer from candidate 1

> 1. Icecaps can melt causing flooding.
> 2. They might not be able to grow crops as it doesn't rain.
> 3. Winters in England will get warmer.

Answer from candidate 2

> 1. Sea levels will rise and flood low areas near the sea.
> 2. There will be droughts and water shortages.
> 3. Farming will change as the climate gets warmer, e.g. growing vines in southern England.

When studying and revising these global topics, be careful not to mix them up. Candidates sometimes become confused between acid rain, global warming and thinning of the ozone layer. They are three different problems with different causes and effects.

Of course, environmental issues are not always tested on a global scale. One topic in the syllabus deals with water pollution and this can be studied at any scale from a local stream to a large sea area.

Look at the question below.

3 Study Figure 4.50 and read the information below.

Figure 4.50 The Cawthorne River

Herons and kingfishers are seen in the area

Precious fragments that must be saved

The Yorkshire Wildlife Trust has recently written to the Barnsley Planning Department concerning the growth of new industrial sites in the area. It is particularly worried about the damage that could occur to the Cawthorne River which is probably the cleanest stretch of river in Barnsley and provides habitat for heron and kingfisher, as well as many other species of birds.

(a) Describe two ways that the growth of new industrial sites could cause pollution. [2]

(b) Describe two possible effects of water pollution on the natural environment in

The question begins by giving you a local example of possible water pollution. Obviously you do not need to have studied the Cawthorne River to answer these questions. They are testing whether you understand possible causes and effects of water pollution. They follow the pattern of the revision questions suggested earlier:

- How is the problem caused?
- How does it affect the natural environment?

People and the Environment

Advice

The question continues the theme of water pollution in the case study.

> **(c)** Name a river, lake or sea you have studied which has been polluted. Describe how the pollution was caused and how it affected people. [5]

It is important to avoid mixing up answers that describe effects. Check if you need to describe the effects of water pollution on people (e.g. unsafe to drink, looks a mess with all the rubbish floating in it), or the effects on the environment (e.g. fish dying in the contaminated water, passed up the food chain).

Throughout the course you will study topics where people have different views about the environment. These different attitudes may affect the decisions which people then make about how they use or protect the environment. The following examination questions test your understanding of how people think about the environment in different ways.

The first question is about how people have different opinions about mining (see Figure 4.51).

> **4** Describe different problems which the Trinity opencast coal mine may cause for local farmers and residents of Aldercar. [4]

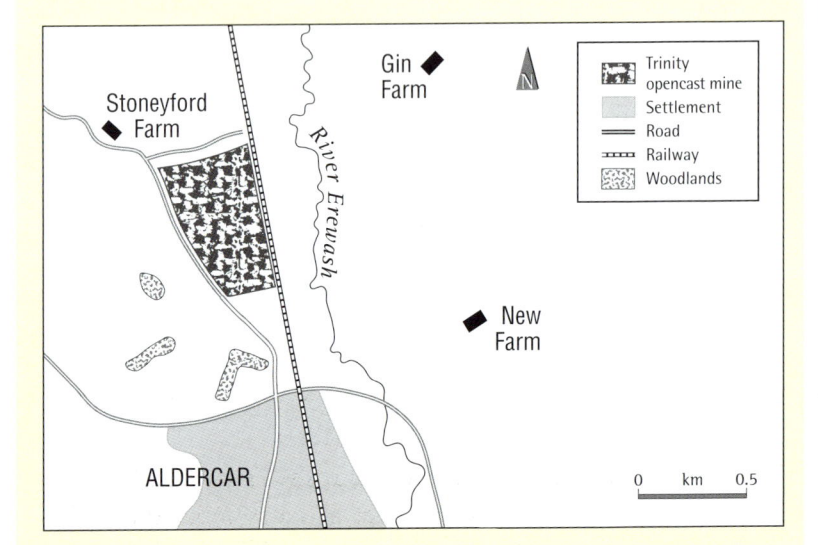

Figure 4.51 The Trinity opencast mine

One candidate suggested the problems shown below.

Candidate's answer

> Local farmers: Noise from the mine may scare animals. Local wildlife which may help pest control may also be scared off. Any land near the mine would be showered by dust when the coal is dug up. So any crops on that land may produce a lower yield.
> Residents: The land doesn't look very attractive and may cause people to move. House prices may also fall. Lorries and trains which transport the coal will cause air and noise pollution.

Examiner's comment

This is an excellent answer which shows good understanding of how people will think about the mine differently. Three problems are suggested for each group of people.

The different attitudes which people may have about the environment are also examined in Paper 3. The following question refers to the map on page 230.

> **5** What benefits and problems might the quarry and works cause for people living in the settlements shown on the OS map? [5]

Question 4 used a location map as a resource. Question 5 instructs candidates to examine an OS map extract to get some help about likely problems and benefits. This question is testing candidates' **understanding** of the attitudes of local people.

The next question looks at the attitudes of people to oil and gas exploration out at sea. To show one group's attitude to this issue, the photograph which goes with this question shows a protest by the Greenpeace organisation (Figure 4.52a).

Examination advice – Unit 4

6 Exploration for oil and gas is now taking place in areas of sea and ocean. Why do some people argue against searching for more oil and gas? [4]

Figure 4.52a Greenpeace protest

Notice that the question only asks candidates to consider one point of view. There are many possible ideas which can be used about both exploration and use of oil and gas; below is a selection of them.

Extracts from candidates' answers

- These fields could leak which would be deadly for the wildlife living in the area and could cause great environmental pollution in the area.
- If it spills out of tankers during transport it can kill birds, fish and other sea animals.
- Burning these fossil fuels releases carbon dioxide which causes problems such as global warming.
- We are using too much fossil fuel and we should be looking towards using alternative energy.
- People think that cleaner forms of energy ought to be exploited first.
- Instead of spending lots of money drilling for oil and gas it could be spent on developing cleaner and safer sources of energy such as solar, hydro-electric and wind power.

One other important topic in this section is about land use conflict in National Parks. This deals with the different ways that people want to use land in National Parks and the arguments that may be caused. The following case study question gives candidates the chance to describe the different attitudes that people have.

See how the three candidates show that people do not always co-operate.

7 Name a National Park which you have studied and describe the conflicts between tourism and other activities which are located there. [5]

Answer from candidate 1

Name of National Park: Peak District
Conflicts: There is not enough parking in villages like Castleton so people block road and driveways. This disturbs the locals as the cars ruin the scenery and sometimes they cannot drive along the roads. There are too many cars causing a lot of congestion at peak times. Bikers and walkers don't stick to the paths which ruins land and causes soil erosion when it rains, this causes conflict with local farmers. A lot of litter is dropped in farms. This could choke and poison the animals which causes conflict with the farmers.

Answer from candidate 2

Name of National Park: Peak District
Conflicts: The army wants to use the National Park for practising firing but there is too much noise for locals and tourists. Farmers say that sometimes gates are left open by walkers which could be dangerous for animals which get out. Locals want the park to be quiet and peaceful which is less likely with so many tourists. Also tourists cause congestion on narrow roads and this also causes pollution with car fumes. Locals have to spend so much money repairing damaged walls and fences caused by visitors.

Answer from candidate 3

Name of National Park: Peak District
Conflicts: There are lots of people who go to the Peak District and many people take their bikes so the grass gets eroded. Many other people go to walk and ruin the park by litter. People take their dogs for a walk and let them chase the sheep. Tourists will ruin the park by going there and kicking the soil with their feet when they walk.

Did you notice that the answer from candidate 1 is **place-specific**, but the answer from candidate 2 is general. Also can you see the difference in quality between answers 1 and 3?

four
People and the Environment
Advice

TASKS

1 The following questions all focus on people and the environment. Decide whether each question is about the **cause**, the **effects** or the **management** of pollution.

   a How do people help to cause acid rain?

   b Suggest two ways to solve the problem of acid rain.

   c Why might pollution in the Mediterranean Sea be dangerous to its wildlife and the people who live around it?

   d How can mining cause damage to the environment?

   e What can be done to reduce the damage caused by mining?

   f Explain why the level of pollution will be greater in some parts of the North Sea than in others.

   g Polluted rivers are a major problem in Britain. Suggest how water quality could be improved. Why is it difficult for people to clean up rivers?

   h Modern farming methods may cause river pollution. Name a river which you have studied and describe how the pollution occurred. How did this pollution affect the river ecosystem?

2 The following topics may all require a case study in the examination. Check the location which you could use as a case study example.

   a How mining and quarrying affects local people in an MEDC.

   b How people can affect the tropical rainforest in an LEDC.

   c Land use conflict in a National Park of the UK.

   d Causes and effects of pollution of a river, lake or sea.

   e Causes, effects and attempts to reduce acid rain.

   f Causes, effects and attempts to reduce global warming.

3 Questions on water pollution, especially in a sea, can include a question on distribution. Answer the following questions which test map skills and understanding.

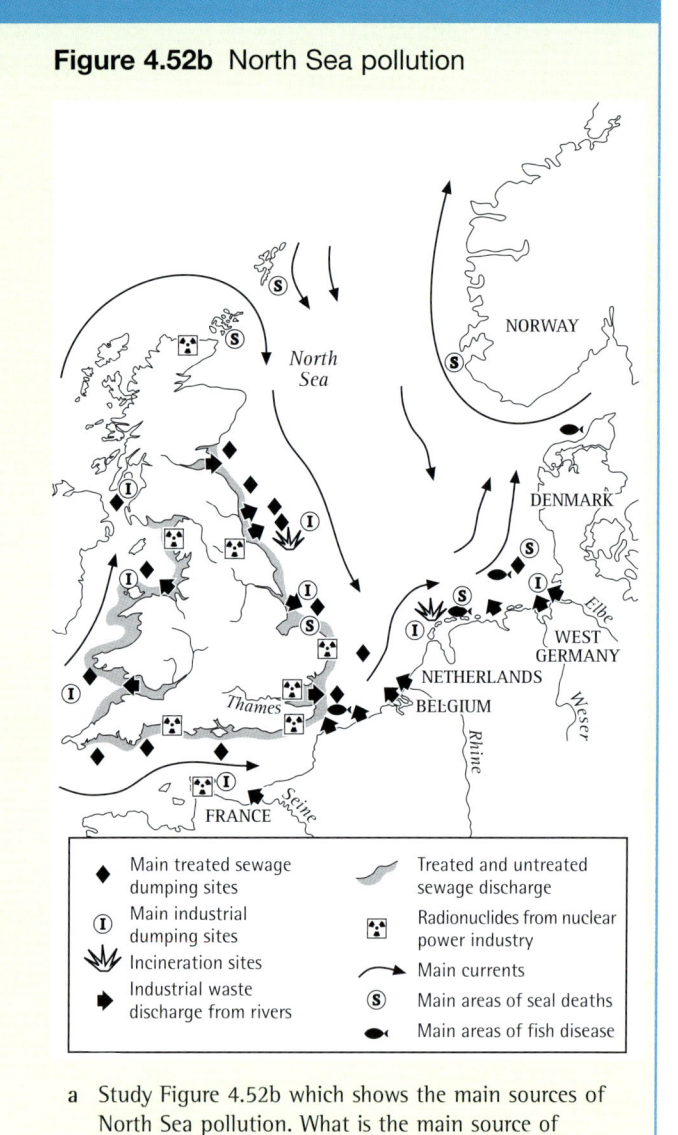

Figure 4.52b North Sea pollution

Key:
- ◆ Main treated sewage dumping sites
- Ⓘ Main industrial dumping sites
- 🌿 Incineration sites
- ➤ Industrial waste discharge from rivers
- Treated and untreated sewage discharge
- ☢ Radionuclides from nuclear power industry
- ⤴ Main currents
- Ⓢ Main areas of seal deaths
- 🐟 Main areas of fish disease

a Study Figure 4.52b which shows the main sources of North Sea pollution. What is the main source of pollution around the UK? [1]

Examination advice – Unit 4

TASKS

b Name a river in Germany which carries industrial waste into the North Sea. [1]

c Which parts of the North Sea do you think will be most polluted? [2]

d Suggest two reasons for the distribution of the main areas of fish disease. [2]

e Suggest reasons why there are main areas of seal deaths in the northern part of the North Sea between the UK and Norway. [3]

4 What do the following questions have in common?

[Clue: think about people.]

a Many people are worried about pollution in the North Sea. Give two reasons why each of the following groups of people would want the amounts of pollution in the North Sea to be reduced:

  i people who own a hotel in a holiday resort on the North Sea coast

  ii the Royal Society for the Protection of Birds.

b Read the information below about the closure of a coal mine in Blidworth, a village in Nottinghamshire.

  Describe the likely impact of the closure of the mine on the community of Blidworth.

PIT CLOSURE BLOW TO VILLAGE
Miners at Blidworth got the news on Monday that they had all been dreading – the pit was to close down. British Coal said that the pit was making a loss of over £10 million.

Figure 4.53 Wind power

c Many people think that areas with landscapes like the one in Figure 4.53 should not be changed. Other people think that wind turbines are a good idea. What reasons might the different groups give?

5 Discuss, with a partner, what attitudes people might have in the three situations described in task 4.

■ People and the Environment

Advice

THE ENTRY LEVEL CERTIFICATE

People and the environment

At the end of the Entry Level Certificate course, there is a Written Test. It lasts for an hour and is worth 30% of your marks. For some of the questions, you will write the answer. For others, you need to draw or shade in or finish something off. Don't forget to take your pencil and ruler with you.

Here is part of the Test. (Don't write your answers in this book!)

1 (a) Look at the map of national parks. How many are in Wales? _____ [1]

(b) On the map, shade in those national parks which reach the coast. [2]

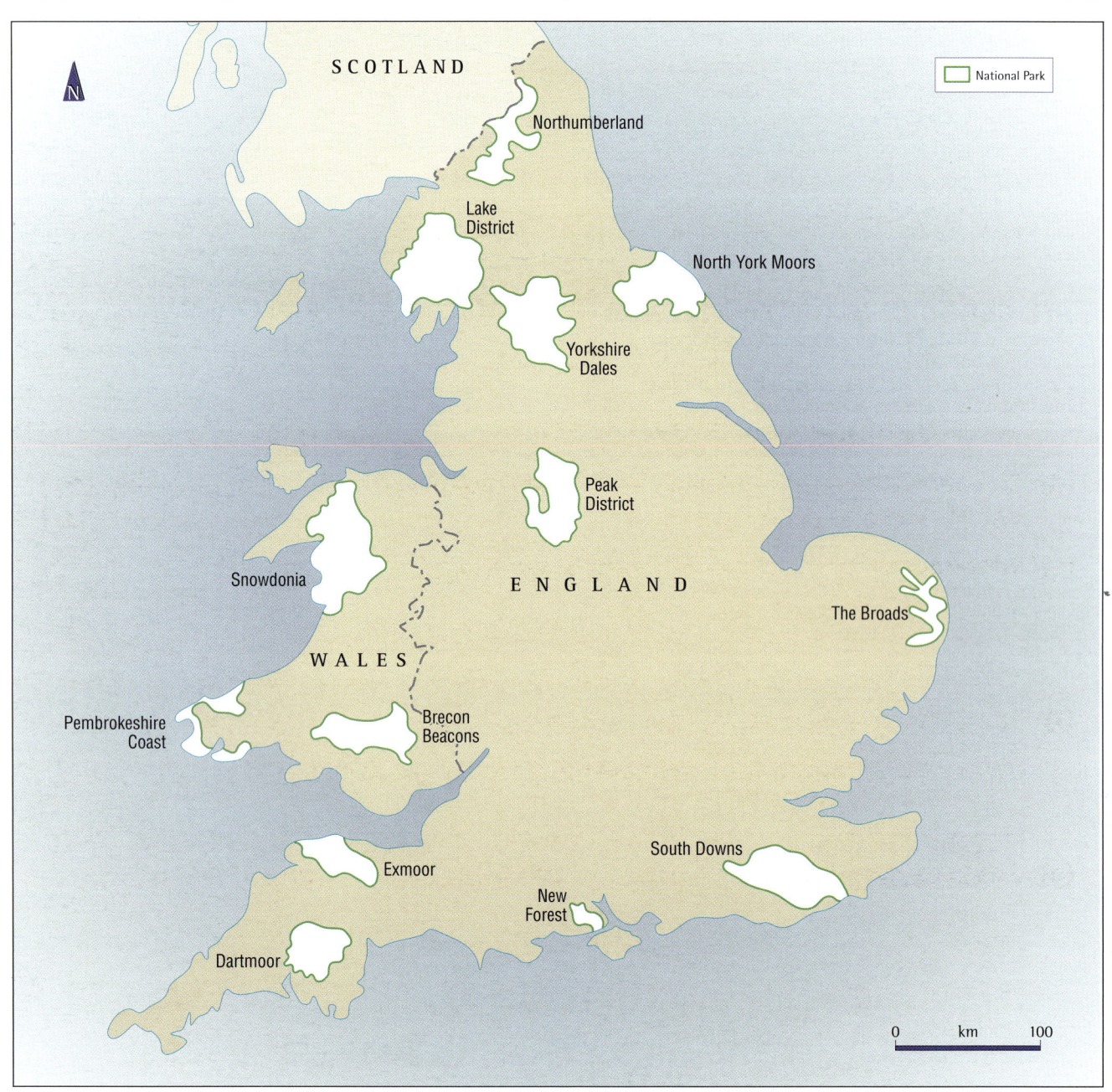

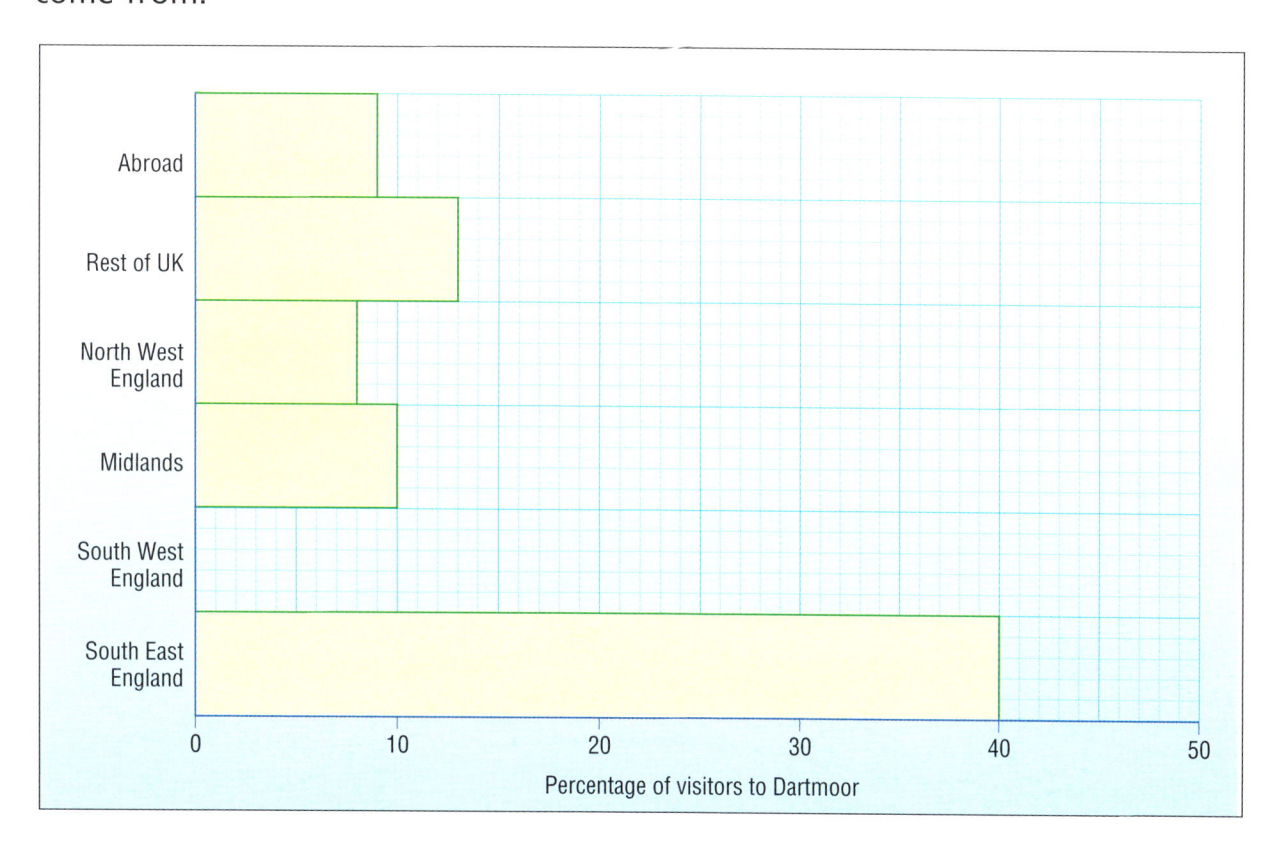

(c) Look at the graph showing where visitors to Dartmoor National Park come from.

How many come from the Midlands? _____ per cent. [1]

(d) 20 per cent come from the South West. Finish the graph off, by drawing the bar for the South West. [1]

(e) Write down two reasons why many people visit national parks.

1 _____

2 _____ [2]

(f) Some people who live in national parks think there are too many visitors.

Write about one problem caused by too many visitors. _____
_____ [2]

(g) Some people who live in national parks want more visitors. Say why. _____
_____
_____ [2]

People and the Environment

Advice

2 (a) Write down one of the uses of coal.

_____ [1]

Look at the photo below. A few years ago, this was an open-cast coal mine.

(b) What is now growing on this land? _____ [1]

(c) Why are there no tall trees here? _____

_____ [2]

(d) (i) Now that mining has finished, suggest one way this land might be used.

_____

_____ [1]

(ii) Why did you choose this land use?

_____

_____ [2]

3 (a) Acid rain is a type of pollution from burning fossil fuels.

Look at the diagram below.

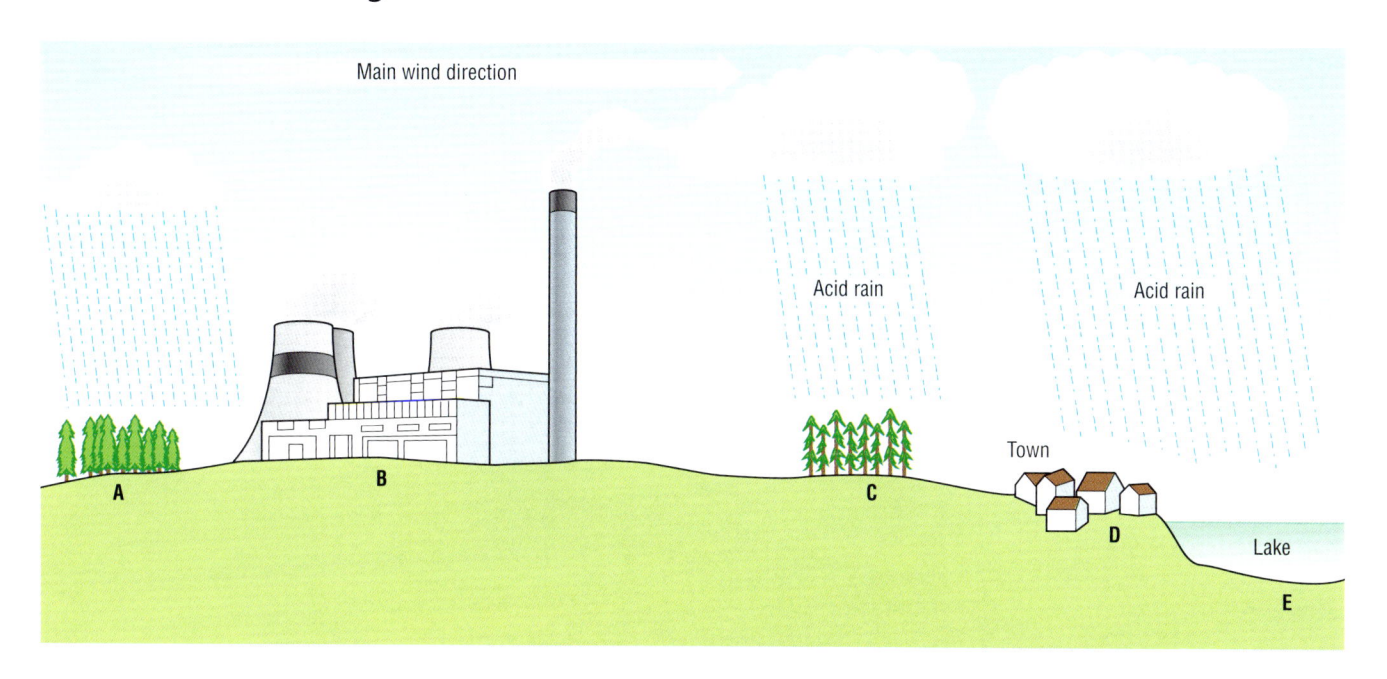

(i) What type of building is B likely to be?

_____ [1]

(ii) What has happened to the trees at C?

_____ [1]

(iii) Why has the same thing not happened to the trees at A?

_____

_____ [1]

(iv) What other effects of acid rain pollution are likely in areas D and E?

Area D _____

_____

Area E _____

_____ [2]

Guidance

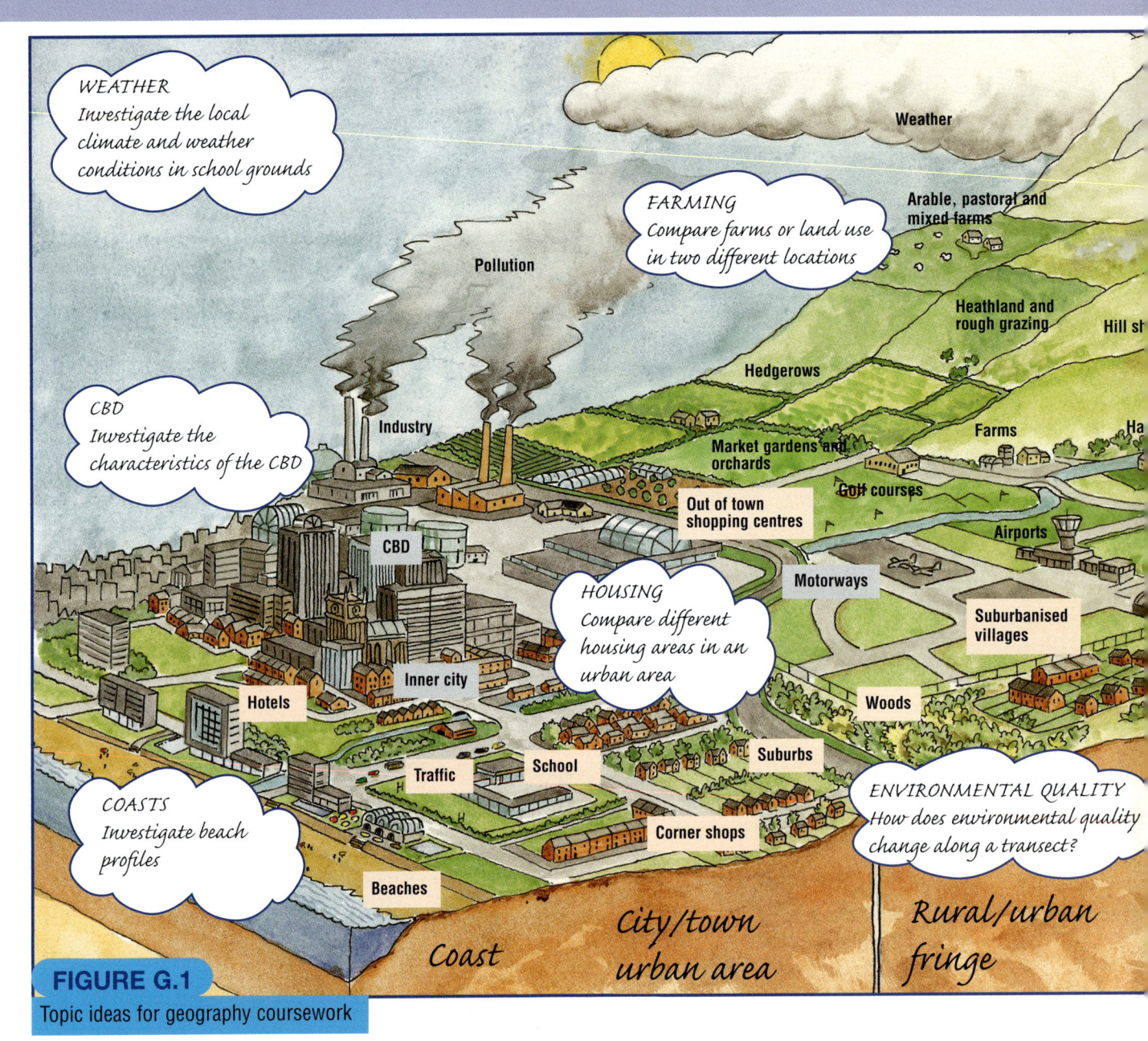

FIGURE G.1 Topic ideas for geography coursework

Labels on figure:
- WEATHER: Investigate the local climate and weather conditions in school grounds
- FARMING: Compare farms or land use in two different locations
- CBD: Investigate the characteristics of the CBD
- HOUSING: Compare different housing areas in an urban area
- COASTS: Investigate beach profiles
- ENVIRONMENTAL QUALITY: How does environmental quality change along a transect?
- Weather, Pollution, Industry, CBD, Inner city, Hotels, Traffic, School, Corner shops, Beaches
- Arable, pastoral and mixed farms, Heathland and rough grazing, Hill sh..., Hedgerows, Market gardens and orchards, Farms, Ha..., Out of town shopping centres, Golf courses, Airports, Motorways, Suburbanised villages, Woods, Suburbs
- Coast / City/town urban area / Rural/urban fringe

COURSEWORK IDEAS

Figure G.1 shows examples of topics you can study for coursework. All but weather are in the examination content. You could choose any topic as long as it is geographical. However, remember that it is best to choose a topic that you have studied so that you include enough geographical words and theory in your coursework.

When choosing a topic you must consider:
- what you are interested in
- fieldwork opportunities
- safety while doing the work.

Titles are suggested in every coursework section in this book. A question can be used as a title. This helps to keep the work clear and the conclusion should be the answer to the question. Avoid titles such as 'a study of the river…' which can make the study vague or descriptive. Think about the geographical terms and theory that apply to the topic and avoid writing a project based on history rather than geography.

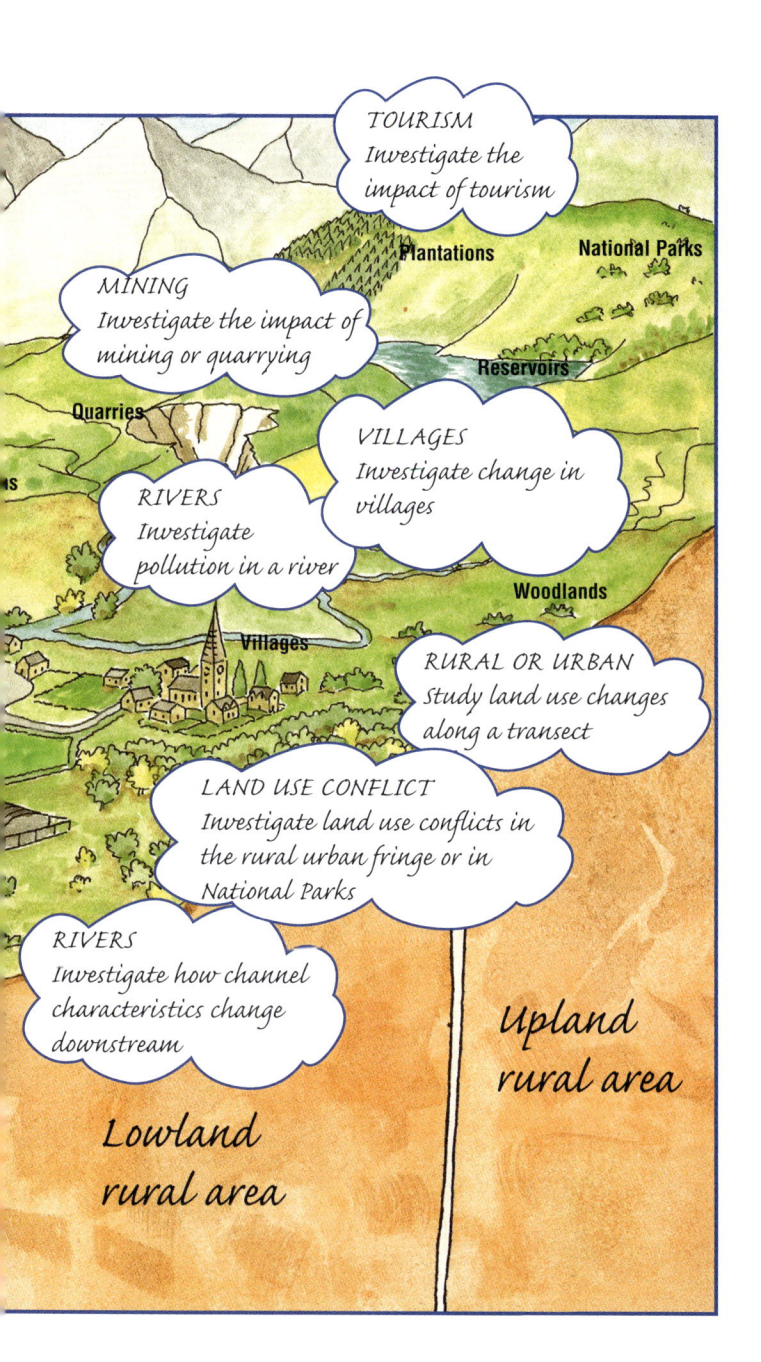

The coursework process

Stage 1 – Choosing a geographical topic

- Think of an idea which interests you.
- Choose a local area which is easy to get to.
- Agree a title with your teacher and read up on the geography topic.
- Write down your aims (what you want to find out).
- Think about what data you need and how and when you will collect it.

Stage 2 – Collecting the data

- Design data recording sheets and produce outline maps.
- Carry out your fieldwork – think about safety.
- Look for other sources of information such as newspapers.

Stage 3 – Processing and presenting the data collected

- Locate your study area on a sketch map.
- Put statistics into tables. Draw a variety of graphs and maps.
- Include labelled sketches and photographs.
- Add your own title, arrows and labels to printed maps and highlight other sources.

Stage 4 – Writing it up

- Write about what your illustrations (maps, tables, graphs and diagrams) show you and include these as you write about them.
- Link clearly to the title.
- Has your study proved geography patterns and trends?
- What are the strengths and weaknesses of the work?
- What else could be done?

TOURISM Investigate the impact of tourism

MINING Investigate the impact of mining or quarrying

VILLAGES Investigate change in villages

RIVERS Investigate pollution in a river

RURAL OR URBAN Study land use changes along a transect

LAND USE CONFLICT Investigate land use conflicts in the rural urban fringe or in National Parks

RIVERS Investigate how channel characteristics change downstream

Upland rural area

Lowland rural area

THE COURSEWORK PROCESS

This can be divided into four stages. Try to plan ahead. For example, think about which graphs you will produce when choosing your data collection techniques. Remember to link to your title clearly at each stage.

■ Guidance

USING ICT IN COURSEWORK
Using ICT for collecting data

ICT such as **laptop computers** can be used to collect data. For example, a spreadsheet could be designed to record and process measurements such as river width and depth. This could be used while at the data collection site. If there is a problem with the data, the tasks can be easily repeated.

Digital cameras have the advantage of being able to view the image and retake it if necessary. DTP software can be used to annotate the photograph on a laptop at each study site.

Digital fieldwork images may be available at school or on the internet. These can be labelled to compare change over time.

Images can be edited and it is easy to copy and paste them into a **word processor**. It is good to have the images included in the written analysis rather than in a separate section.

Data logging equipment can be connected to a portable computer. For example, you could use a flow meter when investigating a river.

Figure G.2 Word processing makes coursework easier

Figure G.3 Using a digital camera so that photographs can be downloaded in coursework

Using ICT in coursework

Figure G.4 Using the internet for coursework data

Figure G.5 Using the scanner to create a base map

Secondary data can be collected from a **CD-ROM** or the **internet**. For example, much census data is available online and local council and tourist board websites may provide background information. Many maps and photographs are available on the internet.

Using ICT to process data

Computers can make processing data easier and faster. For example, questionnaire survey results can be put into a database and sorted. Formulae can be used in spreadsheets to do calculations.

Using ICT to present data

Using ICT to produce graphs and charts can be quick and neat. They should be inserted into a word processor and your analysis written by them. Digital camera images can also be labelled this way. Mapping software could be used at your school to produce digital maps and look for spatial patterns.

Using ICT to analyse data and reach conclusions

Using a word processor can help you to produce clear analysis and conclusions. You can draft and redraft your work to improve and extend it. Sections can be moved around. Charts and images can be included with your analysis. The spell checker and grammar checker can help to avoid mistakes. Do remember to save your work regularly!

Guidance

COURSEWORK ASSESSMENT

A Collection and selection of data – 40 marks

The assessment scheme tells you what to do:

- Choose a geographical question or issue.
- Show initiative in deciding what data is needed.
- Choose appropriate ways of recording data.
- Successfully collect enough data.
- Show that you understand the geography topic and have knowledge of the location studied.

If you are doing teacher-led and group coursework, you need to do some extension work of your own to gain the highest marks.

Figure G.6 Students doing fieldwork

Advice

How to extend teacher-led and group work to ensure that marks for initiative are claimed.

1. Do the same type of data collection
   a. on a different day, e.g. a shopping survey on a Saturday or market day.
   b. at a different time of day, e.g. evening shoppers at an out-of-town centre.
   c. at a different time of year, e.g. tourist visitors outside the main season.
   d. at a different place, e.g. on another stretch of beach or in a different housing area.
2. Use a different method of data collection, e.g. an environmental survey devised by you or your own questionnaire.

B Representation of data – 20 marks

It is important to include a variety of presentation techniques. You could make a list to check that you have different techniques such as line, scatter and bar graphs, maps, pie charts and annotated photographs and sketches. You do not get one mark for every pie chart or graph! Try to avoid too much repetition. Not every item of data collected needs to be put into a graph or diagram. Make sure that you select a technique which is appropriate and that the graph or map links to your title. Every map should have a title, key, scale and North arrow. Label axes on graphs.

Writing up coursework

Writing up your coursework is worth 40% of the marks.

Title
- Display it clearly.

Table of contents
- After numbering the pages, list the major chapters and the page they start on.

Introduction
- Explain the title and aims (purpose) of the study.
- Include maps and describe the study area and why it was chosen.
- Briefly describe the geographical background of the topic.

Data collection
- Describe and explain **how**, **why**, **where** and **when** data was collected.
- Include examples of the types of data collected.

Analysis and interpretation of the results
- Include maps, graphs, diagrams, etc.
- Say what each shows – link to the title.
- Identify patterns, similarities and differences between them.

Conclusion
- Summarise what you have found overall and link to your aims.
- Explain how your findings relate to their geographical background.
- Describe the strengths and limitations of your study.

References
- List books, newspapers websites, CD-ROMS, people consulted and any other resources used.

Appendices
Include:
- tables of data
- examples of data collection sheets
- two completed questionnaires.

C Analysis, interpretation and conclusions – 40 marks

These are hard marks to earn so you must follow advice carefully. You should:

- **Write down and explain your conclusions**. These summary statements must link to your aims.
- **Complete the analysis**. Make sure there is enough data, it is presented clearly and in order and fits the title.
- **Analyse and interpret data by linking to geographical ideas.**

- **Use geographical knowledge to help analyse data and draw conclusions**. Don't copy from textbooks. Try to use geographical terms and ideas when describing and explaining your results throughout your work.
- **Conclude by discussing how reliable your results are**. What went well? What were the weaknesses of your study? Where is it biased? What did you do to get over problems? Did you get any unexpected results? Why?

■ Guidance

HOW TO BE SUCCESSFUL IN THE EXAMINATIONS

Revision

You have now finished your final geography lesson. Revision is a vital part of the preparation for any examination, but how do you revise for your geography examination?

It is very important that you know what you are revising. Is it a case study, a geographical word, a geographical idea, or a geographical skill?

Case study

You will be allowed to choose your own case study. Make sure it fits the question theme and is taken from the correct location. As you learn a case study you should think of a question which you can use it to answer. So, as you revise flooding in Bangladesh, for example, you think about the following question:

> Describe what has been done to control river flooding in a named LEDC.

Why can you *not* use a case study of the Mississippi River to answer this question? (A clue is LEDC.)

To answer questions that focus on a case study you need to know a topic or place in detail. A case study may be of a volcano or earthquake, an area of coastline, one country's population control policy, a city transport network, a farming system, a mining location, an area of water pollution, or many other aspects of the geography course. Therefore it is important that you can write about one particular volcanic eruption rather than volcanoes in general.

Geographical words

During your course you will have learned many new geographical words and terms. It is important that you remember the meaning of words such as subduction zone, life expectancy, fossil fuel and desertification. When revising, it is useful to compile your own **glossary** of the geographical words which you come across. A glossary is a dictionary of key words and terms with their meanings. On page 239 there is a glossary of some of the geographical words used in this book.

A glossary is useful to answer questions such as:

What does 'footloose industry' mean?

Geographical ideas

When revising ideas it is important that you understand what it means and how you might use it with different examples. The idea may be a:

- **process** – such as how earthquakes are caused, or how erosion by the sea forms a stack
- **cause** – why the birth rate of a country may change over time, or what causes acid rain or global warming
- **theory** – how land use zones in a city are different from each other
- **model** – why the tropical rainforest ecosystem can be easily destroyed.

Once you have described or explained the idea you may have to give an example or case study to show how it works. Look at the example below.

Idea: Why do many migrants into cities in LEDCs live in squatter settlements?

Case study: Name a city in an LEDC where many people live in squatter settlements. Describe what is being done to improve their living conditions.

How to be successful in the examinations

Geographical skills

The best way to revise the skills that you may need to use in the examination is by practising them. There are many types of geographical skill. Some common skill questions are shown below.

OS map

Reading (see page 230):

 What is the distance between the churches in Hope and Bradwell? _____ km

 Name a farm in grid square 1583.

Drawing (see page 230):

 Complete the route taken by the road between Grid References 146828 and 184828.

 On the cross-section mark and label the A625 road and the railway line.

Interpreting:

 Describe the relief of the area north of grid line 83.

 Use map evidence to give two reasons why it is difficult to travel from Treherbert to Maerdy.

Graph

Plotting:

 Complete the bar graph by drawing the bar for caravan sites. There are 75 caravan sites.

Interpreting:

 Describe two changes in the amount of energy used between 1985 and 1995.

Photograph

Interpreting (see Figure G.7):

 Use evidence from the photograph to describe the effects of the quarry and works on the landscape and scenery.

Satellite image

Interpreting:

 In which square is St Helens located?

 How is the land use in square B2 different from the land use in square D5? Use the key to work out your answer.

Other maps

Interpreting (see page 116):

 Describe the world distribution of areas of high population density.

Data

Handling:

 Rank the countries shown in the table in order of population growth per year. Rank from highest to lowest.

 Describe the relationship shown by the table between the number of people who live in a settlement and the services available.

You will not know before you open the question paper which area the OS map will cover, what type of photograph will be used, or what type of graph may need completing. However, you can practise your data handling skills as you revise your work.

Figure G.7 Quarry in the Peak District

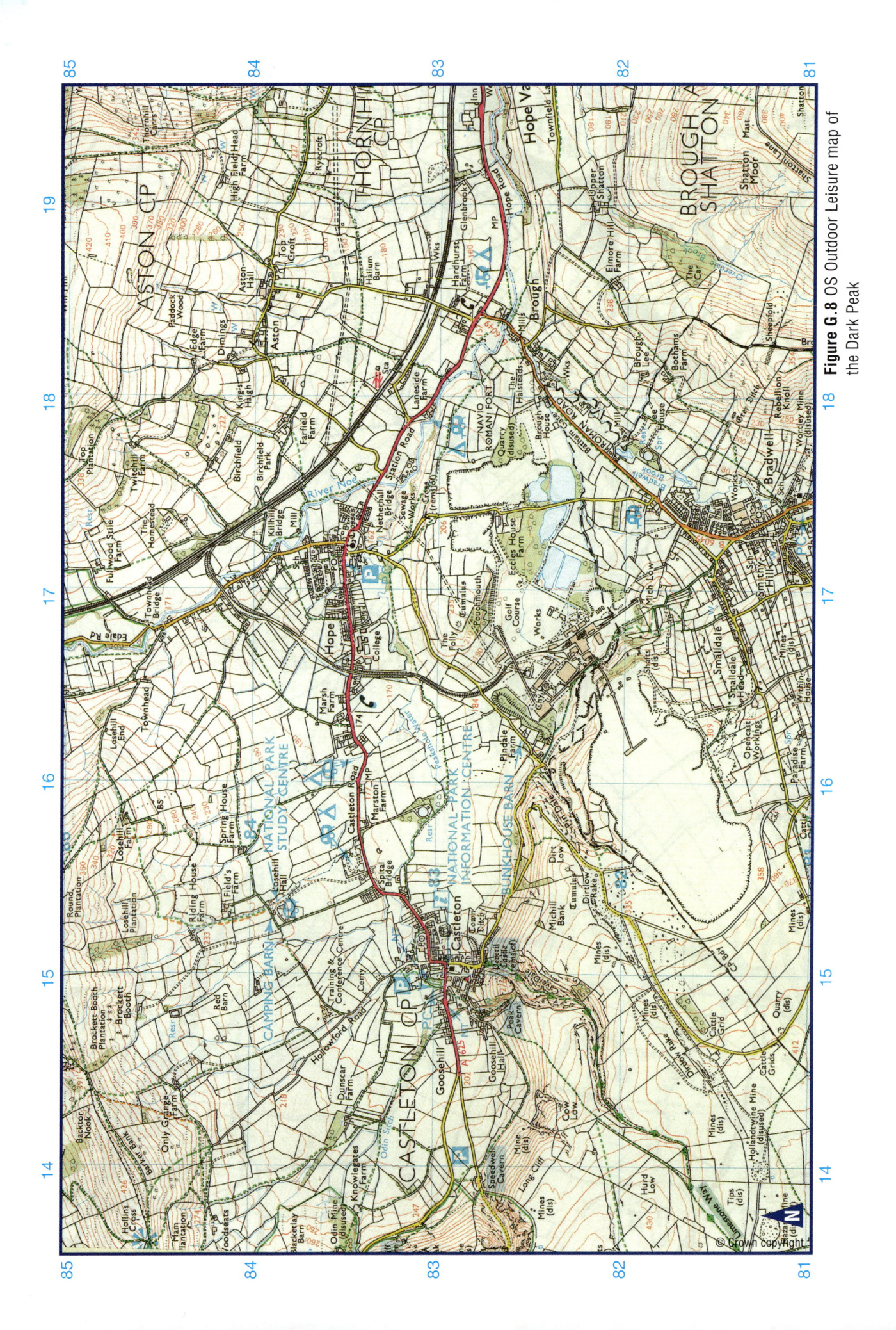

Figure G.8 OS Outdoor Leisure map of the Dark Peak

How to be successful in the examinations

Using your time well

Paper 1 is two hours long and Paper 3 is one hour long.

It is very important to use your time in the examination correctly. You are not going to get your best result if you work too slowly at first and then have to rush to complete other questions. But remember, there is no prize for being the first candidate to finish the examination. So divide up your time and plan your answers carefully.

A simple way to plan your time is to divide up the length of time of the examination between the number of questions which you have to answer. In Paper 1 you have four questions to work through in two hours, so you should aim to spend about 30 minutes on each answer. In Paper 3 you have to answer two questions so spend about 30 minutes on each one. Remember that you can always go back to develop earlier answers or fill in any gaps if you have time at the end of the examination.

Candidates who plan their time well find that they have a few minutes left at the end of the examination before their papers are collected. Do not waste this time. Use it to re-read your answers and use the following checklist:

- Have you failed to answer any section?
- Can you develop your ideas in any section?
- Have you remembered some more information about a case study?

It is always possible to improve some answers when the time pressure is reduced and you are able to think about your answers carefully.

Remember that in the examination you do not have to answer the questions in the order in which they come on the question paper. You may answer the questions in any order. This means that you can start by choosing a question on a subject which you know well. Hopefully by answering this first question well, it will help to get rid of any examination nerves. You can then go on to attempt other more difficult questions with more confidence.

The **mark allocation** is an important clue to timing your answers. The allocation is the maximum number of marks for each answer. It is shown in the examination paper by the figure in brackets ( ) at the end of each question. The mark allocation gives you a clue about how long or detailed your answer should be. Obviously the examiner expects a more detailed answer if there are 5 marks for a question than if there are only 2 marks. So do not write too much detail or an over-long answer if there are only 2 marks available. Write a detailed answer where there are 5 marks allocated.

■ Guidance

THE EXAMINATION QUESTIONS

You need to examine each question carefully. Remember that the questions are not designed to trip you up but to give you the chance to show what you have learned. Your answer must be both accurate and relevant. To do this you need to be familiar with **command words** and **question themes**. Command words tell you what you have to do to answer the question. The question theme tells you what the question is about.

Command words

These can be divided into six types:

1 Simple

Name   Give   State   List   Identify

These are simple command words which provide a clear instruction. They usually show that a short answer is needed.

For example:

- **Name** a fossil fuel.
- Rainforest destruction is one cause of the greenhouse effect. **Give** two other causes.
- **Identify** the coastal landforms at A and B on the diagram.

2 Definition

Define   What is meant by   Give the meaning of

These command words are asking for definitions. The words which you will need to define will be 'geographical' words. You will have seen these words highlighted throughout this book.

For example:

- **Define** the term 'tertiary industry' and give an example.
- Rural depopulation is occurring in many villages. **What is** 'rural depopulation'?
- Bunches Florapost is an example of a distribution industry. **What is meant by** 'distribution industry'?

3 Description

Describe   What

Describe is the most commonly used command word. It instructs you to write about what is at a particular location, what something looks like, or what is shown in a map, graph or photograph. The amount of detail required in your description is shown by the mark allocation.

For example:

- **Describe** two ways to protect the coastline from erosion.

Name an area in the UK or EU where tourism is spoiling the area. **What** is being done to reduce the damage caused by tourists?

4 Explanation

Explain   Why   Suggest   Give reasons for

These questions are testing your knowledge and understanding. You are being told to say why things happen.

For example:

- **Explain** how a stack is formed.
- **Why** do many people continue to live in cities at risk from earthquakes?
- Use evidence from the photograph to **suggest** two difficulties which people living in the village may face.
- **Give two reasons** why large areas of rainforest have been cut down.

5 Identifying differences

Compare   Describe two differences

These command words instruct you to write about what is the same or different between two pieces of information.

For example:

- Describe two differences between the buildings shown in the photograph.

The best way to answer such questions is by using phrases such as 'in contrast' or comparative words to bring out the difference as follows:

- The buildings are older in Photograph A.
- The buildings in Photograph A are small in contrast to those in B which are big.

6 Opinion

Do you think

These command words want you to give an opinion. But you will have to support your opinion with your ideas.

For example:

- People build their own homes in many cities in LEDCs. Do you think this is a good way to improve living conditions in squatter settlements? Give two reasons to support your answer.

Finally on the subject of command words, examine the instructions below.

- Name a volcano you have studied and describe the problems caused by its eruption.
- Many rural areas have few people living there. Name a rural area which you have studied. Explain why there are not many people living there.
- Name a National Park you have studied and describe the conflicts between tourism and other activities which are located there.

These instructions tell you that you must include a **case study** in your answer.

To see if you understand the command words, try writing some possible examination questions, using Figure G.9 below.

For example, 'Name the landform in the centre of the photograph.'

Now try: 'Define…'

'Describe…'

'Explain…'

Figure G.9 The stacks called Old Harry and his wife, Dorset

■ Guidance

Question themes

Each examination question is based on a section of your GCSE course. A theme or topic means that one part of the question leads on to the next. Sometimes when a question follows a theme there may be a change in emphasis within the topic. The question below is based on the theme of employment but the focus moves from employment structure to tourism.

Study Figure G.10.

Country	GDP (per person) (per 1 000)	Infant mortality (per 1 000)	Life expectancy (years)	Number of people per doctor
Canada	$24 800	5.2	79.6	464
Cuba	$1 700	7.4	76.4	275
Mexico	$9 100	25.7	71.7	615
USA	$36 200	6.8	77.3	421

Figure G.10 Development indicators for four countries in North and Central America

(a) (i) Which country is likely to have the poorest **health care**? [1]

   (ii) Give **two pieces of evidence** from Figure G.10 to support this. [2]

(b) Study Figure G.11.

The divided bars were drawn using the following

	Cuba	USA
Primary	25%	2%
Secondary	24%	18%
Tertiary	51%	80%

figures.

(i) Shade the bars and complete the key to show the **employment structure** of Cuba and the USA. [1]

(ii) In Cuba the main employment used to be on plantations growing crops like sugar and tobacco. Now more people are employed in the tourist industry.

In which **employment sector** would the following Cuban people work?

A worker on a tobacco plantation.

PRIMARY   SECONDARY   TERTIARY

A waitress in a hotel.

PRIMARY   SECONDARY   TERTIARY

A worker in a factory making cigars.

PRIMARY   SECONDARY   TERTIARY

[3]

Key
☐ Primary
☐ Secondary
☐ Tertiary

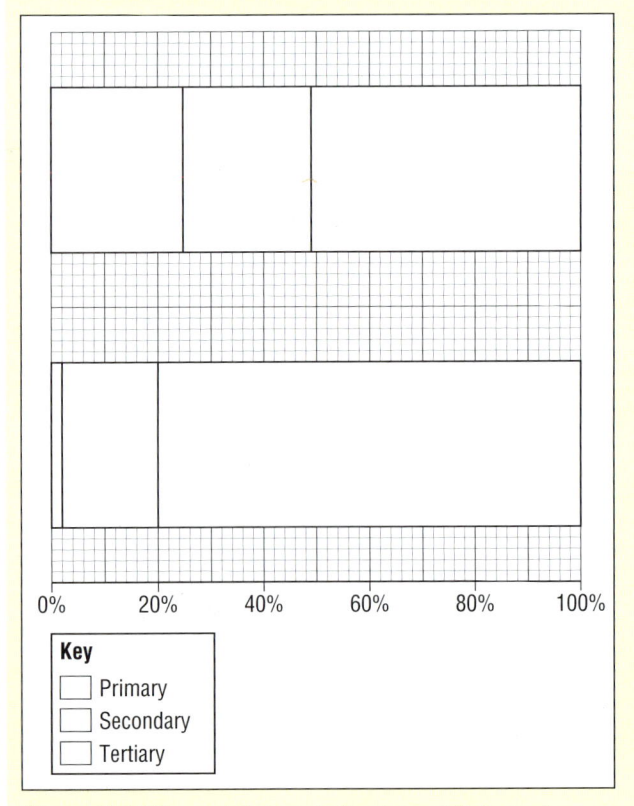

Figure G.11 The employment structure of Cuba and the USA

(c) Study Figure G.12.

(i) How many **hotel rooms** were there in Havana in 1990? [1]

(ii) **Name the area** which did not have any hotels in 1990 but is now an important tourist area. [1]

(iii) Suggest any two **problems which tourism could cause** to people who live along the northern coast of Cuba. [2]

(iv) How might the **growth of tourism** be likely to improve the lives of people who live in LEDCs such as Cuba? [3]

(d) Name an area in the EU which you have studied. Give reasons why the area has become an important **tourist destination**. [5]

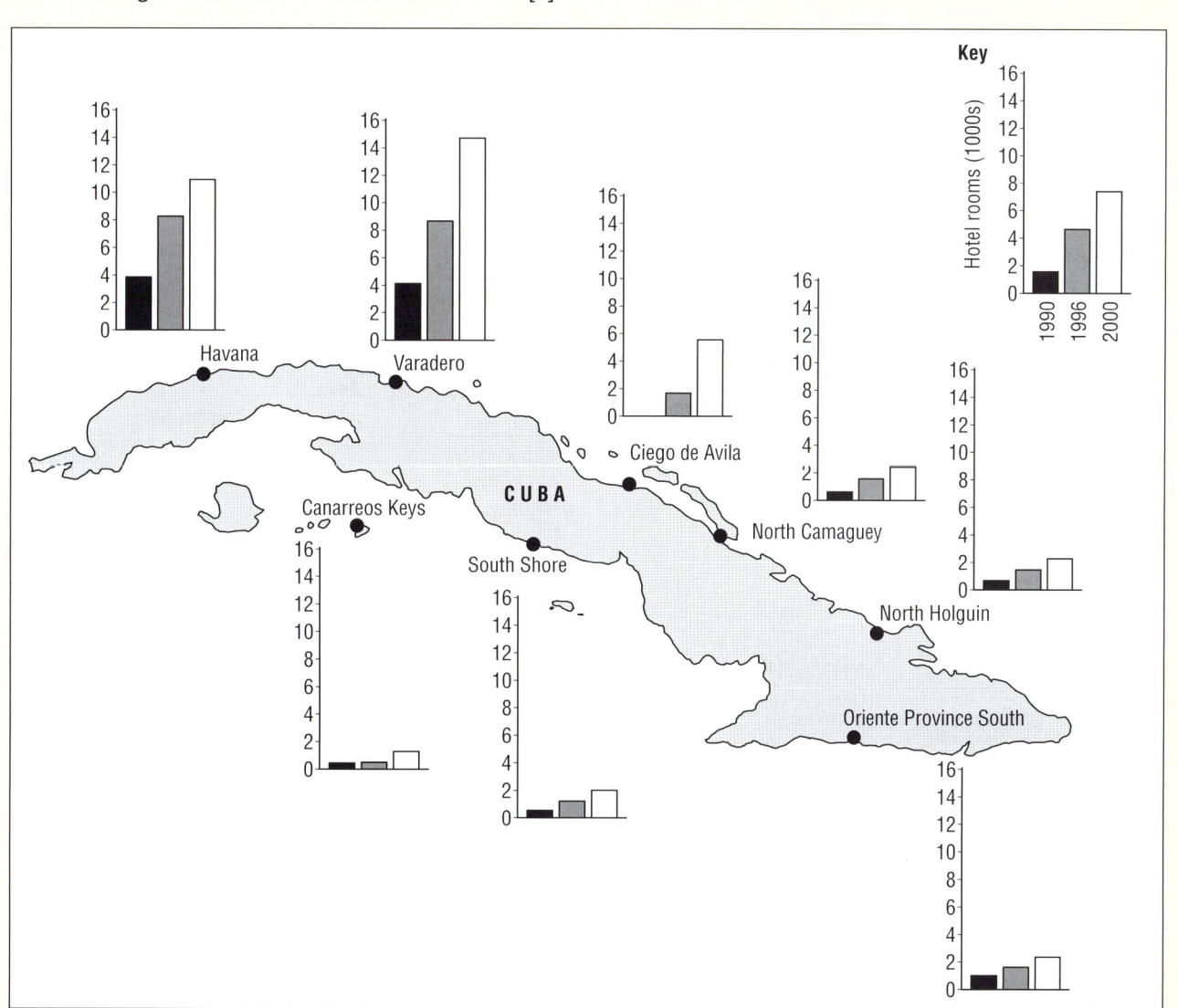

Figure G.12 Number of hotel rooms in the main tourist resorts in Cuba

Guidance

USING QUESTION RESOURCES

A variety of resources will be used in the geography examinations. The main types of resources are:

- **Maps**, e.g. OS map, distribution map on a world scale, large-scale street plan
- **Graphs**, e.g. line graph, pie chart, bar graph, scatter graph
- **Diagrams**, e.g. sketch, process diagram, flow diagram
- **Photographs**, e.g. aerial photograph, close-up photograph, satellite image
- **Data**, e.g. table of figures
- **Text**, e.g. newspaper extract.

It is unlikely that you will have seen the resource before the examination because data, photographs, maps, etc. are selected from many different places. This is not a problem, however, as the question will be testing geographical skills or understanding of the resource.

Questions which make use of resources are varied, as the following selection shows.

Select information from a graph (Figure G.13):

Complete a graph (Figure G.14):

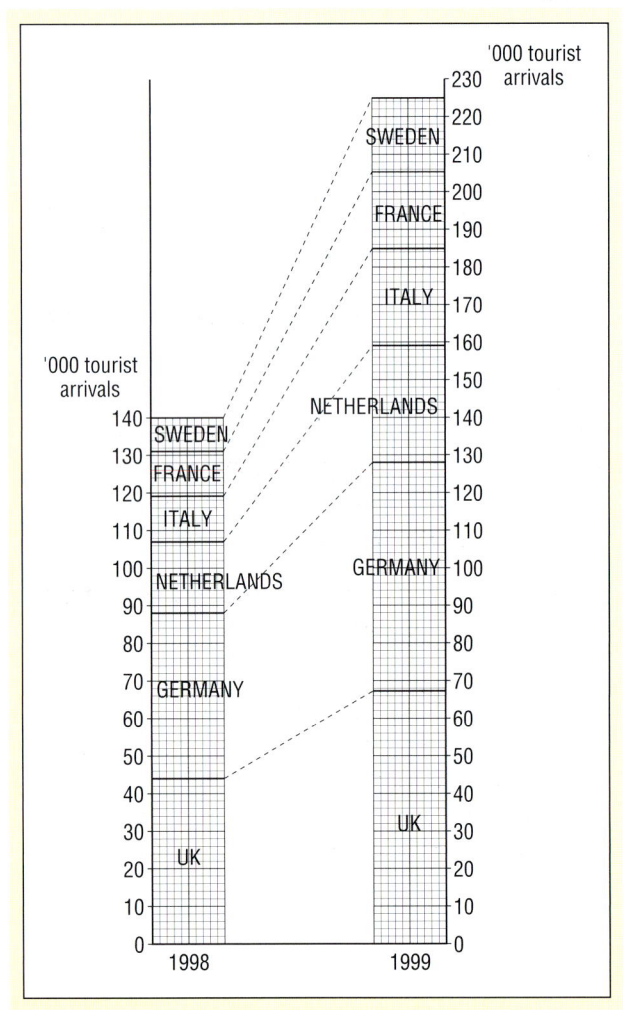

Figure G.13 Number of tourists visiting Bali from six European countries

The graph shows that in 1998 there were 9 000 tourists from Sweden who visited Bali. How many tourists from Sweden went to Bali in 1999?

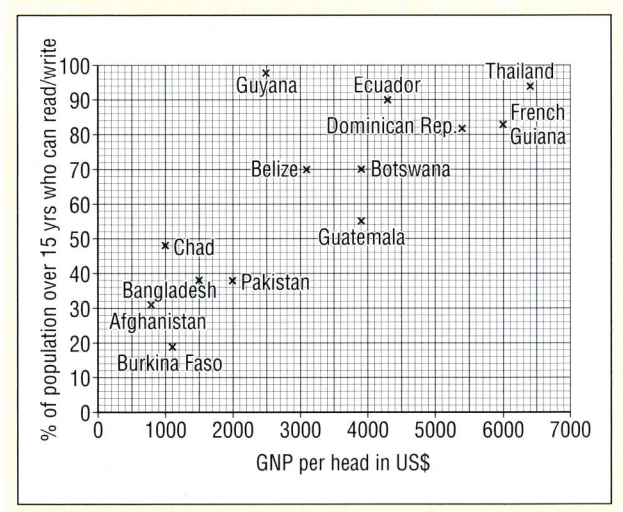

Figure G.14 Scatter graph of GNP per head and percentage population over 15 years who can read and write in selected LEDCs

Use the following information to plot Bolivia on the graph:

GNP per head	US$ 3 000
% of people over 15 who can read and write	83%

Complete a data table by a simple calculation:

Birth rate (per thousand)	Death rate (per thousand)	Population increase
35	15	–

Using question resources

Questions which include a diagram, photograph or map resource usually require interpretation of the resource as shown below:

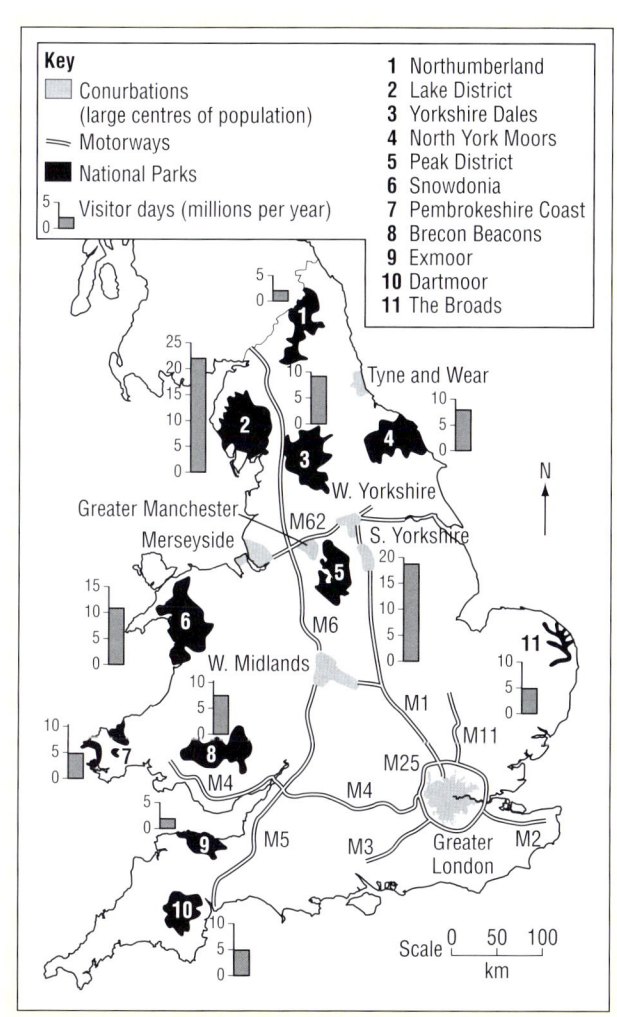

Figure G.15 Number of visitors to National Parks in England and Wales

Which National Park is located west of the M6 and north of the M62?

Suggest two reasons why the Peak District has more visitors than the Broads.

OS map

This resource forms the basis of questions on Paper 3. There are many skills which must be used to interpret these maps.

You can practise them using the Landranger maps on pages 44–45, 103, 122 and 167. Details of the key are on page 123. Examples of maps at 1:25 000 scale are on pages 29 and 230.

A selection of these skills is outlined below.

- Find and give 4- and 6-figure grid references.
- Use the scale and key accurately.
- Describe distributions.
- Label a cross-section.
- Draw a routeway.
- Link the map to another resource, such as a photograph.
- Describe human and physical features.
- Use the map to show your understanding of an idea.

You must study a resource carefully. It will contain information which helps you to answer the question. Resources are not included in examination papers merely to improve their appearance. When studying maps or satellite images, the key is an important aid to understanding the resource.

The following question is an example of using a map and a photograph.

Describe the benefits and problems which the quarry and works might cause for the people living in the surrounding settlements. Use evidence from Figure G.7 on page 229 and the OS map on page 230 in your answer.

Guidance

USING CASE STUDIES

The case study is an important section of each question in Paper 1. It has five marks allocated to it. Questions which refer to case studies are testing your knowledge of real places.

- Name an area which has been affected by erosion by the sea. Describe the effects of erosion on people in that area.
- Name an area where the rainforest is being destroyed. Explain why the rainforest is being destroyed in this area.
- Name an area which has a low population density. Explain why few people live there.

A final reminder of how the case study is marked

If you learn how examiners mark a case study it should help you to write good answers. A case study is marked in 'levels' from Level 1 up to Level 3. To achieve a higher level answer you will need to give details which are related specifically to your named example. This is shown in the following question.

> Name an area which has a low population density and explain why it is sparsely populated. [5]

Mark scheme

Level 1 (1–2 marks):

Simple statements which attempt to explain low population density, e.g.

- no jobs
- high land
- poor climate.

Level 2 (3–4 marks):

More specific statements which explain low population density, e.g.

- few jobs as there are no factories in the area
- high land is difficult to build settlements on
- cold climate/long wet winters.

Level 3 (5 marks):

Uses named example. Detailed and accurate place-specific statements, e.g.

- few jobs in Snowdonia as opportunities are limited to sheep farming, which needs few workers
- high land including many mountains such as Snowdon, which are unsuitable for building
- poor road communications with winding roads, such as the A5, through mountains.

COMMON EXAMINATION ERRORS

Finally in this chapter, some things to avoid in your geography examination.

- Be careful when making your choice of case study. Do not make an incorrect choice. If the question instructs you to choose an example from an LEDC, do not choose one from an MEDC.
- Read the command word carefully. Do not explain when only a description is required.
- Look at the mark allocation. Do not write one full page of information if there are only two marks for a question.
- Check how much time you are taking to answer each question or section. Do not spend half the examination time on the first section and then have to rush through the remainder.
- Use all your time. Do not sit back when you have completed your final answer. You should re-read and check your answer, adding more facts and ideas where you remember them.
- Use all question resources. Do not ignore the map, graph or photograph. It contains information that will help you answer.
- Include the correct units. Do not give a measurement as 2.5 when you mean 2.5 km, or 70 when you mean 70 m.

Glossary

accessible *easy to get to* — 90
adult literacy rate *percentage of population able to read and write by the age of 15* — 129
bar *ridge of sediment deposited across the mouth of a bay attached to land at both ends* — 47
birth rate *number of live births in a year per every 1 000 people* — 72
bus lane *part of a road not available to other vehicles to speed up bus journeys* — 96
commuting *travelling daily from home to place of work* — 105
condensation *water vapour changed to liquid by cooling* — 24
conurbation *large urban area where towns have grown so big that they have merged* — 70
convectional rainfall *rain, often from thunderstorms, resulting from warm air rising in convection currents* — 182
convergent plate boundary *where an oceanic plate collides with a continental plate, resulting in the subduction of the oceanic plate* — 8
core *the centre part of the earth surrounded by the mantle* — 6
counterurbanisation *population change from urban to rural locations* — 105
crust *the shell or skin of the earth, about 5 km thick below the oceans but up to 50 km thick under continents* — 6
death rate *number of deaths in a year per every 1 000 people* — 72
dense *large number per square kilometre* — 68
dependent population *children and old people supported by working adults* — 73
discharge *the flow of water in a river* — 24
distribution *where people or things are located* — 116
divergent plate boundary *where plates are moving apart resulting in sea floor spreading producing new crust* — 9
drainage basin *the area drained by a river and its tributaries* — 24
ecosystem *a community of plants and animals, interacting with each other and their environment* — 182
El Niño *warm ocean current off South America experienced every few years* — 208
enterprise zone *area with special grants and tax advantages to anyone creating employment* — 165
epicentre *point on the earth's surface directly above an earthquake's focus* — 10
eutrophication *rapid growth of plants which reduce oxygen supply in water, caused by excess nutrients* — 196
evaporation *water changed from liquid to vapour by heat* — 24
fallow *land that is left unploughed or unsown for a period of time* — 148
fetch *distance across the sea in which wind builds up waves* — 40
floodplain *flat land forming the floor of a valley, liable to flooding* — 30

focus *underground source of an earthquake* — 10
fold mountains *chain of mountains in continental crust close and parallel to a convergent plate boundary* — 8
footloose *industry which has few constraints on its choice of location* — 152
gentrification *improving housing, including creating new, often expensive homes in run-down inner cities* — 107
green belt *area of countryside around an urban area where most new buildings are not permitted* — 95
greenfield *urban or industrial growth on a previously rural site* — 153
greying population *high, and increasing, proportion of elderly people* — 74
groundwater flow *movement of water through porous rocks* — 24
groyne *breakwater fences to stop longshore drift removing beach material* — 49
guestworker *immigrant to affluent country from poorer country attracted by higher paid work, health care and education* — 78
high order goods *things bought less frequently, expensive* — 91
honeypot *location prone to overcrowding* — 194
hydrograph *graph showing rainfall and a river's discharge at a place over a period of time* — 25
impermeable *rocks which do not let water soak through* — 45
industrial inertia *the survival of an industry in an area after its locational advantages have disappeared* — 152
infant mortality rate *number of babies dying before their fifth birthday, per thousand population* — 129
infiltration *water seeping down through soil* — 24
infrastructure *the basic framework of power and water supplies, transport networks and services such as education and sewerage* — 137
kiss and ride *where the car is driven away as the passenger transfers to public transport* — 97
lag time *the time between peak rainfall and peak discharge as shown on a hydrograph* — 25
levée *embankment alongside a river* — 30
life expectancy *how many years a newborn baby can expect to live* — 129
load *material carried by a river* — 26
longshore drift *movement of sand and pebbles along a beach by waves* — 46
malnourished *inadequately balanced diet* — 132
mantle *the part of the earth between the crust and the core* — 6
migration *movement of people* — 72

multiplier effect *the spiral of growth or decline from the creation or closure of an economic activity* — 137
natural increase *the difference in a year between the number of births and deaths* — 72
neighbourhood centre *group of low order shops serving a community within a town* — 104
overland flow (surface flow) *movement of rainwater across the surface of the ground* — 24
oxbow lake *meander cut off from the main river channel* — 30
park and ride *providing car parks away from town centres with public transport to the CBD* — 97
pedestrianisation *closing streets to traffic* — 91
permeable *rocks which let water soak through* — 45
plate *large piece of the earth's crust* — 7
precipitation *water from the atmosphere such as rain or snow* — 24
raw materials *naturally occurring substances from which the making of all goods starts* — 152
refugee *someone forced to move to live elsewhere* — 79
Richter scale *measure of the power or energy of an earthquake* — 10
salt marsh *area with salt-loving plants on the landward side of a spit or bar, occasionally flooded by sea water* — 47
seismograph *instrument for measuring earthquake vibrations* — 10
sparse *few per square kilometre* — 68
sphere of influence *area served by a settlement, shop or service* — 108
spit *beach extension formed by longshore drift* — 47
subduction *when an oceanic plate is forced beneath a continental plate, melting it* — 9
sustainable *using resources no faster than natural processes can replenish them* — 189
threshold population *minimum number of customers required to keep a business going* — 100
throughflow *flow of water down a slope through the soil* — 24
TNC *trans-national companies, usually run from MEDCs with branch factories worldwide* — 137
tombolo *beach joining an island with mainland* — 47
transform plate boundary *where a plate is slipping past another plate* — 9
transpiration *the transfer of water to the atmosphere through leaves* — 24
water table *the level below which porous or permeable rock is saturated with water* — 24
wave refraction *the bending of a wave as it approaches the shore caused by shallowing water* — 41
weathering *breakdown of rocks by natural agents such as rain, frost, ice and wind* — 43

Place index

Alps	32, 208
Amazon	182–191
Athens	203
Australia	79, 130, 138,
Bangladesh	36–39, 85
Birmingham	104, 106, 152
Brahamaputra	36
Brazil	85, 184, 188
Burkina Faso	132–133, 137
Cairo	88
Calcutta	88
Canada	138
Chernobyl	162
Chesil Beach	47
Chesterfield	165
China	75, 77, 136, 203
Chittagong	38
Consett	166–167
Cookley	102–104
Cutnall Green	107
Czech Republic	203
Dartmoor	193, 194–195
Derbyshire	71, 160, 161, 180
Dhaka	37–39
Doñana	198–199
Dorset	42
Easington	49–50
Egypt	134
Etna	22
Ganges	36
Germany	32, 78, 203
Glasgow	96–98
Guadiamar River	197–199
Hay Tor	194
Himalayas	36
Holderness	48–51
Holmewood	164–165
Hong Kong	136
Hornsea	49–50
Iceland	22
India	85, 144–146
Indonesia	22
Isle of Portland	47
Japan	13, 136
Kenya	73, 158–159
Kidderminster	104, 106–107
Kiruna	166
Kosovo	78
Kyoto	209

Lee Moor	194
Llansamlet	91
London	83
Los Angeles	80
Lynemouth	154
Mappleton	50–51
Menorca	156–157
Merry Hill	104
Mexico	75, 80–81
Milford Haven	200–201
Mombasa	159
Mount St Helens	16–20, 23
Netherlands	32–35
New Zealand	22, 130
North Worcestershire	102, 106–7
Norway	204
Nottingham	165
Paris	83
Peak District	71, 180–181
Pembrokeshire	200
Purbeck	42
Rhine	32, 33–35
River Clyde	96
San Francisco	11, 12–13
São Paulo	85
Scarborough	44, 45, 48, 141
Scroby Sands	163
Sellafield	162
Singapore	136
Solihull	106
South Korea	136, 138–139
Stafford	153
Stoke on Trent	178–179
Sutton Coldfield	106
Swansea	91–95
Sweden	166, 203–205
Taiwan	136
Texas	80
Thailand	75
Thorn Park Farm	141–143
Turkey	12
USA	80–81, 134, 138
Vesuvius	22
West Indies	78
Withernsea	50
Worcester	106
Yellowstone	23

Locations of principal case studies are shown in bold.